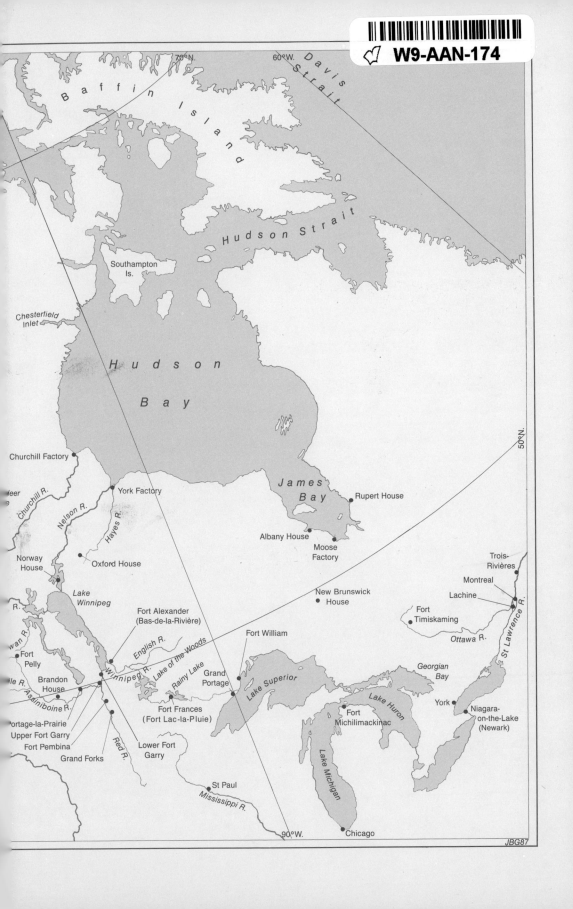

70°N.

60°W. Davis Strait

Baffin Island

Hudson Strait

Southampton Is.

Chesterfield Inlet

Hudson Bay

Churchill Factory

James Bay

Rupert House

Deer

Churchill R.

Nelson R.

Hayes R.

York Factory

Albany House

Moose Factory

50°N.

Trois-Rivières

Norway House

Oxford House

Montreal

Lachine

Lake Winnipeg

New Brunswick House

Fort Timiskaming

R.

Fort Alexander (Bas-de-la-Rivière)

Fort William

Ottawa R.

St Lawrence R.

Georgian Bay

Lake Superior

English R.

Lake of the Woods

Fort Pelly

Winnipeg R.

Rainy Lake

Grand Portage

Lake Huron

York

wan R.

Brandon House

Assiniboine R.

Fort Frances (Fort Lac-la-Pluie)

Fort Michilimackinac

Niagara-on-the-Lake (Newark)

le R.

Portage-la-Prairie

Upper Fort Garry

Fort Pembina

Red R.

Lower Fort Garry

Lake Michigan

Grand Forks

St Paul

Mississippi R.

90°W.

Chicago

JBG87

BY THE SAME AUTHOR:

CAESARS *of the* WILDERNESS

COMPANY OF ADVENTURERS
Volume II

PETER C. NEWMAN

VIKING

VIKING
Penguin Books Canada Ltd., 2801 John Street, Markham,
Ontario, Canada L3R 1B4
Penguin Books Ltd., 27 Wrights Lane, London W8 5TZ
(Publishing & Editorial) and Harmondsworth, Middlesex, England
(Distribution & Warehouse)
Viking Penguin Inc., 40 West 23rd Street, New York, New York 10010, U.S.A.
Penguin Books Australia Ltd., Ringwood, Victoria, Australia
Penguin Books (N.Z.) Ltd., 182–190 Wairau Road, Auckland 10, New Zealand

First published by Penguin Books Canada Ltd., 1987

Copyright © Power Reporting Limited, 1987

Book design by V. John Lee
Design adaptation by René Demers
Printed in Canada by T.H. Best Printing Company Ltd.

Canadian Cataloguing in Publication Data
Newman, Peter C., 1929–
    Caesars of the Wilderness

Bibliography: p.
Includes index.
ISBN 0-670-80967-5 (bound)
ISBN 0-670-81936-0 (leather-bound)

1. Hudson's Bay Company – History.   2. Northwest,
Canadian – History – To 1870.*   3. Fur trade –
Canada – History.   I. Title.

For MICHAEL LEVINE, my guardian angel, whose wisdom
and friendship have made this book and so many of my
endeavours possible.

And for SHIRLEE SMITH, Keeper of the Hudson's Bay
Company Archives, whose patient and knowledgeable
assistance in this project extended far beyond the
call of duty.

I wish also to thank the Hudson's Bay Company for
not even *trying* to influence my judgments during
the research and writing of this book. As in Volume I
of this history, except for granting me unimpeded
access to archives and files, the HBC has had no
involvement—financial or editorial—in this project.
My only debt to the Company of Adventurers still
remains a slightly overdue department store bill—
and the cheque is still in the mail.

"We know only two powers—God and the Company."
— John Rowand
Chief Factor, Edmonton House
Hudson's Bay Company

CONTENTS

Acknowledgements

"AT THE HEART OF GOOD HISTORY," observed Stephen Schiff, critic-at-large for *Vanity Fair*, "is a naughty little secret: good storytelling. A history that isn't implicitly a colorful, twisty yarn is at best fodder for other specialists," he warned. "A historian's richest insights generally come when he asks himself what it would have been like to have been there."

That is my aim in this book: to re-create the interplay of feisty characters and remarkable circumstances that shaped the story of the Hudson's Bay Company during the middle century of its existence. I want to unroll a new map of the Canadian past for contemporary readers not by challenging accepted dates or facts but by following the destinies of crucial individuals and by portraying the subtle confluences of men and women with their geographical, political and emotional landscapes. As I noted in the first volume of this series, history is no more than memories refined—and because memories dim, they must be refreshed.

Like all my works, this is a journalist's book. I have no more claimed the credentials of a historian than I assumed the mantle of a political scientist when I wrote *Renegade in Power* and my other political books, or pretended to be an economist when I was chronicling my various studies of the Canadian Establishment. I regard the much-maligned profession of journalism as an honourable craft that requires no apologies.

Having little patience with cant or the musty ruminations Dylan Thomas once described as "smelling of water biscuits," I have imbued the tales that follow with the bounce and bravado they deserve. Nosing about in the daunting welter of available information, defining themes, tracing dominant personalities who could carry the story forward, I have attempted to extract live metaphors from the Dead Sea Scrolls of Canadian history.

In the research for this book, I owe a primary debt to the fur traders themselves, to all of them jabbing impatiently into half-frozen inkwells by candlelight, meticulously recounting details of their daily exertions. Their records, carefully gathered and lovingly preserved in the HBC section of the Provincial Archives of Manitoba in Winnipeg, are an invaluable source of English Canada's dimly remembered corporate and psychic origins. The assistance of the HBC Archives' senior staff members in the preparation of this book has been invaluable. I am greatly in their debt.

Among the many collaborators who made this book possible,

special mention must be made of those patient souls who read the many pages of manuscript and shored up its tone and tenor:

Professor Timothy Ball, the University of Winnipeg geographer and head of the Rupertsland Society, whose passion is preserving Canadian history and making it more accessible. Even so, his generous advice and thoughtful admonitions went far beyond the call of that admirable quest.

Marjorie Wilkins Campbell, the chronicler of the North West Company, who told me during a 1986 visit about a lighthearted flight in the summer of 1947, gazing down at the South Saskatchewan River from a Tiger Moth. "Every mile, every curve in the river," she remembered, "inspired imagined glimpses of those ghostly canoe brigades." The ravages of her final illness were already visible on her face during our visit, but she was still unflagging in her promulgation of the history of those stirring times.

Dr John S. Galbraith, the Professor of British Empire History at the University of California at Los Angeles, whose book *The Hudson's Bay Company as an Imperial Factor* is a definitive study of the HBC's westward expansion. He vetted my Simpson chapters, adding some elegant touches and corrections.·

Cynthia Good, Vice-President and Editor-in-Chief of Penguin Canada, who not only provided highly enlightened manuscript guidance but has been the effective wagonmaster for the entire project.

Al Hochbaum, the painter, naturalist, essayist and Arctic explorer from Delta, Manitoba, who enlisted his free spirit on my behalf with gratifying results. When we had a difference of opinion about some obscure points of buffalo hunting, he won the day with the retort: "I say this on the basis of having shaken hands with Buffalo Bill at his Circus in 1916—which gives me priority!"

Dr W. Kaye Lamb, retired Dominion Archivist and National Librarian, author of books and numerous articles on the Canadian fur trade, who was kind enough to read my first six chapters literally the day before entering hospital for a dangerous cancer operation.

Martin Lynch, a former assistant news editor of the *Globe and Mail* who now lives amid his extraordinary files in Kaslo, B.C., and **Janet Craig**, the best book editor in the country, who between them tussled with every phrase of the manuscript and improved most of them.

Camilla Newman, my wife, who designed the production sequences for all of us working on the book at various stages. She did much of the research and interviewing, compiled the appendices and edited my rough drafts. Camilla shares credit with the mysterious power of Cordova Bay on Vancouver Island to encourage work that is less frantic yet more productive.

Professor Abraham Rotstein, my good friend and the University of Toronto political economist, who shared his many insights.

Mary Lou Stathers, the great-great-granddaughter of Sir George Simpson, who is devoting her considerable skill to "sorting out all the fur-trade Simpsons into the right family groups," read my chapters about her distinguished forebear. Though Mrs Stathers emphatically does not share my harsh conclusions about the late Governor's antics, I laud her passion and diligence.

There are many others: **George Whitman**, the Bay's former external affairs director, whose fiercely independent spirit and aversion to bafflegab continue to amaze me; **Jean Morrison**, Chief Librarian at Old Fort William, Ontario, who commented wisely on the North West Company material; **Carol Preston**, Managing Editor of *The Beaver*, who has been a wonderfully helpful champion of this difficult enterprise from its very beginning; **Peter Carson**, Penguin's Chief Editorial Director in England, whose good humour and incisive suggestions have been impressive and most welcome; **Hugh MacMillan**, the Ontario archivist who embodies the spirit of the Nor'Westers and gave me the benefit of his knowledge; **Mary Adachi**, who again applied her trustworthy exactness in copy editing; **Kathryn Dean**, who chose and captioned the illustrations; **Pat Harding**, whose charm and diplomatic secretarial skills helped keep me on an even keel in my various roles; **Neil and Brenda West**, who valiantly deciphered the flow of messy pages from my Hermes typewriter, entering each round of revisions into their magic computer and devising ways to make production run more smoothly; **Shawn Cafferky**, who acted as an able editorial assistant; and **Chris Blackburn**, who compiled the index with record efficiency. As always, a salute to the bravura rhythms of **Stan Kenton**.

I am equally indebted to those experts in various aspects of the HBC's history and related areas who allowed me to share their insight and experience. Their names are listed in the Resource People Appendix.

Some notes on style. For the sake of clarity, place names have been modernized and most quotations have been rendered in contemporary English. The title *Caesars of the Wilderness* was first used by Grace Lee Nute in her 1943 epic about Radisson and Groseilliers, but I felt it would be perfect for this volume, expressing as it does both the desolation of the HBC's empire and the assumed majesty of its conquerors.

This book owes its existence to many others not mentioned here, but the responsibility for its imperfections is fully my own.

Cordova Bay, British Columbia   P.C.N.
July 29, 1987

PROLOGUE

"The management of their affairs . . . is like a commercial
tomb, closed with the key of death to all except a favoured few."

—Andrew Freeport writing to
Lord Palmerston about the HBC

HIS REAL NAME was Henry Fuller Davis and he was a Yankee from
Vermont who headed northwest to the Cariboo during the gold rush
of the late 1850s to try his luck. He could neither read nor write—but
he could measure. One rainy night he latched onto the fact that a
twelve-foot strip of land between two of the most productive claims on
Williams Creek had not been properly staked. So he grabbed for
himself that tiny wedge of ground, which quickly yielded gold worth
$15,000 and made him known far and wide as Twelve-Foot Davis.

The bonanza soon exhausted itself, but unlike most of the other
fortune hunters, Twelve-Foot Davis stayed on. He spent the rest of his
life swapping goods for furs with local Indians, competing for a fading
trade with the mighty Hudson's Bay Company. They say he never
forgot a debt and always kept his tiny trading cabins stocked with
emergency provisions as a welcome for weary travellers. According to
one story, when a trapper named Johnny Split-Toe died before collecting
what was due him for his pelts, Davis spent ten years searching for
Johnny's son so that he could pay for them.

During the last half of the nineteenth century, Davis was on the
trading circuit between Soda Creek on the Fraser River, Fort Dunvegan
and Peace River Crossing at the junction of the Peace and the Smoky,
trying with little success to buck the Company store. He grew to
despise the HBC, not for any particular incident but because being a
free trader up against the enormous enterprise proved as tough a way
to scratch a living as there was, especially for a man of his generous, if
somewhat impractical, nature.

He was eighty when he died at Lesser Slave Lake, worn out by a harsh life but respected for his many kindnesses. It took a dozen years for Davis's best friend, a frontier character named Colonel Jim Cornwall, to carry out Twelve-Foot's last wish: that his remains be moved to a hilltop near Peace River Crossing. Cornwall erected a simple gravestone there in the shape of a poplar stump, bearing his late partner's epitaph:

HE WAS EVERY MAN'S FRIEND
AND NEVER LOCKED HIS CABIN DOOR

The grave is there still, but according to local lore (confirmed by Colonel Cornwall before his own death), the real reason Davis had wanted to be buried in that unlikely spot high above the little settlement— directly overlooking the local HBC trading post—was not quite as romantic as the natural beauty of the site might indicate.

"Bury me with my feet pointing downhill," had been Twelve-Foot's final instructions to the Colonel, "so I can piss on the Hudson's Bay Company."

TWELVE-FOOT'S POSTHUMOUS POSTURE was hardly typical, but during the years covered by this volume—from the founding of the rival North West Company in 1783 to the surrender of the HBC's monopoly in 1869—the Hudson's Bay Company aroused every emotion except indifference. The profit-haunted puritans who were the Company's field hands subordinated their personal impulses to remarkably single-minded corporate principles designed to maximize dividends, minimize personal profiles and perpetuate the powers of the royally chartered monopoly. Those who were outside the faith—the HBC's competitors, its parliamentary opponents and the would-be colonizers of its territories—found "the Company of Adventurers of England Tradeing into Hudsons Bay" anything but benign. In an open letter to Lord Palmerston, the British prime minister, Andrew Freeport, an observer of the HBC's methods, noted that "the management of their affairs . . . is like a commercial tomb, closed with the key of death to all except a favoured few . . . its councils unfathomable and its secrets unknown."

Such melodramatic denunciations pointed to a commercial ruthlessness bearing little resemblance to the Company's character during its relatively sedate first century. The early Governors and Chief Factors may have been equally close-mouthed and tight-fisted, but for most of a hundred years after the propitious spring day of the Company's founding in 1670 by Prince Rupert, they had been content to sit in half a dozen forts huddled around the shores of Hudson Bay, bartering axes, guns and blankets for pelts with visiting Cree. Suspended in doldrums of time, place and spirit—asleep "at the edge of a frozen sea," as their critics rightly charged—the Bay men watched the coalescing of their Montreal-based rivals into the North West Company. The energetic young competitors threatened to cut off their fur supplies by establishing inland trading posts along the rivers feeding Hudson Bay. And still they watched.

At first, the HBC reacted not at all, trusting the kindly Providence that had, it seemed, always blessed its uncomplicated commerce. Doing nothing about something as important as a dynamic rival determined to undermine the Company's business created a soporific inertia of considerable power. This was typical of the HBC's operational code—to allow their trading rivals enough latitude to hang themselves. Only when it looked as if the royal adventurers themselves were about to be terminated did the Company spring into action. It took more than a decade for the feud between the two outfits to be fully joined. But once it was, the forests exploded.

As they launched their own long march inland, the HBC traders encountered a breed of buccaneers very different from themselves. Instead of being servants indentured to distant governors, the Nor'Westers were the rampaging free enterprisers of the North American frontier— brave men who had transcended their Presbyterian ethic to mix a little Methodism in their madness. Having adopted a crude form of commercial chutzpah far removed from the grand strategies of British mercantilism and even farther removed from the elegant principle that one should grow rich strictly from other people's labours, these brawny wintering partners were not afraid to plunge into the mosquito-plagued portages of the inland waterways or to spend months in frost-caked lean-tos if it would boost their personal share of profits. This unquenchable impulse—that it was essential to work for oneself and not, like their HBC competitors, for absentee landlords who knew little about the going rate for stamina and defiance—was the incentive that allowed the Nor'Westers to dominate the fur trade and to stay on top for most of four decades.

The Nor'Westers' remarkable exploits fill most of the first half of this book because their story is inextricably woven into that of the HBC, and vice versa. They followed their gutsy instincts, convinced that their unorthodox methods were the only right way of doing things and that no matter how much the Hudson's Bay Governors might wish it, dominance over *le pays sauvage* could no longer be held by waistcoated financiers lounging around mahogany Adam tables in London's

Portaging trade goods at a supply post on the way to the Fur Country

marble halls. Although the Nor'Westers could never obtain a charter to prove it, their hunting grounds eventually extended by right of possession farther than the immense Rupert's Land domain of the Hudson's Bay Company. It was they who developed the first transcontinental trading system. Their profits reflected their fortitude; more than three-quarters of the subcontinent's fur trade moved to their accounts within fifteen years of the NWC's formation. In what turned out to be premature gloating, one of the Montreal Nor'Wester agents proclaimed in feigned protest that *of course* he and his partners did not want to see the HBC go out of business—slyly adding that the Company of Adventurers provided a most useful "cloak to protect the trade from more active opponents."

THE COMMERCIAL WARFARE between the Hudson's Bay and North West companies meant that Canada, which has prided itself on having undergone no revolutions or wars of independence and prissily set itself apart as always having been a "peaceable kingdom," experienced its own equivalent of the American Wild West. The competing fur brigades fought bloody but contained skirmishes in the forests and along the rivers west of the Great Lakes. It was somehow typically Canadian that this struggle was not, as in the American West, concerned with noble assertions of individual liberty against land-hungry cattle barons and black-hatted railway promoters—or even a brave push for collective independence—but was rather an internecine feud between two houses of commerce locked in mortal combat for greater profits.

There was no other commercial feud to equal it.

Ostensibly, the struggle between the HBC and the North West Company was a corporate contest for markets and furs, but it quickly turned into a quest for power and territory. The competition for beaver pelts grew so intense that the northern reaches of America's forests became a battleground.

Both sides settled their accounts in blood. Snipers rode the riverbanks. Loaded cannon were used to reclaim stolen cargoes. Murder and ambush, arson and theft, kidnapping and destruction of property became so common that the act of maiming a competitor was regarded as a condition of doing business. Anarchy escalated to such a degree that in 1803 Britain's Parliament passed the Canada Jurisdiction Act, intended specifically to prevent the abuses that characterized the lawless conflict between the fur-trading companies. But without a resident police to enforce it, the legislation had little effect. In the first eighteen years after these provisions were passed, there is no record of anyone actually being convicted under the law—even though this was the period of the most vicious fighting in the Canadian Northwest.

In one assault, European mercenaries captured the Nor'Westers' main wilderness stronghold. Both sides abused their prisoners, and on the rustic outskirts of the HBC's Red River Colony, twenty settlers and the resident Governor were shot and their bodies mutilated by retainers of the North West Company. Worst of all, by concentrating on massive quantities of liquor as an irresistible lure in the frantic contest for the Indian trappers' bounty, the traders of both companies debauched a civilization, leaving in their wake a dispirited people and nearly destroying a once-proud culture. "It was a bitter war in which each party wielded weapons of trade and violence mercilessly in turn," summarized the Harvard historian Frederick Merk. "From the arsenal of war were drawn raids, the levelling of each other's trading posts, incitation of the Indians and half-breeds to open fighting and secret stabbing and shooting in the shadows of the forest."

Only after the spiral of violence had exhausted itself by the early 1820s in the amalgamation of the two companies' 173 posts under the name and dominance of the HBC did it become clear how close the hostilities between the two firms had come to escalating into all-out war. When the NWC eventually turned in its weapons, the inventory of the Columbia Department alone revealed that its Pacific Coast traders had been armed not only with the usual array of rifles and other small arms but with thirty-two cannon ranging from eighteen-pounders to half-pound swivel guns.

Having won the corporate battle, the Hudson's Bay Company now enjoyed the spoils, lording it over an empire more than twice the size of the princely domain it had originally been granted by Charles II, which had encompassed the then unmapped territory covered by the many rivers draining from nearly every point of the compass into Hudson Bay. The Company's new monopoly stretched from Labrador through to the Pacific Coast and across the continent's northern reaches. The HBC held joint occupancy in what are now the American states of Oregon, Washington, Idaho, Wyoming, and Montana—with outposts as far away as Alaska, Hawaii and San Francisco. This was the moment of the HBC's greatest glory, the time when it held sway over nearly one-twelfth of the earth's land surface. No other commercial enterprise ever achieved comparable sway over so much territory. (The HBC cagily protected its empire against the encroachment of ambitious outsiders by manipulating fur prices, so that challengers soon lost the fiscal will to perpetuate the contest.) During most of the half-century it ruled over this enormous domain, the Company's authority was supreme: it exercised nearly every mandate of a sovereign government, with Sir George Simpson acting as uncrowned king.

It was under Simpson's rigorous stewardship that the HBC exerted its maximum impact on the formation of the Canadian character. As pointed out in my first volume, much of the northern half of North America became a company town, whose inhabitants displayed individuality and imagination at their own risk. Because the little trading posts (or forts, as many were grandly called) were owned and operated by the Company, the prevailing ethic was deference to authority inside their toy ramparts and deference to nature beyond them. These attitudes—the importance of allegiance, of stressing collective survival over individual excellence, of faith in protocol, of respect for the proper order of things—still colour what Canadians do and, especially, don't do.

The most significant historical contribution of both the Hudson's Bay and North West companies was simply that they existed when they did along the still only vaguely defined boundary separating British North America from the United States. "Between 1821 and 1869, it was the skill and perseverance with which the Hudson's Bay Company protected its monopoly trading area between the Great Lakes and the Rocky Mountains that prevented an influx of American settlers that could easily have made the Canadian prairies a second Oregon," noted Dr W. Kaye Lamb, who has written extensively on the fur trade. "The honoured old initials H B C have been interpreted facetiously as meaning 'Here Before Christ'; instead they might more fittingly be taken as signifying 'Here Before Canada.' And if this had not been so, it is unlikely that Canada as we know it today would now exist."

The two companies acted as willing surrogates of the British Empire, occupying for their own purposes the lands beyond its North American colonies. They thus safeguarded these territories until Canada's own awakened imperialistic aspirations took over; this was in time recognized as an essential stage in nation-building.

Similarly, the very fact that these corporate hierarchies existed on the northern side of the border, while the early American fur industry was dominated by individualistic mountain men who competed with Indians for each pelt and liked nothing better than "sniping redskins to watch them spin," fathered permanent characteristics in both societies. The Americans conquered their frontier, sharpshooters against tomahawks, across the ill-famed "Bloody Ground," with the U.S. Cavalry verging on committing genocide in its sixty-nine major attacks on the red man. In sharp contrast, both the Nor'Westers and the Bay men recognized the Indians as long-term trading partners. They formed a relationship based on mutual exploitation. This meant that the Indians were able to trade near-worthless pelts (they had previously killed animals mainly for food) for such desirable goods as axes, guns,

Fort Macleod

blankets and sewing needles; the corporate representatives, on the other hand, got the furs at a fraction of their value on European markets. All parties in the transaction thus had a permanent stake in each other's welfare and in conducting the barter with a modicum of fair play.

The two fur companies fought one another as if they were pursuing a Sicilian vendetta. But they never shot their customers. Frederick Merk, the American history professor who has studied the fur trade of both countries, concluded that the "striking contrast between British and American Indian relations was no mere temporary phenomenon disappearing with the passing of the fur trade. It persisted as long as the red man and the white faced each other in the coveted land of the Far West. Trapper and trader gave way on both sides of the international boundary to miner and cattleman and they in turn to the pioneer farmer. These harbingers of a new day on the American side entered a region of already established strife and perpetuated there traditions two centuries old of Indian massacre and border retaliation. On the Canadian side civilization entered a region reduced by the Hudson's Bay Company to a tradition of law and order. . . ."

THE DEBT TO WATER IN THE NATION'S HISTORY is another dominant trait within the Canadian character nurtured by the fur trade. Novelist Clark Blaise has spoken of "the parenting effect of water on the Canadian

imagination" and no politician jealous of his mandate has ever advocated the export of a drop of the stuff. "Water is very special to
Canadians," Dr Derrick Sewell, a geography professor at the University
of Victoria and specialist on water usage, has commented. "There is no
Indian word for wilderness, because while we may regard it as something separate from us, for them the wilderness is everything—their
dwelling place and source of food, part of their being. To some degree,
Canadians view water with that kind of internal attachment."

The birchbark canoes of the fur trade were propelled by the brawn
and sixth sense of the voyageurs, who were so sensitized to thousands of
miles of river subtleties that they would use clumps of weeds streaming
in fast currents as telltales of their progress. It was this flowing intimacy
with the millions of square miles of wilderness that first created the
notion that Canada might possess a geographical unity all its own.

The land (for its animals) was the quest of these hardy sojourners,
but they depended on water for transportation and supply lines. The
setting for nearly all this book is the network of lakes and rivers that
interlaces Canada's western and northern heartland. Unlike most
countries, Canada was first penetrated by water instead of on horseback.
The animals could not cover enough of the rough terrain or find
enough nourishment to survive in the Precambrian Shield—a rolling
quagmire of rock, matted undergrowth, lakes and streams that covers
nearly half the Canadian subcontinent.

Four key lakes—Huron, Superior, Winnipeg and Athabasca—were
the interconnected hubs whose spokes radiated into the bountiful fur
forests. Onward along three waterways—Hudson Bay, the St Lawrence
and the Columbia—ran the transport routes to market. The water-
highways developed by the early fur traders included many a portage
around rapids, waterfalls and beaver dams, but in the entire length of
the continent, the system was interrupted by few major land gaps, the
longest of them being the twelve-mile Methy Portage in the Churchill
river system at the crest of the Hudson Bay and Mackenzie Basin
watersheds. "The waterways were almost miraculous in their range
and intricacy, and the birchbark canoe a miracle of efficiency," noted
the historian Chester Martin. "A trader could embark at Cumberland
House [an HBC trading post on the Saskatchewan River not far west of
Lake Winnipeg] and, with no portage longer than a single day, could
reach the Arctic Ocean, the Pacific, the Atlantic, or the Gulf of Mexico."

THE FUR TRADERS WHO PEOPLE THIS BOOK possessed an inordinate capacity
for living in desolation. Their stoicism may have bordered on maso-
chism and yet it was much grander than that; any new challenge,

however awkward or dangerous, could not go unaccepted. They were the true caesars of the wilderness—dispossessed Scots and Englishmen seized by the excitement of exploring a New World, determined to live out their boldest fantasies and win fortune in the process.

Their lives were hard and their isolation was hermetic: at Fort Good Hope on the Mackenzie River it took two years for a reply to be received from a letter to England. To the few outsiders who visited their domain, the traders seemed a species apart, men who had voluntarily stepped outside the bounds of civilized society. "I hate the sight of these forts," complained Frederick Ulric Graham, a British baronet who accompanied Simpson on one of his inland journeys. "All the white men living in them look as if they had been buried for a century or two, and dug up again, and had scarcely yet got their eyes open, for they look frightened when they see a stranger."

Their lives may indeed have been harsh, but the best of them savoured the sights, sounds and fragrances of a bewitching land where a man could lose his soul or grasp rare understanding of life's wonders and nature's cycles. The wild flowers forced their green energies through the snow. Deer, moose and ginger fox would watch them from the aromatic forest. The silence of the wild land could cloak emotions or become the catalyst for exhilarating self-discovery. Pretensions fell away like chips from a sculptor's block; character and capabilities were laid bare as stone.

Flashes of humiliation and self-hatred, the cursed immensity of the country, the feats of accomplishment performed without peers to validate one's bravery or compassion—those were the worst emotional ordeals.

Their collective endeavours mapped a continent and claimed an empire, yet with the exception of such grand personages as Sir George Simpson and Lord Selkirk (the utopian Scot who planted Western Canada's first settlement) the men and women portrayed in this book were not aristocrats, innovators or daredevils. They were survivors. They patterned their behaviour around each day's mundane events, leading expedient lives, with the maintenance of shelter and the hunting of food as prevailing priorities. Inclement weather might obliterate overnight a promising pattern of animal tracks, and *that* was often a far weightier matter than the balance-sheet considerations of their distant overlords. Time was as much of a problem as distance, with crucial canoe routes seldom open before mid-May and often frozen shut again by late September. Climate was always the final arbiter of the available options.

The streak of yearning for the freedom of wilderness existence so boldly personified by the men and women who people the pages that follow has endured within the nation's psyche. Most modern Canadians have forgotten or never known about these valiant caesars of the wilderness, yet their lives are marked by the same seasonal rhythms, equally touched by the shared loneliness—the ineffable "northernness" that forms the Canadian character. Those early fur traders learned the hard way why survival is the ultimate Canadian virtue—and why victory so often signals only the postponement of defeat.

Moose Factory on Hudson Bay

I EMPIRE AT RISK

Coat of arms of the North West Company

CHAPTER 1

THE NOR'WESTERS

Never able to establish themselves on Hudson Bay,
the Nor'Westers stepped over the edge of the horizon
and explored virgin lands beyond the known world.

LIKE CRUSADERS OF THE MIDDLE AGES they ultimately failed in their quest
and soiled the banner under which they set out to conquer a continent.
But between 1783 and 1820, the Nor'Westers braved the wilderness
and won. Operating out of their counting houses in Montreal and a
hundred or so outposts connected by an inland navy of two thousand
canoeists, they challenged the power and majesty—the very existence—
of the Hudson's Bay Company and fought the Royal Adventurers to a
standstill.

THE NORTH WEST COMPANY was the first North American business to
operate on a continental scale. Its vast holdings were administered with
greater efficiency and larger civil budgets than the provinces of Lower
and Upper Canada. The NWC's wilderness headquarters, first at Grand
Portage and later at Fort Kaministikwia (renamed Fort William in
honour of William McGillivray, the company's second chief executive
officer), could accommodate nearly two thousand people at the height
of the trading season, its fifteen-foot palisade of pointed timbers enclosing
Canada's first inland metropolis.

The logistics of fur and goods purchasing and the need to co-ordinate
a precariously overextended transportation network led to the development of a remarkably sophisticated trading system (see map on the inside

3

Shooting the rapids in a freight canoe

front cover). The brigades of canoes, loaded to the gunwales with kegs of liquor and packs of trade goods, pushed up from the St Lawrence along the Ottawa and Mattawa rivers, over the height of land and across Lake Nipissing, down the French River to Georgian Bay, through the company's primitive wooden lock at Sault Ste Marie and into Lake Superior. At their northwestern terminus on Superior, the trade goods were trans-shipped into the smaller *canots du nord*, then paddled and portaged up through Rainy Lake, Lake of the Woods and the Winnipeg River into Lake Winnipeg for dispersal along the South and North Saskatchewan rivers and up the Red. The canoes also headed north-west up the Churchill River towards the dreaded Methy Portage that linked the river systems with outlets in the Arctic and Pacific watersheds.

Bringing the furs back to Montreal—the gathering point for their ultimate destination at London's auction markets—meant backtracking over the same route. By the time the Nor'Westers were fully exploiting the prime fur-bearing grounds of the Athabasca Country, the supply line was more than three thousand miles long. These horrendous distances, plus a climate that reduced the period of navigation on northern rivers to less than half the year, created the company's greatest dilemma. Up to thirty months might elapse between the purchase of trade goods and the sale of the furs for which they had been bartered. Every possible shortcut was explored, including an investment of £12,000 "toward making Yonge Street a better road" so that goods in winter could be shipped more efficiently from the town of York (now Toronto) to Georgian Bay.

The Nor'Westers' outposts stretched from Nasquiscow Lake in central Labrador to Fort St James west of the Rockies, north to Fort Good Hope, south to Astoria at the mouth of the Columbia River on the Pacific, across the Prairies and Great Lakes. As well as maintaining posts at nearly every important river junction in what is now northern and western Canada, the NWC established strings of trading forts in present-day Oregon, Washington, Idaho, Montana, North Dakota, Minnesota and Wisconsin. The supply lines converged on a cluster of forty warehouses at Lachine, a cart ride from the partners' headquarters in Montreal.

The most remarkable feature of this wilderness empire was its roots in original exploration. The pathfinders and mapmakers of the North American continent's upper latitudes were the fur traders of the North West Company. With a few dramatic exceptions such as Samuel Hearne, Peter Fidler and Dr John Rae, the HBC's officers for most of a century were content to remain ensconced around Hudson Bay, prepared to allow others to determine the lay of the land.* The Nor'Westers were a more venturesome breed. Peter Pond was the first white man into the Athabasca Country in 1778, and half a decade later the various partnerships exploring the continent's outlying regions had become united in a transcontinental trading company determined to take on the HBC and its hoary charter. The Nor'Westers numbered among their officers some of history's most courageous explorers. Sir Alexander Mackenzie was the first.European to cross North America north of Mexico; he and Simon Fraser hacked their way to the mouths of the torrential rivers that now bear their names. By 1805, the Nor'Westers had started trading past the Great Divide, and Western Canada's founding geographer, David Thompson, was well into his most productive decade of drafting the first workable maps of North America, which included his discovery of the Mississippi's headwaters.

The NWC traders who preceded and followed these and other daring explorers left behind a legacy of alcoholism, syphilis, Mixed Blood babies—and the precise path for the Hudson's Bay Company's subsequent march inland. There was little doubt, as fur-trade historian H.A. Innis put it, that "the North West Company was the forerunner" of

---

*For detailed descriptions of the historic treks of Hearne and Rae, see chapters 13 and 15 of my *Company of Adventurers*, hardcover edition (Viking, 1985), which also chronicles the tentative inland probes of Henry Kelsey, James Knight, William Stuart and Anthony Henday. Peter Fidler's exploits are recounted in Chapter 5 of this volume.

Canadian Confederation, but its more direct accomplishment was to place the huge dominion of land beyond the HBC's territory under the protection of the British Crown.

That these enterprising expansionists deemed each new North West Company outpost to be an extension of the British monarch's reach was the company's most curious gift to posterity, since the Nor'Westers were nearly all either Scots or French—both victims of English imperialism. But they needed London. The manufactured goods essential to the fur trade, such as blankets, axes and particularly the much sought-after guns, had to be purchased in England. London was, of course, also the chief market for dressed pelts, though the Nor'Westers later managed to sidestep that monopoly by trading some of their more valuable sea otter skins directly to Canton in southeast China, navigating half the globe to do so.

The impact of the transcontinental trading routes was pervasive enough to work the magic that helped save Western Canada from being absorbed into the United States. The land had already been claimed through right of exploration by the Nor'Westers and later by occupation of the Hudson's Bay Company. It was a puny scattering of tiny outposts that held the line, but it was enough.

The Nor'Westers' impulse to explore uncharted territories was less the product of an altruistic desire to advance the frontiers of knowledge than a result of the company's infrastructure and the stretch of its traplines. The NWC's profitability depended on constantly moving onward and outward to tap newer and richer animal preserves. That, in turn, meant maintaining an ever-lengthening transportation system with large and multiplying overhead expenditures. Unlike the more sedentary Bay men, the Nor'Westers were constantly in motion. As the beaver lodges in relatively accessible corners were trapped out, the canoes moved ever farther afield—and the longer the network, the less viable it became. No wonder the North West Company's official motto eschewed Latin subtleties, encapsulating its hopes in a one-word, no-nonsense exclamation: "PERSEVERANCE"!

Throughout its glory days, the North West Company sought in vain what the Hudson's Bay Company took for granted: direct sea-access into the continent's midriff and a monopoly sanctioned by royal decree over the trading area within its jurisdiction. "The rivalry was not between two commercial enterprises at all," Daniel Francis, a popular historian of the fur trade, has commented. "Rather, it was a rivalry between two great geographic possibilities. Would the resources of the western hinterland flow southeastward across the Great Lakes and down the Ottawa River to Canada? Or would they take the shorter route north and east, through the stunted forest of the Shield to the swampy shores of Hudson Bay? For almost half a century the answer hung in the balance." Because the Bay route reduced the cost of transportation by more than fifteen hundred canoe-miles, the geographical advantages clearly lay with the London-based Company. Never able to establish themselves on Hudson Bay, the Nor'Westers stepped over the edge of the horizon and explored virgin lands beyond the known world.

Within two decades of their original amalgamation, the Nor'Westers controlled 78 percent of Canadian fur sales and could caustically claim that the Hudson's Bay Company was doing business "as if it were drawn by a dead horse." They ruled the West. Despite perilously over-extended supply lines, during the decade and a half after the turn of the century the Nor'West partners earned net profits estimated at £1,185,000. This meant that original investments of £800 returned £16,000. The NWC also achieved a well-balanced diversification in its fur offerings. In a typical year (1798) their catch included: 106,000 beaver skins, 2,100 bear, 5,500 fox, 4,600 otter, 17,000 musquash (muskrat), 32,000 marten, 1,800 mink, 6,000 lynx, 600 wolverine, 1,600 fisher, 3,800 wolf, 700 elk hides and 1,900 deer hides. Five hundred buffalo robes were a bonus.

They not only grew rich, they also became powerful, forming the fledgling colony's first indigenous commercial Establishment. Unlike the Bay men who went back across the Atlantic at the expiration of their contracts, most Nor'Westers settled down and stayed on. Many of the NWC partners built elegant houses at the foot of Montreal's Mount Royal, capricious castles meant both to display their newly won riches and to proclaim their intention of establishing family dynasties. Their profits helped build the Bank of Montreal into what was briefly North America's largest financial institution, and their favourite hearth, that saturnalian dining phenomenon known as the Beaver Club, became for its time the most exclusive fraternity on the continent.

These knights of the forest regarded themselves as inheritors of that mantle of esteem once worn by gladiators and noblemen, or, more appropriately, Highland clan chieftains—living proof to a hesitant colonial society that ability and application could be spectacularly rewarded. "Sometimes one or two partners, recently from the interior posts, would make their appearance in New York," observed the American historian Washington Irving. "On these occasions there was a degree of magnificence of the purse about them, and a peculiar propensity to expenditure at the goldsmith's and jeweller's for rings, chains, brooches, necklaces, jewelled watches, and other rich trinkets, partly for their own wear, partly for presents to their female acquaintances; a gorgeous prodigality, such as was often to be noticed in former times in Southern planters and West India creoles, when flush with the profits of their plantations."

Irving made fun of "the swelling and braggart style" of "these hyperborean nabobs," noting that the Nor'Westers were not merely traders but in fact proprietors. In sharp contrast to even the most senior employees of the HBC, who laboured for overseas patrons and paltry wages, the ranking Nor'Westers controlled their own destinies. An uneasy alliance of up to three dozen partners, among them Montreal-based Scottish promoters and merchants, the NWC may not have been blessed with a royal charter but its shareholders reaped regal profits. The cost of one share averaged £4,000, and yet yearly dividends of £400 were routinely disbursed at a time when clerks at the NWC's trading posts were being paid £100 per annum.

No wonder the North West Company partners behaved as though they were chiefs of a transcontinental clan, claiming all the traditions and especially the loyalties due in such a feudal structure. Their escutcheons and rituals were designed to strengthen the notion that only within the confines of the corporation could its partners discover and exploit their true natures. Any deviation from set standards was considered treachery. No clan operated with more ruthless efficiency than the North West Company of Montreal.

The organization's hierarchy was not as refined as that of the HBC, which maintained ranks so minutely structured that by accepted protocol Chief Factors, when ordered to perform a duty, had to be "requested," Chief Traders "directed" and non-commissioned officers "instructed"—even when they were talking to one another in the bush. Highlanders entered the NWC as clerks, rising in rank to masters of minor trading posts and eventually, if they produced results, to wintering partners. This latter category, which had no early equivalent within the HBC, gave officers in the field the double incentive of sharing in profits and having a direct voice in formulating policies that would multiply revenues. They were owners as well as operators. At the top of the pyramid were the Montreal agents or directors, who received commissions for their commercial services besides owning a controlling interest of the shares.

This visible, tightly knit command structure helped ignite the NWC's vibrant *esprit de corps*, but what made most of the senior partners so devoted to the common cause was that they belonged not just to the same company or even to the same clan, but often to the same family. At one time or another, there were on the NWC rolls seven Simon

Frasers, four Finlays, five Camerons,* six McTavishes, seven McLeods, eight McGillivrays, fourteen each of Grants and McKenzies and so many McDonalds that they had to differentiate themselves by including home towns in their surnames, as in John McDonald of Garth.† It seemed at times that every partner in the North West Company was blood relative to every other, most of them linking their family trees with that of Simon McTavish, the company's chief founder and guiding spirit. McTavish married a daughter of the trader Charles Chaboillez, whose other daughter became the wife of Roderick McKenzie, a first cousin of Sir Alexander Mackenzie. Simon McTavish's nephew William McGillivray, later the leading partner in the concern (joining his brothers Duncan and Simon), married a sister of John McDonald of Garth, nephew-in-law of McTavish and a cousin of Patrick Small, whose daughter married David Thompson. McTavish had three nephews, two grandnephews, three nephews-in-law, two brothers-in-law, three cousins and one "distant cousin" in the company.

These family connections at least partly compensated for the North West Company's inherent instability as a constantly shifting set of partnerships among the internationally minded Montreal money men and the more earthy and less sophisticated wintering partners. At least eight different agreements were negotiated, and each time the inlanders believed their interests were being subordinated to those of the metropolitan agents who were determined not only to dominate the St Lawrence fur trade but to create business empires of their own. Most of the Montrealers, especially the Frobishers (Benjamin, Joseph and Thomas)

---

*The doughty Camerons originally came from Glenlivet in Upper Banffshire. Aeneas Cameron became chief of the NWC trading post at Fort Timiskaming in northwestern Quebec in 1793. He was succeeded in that post by his nephew Angus, who in turn was followed by *his* nephew, James, with the dynasty completing its eighty-year domination of the district in 1872 with the tenure of James's cousin, Charles Stuart.

†John McDonald of Garth, whose grandfather was wounded at Culloden, was one of the Canadian fur trade's more contentious characters. He often boasted that, as lords of the isles at the time of the Great Flood, the McDonalds had had their own ark on Loch Lomond, and the subsequent survival of their strongest men and fairest women rendered them superior to all Scotland's other clans. Although he was of small physical stature even for that time and was handicapped by a withered right arm, he enjoyed combat and fought several duels, one of them with a Hudson's Bay Company trader named William Tomison over the possession of a well. After his retirement from the NWC at the end of twenty-three years in the fur trade, he built himself a laird's home in Ontario's Stormont County, had sixty tenants cultivating his land and was named a justice of the peace.

and the various McGillivrays (who were all former traders), tried to keep themselves sensitive to the winterers' problems. But officers in the field seldom appreciated the grave difficulties involved in obtaining extended credit sources for the fur trade, the tricky and sometimes questionable tactics required to keep governments in line and the fiscal acrobatics necessary to maintain the prosperity of as volatile an enterprise as the North West Company.

SIMON MCTAVISH, who masterminded the firm's evolution for most of thirty years, remains a shadowy figure in Canadian history. Yet if Paul de Chomedey de Maisonneuve can be credited with the physical founding of Montreal, then it was McTavish with his genius for business organization who transformed the community into a major commercial centre. He repeatedly crowded out smaller Montreal partnerships and struck treaties with American fur companies, hiving their activities into the upper regions of the Mississippi and keeping them there with the persuasively domineering bluster that became his trademark and his chief negotiating weapon. His tenacity, territorial ambition and imperial lifestyle earned him the aristocratic sobriquet "Le Marquis," and he abundantly lived up to both the grandeur and the snobbishness his nickname implied. Lord Selkirk, the Scottish visionary whose colony would ultimately threaten the North West Company, observed during an 1804 visit to Montreal, "McTavish is entirely unequalled here in acuteness and reach of thought—he is admitted to have planned the constitution of the old North West Company by means of which that vast undertaking is kept together."

Born in 1750 on Lord Lovat's estate in Stratherrick, Simon McTavish was the son of a lieutenant in the old 78th, or Fraser's Highlanders, and emigrated to the American colonies at thirteen to apprentice in the Albany fur trade. Described even at that age as a charming young man who loved "good wine, good oysters and pretty girls," he moved to Montreal in about 1775 and began to haggle with the independent traders ranging into the continent's far corners, pushing the idea that the economies of scale inherent in a joint venture would benefit them all, particularly in the face of the HBC's implacable monopoly. By 1790, his firm McTavish, Frobisher & Company dominated the newly formed North West partnership, and he held the controlling interest. The coalition performed economic miracles, but it never achieved the calm possession of authority that the HBC could grandly assume; there were always upstarts ready to finance expeditions inland, knowing the NWC's tenure had no legitimacy beyond tenacious occupancy. The firm's

Simon McTavish

facilities and communications lines were so stretched that it never ceased to be vulnerable.

Instead of relying on royal charters or bureaucratic niceties to enforce their rule over the territories in which they traded, the Nor'Westers under McTavish's direction used the much more direct technique of physically evicting intruders. In 1801, for example, a Montreal free-trader named Dominique Rousseau sent a canoe inland under the command of a Monsieur Hervieu, who eventually set up a tiny emporium just beyond gunshot range of the NWC stronghold at Grand Portage. Duncan McGillivray, Simon McTavish's nephew and a senior NWC partner, immediately ordered him off the site. But Hervieu refused to move until he was shown title to the land, accurately pointing out that he had as much right to be there as anyone else. This legalistic demand for a document the Nor'Westers had never been able to obtain so infuriated McGillivray that he stuck his dagger into Hervieu's tent and slashed it beyond repair, bellowing that the free-trader's throat would be cut next if he ventured farther inland. Hervieu's boss, Rousseau, later took McGillivray to court and won £500 in damages. That legal victory emboldened him to try again, and in 1806 Rousseau dispatched two canoes under a Monsieur Delorme to trade north of Superior. On the trail from the lakehead, the little expedition was intercepted by

Alexander McKay, a Nor'Wester with a mordant sense of humour. Instead of threatening the visitors, McKay ordered his crew to fell trees across the narrow creeks along Delorme's route, and the intruders were soon hopelessly entangled in branches. Frustrated beyond endurance and sensing that their persistent enemy was ready to block their watery path all the way to the Pacific, Delorme and his companions stepped out of their canoes, abandoned their trade goods and walked back to Montreal. Rousseau threatened another court case, but it was never heard; instead, the Nor'Westers paid Delorme back for the jettisoned goods—at the lower Montreal prices, of course.

By the 1790s, more than a hundred canoes were being sent inland annually from Lachine. For the next decade and a half McTavish's influence multiplied exponentially. He was recognized as Montreal's most important and richest merchant. In 1793, at a mature forty-three, he married the beautiful seventeen-year-old Marguerite Chaboillez and purchased, for £25,000, the seigneury of Terrebonne. When he was told that Castle Dunardary, the ancestral home of the chief of the Clan McTavish in Argyll, was due to go under the auctioneer's hammer, he bought that too and received permission to use the clan's armorial bearings. In Montreal, the newlyweds at first occupied a substantial house on Rue St Jean Baptiste, but in 1804 McTavish decided to build his love a northern palace. Angled into a plateau below Mount Royal (between today's Peel and McTavish streets) to allow an unobstructed vista of the St Lawrence River and the rounded mountains beyond, the mansion boasted a flamboyant four-storey façade marked by twin conical towers roofed in tin and a vaulted living-room that promised to become the focal point of Montreal society.

The fur barons tried hard to emulate their role models, the Scottish clan chiefs, by building themselves huge overdone pavilions and carefully keeping score of one another's ostentations. Joseph Frobisher, a Yorkshireman who passed as a Lowland Scot and became McTavish's senior partner, erected an impressive rockpile called Beaver Hall, whose sweeping driveway lined with Lombardy poplars welcomed every dignitary visiting Montreal. William McGillivray moved into Château St Antoine, and many of the lesser partners purchased seigneuries along the St Lawrence.* There was a golden autumn quality about

---

*The only remaining public monument of the fur-trade fortunes is Montreal's McGill University. James McGill had been in the fur trade but gained most of his wealth from banking, timber and land speculation. He bequeathed his summer home, Burnside, plus £10,000, for the establishment of a university—assets that by 1981 were worth $150 million, making McGill the best-endowed university in the country.

their sybaritic lives, with even their most delightful diversions pervaded by a subtle end-of-season mood.

The fur trade was a demanding but highly seasonal enterprise. While the rivers were frozen the Montreal-based *nouveaux riches* devoted their energies to outdoing one another at lavishly catered sleigh rides, card tournaments, private musical recitals and masked balls. One former winterer shod his favourite horse with silver and galloped through the city's poorer districts, scattering showers of coins. He also loved riding into particularly fancy restaurants and ordering the animal a full-course meal. It was a comfortable if self-indulgent existence, but like veterans who can never transcend their time in the trenches, the citified Nor'Westers yearned to recapture the wild freedom and excitement of the frontier. Something, anything, to make the adrenalin pump again.

Those urges found their outlet in February 1785 with the founding of the Beaver Club, which became the quintessential NWC institution. Nothing like it could have been created by the prosaic ramrods then in charge of the Hudson's Bay Company. Despite its astronomical liquor consumption, the Beaver Club was much more than an urban watering hole. Here the Nor'Westers could abandon artificial dignities and re-create those heady times that had given meaning to their lives. Because it was only among their own that such nostalgia was lifted above its more mundane level of providing an excuse to get drunk and break furniture, membership in the Beaver Club was limited to fifty-five fur traders who had spent at least one full season in *le pays d'en haut*.* Club rules were simple but rigidly followed. On admission, each new member had a gold medal struck, engraved with his name, initial wintering date and the club motto: "Fortitude in Distress." These baubles were worn at fortnightly evening meetings, and there was a nominal cash penalty for leaving one's medal at home. The repasts were convened at prestigious local dining-rooms such as Richard Dillon's Montreal Hotel at Place d'Armes or the Mansion House at 156 St Paul

---

*Paradoxically, this eliminated Simon McTavish, who had taken many inland journeys but had never wintered in Indian Country. Eight years after the club's inception, McTavish was allowed to join, perhaps partly because of his proclivity for settling social accounts by winning duels. He had fought a successful duel at Detroit in 1772 against the American land speculator William Constable, and when a Montreal physician named George Selby challenged him because the socially ambitious doctor had not been invited to one of McTavish's balls, the Marquis (who was a crack shot) deliberately missed, leaving the social climber's honour and body intact.

David David was the only Jewish member of the Beaver Club. His medal sold in 1986 at an auction in London for $19,000.

One of four remaining Beaver Club medals. This one was presented to Saskatchewan fur trader Nicholas Montour, who purchased the seigneury of La-Pointe-du-Lac.

Street, where meals were served on the club's own crested crystal and china with matching silver cutlery. The menu consisted of such country delicacies as wedges of pemmican, venison steaks, roasted beaver tails and pickled buffalo tongues. But it was the attendant ritual that really counted. Five toasts were proposed: the Mother of All Saints; the King; the Fur Trade in All Its Branches; Voyageurs, Wives and Children; and Absent Members. Any reveller who deviated in the order of these salutes was fined six bottles of Madeira. Each round was climaxed by the dashing of glasses into the fireplace. After that, a peace pipe was passed around and the serious reminiscing and drinking began.

Usually no one was sober enough to keep minutes of the proceedings, but George T. Landmann, a visiting British officer, left this description of a typical meeting in his *Adventures and Recollections:* "In those days we dined at 4 o'clock, and after taking a satisfactory quantity of wine, the married men . . . retired, leaving about a dozen to drink to their health. We now began in right earnest and true Highland style, and by 4 o'clock in the morning, the whole of us had arrived at such a state of perfection, that we could all give the war-whoops as well as Mackenzie and McGillivray, we could all sing admirably, we could all drink like fishes and we all thought we could dance on the table without disturbing a single decanter, glass or plate . . . but on making the experiment we discovered that it was a complete delusion, and ultimately, we broke all the plates, glasses, bottles, etc., and the table also, and worse than that all the heads and hands of the party received many severe contusions,

William McGillivray and his family

cuts and scratches. . . . I was afterwards informed that one hundred and twenty bottles of wine had been consumed at our convivial meeting."

Landmann's diary noted the presence of a dozen guests at the gathering, which translated into an incredible ten bottles of wine each—but that tally did not include the large quantities of ale, porter, gin and brandy also downed on these occasions. A bill dated September 17, 1808, recorded that thirty-two invitees consumed twenty-nine bottles of Madeira, nineteen bottles of port, fourteen bottles of porter and twelve quarts of ale, as well as unspecified quantities of gin, brandy and negus—a concoction of wine, hot water, sugar and nutmeg. Among the notables who attended Beaver Club dinners were Lord Selkirk, the Arctic explorer Sir John Franklin, the Irish poet Thomas Moore, the American fur magnate John Jacob Astor, Colonel Isaac Brock, then commanding the Montreal garrison, and the Duke of Kent, later the father of Queen Victoria. When the resident Governor-in-Chief, Lord Dalhousie, came to dine on May 14, 1824, he presented each of his companions with a specially designed silver snuff box.*

A highlight of the Beaver Club gatherings was the restaging of *le grand voyage*. Using that narrow window of opportunity between being uproariously drunk and actually passing out, the Nor'Westers would stumble around until they were seated on the floor, arranged two abreast, pretending they were steering a fast-moving *canot du nord*. Grasping fire-tongs, pokers, walking sticks, swords and other likely looking implements as imaginary paddles, they bawled voyageur songs as they stroked ever faster, their eyes glazed, their faces beet-red with exertion. But even make-believe northern canoes must eventually encounter rapids—and that required a change of tactic. With the false shrewdness of the very drunk, the Nor'Westers would consider the possibilities, then clamber up on the dinner-tables and ride the rapids by "shooting" to the floor astride empty wine casks, bellowing a variation on Indian war whoops that verged on Highland battle cries. By this time it might have been four or five in the morning, and the rented dining-room resembled the field hospital of a vanquished army. The few members still upright would adjourn the meeting and stagger home.

The Beaver Club's final gathering was held on March 5, 1827, three years after the death of the elder Alexander Henry, the last of its original members. By then the meeting had mellowed into a sedate

---

*One of these engraved mementoes turned up in 1894 at a New York auction of the personal effects of an actress named Rosina Vokes. It sold for forty-one dollars.

gentlemen's soirée, a decline attested to by the fact that the thirty-two men who were there emptied only sixty-eight bottles.*

THE CLUB'S WILDERNESS OUTSTATION, the place the Nor'West partners treated as the inland nerve centre of the fur trade, was Grand Portage near the head of Lake Superior. But when the boundary settlements between the United States and British North America made it clear that the NWC post would fall south of the new border, the company moved its quarters forty-five miles northeast to the mouth of the Kaministikwia River. There a thousand men built a new trans-shipment centre eventually known as Fort William, and every summer the voyageur-manned canoes would converge on the fort from Lachine and the far-flung hunting grounds. There too assembled the Montreal and wintering partners, laden with gear and self-importance, to negotiate new contracts for the season's catch. "They ascended the rivers in great state," wrote Washington Irving about the partners' processions to Fort William. "They were wrapped in rich furs, their huge canoes freighted with every convenience and luxury, and manned by Canadian voyageurs, as obedient as Highland clansmen. They carried up with them cooks and bakers, together with delicacies of every kind, and an abundance of choice wines for the banquets which attended this great convocation. Happy were they, too, if they could meet with some distinguished stranger, above all, some titled member of the British nobility, to accompany them on this stately occasion, and grace their high solemnities."

Fort William's 125 acres accommodated forty-two buildings massed in a rectangle paralleling the landing docks. Because transportation costs were so high, the Nor'Westers maintained their own workshops, including a cooperage for making kegs and a boatyard for building and repairing canoes. All the warehouses, dormitories and offices were linked to the Great Hall, where the senior partners lived, ate, sat in council and celebrated their large and smaller triumphs. Spacious enough to seat two hundred at a formal dinner, this building was enhanced in its elegant Georgian symmetry by a balconied façade sixty feet long.

---

*A modern version of the Beaver Club was inaugurated by Her Majesty Queen Elizabeth II at Montreal's Queen Elizabeth Hotel in 1959 and now has nearly a thousand members in forty countries—but they don't perform le grand voyage. A major meeting of the Beaver Club was held at the Queen Elizabeth during the Fifth Annual Fur Trade Conference at Montreal in 1985, and the Club entertains Montreal's business elite daily at lunch.

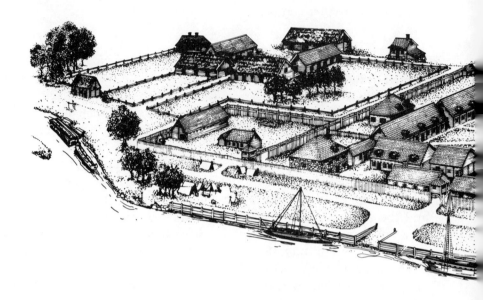

Fort William, the North West Company's wilderness headquarters

Off the main dining-room were four lavishly furnished lodgings for the Montreal agents. The Great Hall's décor included a stern-looking bust of Simon McTavish, a life-size portrait of Lord Nelson and a painting of the Battle of Trafalgar (both attributed to William Berczy), as well as arrays of glittering silver candlesticks and crystal decanters. The NWC's executives dined in comfort every evening, the seating plan tailored to their station within the company's hierarchy. Wild duck, lake trout and buffalo humps were featured, with mutton, beef, fowl, vegetables and butter brought in fresh from the rudimentary farm outside the fort's gates. The daily ration at these sumptuous meals was the equivalent of several pounds of buffalo meat or two whole geese a man, washed down with West Indies rum and French brandy by the barrel.

Each season's rendezvous was climaxed by a gala summer ball. An impromptu orchestra that combined the not always compatible tones of bagpipes, violins, flutes and fifes bleated the lively strains of "The Reel of Tulloch," "The Flowers of Edinburgh" and "The Dashing White Sergeant." Senior partners had first pick among "the ladies of the country" invited to these extravaganzas, and the revelry lasted long into the night. These galas displayed a vigorous mélange of traditions: Scottish reels, Quebec jigs and the more sedate Ojibway steps. While their partners whirled around, the Indian women stood in one place,

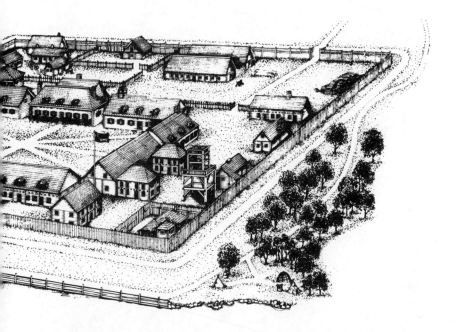

bobbing up and down in time to the music, lifting both feet off the ground at the same time—all executed with rhythmic pacing and dignity. As the hour grew late and the liquor took hold, mock canoe races would be staged, with traders taking their escorts for a "paddle" around the room, ending up in laughing mêlées of buckled legs and groping hands. "At night *bourgeois* and clerks danced in the Great Hall," wrote Marjorie Wilkins Campbell, the unofficial historian of the North West Company, "singing tender Scottish ballads and naughty French songs to the sensuous slipslap of moccasined feet . . . now and again a Chippewa girl's throaty murmur blended with a man's exulting laughter in one of the cabins or from under the canoes beached along the riverside."

When the partners had slept off the after-effects of these revelries, wintering preparations got under way. Brigades of canoes heavy with furs were dispatched at two-day intervals on the return journey to Lachine; the inland partners led their flotillas laden with trade goods into the great Northwest, ready to face another winter trading season. By the end of August, fewer than two dozen maintenance personnel remained at the fort.

The winterers scattered across the Indian Country led isolated but endurable lives. Almost entirely cut off from the outside world, they created a universe of their own that often included country brides and

*Like their earlier NWC counterparts, these HBC men found respite
from the hardships of frontier life at gala balls and Christmas fêtes.*

families. Unlike the HBC, the North West Company placed no restrictions on their traders' taking Indian wives until 1806. These relationships, which were formed at every level of the enterprise, were based on more than sexual gratification, and became vital to the fur trade. The women acted as interpreters, mentors and, through their kinship links, vital conduits into Indian society. Women dressed the hides, made the moccasins, pounded the pemmican, netted the snowshoes and acted as porters when no animal power was available. "What did the Indian women get in return for their labour?" inquired Margaret Atwood in a remarkable essay on the period. "Sometimes they got syphilis or smallpox. They got copper pots instead of birchbark ones, and they got cheap cotton and blanket cloth. They got needles and thread and the pleasure of sewing the coloured trade beads—'mock coral, barley corn, mock garnet, enamelled, blue agate,' and the many more listed in the company's inventories—into beautiful patterns for their men's clothes. They also got acknowledgement of a kind: the company knew their importance, as it knew the importance of the beaver and buffalo."

There is evidence that an active trade in female slaves was sponsored by some of the NWC winterers. When Archibald McLeod, who later became a senior member of the Beaver Club, was stationed at Fort Alexandria on the upper Assiniboine, he noted in his diary: "I gave the Chef de Canard's widow to the amount of 28 plus, & took the Slave Woman, whom next fall I shall sell for a good price to one of the men." James McKenzie, who participated in the Northwest fur trade for twenty-seven years, described in his journal entry of April 9, 1800, how complicated some of these human transactions could become: "This Indian brought his daughter, who deserted in the course of the winter from Morin, at Slave Lake, in order to be returned to her husband. . . . Mr Porter wrote me, by Morin's orders, to sell her to the highest bidder and debit [sic: credit] Morin for the amount. Two advantages may be reaped from this affair; the first is that it will assist to discharge the debts of a man unable to do it by any other means, for he is neither good middleman, foreman, steersman, interpreter or carpenter; the second is that it may be the means to tricking some lecherous miser to part with some of his hoard. I therefore kept the woman to be disposed of in the season when the Peace River bucks look out for women, in the month of May."

There were examples of women and girls as young as nine or ten being traded for horses or kegs of rum, but such transactions were a perversion of Indian custom. More common was the taking of "country wives" in temporary marriages that customarily lasted the length of a Nor'Wester's posting—although many such liaisons endured the stretch of their partners' lives. If the traders' diaries are to be believed, some of these matings were entered into by the men with considerable initial reluctance. Alexander Henry the Younger, who travelled the Northwest accompanied by a tame dancing bear, left behind a sixteen-hundred-page journal describing his encounters with the Plains Indians. Occasionally he would come across some exceptional scenes, such as this one that he recorded in his diary: "[The Gros Ventres] appear to be destitute or ignorant of all shame or modesty. In their visits to our establishments women are articles of temporary barter with our men. For a few inches of twist tobacco a Gros Ventre will barter the person of his wife or daughter with as much sang-froid as he would bargain for a horse. He has no equal in such an affair, though the Blackfoot, Blood, or Peigan is now nearly as bad—in fact, all those tribes are a nuisance when they come to the forts with their women. They intrude upon every room and cabin in the place, and even though a trader may have a family of his own, they insist upon doing them the charity of accepting of the company of at least one woman for the night. It is sometimes with the greatest difficulty that we can get the fort clear of them in the evening and shut the gates. . . ."

On New Year's Day, 1801, Henry awoke with a chief's dark-eyed daughter in his bed. "Liard's daughter took possession of my room," he complained, "and the devil himself could not have got her out." After a month of sparring, he accepted the young woman as his companion. Four years later, while he was away from his post at Fort Pembina, Henry's in-laws were massacred by a raiding party of Sioux. When he later rode out to survey the remains of his family's camp beyond the fort's gates, Henry found only his father-in-law's torso, the skull having been carried off by the raiders as a water dish. "I gathered up the remaining bones of my *belle-mère* in a handkerchief," he lamented, "then I gave a party of three hundred Assiniboines Saulteaux and Cree a nine-gallon keg of gunpowder and a hundred musket balls. 'Go,' I encouraged them. 'Revenge the death of my *beau-père* and his family.'"

A more gentle view of the wild country can be glimpsed in the journals of Daniel Williams Harmon, the God-fearing Vermont-born trader who spent two decades in the Northwest bemoaning, among other things, the loose morals of frontier society. His Sunday-school ethics were particularly affronted by the wanton matings of some NWC traders and their disregard for the sanctity of the Sabbath. After four years of successfully combating temptation, Harmon found himself reluctantly capitulating to the charms of a fourteen-year-old Mixed Blood named Elizabeth Duval. The couple spent the next decade and a half moving from one NWC post to another. In 1819 Harmon was due to leave the fur trade, and there is a moving entry in his diary as he tries to decide how he can follow the usual custom and abandon his country wife. "The union which has been formed between us in the providence of God," he confided to his diary, "has not only been cemented by a long and mutual performance of kind offices, but, also, by a more sacred consideration. We have wept together over the early departure of several children, and especially, over the death of a beloved son. We have children still living, who are equally dear to us both. How could I spend my days in the civilized world, and leave my beloved children in the wilderness? How could I tear them from a mother's love, and leave her to mourn over their absence, to the day of her death?" Harmon opted to take his beloved Elizabeth and their fourteen children out with him; they were officially married at a Vermont Congregational church. The couple founded the New England town of Harmonsville and later moved to Sault au Récollet near Montreal, where Harmon died impoverished but not alone.

Harmon was not the only Nor'Wester to take his wife east. NWC traders George Nelson, James Hughes and J.D. Cameron all took their Indian wives out of the wilderness country, and many more took Métis or Mixed Blood wives with them when their service was complete.

The sons of many North Country liaisons were absorbed into the fur trade, while some of the daughters were sent to the East for convent educations. Because local NWC forts were being charged with maintaining too many wives and children, during its 1806 conclave at Fort William, the Montreal company adopted a new regulation that prohibited its employees from "marrying" pure-blood Indian women (at a fine of £100) to lessen the burden of having to feed and clothe families at company forts. One reason behind this reform was the growing number of retired NWC voyageurs who had chosen to live with women of the country. They had fathered large families and were willing to settle permanently in the Fur Country.

These canoemen provided the essential link with the heartland. It was one of the great ironies of the rampaging empire founded by the Montreal fur traders that it was held together by a remarkable ragbag of magnificent river rats, using the most primitive mode of locomotion there is: raw muscle.

Canoe brigade braving the fog of Lake Superior

CHAPTER 2

THE MAGNIFICENT RIVER RATS

Their exuberant and highly un-Canadian
sense of daring propelled them to risk everything
for a cause as ephemeral as their own brotherhood.

NO SMEAR OF THEIR SWEAT or echo of their ribaldry reaches out to us, yet in their time they were cockleshell heroes on seas of sweet water.

Unsung, unlettered and uncouth, the early fur-trade voyageurs gave substance to the unformed notion of Canada as a transcontinental state. The traditional postcard pastiche of slap-happy buffoons with sly moustaches and scarlet sashes, bellowing dirty *chansons* about pliant maidens—that was not who they were. Their eighteen-hour paddling days were more wretched than many men then or now could survive. They were in effect galley slaves, and their only reward was defiant pride in their own courage and endurance.

Because they could boast of their exploits to no one but themselves, the voyageurs, like a wild and worn-out professional hockey team perpetually on the road, had to concoct their own sustaining myths. No voyageur ever reported meeting a small bear, a tame moose or a wolf that wasn't snarling with blood-lust.

Running through mosquito clouds along boggy portages with 180 pounds or more on their shoulders, strong-arming four tons of cargo through icy rapids while, as one trader told it, "not only hanging on by their hands and feet but by their 'eyebrows,'" the canoemen cherished these daily victories, which became grist for the self-justifying legends that kept them going. The tally of hardship was most clearly visible at the steepest of the killing portages—the plain wooden crosses, sometimes thirty in a group, marking the spot where drowning, stroke,

25

heart attack or strangulated hernia had finally claimed their victims. Out in that witches' brew of a wilderness, they outran their souls and maimed their bodies, and nobody was there to salute them or mark their passage.

Listed in the company ledgers as "engagés," the voyageurs were peons and free spirits at one and the same time. Hired to man the canoes through season after season in the Fur Country, they eagerly signed up for unimaginable toil that cracked their backs and ruptured their intestines but never broke their spirit.*

"They had the pride of champions," noted Hugh MacLennan in *The Rivers of Canada.* "They sprang from European peasants who had never been allowed to leave their villages or their lords' estates . . . but in the West of Canada they were their own masters and lived with the freedom of kings. In the Canadian service far more licence was granted to an independently minded Voyageur than was ever given within the service of the Bay. That is why the Nor'Westers became such great explorers." Indeed, it had been voyageurs (plus some even less acknowledged Indians) who manned the canoes that carried Mackenzie, Fraser, Thompson and the other trail-blazers to fame.

Resident officers of the Hudson's Bay Company, which had to hire Orkneymen and the less tractable Indians instead of voyageurs to man their boats, complained about not having an equivalent to "those natural water Dogs" in their service. The most astute endorsement was delivered by Ramsay Crooks, an executive of the American Fur Company, who requested that voyageurs be exempted from a ban proposed by the United States Congress on Nor'West traders in the upper Mississippi Valley. "It will still be good policy to admit freely & without the least restraint the Canadian boatmen," he wrote. "These people are indispensable to the successful prosecution of the trade, their places cannot be supplied by Americans, who are for the most part . . . too independent to submit quietly to a proper control . . . 'tis only in the Canadian we find that temper of mind, to render him patient, docile

---

*The voyageurs are sometimes confused with *coureurs de bois*, a description reserved for the itinerant, illicit fur gatherers who flooded into the Superior Country during the late 1600s and early 1700s to outrun the Indian middlemen then dominating the trade. The voyageurs' powers of endurance are difficult to exaggerate. Northern historian Alan Cooke, who has portaged a canoe upstream, once observed that the work "may be unfavourably compared with the labour of Sisyphus, whose boulder was, at least, neither fragile nor perishable. The course of his work did not lie along the bed of a mountain stream nor, in the legend, is there any mention of mosquitoes and black flies. . . . All other discomforts of wilderness travel pale beside the continuous torment offered by the hordes of biting insects—this scourge being beyond easy description."

and persevering. In short they are a people harmless in themselves whose habits of submission fit them peculiarly for our business and if guided as it is my wish they should be, will never give just cause of alarm to the Government of the Union." The Canadian identity has seldom since been more perceptively defined.

The voyageurs were not universally revered. Many of the more fastidious NWC partners dismissed them as filthy and profane, much too volatile and sensual to suit the proprietors' Presbyterian predilections. David Thompson disdainfully reported that he had managed to sign up a whole crew of voyageurs for a tough winter journey to the Missouri River because the men wanted to experience for themselves the fabled sexuality of the Mandan women. The most damning indictment was that left by Daniel Harmon: "They are not brave; but when they apprehend a little danger, they will often, as they say, play the man. They are very deceitful, and exceedingly smooth and polite, and are even gross flatterers to the face of a person, whom they will basely slander, behind his back. . . . A secret they cannot keep. They rarely feel gratitude, though they are often generous. They are obedient, but not faithful servants. By flattering their vanity, of which they have not a little, they may be persuaded to undertake the most difficult enterprises . . . all their chat is about horses, dogs, canoes, women and strong men, who can fight a good battle."

The *esprit de corps* that drove the voyageurs to their prodigious physical feats had no clear origins. They could be tender, shyly gathering wild roses to brighten the breakfast table of a trader's wife, or thoughtlessly brutal. They followed the code of the frontier.

There was a strong streak of vanity in the voyageurs' make-up, so much so that before putting into any inhabited port, they stopped to shave, slip on their cleanest shirts and stick plumes in their headgear. Only then would they sweep towards the dock, their boats deliberately angled on collision course. By adroitly backpaddling at the last possible moment, the canoeists would settle their craft, becalmed, at their exact landing spot and each would step ashore with the exaggerated swagger of a lion tamer.

The voyageur subculture was based on custom, dress and circumstance. But it was language that was their unifying ethos; for neither the Indians nor the Nor'Westers enjoyed their advantage of having French as a mother tongue. Unlike the servants of the HBC, the voyageurs were not formless juniors trying to create themselves in the image of their employers. They shared drinks but few assumptions with the *bourgeois* (the NWC's commanding officers, wintering partners and Montreal agents) and were virtually never promoted out of their canoes into more responsible shore billets. If the forts of the Hudson's Bay Company suffered from the harsh discipline that turned them into shorebound Royal Navy frigates, the rowdy voyageurs' favourite hangout, *la cantine salope*, the harlots' tavern at the NWC's summer headquarters, probably had few equivalents this side of a modern motorcycle gang's safe house.

Respect for authority was not the voyageurs' strong suit. They could be reduced to belly-pumping laughter by collapsing a dozy *bourgeois*'s tent over his head or by "accidently" dunking him in an icy stream if he "forgot" to share his private liquor reserve. The dripping, shivering trader would then find himself taunted by derisive catcalls claiming he had just been "baptized." Occasionally, the canoeists would salute a naïve *bourgeois* by "naming" a lobstick after him. A voyageur would climb the tallest nearby pine, lop off all but the top branches and carve the *bourgeois*'s name into the trunk. That ceremony was followed by the firing of guns, loud cheers—and a demand for free drinks from the newly honoured potentate. Most of the *bourgeois* travelled with a personal manservant, but they were not, as an envious HBC surveyor named Philip Turnor reported, carried ashore in feather beds to share the night with female travelling companions.

The universe that counted among voyageurs was self-contained within their canoes. Seniority, muscle and a sixth sense about river navigation determined rank and pay. At the bottom of the scale were the *milieux* who squatted, two abreast, on the middle thwarts and paddled all day according to orders from the *avant* (bowsman) and the *gouvernail* (steersman). These veterans could read the sky and understand the river's moods; they knew how to spot *le fil d'eau*—the safest entry point for shooting rapids. Each brigade of four to a dozen canoes was under the direction of a *guide*, an experienced riverman responsible for daily travel schedules and the safety of the cargo. Paid at least three times as much as the lowly *milieux*, the *guides* were permitted to eat with the *bourgeois* at Fort William and sleep in tents, while their crews had to shelter beneath overturned canoes.

There was one other, pivotal distinction. The voyageurs were divided into two mutually exclusive societies. Those crews taking the freight canoes as far as the head of Superior (or Rainy Lake) were called *les allants et venants* (the goers and comers) or, more frequently, derisively dismissed as *les mangeurs de lard*—a reference to the pork they mixed with their corn gruel. They were usually hired on a per-trip basis and drifted in and out of the trade as the spirit moved them. The aristocrats of the waterways were *les hommes du nord*, the Northmen who wintered in the Fur Country and delivered the payloads. They were the tough professionals who could make their paddles hum, living as close to

The milieux *(squatting) paddled according to orders from the* avant *and the* gouvernail.

nature as Indians. There was one other tiny elite—the crack crews of the express canoes, the light craft reserved for delivering messages and conveying visiting dignitaries.

The exploits of these early voyageurs were so remarkable that in retrospect they appear as giants; in fact, because every pound of excess weight aboard a canoe counted, the ideal voyageur was a compact five foot five. Many a farm boy cursed as he faced the mirror and saw himself grow past the physical limit of the voyageur ideal. Because it was usually the eldest son who inherited the farm while his brothers had little training and few alternatives to fall back on, there was strong family pressure on younger siblings to sign up for the fur trade. Grandfathers who claimed they had followed La Vérendrye westward, cousins and uncles who had worn the voyageur sash filled the tedium of winter nights with many a tall tale of life in *le pays d'en haut*, the wild country north and west of Superior. Sometimes there was little choice. Fathers occasionally signed their sons into the service for three-year stints at whatever wage the *bourgeois* might find appropriate.

At the peak of its activities, the North West Company employed more than eleven hundred voyageurs (and thirty-five *guides*), half of them confined to the shuttle run between Lachine and the head of the Great Lakes. Most of the recruits arrived (with letters of recommendation signed by their local *curés*) from the villages near Montreal—Sorel, Vaudreuil, Longueuil, Rigaud, Île-Perrot, Châteauguay, Chambly and Pointe-Claire—but Trois-Rivières and Quebec also contributed their share. Nearly all were French, but contracts have been found for

Englishmen, Germans, Scots and one West Indian named Bonga.

These contracts (usually signed with a bold X) spelled out not only their pay and length of servitude (three years in the North Country) but even such exact terms as the goods they were granted upon joining. A typical winterer might be given two blankets, two shirts, two pairs of trousers, two handkerchiefs and fourteen pounds of tobacco, though the generosity of distribution depended on each man's rank and experience. Jean-Baptiste Rolland, for example, who signed up on April 24, 1817, as a *milieu* for three years at Lake Huron in the service of a *bourgeois* named Guillaume, was paid £30 a year and given two rods of trade cloth, a three-point blanket, three ells* of cotton, a pair of shoes, one towline, two pounds of soap and three pounds of tobacco.

The voyageurs also pledged themselves "to serve, obey, and faithfully carry out all that the said Bourgeois or any of their representatives to whom they might transfer the present engagement [require], to lawfully respect and honestly do by him, their profit, avoid their damages, to warn them if it comes to his knowledge, and in general all that a good hired man should and is obliged to do; without being allowed to do any personal trading, to be absent from or to leave the aforesaid service, under the penalties set forth by the Laws of this Province, and to lose his wages." This was a vicious enough form of indenture, but what made it worse was that, once inland, the voyageurs were encouraged to go into debt at company stores (which indulged in exorbitant mark-ups) as a way of keeping a grip on their future. Once in hock, they had to work out their debts by further service. The sanctity of their contracts was seldom challenged.

Such peonage must have roused natural resentment, but there were very few documented instances of mutiny. At Rainy Lake on August 3, 1794, the NWC's Duncan McGillivray found a strike in progress, with several brigades of voyageurs refusing to budge unless their wages were increased. It didn't last long. The canny McGillivray noticed some of the ringleaders hesitating and later noted in his journal: "Their minds were agitated with these scruples at the very time that they insisted on a compliance with their demands, and tho' they endeavoured carefully to conceal it, yet a timidity was observed in their behaviour which proved very fortunate for their Masters, who took such good advantage of it, that before night they prevailed on a few of the most timid to return to their duty, and the rest, being only ashamed

---

*An ell was originally the distance between the tip of the middle finger and the elbow, though it became widely varied, so that an English ell was 45 inches, a Scottish ell 37 inches, a Flemish ell 27 inches and a French ell 54 inches.

PARDEVANT LES NOTAIRES de la Province du Bas-Canada à Montréal, y résidant, soussigné; fut present

Alexis Matte de la Sonal

lequel s'est volontairement engagé et s'engage par ces présentes à Messrs. *William McGillivray, Simon McGillivray, Archibald Norman McLeod, Thomas Thain*, et *Henry Mackenzie*, de Montréal, Négocians et associés, sous le nom de McTAVISH, McGILLIVRAYS & Co. & PIERRE DE ROCHEBLAVE, *A.N. McL...*

Ecuier, à ce present et acceptant pour, à leur première réquisition, partir de Montréal en qualité de *Milieu* dans un de leurs canots, pour faire le voyage, et pour hiverner durant *trois années* dans les dépendances du Nord-Ouest dans le Haut-Canada,

qu'sera libre de ce présent engagement qu'à son retour à Montréal, (à la fin de son hivernment) passer par Michilimakinac, s'il en est requis, donner six jours de corvée, faire deux voyages du Fort-William au Portage de la Montagne, ou au lieu d'iceux donner six jours de tems à d'autres ouvrages à l'option des dits Sieurs, aider à porter les canots à trois dans les terres, et avoir bien et dûment soin pendant les routes, et étant rendu aux dits lieux des marchandises, vivres, pelleteries, ustensiles, et de toutes les choses nécessaires pour le voyage; servir, obéir, et exécuter fidèlement, tout ce que les dits Sieurs Bourgeois ou tous autres représentans leurs personnes, auxquels ils pourroient transporter le présent engagement, lui commanderont de licite et honnête, faire leur profit, éviter leur dommage, les en avertir s'il vient à sa connoissance; et généralement tout ce qu'un bon engagé doit et est obligé de faire sans pouvoir faire aucune traite particulière, s'absenter ni quitter le dit service, sous les peines portées par les loix et ordonnances de cette Province, et de perdre ses gages. Cet engagement ainsi fait, pour et moyennant la somme de *Sept Cent* livres ou chelins, ancien cours de cette Province, qu'ils promettent et s'obligent de bailler et payer au dit engagé un mois après son retour à Montréal; et avoir pour équipement une couverte de trois points, une couverte de deux points et demie, six aunes de coton, une paire de souliers de bœuf et un collier, pour la première année et les Gages et conditions du poste où il hivernera pour les autres

reconnoit avoir reçu à compte d'avance *dix piastres l'œuvre six en partant*

s'oblige de contribuer d'un par cent sur ses gages pour le Fonds des Voyageurs. Car ainsi, &c. promettant, &c. obligeant, &c. renonçant, &c.

Fait et passé à Montréal, en l'étude du Notaire soussigné l'an mil huit cent vingt *cinq* le *quinze* de *Février* et ont signé, à l'exception du dit engagé qui, ayant declaré ne le savoir faire, de ce enquis, a fait sa marque ordinaire après lecture faite.

Alexis ✕ Matte

J. N. Mallard

Signing this typical contract with an X, voyageur Alexis Matte agreed to serve in the Northwest for three winters.

to abandon their companions, soon followed the example."

Except for such occasional glimpses, there are few firsthand records of the voyageurs' temperament or physical appearance. Dr John J. Bigsby, secretary of the commission that defined the boundary between Canada and the United States following the Treaty of Ghent in 1814, left behind in one of his diaries a rare description of their tortured features. "One man's face," he wrote, "with a large Jewish nose, seemed to have been squeezed in a vice, or to have passed through a flattening machine. It was like a cheese-cutter—all edge. Another had one nostril bitten off. He proved the buffoon of the party. He had the extraordinary faculty of untying the strings of his face, as it were, at pleasure, when his features fell into confusion—into a crazed chaos almost frightful; his eye, too, lost its usual significance; but no man's countenance . . . was fuller of fun and fancies than his, when he liked. A third man had his features wrenched to the right—exceedingly little, it is true; but the effect was remarkable. He had been slapped on the face by a grizzly bear. Another was a short, paunchy old man, with vast features, but no forehead—the last man I should have selected; but he was a hard-working creature, usually called 'Passe-partout,' because he had been everywhere, and was famous for the weight of fish he could devour at a meal. . . . Except the younger men, their faces were short, thin, quick in their expression, and mapped out in furrows."

They kept their hair long so that a shake of the head would help drive away the marauding summer insects. Short and bulky like Belgian workhorses, they took the pride of dandies in their simple but distinctive dress code. They wore deer- or moose-skin moccasins with no socks, corduroy trousers and sky blue *capots* (hooded frock coats with brass buttons) over red-and-black flannel shirts. The pants were tied at the knees with beadwork garters and held around the waist with crimson handwoven sashes—the famous *ceintures fléchées*. One variation was an embroidered buckskin coat, its seams decorated with bear hair; when caught by the wind after a rainstorm, the garment would make a strange and desolate sound like the ground drumming of a grouse. Choice of hats expressed at least a touch of individuality. Some wore high, scarlet-tasselled night bonnets, others coarse blue cloth caps with peaks, or toques or colourful handkerchiefs wound into turbans. The Northmen proclaimed their vanity by sticking what they called "ostrich plumes" into their headgear, though these were usually dyed chicken feathers—and, sometimes, fox tails.

Almost as much a part of them as their clothes were the voyageurs' canoes. Perfected by the Algonquin tribes of the eastern woodlands, these frail but versatile craft provided the day's transportation, the night's shelter and the centrepiece of pride and conversation. Fashioned from the bark of yellow birches, they were amazing vessels, weighing less than three hundred pounds (six hundred when wet) yet capable of carrying four tons of crew and freight. Birchbark rots slowly, if at all, and is tolerant of frost and heat; it consists of individually layered skins, so that it can be trimmed to any desired shape and thickness without losing tensile strength. Only an axe, a crooked knife and a square or an Indian awl, plus some spruce roots and pitch (spruce gum) were required to build canoes that lasted several seasons. The birch skin was folded around a cedar frame into which were fitted spruce or ash ribs, gunwales, thwarts, stem and stern pieces. Tree roots were used for sewing the birchbark, and resinous gum for caulking its seams.

The large freight canoes (*canots de maître*) that set off from Lachine were thirty-six (occasionally forty) feet long and five feet wide, driven by a dozen men and capable of carrying seventy ninety-pound cargo packages. The smaller *canot du nord*, twenty-four feet long with a beam of just over four feet, required half the crew yet could still hold a ton and a half of freight. Despite their impressive capacities, the vessels were so frail that crewmen did not dare change their paddling positions, and during landings the canoe was never dragged ashore. At the appropriate moment, the crewmen would leap out and gently guide their craft towards the river bank. (These boats were perilously easy to tip. Hugh Mackay Ross, a twentieth-century HBC trader who tried paddling one, wrote in his memoirs: "You really had to keep your tongue in the middle of your mouth; otherwise the canoe would capsize.")

The prow and stern of each vessel were routinely painted with the company flag (its initials in gold letters on the fly of a Red Ensign), a rearing horse or the head of an Indian in war dress, but the best art was reserved for the paddles. The red-cedar paddles came in lengths up to nine feet, depending on their user's position, their surfaces stained a bright blue or green, ornamented by red or black designs. The standard stroking cadence of forty-five dips to the minute could drive a canoe at nearly six knots, though the crews of the express boats were expected to push themselves to a superhuman sixty strokes a minute. The only other way to increase speed was to hoist sail in a following wind. The sail, made of the oilcloth used to cover the freight packages and attached to a temporary mast and boom fashioned from trimmed branches lashed to the thwarts and gunwales, was a jury-rig at best and not often used. But in the right wind and with the proper course and set, the winged canoes could surf along at an expeditious eight knots.

The spring brigades leave Lachine for the long journey west.

EVERY SPRING THE VOYAGEURS would gather at Montreal's Old Market to spend a few days drinking, sparring and relaxing before they took the nine-mile dirt road that bypassed the Lachine Rapids, leading to the North West Company's main staging area and starting point for the brigades west.

The surrounding woods and meadows were still more in bud than leaf as the hectic preparations began for the grand departure. "No camel train across Asia Minor moved with the surety and efficiency of the canoe brigades in the great days of the Canadian fur trade," Leslie F. Hannon noted in an essay on the period. "No European coach or wagon could survive a single mile of the route: there were no roads, only rocks, rapids and white water all the way. Yet cargo losses per voyage were as low as one-half of one percent."

The *bourgeois* appeared appropriately pompous as they paraded their "wilderness look"—ruffles and lace, a brass-handled pistol stuck theatrically into the belt. They gave elaborate farewell picnics for their hangers-on, the coterie of junior partners, clerks, fusty subalterns with small lives and the ladies-always-in-waiting who formed their Montreal circles. An undercurrent of destinies being altered could be felt as the Nor'Westers, gripped by the pageantry of the moment, offered their jaunty Gaelic toast, "On to the High Kanadushka!"—vowing to open up a continent with God knew what riches.

Between rounds of nibbling nippy cheese and gorging themselves on smoked sturgeon, venison and bear steaks washed down with the finest claret and Madeira, the *bourgeois* supervised loading of the freight canoes, self-importantly making certain that bow packs were properly stored before the rest of the cargo was gently fitted onto the flimsy cedar floor boards. When each canoe was packed, its gunwales only six inches above the water, the company flag was raised at the prow and the boatmen impatiently circled offshore until the brigade was in all respects ready.* Just before the final departure signal there would be a momentary hush. The *milieux* hunched over in their starting postures; the *bourgeois* tipped his beaver hat in a farewell salute to shorebound friends; lovers exchanged a final glance. Then the chief *guide*, holding a steersman's pole over his head, lowered his arms in a sudden chop and yelled "*Avant!*" Every paddle sliced into the water, the first of countless strokes that would drive the canoes almost the distance of an Atlantic crossing before coming back to this welcoming hailport. As the brigades—in line formation, two boatlengths apart—disappeared beyond a bend in the river, the voyageurs' mood was jolly. A cloud of laughter seemed almost visible in their wake.

Past Dorval Island and the steep-roofed seigneury mansions they went, following the north shore of Lake St Louis upstream to the first rapids at Ste Anne's (now Ste-Anne-de-Bellevue) at the western tip of Montreal Island. There they halted at a small stone chapel to pray, offer alms and take communion for their time in *le pays d'en haut*. Before leaving Lachine, each canoeman had been given a gallon of rum, the

---

*Each voyageur was allowed forty pounds of personal luggage, including his blanket. As well as the packs of trade goods, provisions for the crew had to be carried because there would be no time to hunt along the way. Boat repair materials (*watape* or fine spruce roots for sewing in bark patches, and pine-gum for waterproofing the seams), towlines, the *bourgeois*'s tent, axes, kettles, kegs of liquor and large bailing sponges completed the standard equipment list. Early brigades consisted of as few as four canoes, but at the height of the NWC's trading cycle, each brigade numbered at least ten canoes. They left Lachine at two-day intervals to stagger traffic through the portages.

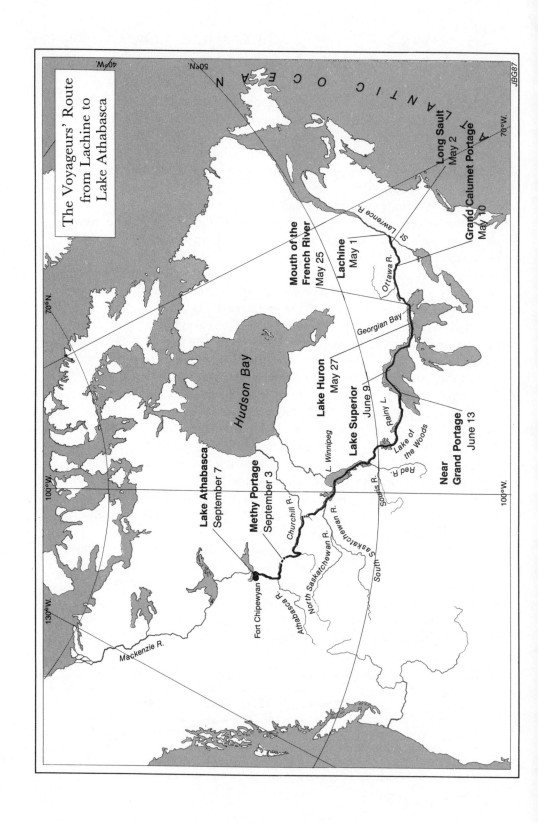

The Voyageurs' Route from Lachine to Lake Athabasca

Lachine
May 1

Long Sault
May 2

Grand Calumet Portage
May 10

Mouth of the French River
May 25

Lake Huron
May 27

Lake Superior
June 9

Near Grand Portage
June 13

Methy Portage
September 3

Lake Athabasca
September 7

ATLANTIC OCEAN

Hudson Bay

Georgian Bay

St. Lawrence R.

Ottawa R.

Rainy L.

Lake of the Woods

Red R.

Souris R.

South Saskatchewan R.

North Saskatchewan R.

Saskatchewan R.

Churchill R.

L. Winnipeg

Athabasca R.

Fort Chipewyan

Mackenzie R.

40°W.

50°N.

70°W.

70°N.

100°W.

100°W.

130°W.

JBG87

official ration for the journey. Typically, the voyageurs sampled a
hearty portion of it on the spot, as if to exorcise the influence of home
and family, of priests and saints. When they set off again, only the thin
echo of the bells of Ste Anne's broke the crystal silence.

Though they were about to launch themselves along the subcontinent's main transportation artery, they passed few settlements. Ever
so rarely was there visible on the far horizon a curling wisp of delicate
smoke from a woodsman's hearth, reminding the voyageurs they were
not completely beyond the tendrils of white civilization. The Ottawa
route, pioneered by Samuel de Champlain in the early 1600s, remained
the primary access into the Great Lakes region until the advent of
the railways and major canal building. From Lachine to height-of-land
on the Ottawa meant a climb of 659 feet, and the subsequent drop to
Georgian Bay was 99 feet. That required passage of thirty-six portages,
but it was still three hundred miles shorter than going up the St Lawrence
and through Lakes Ontario and Erie.

After entering the mouth of the Ottawa (then called the Grand
River or *Grande Rivière des Algonquins*), the voyageurs soon encountered
the Long Sault Rapids, and doffed their headgear in respect to Adam
Dollard des Ormeaux and his seventeen compatriots, besieged there by
a war party of Iroquois in 1660.* Just above the rapids, the voyageurs
first sighted the furrowed brow of the Precambrian Shield, that rugged
mantle of rock, muskeg and water that gives Canada much of its
topography, resources and character.

The journey from Lachine to the head of Lake Superior took seven
to eight weeks, which meant covering an average of about twenty-five
miles a day. That was a considerable feat, since portages of various
lengths and encumbrances had to be negotiated along the way. Portaging meant that the canoe and its load were lifted separately around
waterfalls and impassable rapids for distances of a few yards to twelve
miles—along bush trails, up creviced cliffs and through bogs, with the
men often knee-deep in mud, slithering over slimy boulders. Each
crew member would tuck one of the ninety-pound bales† into the small

---

*They were all dead after a week's battle, except for nine bitter-enders who were
captured, then ritually tortured and eaten. Traces of the bloody struggle were discovered
by Pierre Radisson, one of the founding spirits of the Hudson's Bay Company, and the
site became a shrine. Quebec historians have postulated that Dollard deliberately
sacrificed himself to fend off an attack on Montreal.

†Their size depended on their contents, but each bale weighed exactly ninety pounds
whether it contained trade goods or pelts. This was a subtle anti-pilfering technique
because it was immediately obvious if a bale suddenly seemed lighter than the rest.

of his back, part of its weight borne by a leather tumpline stretched across his forehead so that some of the strain could be absorbed by neck muscles. Then his partner would settle another bale between the carrier's shoulder blades, and the loaded man would dogtrot along the portage trail, knees and back bent, legs pumping, arms swinging free, looking for all the world like a hunchback ape scurrying for cover.

Humping 180 pounds across impassable terrain sounds difficult enough, but ambitious voyageurs could earn a Spanish silver dollar by carrying an extra bale to accelerate the portage crossing. Many did. Pierre Bonga, the only black West Indian known to have been a voyageur, once lugged 450 pounds across an NWC portage, and a Mistassini Indian named Chief Solomon Voyageur is said to have carried the equivalent of eight packs over a half-mile stretch. The most unusual test of strength was the improbable feat of a river man named Montferant, who was reported to have carried loads weighing over 500 pounds across the portage at Grand Calumet from four o'clock one morning to half past ten that night without a rest stop.

The brigades tried hard to avoid portages, preferring to brave all but the worst rapids—a daring option, since the boats they were paddle-handling between the unforgiving rocks were so frail they were susceptible to damage even by a moccasined foot. A frigid dunking of a sweat-soaked body was the lightest penalty for such daring.

Between portages they relentlessly pushed westward, boosting their spirits by mimicking the waterfowl, perfecting the "yole" cry of the loon and the high piercing song of the gulls. To offset the tedium of paddle strokes—as silent and regular as heartbeats—they sang. Like the heave-away sea shanties of the clipper-ship deckhands, the melodies were work songs, a way to ease the tedium of repetitive labour while endowing it with a comforting cadence. In his essay on voyageur songs, the old-world explorer J.G. Kohl noted: "Their song is like the murmur of the river itself. It seems endless. The singers are satisfied when they have found some pleasantly-sounding words which they can adapt to a favourite melody or a refrain giving a good turn to the paddling. The refrain and its constant repetition occupy so much time and place that the story itself in the song at length appears to be a mere makeweight. . . . After each short line comes the refrain, and the story twines itself along like a slender creeping-plant."

Though some songs were filled with *double entendres* more profane than sacred, most of the ditties were romantic re-creations of heroic events. A typical ballad concerned Jean Cayeux, who was fatally wounded by a band of Iroquois while trying to defend his family. As he lay bleeding, he dug his own grave and before sliding into it composed

Voyageurs at dawn

a lament, laboriously writing the words in blood on birchbark. The voyageur's unofficial anthem was an evocative melody called "*À la Claire Fontaine*," which tells how love expired because of the late delivery of a rose bouquet. Music was in the canoemen's souls. At night they loved listening to the rasp of a homemade violin or the twang of a mouth harp. One voyageur dragged part of a wooden door to Fort Edmonton so that he would have a platform to tap-dance on.

When sundown made further progress impossible, the canoes put in to shore. Before it was time to rest, boat hulls had to be patched, an exacting job by torchlight. The evening meal consisted of cooked dried peas or cornmeal mixed with water and bits of lard or suet, a gruel not dissimilar to what the Americans called hominy. Occasionally this tasteless diet was supplemented with a voyageur variety of bread known as *galette*. The recipe was simple: a hole was punched in one of the flour bags, a little water poured in and salt added. The main flavouring came from the cook's unwashed hands, when he kneaded the dough and shaped it into flat cakes to be baked in frying-pan grease. The voyageurs loved flipping these primitive flapjacks by the light of their torches, telling a few more thigh-slappers, smoking one last pipeful, then relaxing their knotted muscles and lamed backs in sleep. With the *bourgeois*'s tent in place, the men tucked in under their upside-down canoes and pulled tarpaulins over their exhausted limbs.

By four in the morning or even earlier, the camp would be stirring with shouts of "*Star Levé!*" (a contraction of "*C'est l'heure à se lever*"). As the rays of the approaching dawn threw trees into relief with just enough light to navigate by, the brigade would depart, paddling quietly through the mist. No one sang until after the eight o'clock breakfast stop. Lunch was either eaten under way or when the crews landed just long enough to boil some tea water and reheat the leftover gruel. Rest periods of five minutes every hour allowed the paddlers to light their pipes, so that distances came to be measured by the number of pipes instead of miles.

FOUR WEEKS OUT OF LACHINE, the canoes swept through the awesome beauty of Georgian Bay's North Channel, squeezed past St Joseph Island to Sault Ste Marie and entered the world's largest lake, Superior.*

Hugging the lofty cliffs of Superior's north shore and bucking angry headwinds, which the voyageurs tried to assuage by sprinkling flecks of tea or tobacco on the boiling sea, the canoes made the final 450-mile dash to Grand Portage, the open sesame to the West first used by Radisson and Groseilliers. Their faces furred with untidy beards, their clothes stiff with two months' sweat, the travellers would land at Pointe aux Chapeaux (today's Hat Point) to wash and change into their finery before racing into the oval harbour of the depot at Grand Portage. The steersman would raise the company flag (stowed since leaving Lachine), the accompanying *bourgeois* would adjust his beaver hat and the vermilion-tipped paddles would glint in the sun as in one final burst of speed the canoes completed their epic voyage.

The cedar-picket stockade of this busy NWC emporium surrounded the complex of sixteen buildings that comprised the main transfer point between the freight canoes arriving with the Montreal trade goods and the North Country canoes bringing in the furs. The crude warehouses and dining-hall where the partners and their clerks discussed policy and celebrated the season's winnings were made of hand-sawn planks, with sloping shingle roofs and window casements painted a deep red, then known as Spanish Brown and later used to paint railway boxcars. Swarms of wild dogs roamed the fort, yelping and begging for scraps. Outside the stockades lived the cows, horses—and the voyageurs.

Even though they had lugged their precious loads from opposite sides of the continent, the canoeists rarely enjoyed the relative comfort

---

*At 31,700 square miles, Lake Superior ranks ahead of every other inland body of water except the Caspian, which is classified as a sea rather than a lake. After 1799, the Nor'Westers eliminated the portage at Sault Ste Marie by building a primitive wooden canal. Because Superior was the hub of the NWC's empire, the company eventually built its own fleet of schooners to ferry heavy goods around the upper lakes. They included the ninety-ton *Recovery*, which survived the War of 1812 by being demasted, covered with pine boughs and hidden inside one of the deep bays of Isle Royale. She later became the largest vessel ever to run the rapids into Lake Huron.

of the trading post. Few Indians or voyageurs were permitted to enter the fort at Grand Portage or the enclosure of the later headquarters, Fort William. There, the exceptions were delinquents destined for the *pot au beurre*—the "butter tub," where they were confined overnight to cool off after particularly vicious brawls. The "butter tub" may have been used as a jail, but it was more of a privy. A blacksmith named Alexander Fraser, who had been caught trading a few moose skins to barefoot passersby so they could fashion new moccasins, was sentenced to twenty days in the *pot au beurre*. In pleading for mercy, he left behind an eloquent third-person deposition, picturing life in that hellhole: "It was a small square building made of hewn logs, without any light, wherein was a quantity of human excrement. That, after being a short time in this confinement, the stench of the place, and the bruises he had received, made this deponent conceive that if he were kept there much longer his health would be destroyed." Gasping for breath, Fraser promised to work a year for no wages if he were released. That offer failed to soften the heart of his overseer, who allowed him out only after the unfortunate Fraser had promised to renew his voluntary contract for *three* full years.

Forced to camp outside the fort's wooden walls, the voyageurs were encouraged to spend their earnings at Boucher's House, a canteen operated by a semi-independent trader named Jean-Marie Boucher, and to run up debts at a nearby "company store." The result was that many voyageurs remained indentured most of their working lives.

Having little else to do, the pork-eaters and *hommes du nord* drank and picked fights. Few rendezvous went by without bullies on both sides dealing out knife wounds, gouged eyes, torn ears and bitten-off noses. What little relief they found was at the harlots' tavern, where they could purchase rum at the equivalent of eight dollars a quart, extra food rations and the temporary favours of Ojibway or Chippewa women. "They have a softness and delicacy in their countenance," confessed a trader named Peter Grant about these resident *poules*, "which rival the charms of some of our more civilized belles."

Before the Lachine brigades could start back with their canoe-loads of fur, they had to lug the trade goods north to Pigeon Lake, a storage depot nine miles inland. That steep trek, usually scheduled before they had recovered from their hangovers, seemed the harshest of their ordeals. It was easier, they sighed, to reach heaven than Pigeon Lake.

By the first week of August, the winterers were growing restive, aware that they had to reach the Athabasca forests within the next two and a half months or face frozen rivers and starvation. The small, manoeuvrable canoes could carry cargoes of three thousand pounds with crews of five, yet their shallow eighteen-inch draft made most streams accessible. (Because there were few birch trees available along the Red and Assiniboine rivers, some local canoes were fashioned out of willow frames over which were stretched raw buffalo hides, fur side in. These floating robes were not good for voyages of any length and had to be unloaded at least once a day to be dried in the sun or over a fire, or they would sink.)

Eventually, an advance storage depot was built on Rainy Lake so that the Athabasca brigades could save fifteen days in each direction by exchanging their loads there instead of going on to Grand Portage. Fort Chipewyan on Lake Athabasca was sixteen hundred miles, or 75 days, from Superior, and the NWC's farthest outpost, Fort Good Hope near the Mackenzie Delta, was a full thousand miles north of Lake Athabasca, which enjoyed only 150 ice-free days. At the topographical dividing point that marked the height of land where the rivers began their long descent to Hudson Bay and the Arctic Ocean, the northern voyageurs paused for a unique ceremony. The senior *guide* would sharpen his knife, cut a bough from a scrub cedar, dip it in ditch water and command each novice in the canoe train to kneel. Thoroughly "blessed" by the wet branch, the newcomers swore allegiance to the Northmen's code of honour: that they would never allow another novice to pass this way without administering a similar oath, and never kiss a voyageur's wife without her permission. The simple ceremony meant more than just another excuse for a celebratory round of drinks. It was no light privilege to stand up and tell the world: "*Je suis un homme du nord!*" —and this was the moment of transmogrification. These tough hombres were willing to risk everything except their pride. "It is questionable," wrote Thomas L. McKenney, an early traveller who witnessed one of the ceremonies, "whether [Napoleon] Bonaparte ever felt this superiority in all departments of mind which so distinguished him, or his achievements, to an extent of greater excitement, than does this poor man . . . in the animating and single belief in his supremacy as a north western voyageur."

Paddling towards Lake Winnipeg was at least a downstream run, but on one stretch of the Winnipeg River ten portages had to be crossed in a single day. When the waterways widened into lakes, the little boats were swung abreast, lashed together, sails hoisted, and the voyageurs would drift north, smoking their pipes, regaling one another with escapades of their recent stay at Grand Portage. The danger in crossing the immense but shallow Lake Winnipeg was its bathtub effect—wind gusts could tip a loaded canoe without warning. That didn't stop the brigades from challenging each other to races. The usual paddling pace of forty-five per minute quickly accelerated to fifty, sixty, even sixty-five. One marathon went on for two days and nights and was called off after forty hours of continuous paddling only because Duncan McGillivray, the accompanying *bourgeois*, ordered a halt. "On the second night of the contest," he later recalled, "one of our steersmen being overpowered with sleep fell out of the Stern of his Canoe which being under sail advanced a considerable distance before the people could recover from the confusion that this accident occasioned; in the meantime the poor fellow almost sinking with the weight of his clothes cried out to two Canoes that happened to pass within a few yards of him to save his life *pour l'amour de dieu*; but neither the love of God or of the blessed Virgin, whom he powerfully called to his assistance, had the least influence on his hard hearted Countrymen who paddled along with the greatest unconcern, and he must have certainly perished if his own Canoe had not returned in time enough to prevent it."

Near the mouth of the Winnipeg River at Bas-de-la-Rivière (later called Fort Alexander) the brigades took on supplies of pemmican. This was the fuel of the Northwest fur trade, the propellant that fed the beasts of burden who manned the canoes. Because every day, almost every hour before freeze-up counted, because the canoes did not have the space to carry adequate food supplies and because there was no time in the eternal rush of the voyageur's sunrise-to-sunset schedule to hunt, pemmican became as essential a part of the fur business as the trade goods. In terms of its bulk, weight and energy-giving properties, it was a remarkably cost-efficient food, with canoemen apparently content to down only a pound and a half of the mundane but highly nutritious substance a day.

Supplied from the plains of the Red and Assiniboine rivers, pemmican, which looked a bit like dehydrated dog food, was made from pulverized buffalo meat mixed with melted tallow and the saskatoon berries then common on the Prairies. (This fruit was a valuable source of vitamin C that helped prevent scurvy.) The ingredients for a ninety-pound bag of pemmican were simple: one buffalo to sixteen pounds of berries. The animal's flesh was cut into flakes or thin slices and hung out to dry in the sun or preferably over fires, a procedure that also served to keep at least some flies out of the mixture. After the meat chunks were thoroughly desiccated, Indian women spread them out and pounded them with stones or wooden flails until they were reduced to a pulp. The animal's hide had meanwhile been sewn into a rawhide sack, which then was half filled with the pulverized shreds. The buffalo's fat, which had been boiling in huge kettles, was now poured hot into the rawhide bags; the berries were stirred in and the sack was sewn shut, its seams sealed with tallow.

Pemmican was eaten either raw, sliced, coated with flour and fried, or cut up into a thick soup called *rababoo*. It required no preservatives and seemed to last forever.* There was considerable dispute about exactly how palatable the stuff really was. Those who ate it staunchly declared there wasn't anything else quite like it, claiming it tasted like nothing but pemmican. The liveliest description of that unmatched flavour is in H.M. Robinson's *The Great Fur Land*: "Take the scrapings from the driest outside corner of a very stale piece of cold roast beef, add to it lumps of rancid fat, then garnish all with long human hairs and short hairs of dogs and oxen and you have a fair imitation of common Pemmican."

Tons of this precious food were required annually for distribution along the northern canoe routes, and the native peoples quickly realized that they controlled a major staple of the fur trade, just as valuable a barter item for liquor, tobacco and knives as animal pelts. To preserve their monopoly, Indians, and later Métis, would occasionally burn the scrub off the land surrounding the trading posts to keep the buffalo herds in their own territories. When pemmican supplies ran out, the voyageurs survived by roasting beaver tails, fishing, shooting the occasional duck or bear, or chewing on herbs and roots. Once in a rare while they would enjoy such local Northwest delicacies as buffalo tongues, dried moose noses or the boiled fetal calf of a buffalo. But most of the time, it was pemmican all the way.

FROM LAKE WINNIPEG, the NWC brigades went south via the Red River towards the upper reaches of the Mississippi; southwest on the Souris River into Missouri Country; or northwest along one of the tributaries of the Saskatchewan River system. With a combined length greater than that of either the St Lawrence or the Danube, the North and South Saskatchewan rivers connect the Lake Winnipeg region with the Rocky Mountains through Blackfoot Country. Starting as glacier melt in those distant plateaus, the sister rivers traverse the Prairies in a huge horizontal Y before joining just east of Prince Albert. Their final cascade into Lake Winnipeg is through the dramatic Grand Rapids, which before damming was an extraordinary sight. The river, a powersurge five hundred feet wide, tumbled through high rock chambers in a drop of more than seventy-five feet in less than three miles.

---

*The *Winnipeg Free Press* of August 10, 1934, reported the discovery by William Campbell of twenty bags of pemmican that had been cached on his northern Manitoba farm eighty years before. After munching a sample, Campbell observed: "It tasted like meat and retained some of its flavour."

The Grand Rapids portage brought the voyageurs to Cumberland House, an NWC pemmican depot beside the Hudson's Bay Company post originally built by Samuel Hearne in 1774.* It would be September by then, and there was a frigid tang of autumn in the air as the wind scudded across the spruce forests under the flaxen rays of the cooling sun. The brigades toiled ever westward, those on the Saskatchewan's upper flank running near the edge of the prairie grasslands and the northern wood country. Canoe brigades ascending the North Saskatchewan were occasionally met by NWC wintering partners from nearby posts bringing saddle horses to allow the accompanying *bourgeois* a spot of buffalo hunting.

The main route out of Cumberland House led to the great Churchill River, which roared down to Hudson Bay from the divide at Lac La Loche, site of the infamous Methy Portage, the longest and toughest on the trade routes. Conquering its twelve-mile trail and climbing its six-hundred-foot elevation under 180-pound packs of freight and furs earned voyageurs the ultimate badge of courage. Crossing this formidable rampart put the canoes in the Athabasca Country, whose gloomy forests eventually yielded more than half the North West Company's profits.

Winter was a frustrating interlude of hunting, gathering firewood, and transporting routine cargoes by dogsled instead of canoe. The voyageurs decked out their animals in gaudy belled harnesses and embroidered felt coats, fitting them with tiny deerskin booties to protect soft paw pads from cracked ice. Travelling mostly at night to avoid snow glare, the men provided the essential courier service between the snowbound forts, fighting cold so intense a veteran trader cried out that "one ought to have his Blood composed of Brandy, his Body of Brass and his Eyes of Glass."

After three or more years in the wilderness the Northmen would return to Montreal, but it was no easy adjustment. River life may have been brutal, but it obeyed natural laws at odds with those of the city. Like sailors at the end of a long passage, the voyageurs, especially the Northmen who had crossed the Hudson Bay divide, found they had become a race apart, outcasts from a world they never made. "Their arrival at Lachine," wrote William George Beers, the observant Montreal dentist who later popularized lacrosse, "is a time of great excitement. The wild picturesque appearance of the men, and the distance they have come, awakens a sympathy for them, and hundreds will go

---

*See *Company of Adventurers*, Chapter 14.

In winter, the voyageurs became couriers, travelling by dogsled between the snowbound forts.

out from town to see them. Their appearance in the city is very odd. They go along the streets, gaping and staring at everything, in such haste and excitement that they run against people and stumble over little obstructions. They . . . roar aloud with laughter at the extensiveness of the ladies' hoops, and the peculiarity of their hats; look in the windows at the jumble of new things, to them, and have hearty laughs at what they consider the absurdities and curiosities of city people."

GIVEN THEIR ABHORRENCE OF DISCIPLINE, the voyageurs must have suffered a shock to their independent spirits when for five action-filled months they found themselves in an incongruous role: they became soldiers for Britain, defending Canada against the Americans in the War of 1812. The Corps of Canadian Voyageurs, formed as an auxiliary unit on October 1, 1812, and disbanded March 14, 1813, was commanded by twenty-seven volunteer *bourgeois* itching in their tailored tunics. Joseph McGillivray, one of the ensigns, reported on the comic tableau of his troops parading with British regulars. "They talked incessantly, called each other pork-eaters, and quarrelled about their rations," he wrote in his diary. "They were guilty of much insubordination, and it was quite impossible to make them amenable to military law. They generally came on parade with a pipe in their mouths and their rations of pork and bread stuck on their bayonets. On seeing an officer, whether general, colonel, or subaltern, they took off their hats and made a low bow, with the common salutation of *Bon jour, Monsieur le Général*, or *le Colonel*, as the case might be, and, if they happened to know that the officer was married, never failed to inquire after the health of *Madame et les enfants* . . . when called to order by their officers and told to hold their tongues, one or more would reply, 'Ah dear captain, let us off as quick as you can; some of us have not yet breakfasted, and it's upwards of an hour since I had a smoke.'"

The voyageurs fought as members of larger units in the battle at Crysler's Farm and the capture of Prairie du Chien. Their best-known exploit was a lightning raid on the pivotal American trading post at Michilimackinac (Mackinac) then commanding the straits between Lakes Huron and Michigan. Under strict orders from Major-General Isaac Brock to capture this strategic fortification, 180 voyageurs and 300 Indians joined 45 British regulars stationed at St Joseph's Island on a three-day expedition to lay siege to the American position. The decisive factor in the garrison's surrender was the presence of two iron six-pounders, artillery pieces lugged along by the voyageurs. Their natural sense of theatrics plus only the vaguest of instincts for self-preservation in the face of danger would have made any enemy flinch.*

THE VOYAGEURS VANISHED from Montreal's hinterland after the demise of the North West Company in 1821. Their songs were heard no more along the rivers and portages. Their lives may not have been blessed with a surfeit of grace, but their legacy endures: their exuberant and highly un-Canadian sense of daring propelled them to risk everything for a cause as ephemeral as their own brotherhood. They have since retreated from the map of their country's consciousness as if they had never existed, leaving history to hand down no precise tally of their achievements.

One problem in attempting retrospectively to plumb the voyageurs' psyches is that there exist no firsthand records of their exploits, no diaries, no letters, nothing but a few songs and the folk memory of men in scarlet sashes having done impossible things. Their own voice is permanently silent.

Only once was a voyageur actually questioned about his brave calling. In 1822, an anonymous septuagenarian who had been a voyageur hitched a ride from Norway House to Red River with the former NWC trader Alexander Ross.† "I have now been," the old man told Ross, "forty-two years in this country. For twenty-four, I was a light canoe-

---

*That untypical interlude was followed much later by a bizarre incident involving so-called voyageurs in an expedition up the Nile. In 1884, Moslem rebels led by the charismatic Mohammed Ahmed, known as the Mahdi, determined to dislodge British and Egyptian forces from the Sudan, had cornered General Charles George "Chinese" Gordon and his troops in Khartoum, a provincial capital on the sixth cataract of the Upper Nile. Sir Garnet Wolseley, the British general charged with organizing an expeditionary force to rescue Gordon, realized he would have to transport his troops up 860 miles of shallow, treacherous rapids above Aswan and remembered the voyageurs from his previous service in Canada, while suppressing the Riel Rebellion on the Red River. Four hundred "voyageurs" (really rivermen then employed in the lumber trade along the Gatineau and Saguenay) were recruited and placed in charge of the troops who paddled eight hundred whalers (enlarged lifeboats) up the turbulent river. The rescuers reached their objective—but it was too late. On January 26, 1885, two days before the expedition arrived, the rebels broke into the city and put Gordon to the sword.

†Ross was a prolific historian of the Red River Colony and its champion office-holder, having at one time or another served as Sheriff of Assiniboia; Councillor of Assiniboia and member of the settlement's Committee of Public Works and Finance; Commander of the Volunteer Corps; Magistrate of the Middle District; Governor of the local gaol; Collector of Customs; ex-officio President of the Court in the Upper District; and Elder of the Presbyterian Church at Frog Plain.

man; I required but little sleep, but sometimes got less than I required. No portage was too long for me; all portages were alike. My end of the canoe never touched the ground till I saw the end of it. Fifty songs a day were nothing to me. I could carry, paddle, walk, and sing with any man I ever saw. During that period, I saved the lives of ten *Bourgeois*, and was always the favourite, because when others stopped to carry at a bad step, and lost time, I pushed on—over rapids, over cascades, over chutes; all were the same to me. No water, no weather, ever stopped the paddle or the song. I had twelve wives in the country; and was once possessed of fifty horses, and six running dogs, trimmed in the first style. I was then like a *Bourgeois*, rich and happy: no *Bourgeois* had better-dressed wives than I; no Indian chief finer horses; no white man better-harnessed or swifter dogs. I beat all Indians at the race, and no white man ever passed me in the chase. I wanted for nothing; and I spent all my earnings in the enjoyment of pleasure. Five hundred pounds, twice told, have passed through my hands; although now I have not a spare shirt to my back, nor a penny to buy one.

"Yet, were I young again, I should glory in commencing the same career again, I would willingly spend another half-century in the same fields of enjoyment. There is no life so happy as a voyageur's life; none so independent; no place where a man enjoys so much variety and freedom as in the Indian country. *Huzza! Huzza! pour le pays sauvage!*"

Sir Alexander Mackenzie

CHAPTER 3

Big Mack

*Thorny as the thistles of his native Scotland, Alexander
Mackenzie was as immovable as the mountains he crossed.
If there ever was such a quality as mulish intelligence he
personified it . . .*

ONE WORD DOMINATED the concerns and conversations of Nor'Westers
huddled around summer campfires and crude winter hearths: Athabasca.
That vaguely defined territory edging up to the shadows of the Rocky
Mountains became the touchstone for the company's aspirations to
greatness.

The full measure of the Athabasca Country—what would later be
called the Mackenzie River Basin—was difficult to grasp, and is still.
In the Western Hemisphere, only two drainage basins—the Amazon's
and the Mississippi's—exceed the size of the Mackenzie's, which
covers an area the equivalent of Western Europe. Three time zones are
required to encompass Athabasca's dimensions, and the Mackenzie,
from its headwaters on the Finlay River to the Arctic Ocean, flows for
2,635 miles—farther than Africa's Niger or the U.S.S.R.'s Volga.

What attracted the Nor'Westers into the Athabasca Country was a
simple law of nature. Covered by matted forests that provided a prime
habitat, chilled by sub-Arctic temperatures that induced its profusion
of animals to grow thick, rich pelts, Athabasca was one of the world's
most lucrative fur farms. The other overwhelming advantage for the
Montrealers was that Athabasca was legally a no-man's land. The
HBC's charter covered only the territory with rivers emptying into Hudson
Bay. Beyond the Methy Portage, the domain of Athabasca clearly
drained in other directions. The HBC was aware of Athabasca's riches

(having sent an illiterate explorer named William Stuart to that far kingdom as early as 1714*), but the Company of Adventurers seemed at that point psychologically unable to field the logistics required to venture that far inland. This was difficult to comprehend because from their starting point in the middle of the continent, the HBC traders were already halfway there. By contrast, the Nor'Westers had to travel forty-three hundred miles from Lachine to the Mackenzie, crossing sixty lakes and 330 portages along the way.

The Nor'Westers had been nibbling at the Far West long before their official amalgamation into one company. An early Nor'Wester named Peter Pangman had marked a spruce tree within sight of the Rockies in 1790, but it was a charismatic murderer named Peter Pond who first plunged into Athabasca.

This combative Connecticut Yankee left home to join the army and escape his father's shoe repair shop at sixteen, noting the event in his diary† using his own strange and barely decipherable phonetic spelling. "Beaing then sixteen years of age I gave my Parans to understand that I had a strong desire to be a Solge. . . . But thay forbid me, and no wonder as my father had a larg and young famerly I just begun to be of sum youse to him in his afairs. Still the same Inklanation & Sperit that my Ancestors Profest run thero my Vanes. It is well known that from fifth Gineration downward we ware all Waryers Ither by Sea or Land and in Dead so strong was the Propensatey for the arme that I could not with stand its Temtations."

After serving in the Seven Years' War, during which he won field commission as an acting captain, Pond went into the Mississippi fur trade but left for the Canadian Northwest in 1775 following the fatal wounding of another trader in a sunrise duel. ("We met the next morning eairley and discharged pistels in which the pore fellowe was unfortenat.") The Saskatchewan River tributaries were by that time swarming with independent traders. At the mouth of the Sturgeon River near modern-day Prince Albert, Saskatchewan, for example, seven different partnerships were represented. In the spring of 1778, the frontiersmen working out of this post pooled the season's remaining trade goods and chose Pond to lead an exploratory five-canoe probe into the heart of the Athabasca territories. This foray was nothing more

---

*See *Company of Adventurers*, Chapter 11.

†Pond's journal, which ends abruptly in mid-sentence, was preserved as a curiosity mainly because of its unique language. The pages describing his pivotal Athabascan exploits were unfortunately lost when they were used to light a kitchen fire.

The view from Methy Portage

than a pragmatic response to the circumstances in which the winterers found themselves, but the tactic was to prove an essential breakthrough for the Nor'Westers. If the assault on Athabasca were started at mid-continent instead of from the head of Lake Superior, the anticipated fur trade could become a practical proposition. Pond pushed up the Churchill River, his voyageurs paddling through virgin spruce forests until they reached Methy Portage. The first white men to struggle up the cliff towering six hundred feet over the Clearwater as it flows towards the Athabasca River, they marvelled at the verdant panorama. One lyrical description of the view from the top of Methy was that of Lieutenant John Henry Lefroy, a Royal Artillery surveyor who visited the site in 1844: "It is celebrated for the view from the north end. It is a wide and regular valley, of great depth, stretching for a distance of thirty miles to the west. The sun was just setting as I arrived there, the light glancing from the nearer foliage, and filling the distance with golden haze; there is not that variety in the autumnal tints of a forest here which makes those of Canada so wonderful, but quite enough to compose a very beautiful picture. A portion of wood in the distance was burning, and there was an uncommon felicity in the manner in which the columns of smoke rose up against a dark mass of Pines which crossed the valley behind them. The Clearwater river winds through the midst, some-times expanding into a placid little lake, then diminishing to a thread of light barely caught among the trees. Upon the whole I have seen few views more beautiful."

After setting up a crude log cabin forty miles south of Lake Athabasca,

Pond and his voyageurs settled in for the winter's trading with the Chipewyan. On July 2, 1779, they were back at Cumberland House, starving but hauling 140 packs of superb dark pelts, having been forced to leave an equal quantity behind in a secret cache because the little brigade would have sunk under the full load.

Pond spent the following season in Athabasca with similarly impressive results and became a full partner in one of the first NWC amalgamations.* Caught by an early freeze-up, he spent the winter of 1781–82 at Lac La Ronge, where he met Jean-Etienne Waden, the Protestant son of a Swiss professor, who had come to Canada with Wolfe's army.† The opportunities of the fur trade quickly led Waden into a share of the new North West Company, but he was part of a faction that opposed the granting of the entire Athabasca district to Pond. One March night the two men quarrelled and Waden was fatally wounded, though the exact circumstances of the fight were never established and the murder might have been committed by a Pond subordinate with the grand name of Toussaint le Sieur. Pond escaped retribution and fled the Northwest. Five years later the intemperate Yankee was back in the Athabasca Country trading opposite John Ross, who had left the NWC to join an ambitious competing fur partnership called Gregory, McLeod & Company. During a quarrel with Pond about supplies, Ross was killed, though it was one of Pond's men, a Canadian named Péché, who was charged (but not convicted).

By this time, Pond was forty-six, an old man in the brotherhood of the trade, and his reputation for violence had lost him the respect of his peers. He did spend one more season in the Athabasca Country, working on a chart he swore would revolutionize the geography of the day and teaching all he knew to an eager neophyte named Alexander Mackenzie.

Pond kept busy that long winter drafting a map depicting a mythical North West Passage, convinced by his conversations with local Copper Indians that the Pacific Ocean lay within easy access of the rivers linked to Lake Athabasca. He planned to present his theory to Catherine II, Great Empress of all the Russias, who was known to be

---

*During his journeys, Pond observed outcroppings of tar sand, the black gold that would eventually become the impetus for grand-scale oil extraction. At the time, he was impressed with the dark substance oozing from the banks of the Athabasca River only because it was useful for caulking canoes.

†In 1761 Waden had married Marie-Josephte Deguire, and their daughter Veronique became the wife of the Reverend John Bethune, Montreal's first Presbyterian minister. The Bethunes' son Angus was an active NWC partner and great-grandfather of Norman Bethune, the Canadian surgeon who became a hero of the Chinese Revolution.

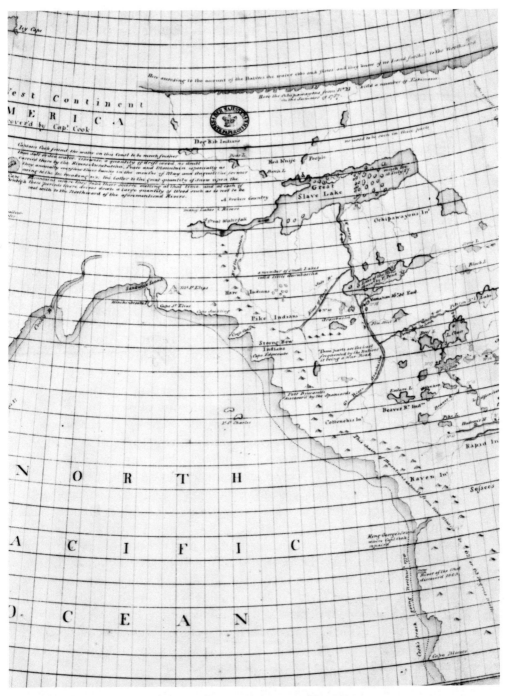

Part of Peter Pond's map, showing the imaginary
Cook's River (upper left) a short distance away from Great Slave Lake

interested in northern exploration. Working by the flicker of candlelight and using ink that often had to be thawed, Pond drew and labelled the two "Great Rivers" he postulated ran to the Pacific. The geography of his scratchings proved to be mostly imagination, but he inspired the eventual discovery by the twenty-four-year-old Mackenzie of the river that now bears his name, and his subsequent push to the Pacific. In the spring of 1788, Pond left the Fur Country forever, to die in impoverished anonymity nineteen years later in the wilds of New England. His protégé, Mackenzie, journeyed to the NWC's Superior headquarters, determined to obtain official blessing for his dream of seeking the Pacific using one of Pond's suggested routes.

ALEXANDER MACKENZIE is a legitimate Canadian hero, having been the first to pass the test of crossing the country that two centuries later would confer similar status on his handicapped successors: Terry Fox, Steve Fonyo and Rick Hansen. Mackenzie's physical feat of having been the first white man to take an expedition across the upper continent—thirteen years before Meriwether Lewis and William Clark led a much larger and better-equipped force to the more southerly American shore of the Pacific—overshadowed his considerable contributions to the politics of the fur trade, to international diplomacy and to Arctic literature. The first Nor'Wester more interested in creating a global British commercial empire than in the gathering of pelts, he envisaged the linking of the North American fur trade to the exotic commerce of the Orient, with Britain's growing manufacturing strength forming the third side of the triangle. It was a dream of high statesmanship. "At one moment," wrote Dr W. Kaye Lamb, the former dominion archivist, in a perceptive essay introducing the explorer's journal, "Mackenzie is hard put to it to overcome a few yards of rapid current, at another he is thinking of trans-Pacific commerce with Canton. He may be standing waist deep in a rushing river, holding on to a wrecked canoe, but this battered craft is still the needle drawing behind it a thread which, knotted with those drawn across the world's greatest oceans by Cook and Vancouver, will form the basis of a network on which Canada still depends for economic survival. Mackenzie may have been, from a military point of view, almost unarmed, yet the permanent effects of his penetration of territory were at least comparable to Marlborough's leading an army to Blenheim."

The official portrait of Mackenzie by Sir Thomas Lawrence that now hangs in the National Gallery of Canada reveals a sensitive, almost pious face, its set jaw contradicting the dreamy eyes—a self-contained man fully aware of his worth. There is no texture of wilderness in Mackenzie's features, little residue of his superhuman struggles down wild rivers, yet the man's virility and physical prowess shine through. He once snowshoed seven hundred miles to attend a Christmas dinner, and paddled a freight canoe seventy-two miles in one stretch of daylight, against headwinds and in temperatures so frigid his voyageurs resorted to wearing mittens. Like most of his confrères, he enjoyed several open-air romances* but did not marry until he was forty-eight, settling down at last with a perky fourteen-year-old Scottish lass. Thorny as the thistles of his native Scotland, Alexander Mackenzie was as immovable as the mountains he crossed. If there ever was such a quality as mulish intelligence he personified it, convinced that his inherent arrogance sprang from superior intellect.

In his daily dealings with Indians and voyageurs he was often suspicious and curt, treating them as inferior creatures to be manipulated for his own purposes. Unlike Samuel Hearne, who surrendered himself to his soulmate and guide, Matonabbee, Mackenzie never developed a bond of friendship with English Chief, the leader of the Indians who accompanied him to the Arctic Ocean. "The English Chief was very much displeased at my reproaches," Mackenzie noted in his journal, "and expressed himself to me in person to that effect. This was the very opportunity which I wanted, to make him acquainted with my dissatisfaction for some time past . . . he accused me of speaking ill words to him . . . [and] concluded by informing me that he would not accompany me any further . . . [later] I sent for the English Chief to sup with me, and a dram or two dispelled all his heart-burning and discontent . . . I took care that he should carry some liquid consolation to his lodge, to prevent the return of his chagrin."

Although he was always careful to husband his energies and planned his life with a sure instinct for beneficial self-preservation, his natural reserve would occasionally break. In the spring of 1797, while the NWC canoe brigades were preparing to leave Lachine, Mackenzie and William McGillivray, then sharing Montreal lodgings, lunched with George Landmann, the visiting officer from the Royal Engineers. "We sat down," Landmann later reported, "and without loss of time, expedited the lunch intended to supersede a dinner, during which time the bottle had freely circulated, raising the old Highland drinking propensity, so that there was no stopping it; Highland speeches and sayings, Highland

---

*Mackenzie sired at least two Mixed Blood children: Maria, who later married Robert Munro, a Scottish widower; and Andrew, who stayed in the fur trade and died at Fort Vermilion on March 1, 1809.

reminiscences; and Highland farewells, with the doch and dorich, over and over again, was kept up with extraordinary energy, so that by six or seven o'clock, I had, in common with many of the others, fallen from my seat. To save my legs from being trampled on, I contrived to draw myself into the fire-place, and sat up in one of the corners, there being no stove or grate ... I there remained very passive, contemplating the proceedings of those who still remained at table, when at length Mackenzie ... and McGillivray ... were the last retaining their seats. Mackenzie now proposed to drink to our memory, and then give the war-whoop over us, fallen foes or friends, all nevertheless on the floor, and in attempting to push the bottle to McGillivray at the opposite end of the table, he slid off his chair, and could not recover his seat whilst McGillivray, in extending himself over the table in the hope of seizing the bottle which Mackenzie had attempted to push to him, also in like manner began to slide to one side, and fell helpless on the floor."

Just why this singular but fallible man fought with such unremitting fierceness to achieve his vision of the fur trade can never be fully ascertained. His unusual apprenticeship seems to have been devised for straightforward commercial ambitions—the natural quest of an expansion-minded business executive determined to extend his territory. Certainly, he was obsessed with serving the best economic interests of Britain by squaring the circle of the island nation's trade routes—in effect discovering the North West Passage that English seamen had been trying to find for nearly two centuries, even if that channel now ran by land and water through the middle of the continent.

Born to a prominent Stornoway family in 1764, Mackenzie was left motherless very young. His father emigrated to New York, where he eventually became an officer in the Loyalist forces fighting the American insurgents. Young Alexander was reared mainly by two aunts, who sent him to Montreal for his schooling. At fifteen, he joined a counting house headed by John Gregory, a pioneer of the inland fur barter, whose canoe brigades had been among the first to reach the Saskatchewan Valley. Mackenzie spent five formative years learning the business side of the trade, and when Gregory decided to join the Nor'Westers, Mackenzie went along as a partner.

His posting to the Athabasca Country, first as Peter Pond's assistant and later as his successor, was one of those satisfying coincidences of history that fix an individual precisely at the time and place in which circumstances allow him to realize his aspirations. Pond's theory that two broad rivers connected Great Slave Lake north of Lake Athabasca with the Pacific Ocean by only six paddling days to the west was a bit of geographical fancy because it assumed that the northern extensions of the Rocky Mountains ended at 62° north and that Great Slave Lake was at least a thousand miles farther west than it actually was. But in happy ignorance Mackenzie resolved to follow one of Pond's mysterious streams to its mouth and stake a claim to the Pacific shore.

So excited was he by the secret instructions he received to this effect at the 1788 summer meeting in Grand Portage that he returned to Athabasca in a record fifty-two days, cutting two weeks off the usual travel time. His first cousin Roderick McKenzie,* assigned to be his assistant, built Fort Chipewyan, a new NWC regional headquarters post on the southern shore of Lake Athabasca, while Mackenzie prepared for his dash to tidewater.

AT NINE O'CLOCK on the morning of June 3, 1789, a flotilla of four flimsy canoes unceremoniously departed from the Fort Chipewyan mud strip and pushed off into the lake. In his pocket Mackenzie carried rubles for trading with the Russians he expected to meet on the way. The explorer was accompanied by the voyageurs François Barrieu, Charles Ducette, Joseph Landry, Pierre de Lorme and John Steinbruck, two of whom brought their wives, and a small Indian party under the leadership of English Chief, who eighteen years before had been among the Indians accompanying Samuel Hearne to the mouth of the Coppermine. A separate canoe bearing an NWC clerk named Laurent Leroux went along to establish a supply camp at Great Slave Lake.

That first day, the travellers made it across the west end of Lake Athabasca and started descending the Slave River. They still faced the sixteen-mile stretch of rapids between present-day Fitzgerald and

---

*The resident intellectual of the Northwest fur trade, Roderick McKenzie started a library at the new Fort Chipewyan, arranging to have an eclectic collection of books shipped, paddled and portaged from England. The library grew so large it eventually had to be catalogued and housed in its own building. Under McKenzie, the desolate fort (the only NWC post that was painted inside) was known as "Little Athens" and became an important social influence. After a decade a new post was built across the lake, on the site of the present Fort Chipewyan.

The last of the original buildings at the second fort, the residence of the former Chief Factor, was torn down in 1964. Except for some fading footpaths, all that remains of this once-great facility is the base of the sundial that marked the time of day until the 1940s. Indians at the isolated settlement, 380 miles north of Edmonton, in the spring of 1987 settled one of Canada's largest outstanding land claims. After twenty years of negotiation, local Cree were given $26.6 million cash plus hunting rights to three million acres of nearby Wood Buffalo National Park. Fort Chipewyan has only five miles of streets and one general store—plus a beer parlour named for the old explorer: The Peter Pond Hotel.

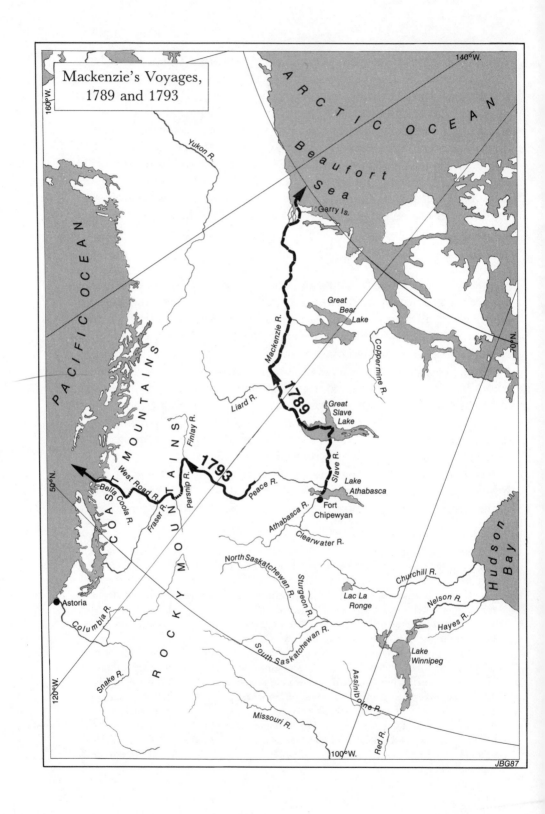

Mackenzie's Voyages,
1789 and 1793

Fort Smith. It was snowing and the little birchbark canoes were toys in the face of a vindictive northwest wind. On the morning of June 9, after six portages and the loss of one canoe, they reached Great Slave Lake and found it still frozen. For the next twenty days Mackenzie led his men along the lake's swampy shore, slipping between floes, avoiding the many beaver ponds, trying to snatch sleep in the extended daylight of June nights. Temperatures dropped so fast that each morning the lake was edged with ice a quarter of an inch thick—this at the time of the summer solstice. (Mackenzie was in fact travelling during what geographers call the Little Ice Age, when ice would have stayed longer in the spring and arrived earlier in the fall.) The entry to the Big River—later to be called the Mackenzie—proved difficult to find because the lake at that point is a confusing pattern of shallows, marshes, dead ends and mud bars. A local Dogrib was persuaded to join the wallowing cavalcade and English Chief vowed to cut the newcomer's throat if he didn't lead them to safety. The Dogrib was terrified of the wild monsters he had been told guarded the Big River and tried repeatedly to escape; Mackenzie finally had to pinion the fellow by sleeping on the edge of his vermin-infested coat. At last, on June 29, they found the entry and headed downstream, but the unrelenting rain soaked them to the skin and they felt as though they were drowning between the clay banks of the broad river, bailing more often than paddling their canoes.

The river initially flowed west, raising Mackenzie's hopes that the Pacific Ocean might appear around one more bend. But then the stream turned due north, and by July 10 (at a latitude of 67°47′N) Mackenzie realized that this was no shortcut to a still distant ocean. "It was evident," he noted in his journal, "that these waters emptied themselves into the Hyperborean Sea; and though it was probable that we could not return to Athabasca in the course of the season, I determined to penetrate to the discharge of them."

By this time not only the cowed Dogrib but all the Indians and the voyageurs had seen enough. They begged Mackenzie to turn back, and to their surprise he promised he would, if they didn't touch an ocean shore within a week. "I also urged the honour of conquering disasters and the disgrace that would attend them on their return home without having obtained the object of the expedition," he noted later in his journal. "Nor did I fail to mention the courage and resolution which was the peculiar boast of the Northmen. . . ."

The puny expedition had by now lost most of its sense of purpose and direction; the battered canoes meandered unresisting down the broad torrent hissing under their narrow beams. Only the occasional abandoned native settlement broke the monotony of steep banks dotted with dwarf trees. The few fox or hare they shot had a strange whitish grey hue and unusual socks of downy fur covering their feet. As the season advanced, the sun merely teased the horizon, and their meagre provisions were nearly exhausted. Out of desperation, Mackenzie kept landing to climb nearby hills to see where the river was leading them, but the view was never clear enough to show the way.

The air of doom hanging over the cursed river grew more tangible as the Indians spotted a deserted encampment, its tent poles fashioned from whalebone. They knew then that they had entered the land of their ancestral enemies, the Eskimos.* Time was measured in hours instead of days now, and Mackenzie's observations placed the forlorn brigade at about 69° north, just downstream from present-day Inuvik. They pressed on, heading west through freezing shallow water. Dispirited beyond the point of fear, they landed at what is now called Garry Island, but it was too foggy for them to estimate their position.

That night (July 14, 1789), it finally happened. At four in the morning Mackenzie awakened and sat bolt upright; his belongings were wet. Since there was no wind, the only explanation had to be an incoming tide—the conclusive signature of an ocean. After a few hours of paddling out from the dank coast into the Beaufort Sea, Mackenzie and his men hurried away from the godforsaken shore, knowing they had beaten the odds, but to little purpose.

By September 12 they were safely back at Fort Chipewyan. They had been gone 102 days. They had covered more than three thousand miles, survived unspeakable hardships—and discovered only that what they were seeking must be elsewhere.

WHEN MACKENZIE REPORTED HIS MEAGRE FINDINGS to the following summer's NWC conclave at Lake Superior, he was politely ignored. That not-unexpected reaction hardly upset him, because by then the disappointed explorer had another expedition in mind. On his return journey, Mackenzie had learned that nomadic bands of Eskimos traded with white men in ships to the westward, though local Indians warned him the natives of that far country were giants with wings who could kill with their eyes. Shortly afterward, during one of his journeys out of the Athabasca, Mackenzie had met Philip Turnor, a surveyor for the Hudson's Bay Company, who persuaded him that he needed to study

---

*The deep-seated distrust, sometimes reaching homicidal hostility, between Indians and Eskimos remains a mystery. For a discussion of some of its underlying causes, see *Company of Adventurers*, hardcover edition, pages 253–54.

surveying and astronomy in England if he intended to become a serious explorer. Turnor had located the true position of Fort Chipewyan at longitude 111° west, which, if true, meant that it was considerably farther from the Pacific than Pond had originally postulated. Mackenzie's mercenary instincts were also aroused; he was pleased to learn that the British Parliament had posted an award of £20,000 to the discoverer of the North West Passage.

After a winter in England spent honing his surveying skills, Mackenzie returned to the Athabasca determined to follow Pond's second "Great River" of the Northwest to its mouth. He moved out to winter at a fork of the Peace River.

ON MAY 9, 1793, Mackenzie departed on his greatest adventure. With him was an NWC clerk named Alexander McKay, six voyageurs (Jacques Beauchamp, François Beaulieux, Baptiste Bisson, François Courtois, Charles Ducette and Joseph Landry), two Indians and a large friendly dog. They were crowded into a specially built twenty-five-foot canoe light enough for two men to portage, yet capable of carrying three thousand pounds of pemmican, beans, flour, rum, guns and trade goods. As they paddled west under a cool spring sun, the customarily stoical Mackenzie was moved to write in his journal: "This magnificent theatre of nature has all the decorations which the trees and animals of the country can afford it. Groves of poplar in every shape vary the scene; and their intervals are enlivened with vast herds of elks and buffaloes. The whole country displayed an exuberant verdure; the trees that bear a blossom were advancing fast to that delightful appearance, and the velvet rind of their branches reflecting the oblique rays of a rising or setting sun, added a splendid gaiety to the scene."

By mid-May they were under the brow of the still snowbound Rockies. Game seemed plentiful, but Mackenzie was nervous that gunfire might frighten local Indians. Finally it was the dog that chased down a buffalo calf for the evening's repast. The gorges narrowed the next day, squeezing the river into rapids between perpendicular cliffs. The crew had to disembark, towing the canoe with a 180-foot line while Mackenzie led his troops up impossible rock-faces, cutting miniature ledges as he ascended the slippery slope. The men stepped from his shoulders to the shaft of his axe, embedded in whatever root he could reach, creeping up the near-vertical surface, trying not to glance at the waters raging below. The canyons of the Peace echoed with the rumble of distant rockslides as the stream disintegrated into a sequence of waterfalls. They struck out overland, chopping their way through the brush and forest on the bone-chilling margin of the Rockies. Sulphur pools bubbled unheeded as they hacked their way through moss-hung branches, advancing less than three miles a day. They collapsed exhausted by four o'clock in the afternoon, sleeping where they fell, their backs wedged against large tree trunks as protection from rock- and mudslides. Their moccasins were in useless tatters; every step was agony. In case they perished among the slides of these malignant hills Mackenzie scribbled a note, stuffed it into an empty rum keg and kicked the thing into the river.

They were near the height of land now, marching silently through the halo of clouds that blotted out the earth except for mountain peaks that appeared to float in these elevated misty seas. At the juncture of the Parsnip and Finlay rivers they halted, not sure which way to go. Then, heeding the advice of an old Beaver Indian they had met along the way, they turned south into the Parsnip. The turbulent tributary was in flood, inundating the beaver meadows that lined its banks, and their progress was halted by so many rapids that the crew threatened mutiny. The travellers were too dispirited to talk or even pray.

Then, some unexpected luck. Camped in that high hard land was a small band of Sekanis, people of the rocks. Understandably nervous about this unexpected incursion of palefaced scarecrows, they took up their weapons, but Mackenzie reassured them with the simple gesture of walking up to the closest warrior and placing an arm around his shoulders. In the translated conversation that followed, one of the Indians recalled obtaining bits of iron from other tribes that had gone down to a big stinking lake (the Pacific Ocean) to trade with white men who arrived in ships "as big as islands," but he would not or could not tell how to get there. Mackenzie tried to bribe him with hunks of pemmican, beads, a knife—but no, he claimed he knew nothing about the "Great River" flowing into that stinking lake.

The phrase "Great River" was used so often in the interchange between the Sekanis and the expedition's interpreter that Mackenzie memorized it. Next morning he was feeding bits of sugar to a young Sekani boy when he overheard one of the adults mentioning the "Great River." He confronted the man and had him sketch its location on bark with a chip of charcoal. The drawing showed a route farther along the Parsnip, across a chain of small lakes and portages, down to the "Great River," which the Indian warned was the home of warlike tribes who lived in houses built on islands. The stinking lake, he estimated, was a moon's journey away.

Setting out with renewed vigour, the expedition reached the little lakes, where a well-travelled path of 817 paces led across a ridge to a sister body of water. Each was a source of rivers that flowed in opposite directions.* Mackenzie was jubilant: he had reached the Arctic-Pacific divide. All he had to do now was to follow the new river to the sea— downstream all the way.

Next day Mackenzie and his men celebrated their luck, shooting down the river, their reflexes dulled by their easy passage. Suddenly the canoe was deep in white water exploding into rapids. The boat slammed into a rock, almost went over on its port side, was thrown onto a gravel bar and then back into the maelstrom, where its stern was pounded against a boulder—the force of the impact heaving it against the opposite shore and caving in the bow. Trying to steady what was left of their craft, one of the voyageurs grabbed the overhanging branch of a tree, but instead of holding the boat inshore, it catapulted him into the bush. The canoe, still somehow floating, was tossed into a shallow cataract that damaged its bottom, then spewed it out into a calm eddy. Some supplies and many musket balls were lost; the canoe had been reduced almost to kindling.

That night the shaken voyageurs gathered for comfort around an early campfire. It was almost their last. One of the voyageurs carelessly puffed a pipe while strolling over the gunpowder spread out to dry— very nearly, as Mackenzie noted in his diary, putting "a period to all my anxiety and ambition." Next morning they rebuilt the canoe, which now looked more like a patchwork quilt than a boat, and resumed their voyage. On this western slope of the Rockies there was little indigenous food supply; Mackenzie buried a ninety-pound sack of pemmican one night, and his men built a campfire over the hole to hide any trace of the cache for their return journey. Farther along, now on the Fraser, the travellers entered the land of the Carriers,† a fierce tribe of Indian middlemen who did not welcome white traders. After being greeted by a volley of arrows, Mackenzie landed on the opposite shore and beckoned to the chief, spreading beads on the ground in a gesture of giving— but first stationing one of his sharpshooting voyageurs in the brush to cover him in case of trouble. After some hesitation, the Carriers crossed the river in a dugout canoe and the palaver began. Drawing pictures in

---

*The first body of water, present-day Arctic Lake, is the source of the Parsnip and ultimately the Peace and the Mackenzie; the second, Portage Lake (with the adjoining Pacific Lake), is the source of James Creek (Mackenzie called it the Bad River), a tributary of Herrick Creek and ultimately of the McGregor River, which flows into the Fraser. Mackenzie mistakenly believed the Fraser to be the Columbia.

†So called because the widows of Carrier warriors carried their husbands' ashes with them for three years.

the mud to make themselves understood, the Indians told Mackenzie the "Great River" was blocked by cascades that could not be crossed. The stinking lake could be reached only by land.

Mackenzie was puzzled. For six years he had been dreaming that Pond's "Great River" would carry him to the Pacific. Should he now abandon that quest for an alternative route scratched on a forlorn beach by an Indian with uncertain motives? He decided to do just that, partly because the Fraser was veering south instead of west and partly because he knew he could not keep his men on the river much longer. "I determined to proceed with resolution, and set future events at defiance," he boasted in his journal.

After reaching a point on the Fraser about midway between the present-day towns of Quesnel and Williams Lake, he headed back up the river to somewhere near its junction with a western tributary, which Mackenzie called the West Road River (also known as the Blackwater). He and his men cached their canoe and much of their food and powder and set off westward on foot along a trail to the north of the West Road. The land route was so hard to follow when they found it on July 4 that Mackenzie enlisted a guide who promptly threatened to desert. To ensure his presence overnight, Mackenzie took him to bed, confiding to his journal: "My companion's hair being greased with fish oil, and his body smeared with red earth, my sense of smelling threatened to interrupt my rest; but these inconveniences yielded to my fatigue, and I passed a night of sound repose." The Nor'Westers were passed along to a relay of guides and, once over the coastal range, entered the rain forest of the Pacific, warmed and wetted by milder breezes that made the cedar, hemlock and fir grow too large to hug. Welcomed by local Bella Coola Indians who lived in a highly developed, salmon-dependent culture, the explorers were feasted; their hosts even lent them a replacement canoe for the final dash to the ocean along North Bentinck Arm and down Dean Channel. The tang of salt spray was in the air now; the pearly sky was flat. It was a moment for drums and flags—but understatement was the order of the day. Mackenzie's journal barely mentioned his first hint of the Pacific. It was casually tossed in at the end of a lengthy diversion about local architecture: "In the house there were several chests or boxes containing different articles that belonged to the people whom we had lately passed. If I were to judge by the heaps of filth beneath these buildings, they must have been erected at a more distant period than any which we had passed. From these houses I could perceive the termination of the river, and its discharge into a narrow arm of the sea."

Next day Mackenzie set out to touch the ocean, guided by his Bella

Coola friends. They reached King Island at the top of Fitz Hugh
Sound and were confronted by three canoes of Bella Bellas, hostile
natives whose chief menacingly recounted a mysterious tale of an earlier
unpleasant confrontation with white men, and threatened Mackenzie's
crew. The Nor'Westers escaped by paddling to a nearby cove, where
they spent an uneasy night. Two more war canoes appeared next
morning and his crew begged Mackenzie to flee before they were all
slaughtered. As he was leaving, he made his best-remembered statement.
On the southeast face of the large rock that had served as his nocturnal
rampart, the proud Highlander used a mixture of vermilion and bear
grease to daub, in large letters, the laconic summary of his incredible
journey:

ALEX MACKENZIE
FROM CANADA
BY LAND
22d JULY 1793*

Next morning the party started home, and thirty-three days later
the ten men and the large friendly dog were back in Fort Chipewyan.
Having covered 2,811 miles, Mackenzie jotted a final entry in his
journal: "Here my voyages of discovery terminate. Their toils and

---

*Patterning himself on Mackenzie, William Clark, who with Meriwether Lewis was the
first American explorer to reach tidewater on the Pacific, carved into a tree the words:
"WM. CLARK, DECEMBER 3D 1805 BY LAND FROM U.STATES IN 1804&5."
Meriwether Lewis was more wordy. As the party was about to leave on the return
journey to St Louis, he posted a sign that read: "The object of this last is that through
the medium of some civilised person who may see the same, it may be made known to
the world that the party consisting of the persons whose names are hereunto annexed
and who were sent out by the Government of the United States to explore the interior of
the continent of North America, did penetrate the same by way of the Missouri and
Columbia Rivers, to the discharge of the latter into the Pacific Ocean, at which they
arrived on the 14th day of November, 1805, and departed on their return to the United
States by the same route by which they had come."

The American expedition, consisting of forty-five men and a Newfoundland dog,
spent two years in the field and all one winter on the Pacific shore. Although Lewis and
Clark quickly established themselves as twin icons in the American exploration hall of
fame, at least one contemporary observer, David McKeeham, wrote to remind them of
Mackenzie's greater, if less heralded, achievement: "Mr. M'Kenzie with a party
consisting of about one fourth part of the number under your command, with means
which will not bear a comparison with those furnished you, and without the *authority*,
the *flags*, or *medals* of his government, crossed the Rocky mountains several degrees
north of your route, and for the *first time* penetrated to the Pacific Ocean. You had the
advantage of the information contained in his journal, and could in some degree
estimate and guard against the dangers and difficulties you were to meet. . . ."

Mackenzie's rock inscription on Dean Channel

their dangers, their solicitudes and sufferings, have not been exaggerated in my description. On the contrary, in many instances, language has failed me in the attempt to describe them. I received, however, the reward of my labours, for they were crowned with success."

He had been the first across the North West Passage, that mysterious and, as it turned out, barely existent route to the Orient that had been the chief geographical goal of European explorers ever since Christopher Columbus first set out to seek it three centuries before. "Mackenzie," Hugh MacLennan has noted, "introduced a new reality, just as Columbus's lost quest drew an entire hemisphere into the story of civilization. How strange that a Canadian birch-bark canoe without a name, last in a long succession of canoes from Champlain's first one, should have earned a place in the company of ships like the *Santa Maria* and *Golden Hind!*" Still, Mackenzie had not pioneered a feasible new trading route, nor could he claim to have discovered the Bella Bella country. The white men encountered there by the Indians had sailed into the same channel forty-nine days earlier in a cutter charting the inlet for Captain George Vancouver, then on a voyage of exploration on behalf of George III.

The anticlimax of having to spend the winter in the mundane preoccupations of the fur trade taxed Mackenzie's nerves. Physically exhausted and emotionally crippled by having led two expeditions dedicated to the glory of extending British commerce and failing both times, he imploded into what seems to have been a nervous breakdown. He spent that long, lonely season pacing the floor of his snowbound hut, trying aimlessly to complete his appointed task of producing a fair copy of his wilderness journals, and finding it impossible to concentrate. Writing to his cousin Roderick, Mackenzie confided his innermost thoughts, disjointedly apologizing that the draft of his revised journal was not enclosed for his cousin's perusal: "Last fall I was to begin copying it—but the greatest part of my time was taken up in vain speculations—I got into such a habit of thinking that I was often lost in thought nor could I ever write to the purpose—what I was thinking of—would often occur to me instead of that which I ought to do—I never passed so much of my time so insignificantly—nor so uneasy— Although I am not superstitious—dreams amongst other things—caused me much annoyance—I could not close my eyes without finding myself in company with the Dead—I had visions of late which almost convince me that I lost a near relation or a friend—It was the latter end of January when I began my work—thinking then I had time enough— though the reverse is the fact—and I will be satisfied and so must you, if I can finish the copy to give you reading of it in the Spring—I find it a work that will require more time than I was aware of—for it is not a quarter finished."

In an even more telling sequel, he explained to McKenzie why he was determined to attend the following summer's NWC conclave at Grand Portage: "I am fully bent on going down. I am more anxious now than ever. For I think it unpardonable in any man to remain in this country who can afford to leave it. What a pretty Situation I am in this winter. Starving and alone, without the power of doing myself or body else any Service. The Boy at Lac La Loche, or even my own Servant, is equal to the performance of my Winter employment."

STILL ONLY THIRTY YEARS OLD, Mackenzie left Athabasca the next summer, vowing to quit that accursed country forever and to turn his attention to a continental strategy for the fur trade. At the Grand Portage meetings the NWC partners were reasonably impressed with the tally of his performance, voting him an extra share of stock as a reward, particularly since he had achieved what the Hudson's Bay Company, originally chartered to discover the North West Passage, had failed to accomplish. Some of his more practical colleagues, however, carped at the exorbitant mark-up on his glory, noting that the Mackenzie expedition had cost £1,500 without adding a single pelt to their storehouses. The winterers at that 1794 gathering, unhappy about their share of profits and feeling frustrated that the Montreal agents were supplying goods inferior to those of the HBC, cornered Mackenzie with their complaints. They found him, if not rebellious, at least open to suggestions for drastic reform of the Canadian fur trade. It was Mackenzie's contention that the company should negotiate a merger with the Hudson's Bay Company, and that the joint organization should plunge into the Pacific trade before it came to be dominated by the aggressive Americans. On his way east from Superior, Mackenzie stopped off at Newark (Niagara-on-the-Lake) and called on John Graves Simcoe, Lieutenant-Governor of Upper Canada, to advocate his radical proposal. That November, back in Montreal, he prepared a lengthy treatise of his views for Lord Dorchester, then Governor-in-Chief of British North America. The expanded, royally chartered fur monopoly he visualized would have opened a transportation route through the Rockies and established a large harbour on the Pacific to take control of the West Coast trade across the ocean to China, the whole network being controlled, round Cape Horn, from London, with an amalgamated NWC and HBC at the heart of the empire.*

Simon McTavish had very mixed feelings about the Mackenzie proposals. It was clearly in the Marquis's self-interest to keep Montreal—and thereby his personal influence—dominant in the fur trade. The highly profitable infrastructure he had set in place would topple if Hudson Bay and the Pacific Coast became the transportation hubs of the amalgamated companies. Yet there was no doubt the shorter routes offered decisive cost savings, and so McTavish did the only sensible thing—he became determined to claim a Pacific port and, more immediately, to negotiate for direct access to Hudson Bay. Earlier he had spent several winters in London, appealing to William Pitt for repeal of the HBC charter. When the British Prime Minister pointed out that this would require an Act of Parliament he was not prepared to sponsor, McTavish lost patience and in 1803 dispatched an armed detachment and a supply ship to establish four outlaw trading posts on Hudson Bay. That venture failed because the HBC immediately went into its traditional defensive stance: it did nothing and waited for the impossible Hudson Bay climate to take care of its temporarily housed enemies. At the same time, the London-based Company's resident factors persuaded most of the Cree to stay away from the NWC posts, and after three years of lacklustre results the Nor'Westers razed their tiny forts and retreated from that unfriendly place. The NWC's agents had meanwhile been unsuccessfully tempting the HBC Governors to sue their firm for trespassing, hoping the resultant test case would reveal the royal charter's dubious legality. The Committeemen waited out their

---

*He even extended the scheme from furs to fish, planning to establish a new firm called the Fishery and Fur Company. Its whaling ships would trade items to the Northwest Coast from Nootka Sound, the harbour on the west coast of Vancouver Island that had sheltered Captain James Cook in 1778. He visualized posts being built at the mouth of the Columbia River and at Sea Otter Harbour, in the north. Mackenzie presented this plan to the Colonial Office in London twice in 1802, but no action ensued.

opponents and won the battle. The dynamics of delay had triumphed once again.

Mackenzie enjoyed a brief holiday in London before returning to Montreal, where he became a member of the Beaver Club and befriended the Duke of Kent, who had been sent to Quebec in command of the 7th Regiment of Foot (Royal Fusiliers). Although he was fully occupied as an agent in Simon McTavish's trading firm, Mackenzie became more and more interested in a Detroit-based interloper calling itself Forsyth, Richardson & Company. He was bound by agreement to remain a North West Company partner until 1799, yet he felt increasing irritation with McTavish's authoritarian style of management. The even more frustrated winterers began to regard him as their spokesman, although as the fifth of five co-partners in the McTavish trading company, he had no real power. Sensing his star partner's alienation and wanting to isolate him from the grumbling winterers, McTavish posted Mackenzie to New York as the NWC's resident agent. That transfer only served to whip up the explorer's anger because in his regular contacts with American fur traders he very quickly recognized they were about to outrun the Canadians to the Pacific.

The break came during the 1799 annual meeting of NWC partners at Grand Portage. At the very first session, Mackenzie rose in his place to declare that he would not be renewing his contract and had resolved to withdraw from the company. Agitated winterers immediately passed a resolution stating that Mackenzie alone enjoyed their confidence, asking him to reconsider. McTavish sat out the exchange in imperious, glacial silence, refusing to add his voice to those urging Mackenzie to stay. Mackenzie stalked out of the hall, later confessing that he had been so angry the gesture made him forget "that which we seldom lose sight of," his self-interest. Adding to the hurt, his place in the NWC partnership was taken by his beloved cousin Roderick. Describing the incident, Alexander Henry the Elder, who was there, noted: "The old North West Company is all in the hands of McTavish and Frobisher, and Mackenzie is out. The latter went off in a pet. The cause as far as I can learn was who should be the first—McTavish or Mackenzie, and as there could not be two Caesars in Rome, one must remove."

Mackenzie stormed back to Montreal and soon afterward embarked for England, where he sought solace among bluebloods who treated him as a colonial hero. He fitted perfectly into British society of the day, an exuberant, bearded fur trader fresh from his historic trek across an unknown continent—an ideal celebrity for the salons of aristocrats caught up in the patriotic fervour of that golden period in British history between Lord Nelson's victories at the Nile and at Trafalgar. He had his portrait painted by the King's Painter-in-Ordinary and with the aid of a ghostwriter named William Combe* published a 550-page book about his exploits, bearing the imposing title *Voyages from Montreal, on the River St. Laurence, through the Continent of North America, to the Frozen and Pacific Oceans in the Years 1789 and 1793; With a Preliminary Account of the Rise, Progress, and Present State of the Fur Trade of That Country.*

The instant bestseller publicized Mackenzie's vision of a world-spanning trade organization, outlining details of his proposals for a grand coalition between the amalgamated Canadian fur organizations and the East India and South Sea companies. At another level, it was an exciting reprise of the explorer's discoveries, told without the exaggerated self-importance that characterized travel writing at the time.† "These voyages will not, I fear, afford the variety that may be expected of them," he wrote in his preface; " . . . I could not stop to dig into the earth, over whose surface I was compelled to pass with rapid steps; nor could I turn aside to collect the plants which nature might have scattered on the way, when my thoughts were anxiously employed in making provision for the day that was passing over me. I had to encounter perils by land and perils by water; to watch the savage who was our guide, or to guard against those of his tribe who might meditate our destruction. . . . Today I had to assuage the rising discontents, and on the morrow, to cheer the fainting spirits of the people who accompanied me. The toil of our navigation was incessant, and oftentimes extreme; and in our progress over land, we had no protection from the severity of the elements, and possessed no accommodations or conveniences but such as could be contained in the burden on our shoulders, which aggravated the toils of our march, and added to the wearisomeness of our way."

NWC spies sent back regular reports on Mackenzie's activities and

---

*A soldier, waiter, teacher and cook, Combe became one of the most popular English authors during the early nineteenth century. His satirical verse, *Tour of Dr Syntax in Search of the Picturesque*, was followed by a long series of sequels, but he was as profligate with his money as with his pen and wrote the Mackenzie book while in a London debtors' prison.

†Among the volume's most interested readers was Napoleon Bonaparte. That French connection came to light years later in the correspondence of a Scandinavian monarch, Napoleon's former marshal Jean-Baptiste Bernadotte, who ruled as Charles XIV of Sweden. According to Bernadotte, Napoleon had intended to negotiate a treaty with the United States that would have permitted him to use New Orleans as a base of attack against British North America, with his troops sneaking up the Mississippi and taking Canada by surprise. The Mackenzie journals were purchased and translated into French, but the expedition was permanently delayed when Napoleon launched his disastrous Russian campaign instead. The special edition, stamped with Napoleon's personal eagle insignia, was found after his death among his possessions on St Helena.

remonstrations. "You know him to be vindictive," tattled John Fraser, the Marquis's cousin and London-based partner. "He has got an entire ascendant over your young Men, and if driven to desperation he may take steps ruinous to you. He has told myself Your Nt. West business will be completely ruin'd; to others he has thrown out most violent threats of revenge, and I have had some hints too extravagant to mention." But Mackenzie was reaping too much honour and glory to worry about such sniping. He attended a grand ball given in his honour by fellow Scots at Ayr, south of Glasgow, and early in 1802 was knighted by George III, in part thanks to the good offices of his friend the Duke of Kent. That knighthood, the first to be conferred by a British sovereign on a Canadian fur trader, added a splendid patina of grandeur to all of Mackenzie's subsequent schemes.

He visited Montreal regularly, especially when he heard that plans had been hatched for a full-scale challenge to the North West Company's domination, with Parker, Gerrard & Ogilvy, a large local concern, forming a combine to include the Forsyth, Richardson firm as well as Leith Jamieson, a Detroit partnership. By 1798 these disparate operations had been united into an organization officially known as the New North West Company but quickly dubbed the xy Company, a name derived from the "xy" insignia on its kegs and its bales of furs. (The initials were picked because they followed alphabetically the nw markings of its rival.) At first, the Nor'Westers dismissed the upstarts as "Potties"—a corruption of either *les petits* or *les potées*, a colloquialism meaning men made of putty. In other words, softies. The newcomers put together a small but highly efficient woods operation stretching all the way to the Athabasca that rocked the established trade of the Nor'Westers and cut further into the fur supplies reaching Hudson Bay.

The competition remained manageable until Mackenzie brought his prestige and active presence into the concern, which changed its name to Alexander Mackenzie & Company. The nwc was being hurt badly, and during the 1801 meeting at the head of Lake Superior, McTavish proposed a revamping of the company, enlarging its scope of operations and raising its share capital as part of a new, twenty-year agreement. He was fifty years old now, tending to snap at lesser mortals, particularly when one winterer after another rose to complain that the Potties were moving in on their territories and gaining ever-larger portions of the trade. McTavish rewarded his most hardened and experienced traders with extra stock and sent them back into the critical fur regions with orders to drive the Potties out any damn way they chose. The battle had been joined.

By this time, the xy traders had built forts alongside many of the nwc establishments, including a miniature headquarters beside Grand

Portage; prices were cut and wages inflated; all three companies were flooding the West with rum and brandy. The new partnership had only half the NWC force in the field, but its winterers were at least as tough and even more determined. Angry traders spied on one another, ambushed pemmican-laden canoes, bribed Indians with excessive trade goods and even more outrageous promises. The violence grew worse with each season, and because of the inaccessibility of the venue no legal action was taken. Crimes simply went unpunished. That changed, at least in theory, when an NWC clerk named James King was shot by the XY's Joseph Maurice Lamothe at Fort de l'Île on the North Saskatchewan in 1802. A band of nearby Indians had sent a message to the fort that they had valuable pelts to trade, and both men set off to claim them. They spent a night on the trail, sleeping together inside a leather tent, exchanging small talk, enjoying the camaraderie of the wilderness. They agreed that the best way to split the booty would be for each trader to deal with those Indians who had credit with his company. Next day, when King was loading his furs, several packs were missing, and his Indians told him they had already been bartered. Suspecting Lamothe, he walked over to his fellow trader, accused him of having broken their accord and asked for the furs back.

"Would you give them up if you were me?" an angry Lamothe demanded.

When King agreed that he would not, the enraged Lamothe yelled, "Then you will not have mine!"

As King reached for one of the packs, Lamothe drew his pistol and shot him dead, in full view of a dozen witnesses. The murderer was acquitted at a trial in Montreal because the presiding judge could not decide who had proper jurisdiction over the Indian Country where the crime had been committed. In direct response to this atrocity, the British Parliament passed the Canada Jurisdiction Act on August 11, 1803, ordering that offences committed in the Indian territories be tried in the courts of Lower or Upper Canada and that roaming magistrates (nearly all Nor'Westers, as it happened) be empowered to arrest anyone charged with a crime.

By 1802, the working capital of Mackenzie & Co. was nearly equal to that of the older NWC partnership. It had only 520 men in the field, compared with McTavish's 1,058 (assigned to 117 permanent trading posts), but was producing almost as much fur. Mackenzie had meanwhile been busy in England trying to buy control of the Hudson's Bay Company. The offer of £103,000 in Exchequer bills delivered through an intermediary was very nearly accepted. The deal was not consummated mainly because a majority of the HBC stock was held either by trustees or by minors who could not transfer their shares without a court action. This the Committeemen were determined to avoid, because they did not want news of the transaction made public.

THE ESCALATING VENDETTA came to an abrupt resolution when Simon McTavish, whose hatred of Mackenzie had fuelled so much of it, died unexpectedly on July 6, 1804, leaving a young wife, four children and his uncompleted dream mansion. They buried him in its garden, and the top-hatted mourners gathered for tea under the swaying pines.*

With the Marquis's autocratic presence removed, Mackenzie and William McGillivray, who succeeded McTavish, took only four months to negotiate a merger. The agreement provided for creation of a hundred shares in a revamped NWC, a quarter of the stock being allocated to the XY partners. But there was one codicil: because of his stormy temperament and because he had been so dominant in both companies, Mackenzie was precluded from actively participating in the new partnership. It was the supreme irony of Mackenzie's dashing career that his ambition nearly succeeded in wrecking the company he had sought to dominate; in the process, he lost his influence over the trade that might have allowed him to put into place some of his grander designs. Briefly elected to the Legislative Assembly of Lower Canada,

---

*McTavish's vault, located just to the west of the half-finished building, was eventually covered with a mound of earth to keep out vandals, and today the founder of Montreal's commercial life lies in an unmarked and invisible grave. The mansion was demolished in 1821 and eventually made way for Ravenscrag, the estate built by Sir Hugh Allan, the shipping and railway magnate whose $356,500 contribution to the Tory party triggered the Pacific Scandal of 1873, causing the only post-Confederation defeat of Sir John A. Macdonald's government. Allan, who was a staunch Presbyterian, also managed to corrupt Montreal's Catholic clergy so thoroughly that he once had a priest demoted for not supporting a municipal subsidy for one of his railway projects.

The McTavish estate was settled on the late Marquis's elder son, William. The sad, brief lives of the great Nor'Wester's four children are reflected in a pathetic tablet found at Chiswick parish church in London:

> In a vault beneath this church are deposited the remains of William McTavish, who died in his 22nd year at Strand-on-the-Green on the 4th May, 1816, and Anne McTavish, who departed this life at Bridport on the 22nd May, 1819, in her 20th year, and Mary Pasky, sister of the above, who died in her 22nd year at Sidmouth, on the 9th June, 1819.

> Lord, make me to know mine end and the measure of my days, that I may know how frail I am.

> Simon McTavish, Esqr., 4th [child] and last son of Simon McTavish, Esqr., of Montreal, died at Ramsgate 9th October, 1828, aged 25 years.

The dynastic dream of Montreal's founding merchant was ended.

he found political debate boring and except for one brief visit in 1810, he left North America for good in 1805.

Back in Britain, Mackenzie lived on his book profits and fur-trade earnings, married a teenage member of his own clan in 1812 (Geddes Mackenzie of Avoch*) and retired to his father-in-law's estate in Ross-shire on Moray Firth not far north of Inverness and Culloden. In his last preserved letter, written like so many others to his dear cousin Roderick, he complained about his health ("I have at last been over-taken with the consequences of my sufferings in the North West") but seemed more concerned about his distance from the scene of the action, lamenting: "Most of the prominent events I learn from the public prints." That final communication is muted, concluding on a domestic note: ". . . Lady Mackenzie is sitting by me, and the children are playing on the floor. . . ."

A few months later, on his way by stagecoach from Edinburgh to Ross-shire, he was suddenly taken ill near Dunkeld† and died at a roadside inn. Fifty-six years old, Mackenzie was probably the victim of Bright's disease, which had progressively destroyed his kidneys. Some years later, a fire swept through the estate at Avoch, burning most of his manuscripts and papers.

The Mackenzie legend has outgrown the man. "In a longer vista of time than we at present command," concluded Roy Daniells, his most thoughtful biographer, "Canadians will probably see the voyages to the Arctic and Pacific as the Greeks saw the fabulous voyage of the Argonauts to fetch the fleece."

There is implicit in the life of Sir Alexander Mackenzie, who came by land to taste the brine of the Pacific, an enduring sadness that this monument of a man who vowed to alter the world to his specifications could not have had his way.

---

*It certainly was a close-knit family. Not only Geddes herself but her great-grandfather, grandfather, father and twin sister all married within their own clan. Her great-grandfather George married twice, fathering thirty-three children.

†A good place for a Highland lad to die: in 1689, five thousand Highlanders in the Jacobite cause battled twelve hundred Covenanters holding Dunkeld for the government of William and Mary. At the Pass of Killiecrankie nearby, on July 27, 1689, Bonnie Dundee's Jacobites mauled a superior government force of four thousand men under General Hugh Mackay. Bonnie Dundee was killed in the moment of victory. Shortly after Killiecrankie, the Highlanders drove on Dunkeld, from which they later withdrew. Canada's second prime minister, Alexander Mackenzie, was born in Dunkeld on January 28, 1822, just twenty months after Mackenzie the explorer died there.

The Mackenzie River Delta

Descending the canyons of the Fraser

CHAPTER 4

Storming of the West

"We had to pass where no human being should venture. . . ."
— Simon Fraser

FOR A FULL DECADE after Mackenzie's magnificent forays, the distant territories west of the Rockies' height of land were left undisturbed. The rivers that slithered off the eastern shoulders of the mountains had become the turnpikes of the fur trade, coursing through the prairie lands and forests towards the great trading depots at Fort William and York Factory. But west of the unnamed peaks of the forbidding ranges there was nothing—no probe for an exit to Pacific tidewater when it was becoming desperately urgent to find one.

Short-term greed for pelts continued to drive the NWC winterers into untrapped districts, especially regions beyond the reach of the Hudson's Bay men, but in the longer term the company realized that American advances might soon close off overland access to the Pacific. The treaty that ended the American War of Independence and the Louisiana Purchase of 1803 had transformed the former Thirteen Colonies from a seaboard nation to half a continent. No longer were the Nor'Westers free to range down the bountiful valleys of the Mississippi and Missouri into what is now the American heartland. By 1805, Lewis and Clark had crossed the main ridge of the Rockies at Lemhi Pass (on the present-day Montana-Idaho border) and followed the Clearwater and Snake rivers to the estuary of the Columbia.

The struggle to discover an economic passage through the Canadian Rockies took more than ten years to resolve.

Simon Fraser

Simon McTavish's nephew William McGillivray, who had served his apprenticeship as the company's first non-French inland clerk and had taken over command of his uncle's company, knew his most pressing priority was to gain trading access to the Pacific. Because the Nor'Westers were cut off from Hudson Bay, only an accessible route across the Rockies (connected to England via Cape Horn) could ease the killing expense of maintaining his company's continental transportation network, and only a link into the lucrative fur trade with China could gain the profits necessary to keep the whole enterprise afloat.

Of the large rivers that fall west of the mountains, the Skeena, Nass and Stikine discharge too far north to have been useful to the fur trade, leaving only the Columbia and Fraser to be profitably explored. That last, then-unnamed, river, which had already been partly travelled by Mackenzie, was chosen for the initial assault on the misty province beyond the setting sun.

Picked to undertake this perilous enterprise was Simon Fraser, the most heroic and least attractive of the NWC explorers. Grumpy and forbidding, this brooding Vermont-born Scot demonstrated all the obstinacy but little of the charm of his heritage. His soft, pasty face, sloping forehead and trout-mouth gave him a permanently sour look. He was an awkward, uninspiring man. His mother, Isabella Grant (daughter of the Laird of Daldregan), had fled to Canada when her husband died in prison during the American War of Independence, and had settled in Cornwall Township on the St Lawrence River. After two years' schooling, Simon became a clerk in the North West Company and in 1801, at the age of twenty-five, had been promoted to full partnership. During the company's conclave at Fort William four years later, he was assigned twin tasks: to lead the expedition that would establish a new Western Department by planting a string of trading posts past the Great Divide, and to follow what the Nor'Westers believed to be the Columbia River to its mouth. Little was known about that rumoured waterway except that dependable captains of three countries—Bruno Heceta of Spain, W.R. Broughton of England and Robert Gray of the United States—had located its broad mouth at about latitude 46° north. Sir Alexander Mackenzie had correctly suggested that the river provided the most plausible access to the Northwest, but wrongly assumed he had travelled along its upper waters in 1793. If American competition on the Pacific was to be forestalled, Simon Fraser had to move fast.

That first winter Fraser and his small party followed Mackenzie's route along the Peace and Parsnip rivers, building several trading posts, among them Fort McLeod, the first permanent white establishment between Alaska and California. The following season he moved deeper into unknown territory and reached Stuart Lake, where his men erected a squat of huts known as Fort St James, which would evolve into a pivotal outstation of the fur trade. Fraser was so entranced by the majestic beauty of the landscape that he named the district New Caledonia, after the Scotland of his mother's fables.* He was determined to start down the mysterious "Great River" (which he confidently assumed to be the Columbia) in the summer of 1807, but supplies reached him too late in the season. He waited, fretting, until the spring of 1808.

According to Bruce Hutchison, who wrote its definitive portrait, Fraser's river (eventually named after him) "is one of the basic political and economic facts of America. . . . The life of Canada from the beginning

---

*The country was known to the Romans as Caledonia, and the term "Scotland" was first used in the eleventh century. Scots who emigrated kept establishing New Caledonias wherever they went.

has flowed mainly down two channels, the St. Lawrence in the east and the Fraser in the west. . . . Measured by size, by economic consequence, by political influence, the Fraser is a continental force." The river itself shoots 850 miles from its source near Yellowhead Pass on the western slopes of the Rockies north, west and south to the Pacific in a vaguely S-shaped descent between rugged mountainsides and through snarling cataracts.

At five o'clock on the morning of May 28, Fraser and his two lieutenants, John Stuart and Jules Quesnel, plus nineteen voyageurs and two Carrier Indians, set out in four canoes aptly christened with such brave names as *Perseverance* and *Determination*. Floating down the relatively calm waters between Fort George (now Prince George) and Soda Creek, they sighted a succession of Indian villages. The moccasin telegraph had been working overtime, passing along news of the intruders' progress and, curious to learn his intentions, the natives gathered in one of the larger settlements and invited Fraser ashore. The Nor'Wester made the most of the occasion, donning his topper and having himself grandly carried to land on the shoulders of two brawny voyageurs. Speaking through an accompanying interpreter, Fraser addressed an open-air rally, attempted some faith-healing by treating sick youngsters with tincture of opium and demonstrated the power of his "thunderstick." "These Indians," he noted in his journal, "had heard of fire arms but had never seen any, and they evinced a great desire of seeing ours and obtaining explanations as to their use. In compliance, we fired several shots whose reports astonished them so as to make them drop off their legs."

The impressed natives donated a slave to the expedition. Although the man was touted to be useful as a guide, Fraser dismissed his warnings of impassable waters ahead that would swallow his canoes as the whimperings of a superstitious primitive. His attitude towards Indians, in this and other matters, was oafishly condescending. The diary he kept mentions that "their singing makes a terrible racket" and "their women's hair is dirty and smelly." He thought the several dyed dog-hair blankets given him attractive mainly because "they resembled, at a distance, Highland plaid." Although he was serenaded and feasted at one Interior Salish village, Fraser noted sarcastically that "however kind the savage may appear, I know that it is not in their nature to be sincere in their professions to strangers. The respect and attention, which we generally experience, proceed, perhaps, from an idea that we are superior human beings . . . at any rate, it is certain the less familiar we are with one another the better for us."

After this interlude, the exploration party was swept once more into the canyons of the Fraser, a stretch of the roughest water ever traversed. "In a sense the Fraser does not flow at all," wrote Hugh MacLennan in his study of Canadian rivers. "It seethes along with whirlpools so fierce that a log going down it may circle the same spot for days as though caught in a liquid merry-go-round. It roars like an ocean in storm, but ocean storms blow themselves out while the Fraser's roar is forever." Spumes sluice down the narrowing riverbed, force-fed by the melting snow, moving with such speed and power that they hurl large fish bodily from the current.

Travelling through this maelstrom had less to do with boat handling than with acrobatics. The Nor'Westers had entered a world without choice: to attempt the only available portages—which meant hacking precarious footholds in the rock-faces overhanging the mad stream—made just as little sense as staying in their flimsy birchbark canoes and braving this hellish excuse for a river. Even Fraser's taciturn nature yielded to the terrors facing him. In the journal tallying each harrowing escape along the route, he uncharacteristically allowed himself the use of an exclamation mark in lamenting the nature of his mission: "... a desperate undertaking!"

Having decided to proceed, Fraser and his men inched along rock ledges so narrow it was often difficult "even for one person sideways" to make headway, and all but impossible to portage canoes: "We cut steps ... fastened a line to the front of the canoe ... some of the men ascended in order to haul it up, while the others supported the canoe upon their arms.... Our lives hung as it were upon a thread; for failure of the line or a false step of one of the men might have hurled the whole of us into eternity."

On June 9, at French Bar Canyon, about halfway between the mouth of the Chilcotin River and present-day Lillooet, the men faced a gorge with sheer walls and cliff edges almost meeting at the top, forming a roof over the cascades below. "Here," Fraser noted on what must have been water-soaked pages, "the channel contracts to about 40 yards, and is enclosed by two precipices of great height, which, bending towards each other, make it narrower above than below. The water, which rolls down this extraordinary passage in tumultuous waves and with great velocity, had a tremendous appearance. It being absolutely impossible to carry the canoes by land, all hands without hesitation embarked as it were *à corps perdu* upon the mercy of this Stygian tide. Once engaged the die was cast, and the great difficulty consisted in keeping the canoes within the medium, or *fil d'eau*, that is to say, clear of the precipice on one side, and of the gulfs formed by the waves on the other. However, thus skimming along like lightning, the crews, cool and determined, followed each other in awful silence, and when we arrived at the end, we stood gazing on our narrow escape from perdition."

Near Jackass Mountain, south of present-day Lytton, the going got even rougher. One of the voyageurs rode an overturned canoe three miles downstream, holding on for dear life with his legs and dancing with his spine as if he were on the back of a bucking bronco.

No relief. At Black Canyon, downstream from the present twin railway communities of North Bend and Boston Bar, expedition members were forced to claw over slimy outcrops, dangle from primitive rope ladders and balance on precariously hung log booms devised by local tribes. The men were by now exhausted beyond endurance and discouraged beyond caring. The conquest of each new trial-by-terror only meant encountering yet another, even worse, obstacle. Hell's Gate was next. The river narrowed into a giant crevice where torrents eighty-five feet deep had been heightened an extra hundred feet by the spring runoff. "I have been for a long period among the Rocky Mountains," Fraser confessed to his diary on this ultimate rainy day of his soul, "but have never seen anything like this country. . . . I cannot find words to describe our situation at times. We had to pass where no human being should venture. . . ."

But even here there was a footpath indented into the precipice by Indians who had come this way for generations. Fraser described "steps . . . formed like a ladder or the shrouds of a ship, by poles hanging to one another and crossed at certain distances with twigs, the whole suspended from the top to the foot of immense precipices and fastened at both extremities to stones and trees," and how he and his crew scrambled up these flimsy supports like grateful monkeys on a string.

That final hurdle behind them, the waterlogged Nor'Westers headed towards the ocean. Gulls were wheeling overhead. Just beyond the river's silty delta they could see a broad gulf set with jewelled islands. But true to the character of this expedition, Fraser's problems were far from over. On July 2, 1808, just before they broke through to tidewater, the boats were surrounded by hostile Musqueam Indians. Fraser noted that they were "singing a war song, beating time with their paddles upon the sides of the canoes, and making signs and gestures highly inimical." The following day, after more of the same, he wrote: "We, therefore, relinquished our design and directed our thoughts towards home." He did reach the ocean but had no time to look around and check his longitude, snatching only a fast latitude reading—just above 49° north. That was enough to confirm his worst fears: the muddy mouth of the river he had just run was clearly not that of the

Columbia, which three master seamen had located near the 46th parallel.

The return voyage was worse than the original journey because the region's Indians, sure that the party of white men would perish in their attempt to ride the river, now did not want them to leave alive. Boulders were hurled down at the explorers' canoes; showers of arrows met some of their attempts to land for food. But thirty-three days after leaving the Pacific foreshore, Fraser and his men were back at Fort George, having accomplished little beyond proving decisively that what they had discovered was not the Columbia and that the Fraser was not a navigable fur-trade route.

AFTER BOTH MACKENZIE AND FRASER had proved it was impossible to send freight canoes through the mountains, it became evident that the only effective way to move goods to the Pacific side was to go around them. That required a successful expedition down the serpentine Columbia to its saltwater mouth. The Nor'Wester who accomplished that difficult task as well as the mapping of one-third of the previously blank subcontinent was a remarkable geographer named David Thompson.

Thompson stood out among his colleagues. He was not Scottish but of Welsh descent, and was not only prodigiously literate but left behind thirty-nine volumes of journals that rank (or should) as major contributions to the early history of Canada. He cared little for the fur trade but walked and canoed fifty-five thousand miles, pacing off the country he was determined to chart. During his stewardship as chief topographer of the North West Company, Thompson not only mapped the Columbia River system to the Pacific but also pinpointed the sources of the Mississippi, explored the upper region of the Missouri and the southeastern interior of British Columbia. He also did the original surveys of the Muskoka country between the Ottawa River and Lake Huron and laid out Quebec's Eastern Townships. He later surveyed much of the border between Canada and the United States. "Elliott Coues's description of Thompson as the greatest geographer of his day in British America errs, if it errs, only in being an understatement," wrote Professor Richard Glover in his introduction to a modern edition of Thompson's journals.

Despite his sterling qualifications, Thompson seemed ill-fitted for the crude ethics of frontier life. His upright approach to the circumstances in which he found himself prompted the modern explorer Joseph Burr Tyrrell to exclaim that Thompson continually bore "the white flower of a blameless life." Such attempts at beatification were based less on

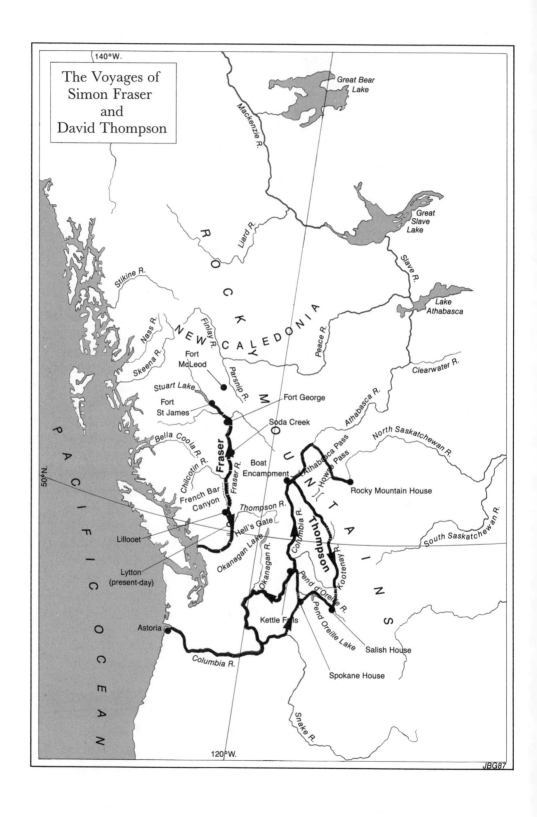

The Voyages of
Simon Fraser
and
David Thompson

140°W.

Great Bear
Lake

Mackenzie R.

Great
Slave
Lake

Liard R.

Slave R.

R
O
C
K
Y

Stikine R.

Lake
Athabasca

NEW CALEDONIA

Nass R.

Finlay R.

Peace R.

Skeena R.

Fort
McLeod

Clearwater R.

Parsnip R.

Athabasca R.

North Saskatchewan R.

Stuart Lake

Fort
St James

Fort George

M

Bella Coola R.

Soda Creek

O

Fraser

Chilcotin R.

Boat
Encampment

Athabasca Pass

Howse Pass

U

Fraser R.

N

Rocky Mountain House

50° N.

French Bar
Canyon

T

Columbia R.

A

Thompson R.

Thompson

I

South Saskatchewan R.

Lillooet

Hell's Gate

N

Okanagan Lake

Kootenay R.

Lytton
(present-day)

Okanagan R.

Pend d'Oreille R.

S

P
A
C
I
F
I
C

Astoria

Kettle Falls

Pend Oreille Lake

Salish House

Columbia R.

Spokane House

O
C
E
A
N

Snake R.

120°W.

JBG87

Thompson's professional accomplishments than on his carefully groomed appearance and personal habits. He didn't smoke, swear or drink and not only had thirteen children by his country wife but stayed faithful to her for sixty years. His idea of relaxing after a strenuous paddle was to gather his voyageurs around him and read aloud in French from the New or Old Testament, explaining the Word of God to his uncomfortable charges.

According to his contemporaries, he was an immensely talented storyteller. Dr J.J. Bigsby, who helped him survey the boundary between Canada and the United States, described how Thompson could "create a wilderness and people it with warring savages, or climb the Rocky Mountains with you in a snow storm, so clearly and palpably, that you only shut your eyes and you hear the crack of the rifle, or feel the snow flakes melt on your face as he talks."

Thompson not only denied himself alcohol but also tried to deny it to others. No post under his jurisdiction was allowed to use liquor in the trade. On one trip into the Kootenays, he was ordered by his superiors to include two kegs of rum among his provisions. He fastidiously tied them onto the back of his most spirited packhorse; within hours the kicking, bucking animal had staved in both barrels, and Thompson wrote an accurate report in clear conscience to NWC headquarters about what he had done.

His view of Indians bordered on reverence. He blamed Europeans for every wrong committed in the New World, paying elaborate homage to the natives' way of life, their ethics, religions and customs. He believed nature had been in perfect balance with the red man until the rum-besotted traders had desecrated the natural paradise. "Writers on the Indians," he complained in his journal, "always compare them with themselves, who are all white men of education. This is not fair. Their noted stoic apathy is more assumed than real. In public, the Indian wishes it to appear that nothing affects him. But in private, he feels and expresses himself sensitive to everything that happens to him or his family. On becoming acquainted with the Indians I found almost every character in civilized society can be traced among them—from the gravity of a judge to a merry jester, from open-hearted generosity to the avaricious miser."

There was a wide mystical streak in the man. He worshipped beavers as deities and claimed to have been challenged to a card game by the Devil. (Thompson reported that he beat Lucifer, but as a result of that match, he swore off cards forever.) The Indians called him *Koo-Koo-Sint* ("the man who looks at stars") and marvelled at his extra-terrestrial obsessions. "Once after a weary day's march," he noted, "we sat by a log fire. The bright moon, with thousands of sparkling stars, passed before us. The Indians could not help enquiring who lived in those bright mansions and, as one of them said, he thought he could almost touch them with his hand. I explained to them the nature of these brilliant planets. But I am afraid it was to no purpose. The Indians concluded, 'The stars are the abodes of the spirits—of those who have led a good life.'"

As ardent a naturalist as he was a navigator and astronomer, Thompson described every species of moss he could find; while being bitten by mosquitoes he studied the insects' devouring tactics under a magnifying glass, and he was the first to take the temperature of a reindeer's blood. As he led three suffering companions on a leash through a winter whiteout, he discovered that one factor governing the severity of snow blindness is eye colour; blue-eyed people suffer the most, dark-eyeds the least. He compiled Indian language dictionaries, could speak four Indian tongues (Chipewyan, Mandan, Peigan and Kootenay) and some of his bird observations have never been equalled for their evocative sensitivity: "No dove is more meek than the white prairie grouse,* with its pleasing cheerful call of *Kabow-kabow-kow-a-e*. . . . I have often taken these birds, with their deep chocolate feathers against a background of beautiful white brilliance, from the nest. I provoked them all I could without injuring them. But all was submissive meekness. Rough humans as we were, sometimes of an evening we could not help enquiring, 'Why should such an angelic bird be doomed to be the prey of carnivorous animals and birds?' But the ways of Providence are unknown to us."

With these and other virtues being paraded at every available opportunity, it was little wonder that his contemporaries tended to dismiss him as being too good to be true. The modern fur-trade historian Richard Glover shrewdly rejected the geographer's goody-goody reputation by pointing out that the man "may perhaps be correctly diagnosed as suffering that common Puritan disease, a consciousness of his own virtue which was too strong and determined to enable him to recognize when he was doing wrong; and if he ever did realize that he made mistakes he was certainly not in the habit of admitting them."

In the end, what really mattered was his skill as a surveyor—and that was superlative. Thompson's map of the NWC empire, displayed at Fort William's Great Hall,† became the matrix for every atlas of western

---

*Thompson probably had encountered a willow ptarmigan.

†A copy of the map is now on public view in the Archives of Ontario in Toronto.

Canada published in the next seventy-five years. His almost uncanny ability to delineate the contours of the wild land owed little to any privilege of his upbringing. Born of Welsh parents, he was fatherless when he was two, and his mother, unable to support her family, placed him in a charity institution called Grey Coat School, near Westminster Abbey. The young Thompson spent his free time reading adventure books such as *Robinson Crusoe* and touring the abbey memorizing the epitaphs of the great men and women buried there. He studied navigation in hopes of a career in the Royal Navy but joined the Hudson's Bay Company as an apprentice instead, leaving England in 1784 when he was fourteen. His first assignment was to Churchill, then under the distinguished governorship of Samuel Hearne. The youngster helped him copy some of his famous journal, though no real friendship developed between them.

After a brief stint at York Factory, Thompson was sent inland to serve at a post on the South Saskatchewan River. Two days before Christmas 1788, while hauling a sled of firewood, he fell and fractured his leg. That accident, which laid him up at Cumberland House for most of the next year, temporarily removed him from the daily pressures of the fur trade. It was Thompson's great good fortune that Philip Turnor, the HBC's resident surveyor, spent a winter with him explaining the rudiments of surveying. His mentor gave him an old Dollond sextant, and ever afterward Thompson took sightings wherever he went, gradually filling in the vast empty spaces on his map.

After several unsuccessful attempts to find a direct navigable route from Hudson Bay to the Fur Country of the Athabasca, Thompson decided to leave the HBC and defect to the service of its chief rival. Certainly, he must have been bored during his early service on Hudson Bay, feeling that his skills were severely underutilized and confiding to his journal, ". . . for all I had seen in their service neither writing nor reading was required. And my only business was to amuse myself, in winter growling at the cold and in the open season shooting Gulls, Ducks, Plover and Curlews, and quarrelling with Musketoes and Sand flies." Thompson's own rationale for his decision was that it was against his honest nature to pretend any longer he was interested in trading furs when what he most wanted to do was survey the country. When he received a letter from Joseph Colen, his supervisor at York Factory, forbidding him to spend Company time on any more surveys, he knew he had to resign. Just before he left, Thompson had been offered a promotion with the unusual title "Master to the Northward." If he had accepted that grand post, the fur trade would have had to become his full-time occupation. More to the point, he would have had to expend all his energies not only in commercial pursuits but also in the active leadership of his fellow traders. Despite his talents, Thompson did not feel qualified to manage the lives of others, preferring to commune silently with the sun and stars through his instruments. That obsession may have been the ultimate reason for his desertion. His actual defection took place in the spring of 1797, when Thompson walked the seventy-five miles from an HBC post on Reindeer Lake to Alexander Fraser's house on the Reindeer River, having made certain before his irrevocable act that the NWC would welcome him into its service.

AT THE NWC'S ANNUAL CONCLAVE the following summer Thompson was assigned to survey (at four times his HBC salary) the new boundary between the United States and the company's territories. He traced the Red and Assiniboine rivers, found the gurgling springs where the Mississippi originates (in what is now northern Minnesota) and at Lac la Biche met and fell in love with a gentle fourteen-year-old Mixed Blood named Charlotte Small, the daughter of a prominent NWC *bourgeois*, who proved to be an invaluable lifetime helpmate. During the next half-decade he surveyed many of the lakes, rivers and trading posts of the Northwest, all of it the perfect preparation for his journey down the Columbia.

That confusing river had baffled the early geographers. Its tributaries, joining it from nearly every quadrant of the compass, are often substantial rivers in their own right—the Kootenay, which at one point runs parallel to the Columbia but in the opposite direction; the placid Okanagan; the Pend d'Oreille; and the magnificent Snake, whose drainage area would one day become the HBC's main trapping preserve. The source of the Columbia is a cool lake high in the Rocky Mountain Trench south of present-day Windermere, B.C. From there, the river wends deceptively for most of two hundred miles northwest before it doubles back on itself, then surges past the Selkirk Range and winds south and west towards the ocean. Its drop of 2,650 feet between source and sea makes it the most powerful of the West Coast rivers.

Thompson first sighted the upper reaches of the Columbia in 1807, after setting out with Charlotte and their three young children from Rocky Mountain House. The small party reached the azure glaciers of the high Rockies and, looking towards his river of destiny, Thompson prayed that God in his mercy would guide him to where its waters joined the ocean.

That quest would take another four years to satisfy. In contrast to the commando tactics of Mackenzie and Fraser, the sensitive Welshman chose to blend into the territory, spending the next three seasons on exploratory journeys to various sections and tributaries of the Columbia but never able to commit himself to its full exploration. Then, in 1810, as he was on his way back to Fort William, Thompson was ordered to the Pacific.

He set off immediately with a large, well-equipped party up the North Saskatchewan River, bound for Rocky Mountain House. In his conquest of the Columbia, Thompson had to overcome not only the river's geographical puzzles but the active resistance of the Peigan Indians who guarded the routes to its headwaters. The Peigans feared the white intruders would disrupt their trading patterns by supplying guns directly to their traditional enemies, the Kootenays. Thompson's most immediate problem was that one angry band of Peigans, who knew he had traded guns to the Kootenays, blocked Howse Pass (roughly halfway between the modern resort towns of Jasper and Banff), the entry point he had used for his previous treks into the mountains. Thompson divided his party into two groups. He left the main canoe flotilla behind and rode ahead on horseback with his own companions to scout and hunt for food. When he got back to the previously arranged rendezvous, the canoes had not yet arrived. He sent his Indians forward to reconnoitre, warning them not to fire their guns in case they tipped off their presence to the Peigans. The search party promptly came crashing back. They had run up against the Peigan blockade, fired a warning shot and fled. At this point, Thompson lost his nerve. Instead of waiting for his main force to arrive, he ran for his life and spent the next three weeks cowering alone in a wooded gully in the nearby hills. There he nearly starved to death, being too paralysed with terror to sneak out and shoot game.

The main flotilla of canoes had meanwhile passed Thompson's hiding place and arrived uneventfully at Rocky Mountain House. Alexander Henry the Younger, an NWC partner on his way west to join Thompson, got to the post on October 5. Assuming that Thompson was upriver, having originally gone to scout *ahead* of his troops, Henry set himself the difficult assignment of sneaking the canoes upstream past the Peigan war party. Hostile Indian scouts were hanging around the post, looking intentionally ominous, and when Henry tried to send boats through on a dark night, they were stopped and ordered back to the fort. The problem was that the Peigans assigned to loiter near Rocky Mountain House sent word to their platoons on the river as soon as any canoe activity was sighted. To fool them, Henry dispatched empty canoes downstream, and invited the Peigans at the fort in to drink. He laced their rum with opium and, when they blissfully passed out, ordered the canoes back, loaded them and managed to slip past the river guards who had received no warning of their departure.

Henry was congratulating himself on his successful ruse when a voyageur who had been with the advance party arrived to report that Thompson was on the *other* side of Rocky Mountain House. An exasperated Henry marched back and finally located the trembling geographer on the north bank of the river at the top of a hill three hundred feet above the water, in a gully so thickly treed that he did not spot Thompson's tent until he was within ten yards of it. The grounded explorer had been living mainly on berries for twenty days and seemed beyond the point of being able to make rational choices.

Henry urged him to join the main party upriver, pointing out that even if the Peigans were on the warpath, they were dependent for their arms and ammunition (and rum) on the Nor'Westers and would hardly dare spark too decisive an incident. But Thompson, still wild-eyed, could not be persuaded. He insisted on abandoning the North Saskatchewan and Howse Pass route, deciding instead to break through the mountains at an unknown dip near the headwaters of the Athabasca River. The month-long delay, Thompson's refusal to take the easier route through the Rockies, and the three months he spent in a winter camp waiting for the weather to yield cost him valuable time. During the nightmarish trek through Athabasca Pass, all but three of his original thirteen companions deserted him, arriving back at Rocky Mountain House cursing the weather and Thompson's faltering leadership.

Thompson reached the Columbia at Boat Encampment, near the confluence of the Columbia, Canoe and Wood rivers, and here his men built a new boat. Only a quartet of survivors managed to get down the length of the Columbia, having made an unnecessary, six-hundred-mile detour when Thompson chose to avoid Howse Pass and seek a new route to the north. They finally built an awkward canoe out of split cedar held together by pine roots. But instead of floating down the river, they decided, in a search for added manpower, to *ascend* the Columbia and cross over to the Kootenay.*

---

*Trying to reconstruct Thompson's journey is difficult because after his harrowing crossing of the Rockies at Athabasca Pass and negotiating the Wood River, he followed a circuitous route: he ascended the Columbia from Boat Encampment (at the top of the Big Bend), crossed over from Columbia Lake at Canal Flats to the Kootenay, went down the Kootenay into what is now Montana, crossed over to the Clark Fork (a big tributary river that flows into Lake Pend Oreille in Idaho, and flows out as the Pend d'Oreille River and ultimately reaches the Columbia, in Canada, downstream from Trail, B.C.), and then went across to Spokane House, fairly close to the present-day Spokane. (He had established Spokane House, on the Spokane River, a couple of years earlier.) He didn't go down the Spokane River to the Columbia but took a more

On July 12, 1811, they found seals playing around their boat, smelled salt in the air and broke out the company flag. Two days later, Thompson rounded Tongue Point. Four newly built log cabins were already holding that hallowed ground. The newcomers had arrived by sea on March 22, representing John Jacob Astor's Pacific Fur Company, an offshoot of the American Fur Company. They feasted the Nor'Westers with a magnificent duck dinner, urging Thompson to abandon his vow of abstinence and join in the Madeira toasts to his exploits. He refused. After canoeing to the open Pacific the next day, he set out on his return journey. That undertaking was just as complicated as his original trip, taking more than a year to complete.*

---

complicated route which brought him out to the river at Kettle Falls, opposite the point where the Kettle River merges with the Columbia. Then he went downstream on the Columbia. (The party had travelled overland from the Pend d'Oreille River, somewhere near the present village of Usk, Washington, to Spokane House, and by land from Spokane House to Kettle Falls, using horses they had obtained locally.) The party built a new canoe at Kettle Falls and embarked on July 3, 1811. This was the first time they were going downstream on the Columbia. Thompson fixed the latitude of Astoria at 46°13'56" north and the longitude at 123°36'16" west.

*The party left Astoria on July 22, 1811, and headed upstream. They then turned up the Snake for fifty-six miles, got eight horses from the local Indian band, and a couple of days later (August 11) were again at Spokane House. By land they went to Kettle Falls, built a canoe, and were set to continue on September 2, eventually arriving at Boat Encampment. They didn't find the men and goods they expected, and set off up the Canoe River, taking nearly four days to go forty-eight miles. Then two men in a small canoe caught up to them, reporting that reinforcements had arrived. The forty-eight miles downriver took them only a few hours. Thompson then sent a party of nine men, with goods, downriver to Kettle Falls to supply the lower posts like Spokane House. He got more supplies, and on October 21 set out downriver, making it through ice on the Arrow Lakes, to reach Kettle Falls on October 30. Here he expected to find men and horses. There being none, his party set off on foot on November 1, reaching Spokane House on November 3. They then went to what he called the Salish River (the Clark Fork), getting there on November 13. They moved by land up the river, finding Salish House wrecked and a tent full of Kootenay Indians killed by Peigans. On November 24 John George McTavish and James McMillan arrived with fifteen men, ten horses and twelve hundred pounds of trade goods. Thompson and his men continued to repair and rebuild the wrecked post, and by December 16 they were all under shelter. In February, Thompson and two of his men explored the territory to the southeast (to Missoula, Montana). On March 13 they set off for Kettle Falls, where they built four more canoes and on April 22 set off upstream. On May 5 they arrived at Mountain Carrying Place (Boat Encampment). Thompson and three hunters set off on snowshoes, reaching the height of land (Athabasca Pass) on May 8 and arriving at the house of William Henry (near Jasper) on May 11. On May 13 they embarked on their journey to Fort William, which they reached on July 12, 1812. Three days later a vessel arrived bearing word that the United States had declared war on Britain. They set out again and reached Montreal unharmed in mid-August.

David Thompson in the Athabasca Pass, 1810

After such hardship Thompson decided to leave the Northwest permanently. "Thus I have fully completed the survey of this part of North America from sea to sea," he summarized in his journal, "and by almost innumerable astronomical observations have determined the positions of the mountains, lakes and rivers, and other remarkable places on the northern part of this continent; the maps of all of which have been drawn, and they are laid down in geographical position. This work has occupied me for twenty-seven years."

David Thompson retired from the fur trade the following year to Terrebonne, Quebec, and spent the next twenty months completing his ten-foot-long map of the Northwest, delineating the 1.5 million square miles of the territories he had travelled and showing the precise location of the North West Company's trading posts.

JOHN JACOB ASTOR, who had beaten the Nor'Westers to the Pacific Coast, is best remembered as the man who made his fortune by being the first person to grasp the real-estate potential of New York, capturing owner-ship of more houses, commercial buildings and entire downtown blocks

John Jacob Astor

than any other individual has been known to own in one large city. He not only became the richest American of his generation but also founded one of the most enduring family dynasties, his descendants achieving dominant status within the United States and, later, British circles. The Astors could automatically count themselves as high society on both sides of the Atlantic at a time when the Vanderbilts were still struggling for social recognition and J.P. Morgan was dismissed as being *nouveau riche*.

He may have been a role-model for a fledgling society emulating anyone who had hacked a fortune from the new land, but John Jacob Astor was in fact a monumental boor—a vulgar barbarian in morning coat whose manners were damned in the diary of James Gallatin, a son of Thomas Jefferson's Secretary of the Treasury: "He dined here last night and ate his ice cream and peas with a knife." The less well-known coda to that famous gaffe was Gallatin's report of another meal at which Astor after the main course not only wiped his dirty fingers on the gown of the lady seated next to him but also shattered the cosy postprandial atmosphere by blowing his nose into his cupped hand.

A self-made man who worshipped his creator, Astor was born at

Walldorf* on the fringes of Germany's Black Forest and left his father's butcher shop in 1779 at sixteen to follow his brother George to England, where he helped run a small musical instrument business. Three years later he had saved enough to buy a steerage ticket to America and left for the New World carrying his total wealth (£5) and seven flutes. On the way across the Atlantic he overheard some Hudson's Bay Company officials discussing how much money could be made in furs by traders operating independently of the large companies. His fellow passengers remembered Astor mainly because every time a storm came up, he would put on his best clothes, explaining that if the ship went down and he was rescued, at least he would have saved his one good suit.

The New York in which he landed was a swamp with a population of less than thirty thousand, no sanitary facilities and a future downtown that was still farmland. Astor's start as a pedlar of sweet cakes along the settlement's streets soon gave way to a better job (at two dollars a week) beating the dust out of furs and packing them for shipment to the London auction markets. From that, it was a quick step to becoming an apprentice fur trader, venturing into the Iroquois territory north of Albany with a sixty-pound pack on his back, tramping through twenty miles of bush a day. The young Astor was inordinately successful because he managed to drive a hard bargain while ameliorating his technique by playing the flute and speaking to the Indians in their own languages—a skill first exhibited when he had to learn English virtually overnight after leaving Germany. Persuading the Indians to part with their pelts for a fraction of their worth was what had originally attracted him to the business. But when a New York fur merchant sent him to England and he realized that beaver skins traded for inferior trinkets could fetch 900 percent profit, Astor knew he had found his true *métier*.

In New York, he had married Sarah Todd, the daughter of his Scottish landlady, who not only brought him a sizeable dowry—and free room and board—but turned out to be a fine businesswoman. As their trade grew, she eventually charged him a usurious $500 an hour to grade the furs he collected on his treks through the Catskills, the thick forests of New Jersey and Long Island swamps—and he was glad to pay it.

---

*The namesake of New York's Waldorf-Astoria Hotel, built by John Jacob's great-grandson, William Waldorf Astor, in 1897.

One of the few altruistic clauses in the original Astor's will provided for the construction of a large and elaborate home for the poor in his home town. During the Second World War it was taken over by the Nazis and converted into a barracks for the *Bund Deutscher Mädchen*, the Aryan teenage girls who indentured themselves into becoming mothers of blond and blue-eyed babies sired by high-ranking SS officers.

New York in the early nineteenth century

By the turn of the century Astor, who was rumoured to be worth $250,000, decided to enter the China trade. That exotic commerce was centred at Canton, the busy port upstream from the Pearl River Delta that had become the trading capital of the South China Sea. The East India Company had operated there since 1685 and eventually thirteen "factories" had been opened to buy and sell most of China's imports and exports. The most unsavoury—and most profitable—aspect of that trade was the Turkish and Indian opium brought in by British mer-chantmen and sold to the Chinese. Profits from that degrading commerce were used to buy the tea and silks imported across the Pacific. Because one of the most desired western goods in China was luxury fur, a quarter of the pelts auctioned off in London found their way into the Chinese market.

With the French Revolution and other European discontinuities, that flow was disrupted, and Astor, seeing an opportunity to trade directly with Canton, dispatched his first chartered vessel there in 1800. It was loaded with 30,573 seal skins, fox, otter and beaver pelts and 132 barrels of ginseng, a root-plant then harvested in America that had become a popular Chinese aphrodisiac and cure-all. Vessels in the China trade, which had tea as the main return cargo, could take up to three years for the round trip. But the profits were so phenomenal that soon Astor had built himself a fleet to exploit the trade.* He envisaged a world-spanning business empire that would give him supremacy over a triangular, highly lucrative commerce. It involved gathering furs from the untapped regions of the Pacific Coast (the Chinese were willing to pay $100 for sea otter pelts, available mainly in Pacific waters); transporting them to Canton; loading up the ships there with tea (plus spices and silks) for the run to New York; reloading with trade goods (beads, bells, blankets, rum) for the sail around Cape Horn and back to the American West Coast—where the Indians supplied the furs. What this grandiose but entirely feasible scheme required was a tidewater port on the Pacific Coast—and the mouth of the Columbia River, so recently charted by Lewis and Clark, was the ideal spot. That distant and as yet unoccupied harbour was to become the capital of Astor's fur-trading empire, drawing its pelt supplies from the trading posts he eventually established up the Missouri and Columbia. This, roughly, was the Oregon Country, a vast, temperate stretch of forests, mountains and valleys on the Pacific side of the continent, still *terra incognita*, its only boundaries the northern margin of California, occupied by Spain, and the even less clearly determined southern edge of Alaska.†

Later, during the run-up to the War of 1812, a U.S. embargo suddenly forced ships to stay in port. Astor already had the *Beaver* loaded and ready to go. To lobby for an exemption, Astor sent a "Distinguished Mandarin" named "Punqua Wing-chong" dressed in fine

---

*Its flagship was a 111-foot steam-powered sailing ship, the *Beaver*, which could cut the passage time to Canton in half. When Astor launched a sister ship called the *Magdalen*, John Cowman, its newly appointed captain, reported that the insurance company underwriting the vessel insisted she be equipped with a chronometer. Astor refused to buy the instrument, claiming the $500 cost was the captain's responsibility. Cowman quit his command and, six weeks after *Magdalen*'s departure under a new master, sailed for Canton in a rival vessel. His navigation skills brought him back to New York well ahead of the *Magdalen*, in time to outdo Astor at local tea auctions, causing his former employer a $70,000 loss.

†Russian fur merchants had been landing on the Alaska coast since Vitus Bering's dramatic voyages of the early eighteenth century (see *Company of Adventurers*, pages 225–27), and by 1799 the Russian-American Company had been formed to take over the trade. Sitka (New Archangel) was founded as the main trading post in 1804, but the Russians were cut off from most of the huge China market because the Chinese emperor permitted only a limited number of their pelts to be brought in via a tiny border settlement in northern Mongolia named Kiakhta. To avoid having to purchase their supplies and trade goods from visiting American skippers, the Russians sent an expedition south and managed to establish an agricultural colony in California. Finally, in 1821, the Tsar prohibited all foreign commerce on the Pacific Coast north of latitude 51°.

silks to Washington, claiming his father had died and that he had to return home immediately—aboard the *Beaver*, of course—for the state funeral. Permission was granted and the ship sailed off—without its exalted passenger, who returned to his former incarnation as an Oriental deckhand on another of Astor's vessels. Because the *Beaver* was the only tea carrier to return with a cargo that season, Astor raised prices and cleared a $200,000 profit.

Although Spain, Britain and Russia all laid claim to the Pacific Coast of North America, John Jacob Astor was determined to put forward Washington's rights by the authority of occupation. "Oregon was the specific prize at the centre of the conflict," wrote Kenneth Spaulding in his study of the Far West, "bounded by the Louisiana Purchase on the east, by Russian Alaska and the territory of the North West Company on the north, by the Pacific Ocean on the west, and by Spanish settlements on the south, it lay like a hollow center among contending interests and nations. . . . The beaver were there and the price was right; the risks were to be assumed with the rewards. . . . The country was open, beautiful, untrodden, and the hostile Indians would help keep it that way."

Astor chartered, as the instrument of the monopoly he hoped to establish, the Pacific Fur Company, and persuaded four fairly senior but disaffected Nor'Westers and a dozen experienced canoeists to join his new firm. In typically boisterous fashion, the boatmen arrived from Montreal for their New York posting in proper voyageur style. "They fitted up a large but light bark canoe," reported Washington Irving, "such as is used in the fur trade; transported it in a wagon from the banks of the St. Lawrence to the shores of Lake Champlain; traversed the lake in it, from end to end; hoisted it again in a wagon and wheeled it off to Lansingburg, and there launched it upon the waters of the Hudson. Down this river they plied their course merrily on a fine summer's day, making its banks resound for the first time with their old French boat songs; passing by the villages with whoop and halloo, so as to make the honest Dutch farmers mistake them for a crew of savages. In this way they swept in full song and with regular flourish of the paddle, round New York, in a still summer evening, to the wonder and admiration of its inhabitants, who had never before witnessed on their waters, a nautical apparition of the kind."

Staking claim to the trans-shipment port at the mouth of the Columbia River required a complicated exercise in logistics. Astor sent one group by land and another by sea. The foot party of sixty-four men and one woman was placed in the charge of a U.S. Cavalry captain named Wilson Price Hunt, who earned his reputation as a man who could be depended upon to bungle, so that whenever a decision had to be made about which way to go, he inevitably headed down the wrong trail. His party travelled most of two years, covering more than twice the actual distance involved because Hunt so often had to double back over his own path. By the time they staggered to their destination in the winter of 1812 they had eaten all their horses, including the nag whose hide they tried to make into a boat, which promptly upset, drowning its occupants. One of their party, John Day, had lost his mind; some of the others were on the point of insanity and all were well into the throes of starvation.

To command the *Tonquin*, the ship designated as the sea element of Astor's drive to the Pacific, he recruited a loony naval officer (on leave of absence) named Lieutenant Jonathan Thorn, who had taken part in the U.S. Navy's raid on Tripoli in 1804. His behaviour made the ill-starred Captain Hunt seem saintly. The kindest assessment of Thorn was that of the former Nor'Wester Alexander McKay, who whispered to one of the ship's mates: "I fear we are in the hands of a lunatic."

The captain of the *Tonquin* treated his ship's company of thirty-three sailors, clerks, partners and voyageurs with wanton cruelty, during an era when any sea voyage was hardly a benign occupation. Thorn's response to the mildest questioning of his most ludicrous orders was to draw his pistol and threaten to shoot anyone within range. He ordered all lights out by eight o'clock, promising to blow off the head of anyone caught not obeying his instructions. When the ship stopped off at the Falkland Islands to take on water, three of the most senior fur traders aboard and five other men went ashore, where they found two neglected graves whose headstones required repairs. They were completing this task when Thorn ordered the vessel under way. The shore party tumbled into their beached rowboat and desperately tried to catch up with the *Tonquin*. The distance between the two vessels widened and it was only when the cousin of one of the men in the small boat put a gun to Thorn's head that he hove-to and allowed the frantic rowers to catch up. When the ship reached the Sandwich Islands (Hawaii), some of the crew deserted, but one seaman named Aymes was so conscientious that when he missed the liberty boat, he hired a native canoe to take him out to the *Tonquin*. An entry in the journal of Gabriel Franchère, a clerk on the voyage, describes what happened: "On perceiving him, the captain ordered him to stay in the long-boat, then lashed to the side with its load of sugar-cane. The captain himself got into the boat, and, taking one of the canes, beat the poor fellow most unmercifully with it; after which, not satisfied with this brutality, he seized his victim and threw him overboard!"

The Tonquin entering the Columbia River, March 1811

By the time the ship arrived off the mouth of the Columbia on March 22, 1811, the crew was ready to mutiny—but the ordeal was not yet over. The estuary was obstructed by a dangerous sandbar. Thorn insisted on launching a boat to sound the channel even though a storm was brewing and the water was far too rough for safe navigation. The boat overturned, drowning five men, but instead of waiting out the high winds, Thorn ordered another boat into the channel and lost it too, with three more casualties. Two weeks later, the survivors had selected an appropriate site for Astor's western headquarters, christening it Astoria. On June 5, the *Tonquin*, with twenty-three of her original crew aboard, sailed north to barter for sea otter skins. When the ship put into Clayoquot Sound, one of the many inlets that scallop the west coast of Vancouver Island, Thorn lost his temper with the local chief, flung a pelt in his face and ordered him off the ship. His mates, sensing that the insult might have dire consequences, begged Thorn to hoist sail and leave, but that only persuaded the obstinate captain to stay. Next morning, large canoes arrived, their occupants waving otter skins above their heads—indicating willingness to trade. Thorn beckoned them aboard. Soon more canoes arrived, one after another, and the Indians crowded the decks. Two of the Nor'Westers warned Thorn that the situation was getting out of control, but that blinkered martinet kept exchanging furs for more and more knives, confident his guns could handle any trouble that came along. At a pre-arranged signal, the Indians drew their daggers. With a war whoop they attacked the crew, slashing throats and pushing the surviving wounded over the side, where the women in newly arrived canoes finished them off with their paddles. Thorn was quickly put out of his misery. One survivor was the Indian interpreter who eventually made his way back to Astoria with the gory details; the other was James Lewis, the ship's clerk, who though grievously wounded managed to pull himself near the *Tonquin*'s powder magazine. Next morning the Indians climbed back aboard to claim their booty and loot the ship. Lewis waited until he sensed that the full complement of boarders was preoccupied, then lit a fuse and blew them—and himself—skyhigh.

DESPITE THIS DISASTER, the morale of the traders at Astoria remained high. Not only had they reached their objective and erected John Jacob's new West Coast terminus, but the unexpected arrival of David Thompson had prompted them to expand their sphere of operations inland, certain they could meet the Nor'Westers on their own ground and triumph. Astor's agents built trading posts on the Okanagan and Kootenay rivers, at Spokane, and all the way up the Okanagan Valley and across to the Thompson River at what is now Kamloops, B.C. They inevitably became trade rivals of the NWC, but for the first while it was only token jousting, as this report of a duel between an Astorian and a Nor'Wester indicates: "Mr. Pillet fought a duel with Mr. Montour of the North-West, with pocket pistols, at six paces; both hits; one in the collar of the coat and the other in the leg of the trousers. Two of their men acted as seconds, and the tailor speedily healed their wounds."

In the summer of 1812, while Napoleon was preparing to invade Russia, the United States declared war on Great Britain and for the next two years invaded and harassed its territories in North America. Using that conflict as a pretext, in the autumn of 1813 the NWC decided to pursue its Oregon venture and dispatched a hundred men under the command of John George McTavish and John Stuart down the Columbia.* They laid siege to Astoria, aided by rumours of war that threatened the continued safety of its occupants, specifically that the Royal Navy's twenty-six-gun sloop HMS *Racoon* was on her way around Cape Horn assigned to shell the embattled fort. The former Nor'Westers occupying the American outpost felt they had been abandoned by their own supply ships and began to talk surrender. (Astor had actually dispatched two ships to Astoria. The *Beaver*, then trading furs in Alaska, continued on to Canton where, hearing of the declaration of war, she stayed put. Another supply ship, the *Lark*, was wrecked off Hawaii.) It was hardly one of history's more savage sieges. The Astorians, most of whom were former Nor'Westers, were decidedly uncomfortable defending a fortress flying the Stars and Stripes when their home country was at war with the United States. They had not only friends but relatives among the besiegers, so whenever the attackers ran out of food, the defenders would quietly sneak out and offer them a snack. Finally, on October 16, 1813, Duncan McDougall, who was in charge of the fort, had the bright idea that instead of surrendering he would sell Astoria to

---

*Stuart, who had been first lieutenant to Simon Fraser, was appointed supervisor of the NWC's New Caledonia district. On his way down to help McTavish, he left the Fraser River at the foot of navigation for southbound travellers (Fort Alexandria), went overland by horse to Kamloops, and then passed along the west side of Okanagan Lake to the Okanagan River, a tributary of the Columbia. Once Astoria was in the NWC's hands, that route, which came to be known as the Okanagan Trail, became the main supply line for the entire region, taking the place of the long and awkward transshipment alternative eastward to Fort Chipewyan and through Fort William to Montreal. After the Oregon Treaty of 1846, the route was shifted directly from Kamloops to the Fraser. Eventually, the traffic moved to the Cariboo Road, which ran along the Fraser Canyon between Yale and Barkerville, the route now followed in part by the Trans-Canada Highway.

the friendly invaders. The price was a bargain, with the inventory (worth about $100,000) of otter and beaver pelts going for less than half-price (about $40,000). Part of the deal was that McDougall and most of the senior Astorians would be admitted back into the NWC as partners.

HMS *Racoon*, her Royal Navy colours flying, appeared eight weeks later. William Black, her captain, could hardly believe his bad luck in having sailed eighteen thousand miles to this collection of shacks, which his four-pounders could have flattened before breakfast. Worse still, the purchase of Astoria by the Nor'Westers had deprived him of the right to claim the furs as prize money. He was so annoyed he decided to stage the takeover ceremony anyway. The voyageurs were rounded up, equipped with muskets and drilled to distraction by the ship's officers into a wobbly formation resembling a guard of honour. Resplendent in his dress blues, Black ordered the Union Jack majestically hoisted. He broke out a bottle of Madeira, toasted His Majesty, renamed the post Fort George and ordered his quasi-militia to fire a proper salute. This they achieved in three rowdy rounds, one of the Nor'Westers very nearly shooting himself in the face.

Astor was beside himself when he was told of his fort's ignominious surrender, exclaiming: "While I breathe and so long as I have a dollar to spend, I shall pursue a course to have our injuries repaired!" He collected dividends of more than $1 million on his fur operations well into the 1830s, but Astor had by then become more intrigued by real estate development, riding nightly through the New York suburbs so he could foreclose on the properties of overextended farmers.

By 1844 Astor had acquired a fortune of $20 million in a country with private-sector capitalization of little more than $200 million. His last days were pitiful. He was North America's—and probably the world's—richest man, and yet he complained bitterly that one of his grandchildren had put more butter on his bread plate than he could possibly eat. Critically ill, Astor was kept alive to his eighty-fifth year by taking his daily nourishment from a wet nurse and being tossed about every morning in a blanket to get his circulation going. Only days before his death, he insisted that a destitute elderly woman pay the piffling rent for a flat in one of his houses. When his agent informed Astor that she was too sick and too poor to meet her obligations, he flew into a rage and demanded that the man go back and force her to pay up. The agent reported the conversation to Astor's son William, who gave him the equivalent of the unfortunate woman's rent so that the realtor could go back to Astor and claim the bill had been paid. The millionaire grumped with satisfaction: "There, I told you she would pay it, if you went the right way to work with her." John Jacob Astor died a few days later on March 29, 1848, presumably a satisfied man.

TO CONSOLIDATE THEIR HOLD on the strategically important mouth of the Columbia, the Nor'Westers had decided at the 1812 Fort William meeting to dispatch a sea party as a supplement to the overland expedition under John George McTavish. This contingent, commanded by Donald McTavish (Simon's first cousin) and John McDonald of Garth, boarded the 350-ton *Isaac Todd*, an armed merchantman built at Trois-Rivières, Quebec. They sailed to England with a load of pelts—and a crew of voyageurs to man the NWC's future trading canoes on the Columbia. The furs took many weeks to sell, and it wasn't until March 1813 that the *Isaac Todd* was ready to sail away in convoy with the Royal Navy's thirty-six-gun frigate *Phoebe*. McTavish and McDonald were dining at the main hotel in Portsmouth on the eve of departure, when word came that most of their voyageurs, who were celebrating their departure with a drinking spree, had been shanghaied by a Royal Navy press-gang and were already aboard a training ship. McTavish freed them by interceding with the port admiral, who happened to be a relative of the NWC agent's brother-in-law, Lord Grey, then leader of the Whigs.*

Armed with twenty guns, the *Isaac Todd* took an unprecedented thirteen months to reach Astoria. "It might have been better if she had only six guns well managed," McDonald of Garth noted in his journal. "We had on board cannon balls enough for a line-of-battle ship. She proved to be a miserable sailer, with a miserable commander, a rascally crew and three mates." The *Phoebe* was diverted to fight the American frigate *Essex*, which she captured off Valparaiso harbour, and the *Isaac Todd* finally slipped alone into Astoria on April 23, 1814.

That same season, the battered little ship took on a load of furs and sailed another eight thousand miles to Canton, as did the NWC's 185-ton *Columbia*, which arrived at Astoria three months after the *Isaac Todd*. Trade through Canton, operating under the East India Company's

---

*One extra passenger did sneak aboard the *Isaac Todd* that night—a spunky Portsmouth barmaid named Jane Barnes, who signed on, according to her personal claim, to do whatever needlework might be required on the voyage. Described as being "coarse" and "illiterate," the first white woman on the Columbia did not have an easy time of it. McTavish himself took up with her, but then found an alternate entanglement with a Chinook woman. The other traders could only laugh at Barnes's social pretensions and resented her insulting attitude towards native women. On the way back to England via Canton she found a husband in the ship's commander and returned to Astoria briefly in 1819. According to Alexander McKenzie, a clerk serving there at the time, she had not improved with age. "I should offend your modesty," he wrote to a friend, "were I to mention specimens of what she intended as wit and humour during her stay with us."

monopoly, was complicated by byzantine customs regulations.* A special edict allowed the Nor'Westers to sell their furs for cash instead of merely bartering them for Oriental products like most other importers, but it proved to be not a particularly profitable venture. "The expense attending the sending of our own vessels to China is too heavy," complained William McGillivray in April 1816. "The Partners of the North West Company do not understand the management of ships or captains. Collecting and trading skins is their real business."

That business was under intense pressure from the Hudson's Bay Company in the Northwest and from American freebooters in the Southwest. The American case rested mainly on that costly display of pretension by Captain Black of HMS *Racoon*. The protocol-encrusted naval officer's formal takeover of the tiny fort on behalf of his monarch lent authority to the case that Astoria had not been sold but captured as an act of war and, according to the terms of the Treaty of Ghent, all territories seized by force had to be returned. The British, who regarded the western coast of North America with an attitude that could not even be dignified as benign neglect, surrendered their claim. But the Nor'Westers dug in. Their take of furs from the district had doubled, they had financed the establishment of a chain of inland posts and felt very much at home in the lush Pacific land, free from the burden of having to struggle against the fierce climate of their northern territories.

Late in 1817, the *Ontario*, an American naval sloop, sailed into the mouth of the Columbia carrying a government commissioner named James B. Prevost to retake formal possession of the fort. When James Keith, then the NWC's resident chief, flatly rejected the appeal, Prevost tacked his proclamation on a board nailed to a tree and left. Shortly afterward, the *Blossom*, a British man-of-war, arrived with orders from

---

*According to Hilary Russell, who studied the trade and especially the involvement of Angus Bethune, who was the NWC's representative aboard the *Isaac Todd*, on "all foreign vessels trading in China, the cargo was ferried twelve miles to Canton in chop boats. Before the hatches of a foreign vessel could be opened, the superintendent of customs or his representative calculated the tonnage duties due. This was done by multiplying the length of the ship by the breadth amidships (in a Chinese unit equal to 14.1 inches) and dividing the product by 10. This figure was paid in taels, one of which equalled about 1.4 dollars. In addition, a standard charge of 1950 taels was exacted for 'cumsha'—presents—which were distributed to the Emperor, his officials and soldiers, and the 'poor.' These sums were paid through a Chinese security merchant, who was authorized to trade with foreigners and who was responsible for the conduct of the ship. The supercargo was obliged to transact all business through the security merchant and linguist. The latter was licensed and appointed by the superintendent of customs, as were the 'tidewaiters' who watched the ship to prevent smuggling."

the Colonial Office that the post should be handed over. That too carried little weight with Keith. The Stars and Stripes was hoisted over the post, but the American and British governments eventually signed a convention that allowed the Oregon Country to be used jointly by citizens of both jurisdictions, and this arrangement lasted until 1846.

But at headquarters these Pacific pursuits were relatively minor in the North West Company's lexicon of priorities. It was suddenly being threatened by a revived Hudson's Bay Company, whose factors were challenging the Montrealers at every river bend.

Liquor in the fur trade

CHAPTER 5

Howling with the Wolves

"When you are among wolves, howl."

—Colin Robertson
NWC/HBC Trader

IN THE CHARGED ATMOSPHERE OF MULTIPLYING confrontations, the two companies fought one another with hardening determination and, once the Bay men had moved fully inland, with the bravado reminiscent of a civil war. The chief victims of that wilderness imbroglio were not the men who traded the furs but the Indians who supplied them.

Canadians have traditionally prided themselves on the fact that after the turn of the nineteenth century there were relatively few armed confrontations between white and red men—certainly nothing on the scale of the Indian wars fought by the U.S. Cavalry. But this difference does not justify the smug assumption that white men north of the 49th parallel treated the native population with compassion and respect. On the contrary, the unrestrained use of liquor in the Canadian fur trade ranks as one of history's more malevolent crimes against humanity.

The Nor'Westers and the Bay men were equally guilty of encouraging and benefiting from that debauching commerce—though the London Company did not initiate the practice and gradually put an end to it once the two firms were amalgamated. In *The Owners of Eden*, Robert MacDonald, an Alberta historian highly sympathetic to the Indian cause, has noted that "'The Honourable Company' . . . opposed the liquor trade, until the time when they felt the competition had made its sale a matter of economic survival." The late Frank B. Walker, former editor-in-chief of the *Montreal Star* and before that an executive with the HBC's head office in Winnipeg, once made the argument that it was impossible for isolated Company post managers to persuade Indians to bring in their furs except by treating them with justice. "That applied particularly to the liquor trade," he claimed. "It wasn't profitable to have drunken Indians. They weren't good trappers and they could be highly dangerous. Canada was not at all like the American experience, with a big fort and cavalry standing by. Usually, it was one Bay factor and his nineteen-year-old clerk, surrounded by four or five hundred Indians at trading time. There was no way the HBC wanted them drunk. You can't stare down four hundred drunken Indians."

Unfortunately, that kind of retrospective reasoning had little impact on what happened in the Canadian Northwest during the early 1800s.

Liquor became the currency of the fur trade. The initial utility of rum and brandy was based mainly on the fact that it was the most cost-effective item to carry inland, much less bulky in its concentrated form than such standard goods as blankets, axes, guns and bolts of cloth. Also, once addicted, the Indians could not get enough of the white man's deadly nectar and lost their ability or willingness to bargain patiently and shrewdly for their booty of furs. It was not long before the buyers of both companies realized that the way to manipulate their trading standards most profitably was by diluting the liquor rations with water. The Nor'Westers, who purchased their liquor supplies in Montreal from Caribbean exporters, would mix a nine-gallon keg of powerfully concentrated (132-proof) rum with anywhere from thirty to seventy gallons of water. This so-called High Wine was diluted according to whatever minimum the traffic would bear. In Cree or Assiniboine country, three to four parts water was the going formula; for the Blackfoot, the brew was reduced to seven or eight parts water, giving birth to a frontier cooler known as "Blackfoot Rum." The Indians, incidentally, quickly caught on to the white man's cheating ways. They would test the strength of any vintage by spitting a mouthful on a fire: good liquor would flame up dramatically, but if it were too weak, the potion would quench the flames. And that was how the term "firewater" originated.

As much as fifty thousand gallons of liquor was imported into the Fur Country each season. When mixed with water that probably amounted to at least a quarter of a million gallons—an appalling total, considering that the interior at the time had a native population of about one hundred and twenty thousand, including women and children. More than a third of the NWC freight stowed in the canoes heading west consisted of ninety-pound kegs of rum. As well as being a straight-out swap for pelts, alcohol served as an integral part of the gift-giving

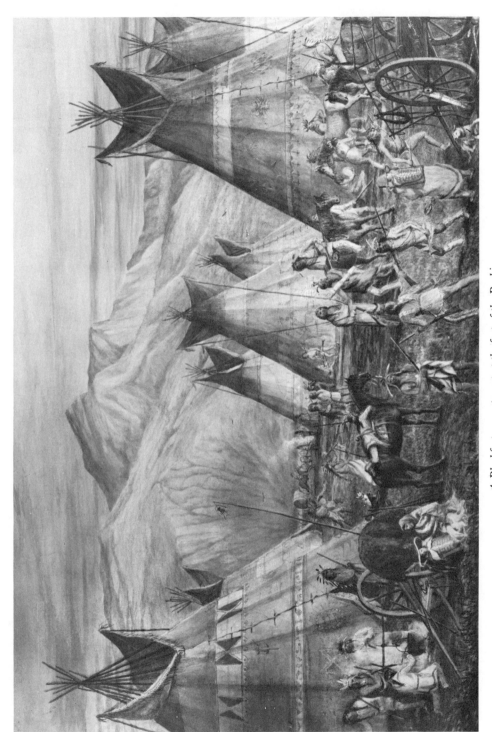

A Blackfoot encampment at the foot of the Rockies

ceremony that preceded the actual trading process. While the possession of adequate stocks of rum and/or brandy (and tobacco) became
essential, the traffic in such staples as guns, axes and blankets continued to
predominate at most posts.

In 1786, the HBC's William Tomison had become so upset at the
Montrealers' indiscriminate abuse of rum that he led a group of his
colleagues in dispatching an official letter to the resident British
Commander-in-Chief for Canada. "Good Sir," read the petition, "it
grieves us to see a body of Indians destroyed by a set of Men, merely
for self Interest, doing all in their Power to Destroy Posterity, so we
hope that your Excellency will make such regulations as will preserve
Posterity, and not be Destroyed by fiery double Distilled Rum from
Canada." After a journey up the Saskatchewan the following year,
Tomison complained to London that "the Canadians is [sic] going
through the Barren Ground with Rum, like so many ravenous Wolves,
seeking whom they may devour."

Yet less than half a decade later, the Bay men were openly trafficking
in a potent concoction called English Brandy, trading booze for furs
with as much aplomb as the Nor'Westers they had so recently condemned. The formula for making English Brandy was nothing if not
simple: raw gin plus a few drops of iodine to simulate the ochre shade
of the Nor'Westers rum.* Nor was any attempt made to hide the
shameful commerce. When there was a ban in England on the domestic
distillation of grain during the Napoleonic Wars, the London Committee
dispatched stills to be erected at York Factory, Albany and Moose. By
1820 even a small HBC post like Fort Waterloo on Lesser Slave Lake was
distributing its quota of 369 gallons per season; that meant dragging
nearly two tons' worth of the concentrated grog across portages and
rivers 1,350 miles from the nearest supply point. The HBC gained such a
black reputation for its liquor trade that many years afterward, during
a parliamentary debate, Lord Palmerston, the British Prime Minister,
crudely interjected that "the Company's function should be to strip the
local quadrupeds of their furs—and keep the local bipeds off their
liquor." The most devastating summary of the HBC's attitude, which
accurately reflected the prevailing frontier ethic of the time, was Douglas

---

*When iodine supplies ran low, a squirt or two of chewing tobacco provided the appropriate
hue. A slightly more sophisticated blend was featured by the American Fur Company,
which added to the base of water and raw alcohol doses of a medicinal painkiller
(tincture of opium), overfermented wine, pepper and sulphuric acid. These and similar
recipes raise the valid question whether the Indians who drank such rotgut got drunk or
became sickened by the bizarre mixtures.

The trade in liquor debauched families and decimated Indian culture.

MacKay's comment in *The Honourable Company*, a lively Company history by an HBC official. "Drunken Indians," observed MacKay, "were among the casual inconveniences of fur trading."

Even if their field tactics varied little, the approaches of the two companies were subtly different. The Nor'Westers seemed convinced that drunken Indians were jolly hunters, as reflected in this typical entry from Duncan McGillivray's journal. "The love of Rum," he enthused, "is their first inducement to industry, they undergo every hardship and fatigue to procure a Skinfull of this delicious beverage, and when a Nation becomes addicted to drinking, it affords a strong presumption that they will soon become excellent hunters." The HBC factors believed the opposite: that the only good trapper was a sober trapper. But no matter what they thought or said, both concerns continued ladling out the booze. The daily tot was habit-forming, and once under the influence most Indians would trade only if firewater was included in the transaction.

The effect on their minds and bodies, on their families and culture, was ruinous. Firsthand reports from the Northwest described scenes so distressing that hardened fur traders could barely find words to express what they had seen. When he returned from the Blackfoot Country, Duncan McGillivray confided to his journal what he had witnessed: "Men, women, and children promiscuously mingle together and join in one diabolical clamour of singing, crying, fighting, &c and to such excess do they indulge their love of drinking that all regard for decency or decorum is forgotten:—they expose themselves in the most indecent positions, leaving uncovered those parts which nature requires to be concealed—a circumstance which they carefully avoid in their sober moments, and the intercourse between the sexes, at any time but little restrained, is now indulged with the greatest freedom, for as chastity is not deemed a virtue among most of the tribes, they take very little pains to conceal their amours, especially when heated with liquor." At about the same time, Daniel Harmon, the puritanical New England fur trader, recorded in his diary this sad scene from a trip into the northern reaches occupied by Chipewyans: "To see a house full of drunken Indians, consisting of men, women and children, is a most unpleasant sight; for, in that condition, they often wrangle, pull each other by the hair, and fight. At some times, ten or twelve, of both sexes, may be seen, fighting each other promiscuously, until at last, they all fall on the floor, one upon another, some spilling rum out of a small kettle or dish, which they hold in their hands, while others are throwing up what they have just drunk. To add to this uproar . . . a number of children, some on their mothers' shoulders, and others running about and taking hold of their clothes, are constantly bawling, the older ones, through fear that their parents may be stabbed, or that some other misfortune may befall them, in the fray. These shrieks of the children, form a very unpleasant chorus to the brutal noise kept up by their drunken parents, who are engaged in the squabble."

Another report described in explicit detail some of the worst abuses that resulted from too much drinking: "Every one knows the passion of the savages for this liquor, and the fatal effects that it produces on them. . . . The village or the cabin in which the savages drink brandy is an image of hell: fire [i.e., burning brands or coals flung by the drunkards] flies in all directions; blows with hatchets and knives make the blood flow on all sides; and all the place resounds with frightful yells and cries. . . . They commit a thousand abominations—the mother with her sons, the father with his daughters, and brothers with their sisters. They roll about on the cinders and coals, and in blood."

Diamond Jenness, the New Zealander who became recognized as Canada's most knowledgeable anthropologist through his studies of native cultures, flatly declared in his definitive work, *The Indians of Canada*, that "whisky and brandy destroyed the self-respect of the Indians, weakened every family and tribal tie, and made them, willing or unwilling, the slaves of the trading-posts where liquor was dispensed to them by the keg. . . . Disease and alcohol demoralized and destroyed the Indians just when they needed all their energy and courage to cope with the new conditions that suddenly came into existence around them. The old order changed completely with the coming of Europeans."

There were innumerable testimonies to the havoc caused by liquor, but one of the most brutal was reported by Alexander Henry the Younger. "We may truly say that liquor is the root of all evil in the North West," he wrote, and went on to detail a horrifying example of its effects: "The Indians continued drinking. About ten o'clock I was informed that old Crooked Legs had killed his young wife.... By sunrise every soul of them was raving drunk—even the children.... In the first drinking match a murder was committed. L'Hiver stabbed Mishenwashence to the heart three times ... Grande Gueule stabbed Capot Rouge, Le Boeuf stabbed his young wife in the arm ... Old Buffalo, still half drunk, brought me his eldest daughter, about nine years of age, in hopes I would give him a keg of liquor...." On another occasion Henry described what happened to an elderly Indian who, suspecting his young wife of infidelity, got blind drunk and stabbed her three times. When the woman had recovered, she plotted with her family to get even. After a drinking match, her relatives held her husband down while she "applied a fire brand to his privates, and rubbed it in. She left him in a shocking condition, with the parts nearly roasted."

How progressively hardened the frontiersmen became to the agony they had caused is dramatically revealed in this afterthought from Henry's journal: "Little Shell almost beat his old mother's brains out with a club. I sowed garden seeds."

Such inhumanity amounted to the anaesthetizing of the First Nations and helped promote the then-prevalent stereotype of Indian as "abject supplicant or outrageous maniac." Blair Stonechild, the head of the Department of Indian Studies at Saskatchewan Indian Federated College in Regina, has argued persuasively: "On the subject of alcohol abuse, Indians have not been dealt with fairly. Everyone is familiar with the stereotype of the 'drunken Indian,' and the Indian inability to deal with liquor. In Central America, where Indians had developed alcoholic beverages, a very firm approach was taken. Under the laws of Nezahualcoyotl, any official of high rank found intoxicated was immediately executed. Commoners were dealt with more leniently. The first time, the person's head was shaved in public and his house was knocked down. The second time, he was publicly executed. Surely these laws were more effective than today's approach of sending drunkards to halfway houses."*

---

*That notion, in highly modified form, has appeared in modern Canada; at Norway House, for example, the Indians are so concerned that no liquor be drunk in their "dry" community that they once had a constable of the local Royal Canadian Mounted Police detachment arrested for keeping "hooch" for his own consumption.

Historian Robert MacDonald made a telling point about why the natives took to liquor with so much abandon: "The Indian had never before tasted alcohol. He had no customs of social or convivial drinking. But he did have beliefs and rituals which required hallucinogenic experiences such as visions. Here, suddenly, was a surprising and powerful intoxicant. The trader encouraged him to use it to excess—the missionary exhorted him not to use it at all; *never* was it represented to him as something to be used *in moderation*." That was true, but most of the fur traders misinterpreted the Indian's reaction to the rum and brandy, concluding he was in some genetic or chemical way inferior. Typical of this view was the comment of historian Robert Pinkerton, who viewed Indians as childish savages devoid of morals. "It is commonly understood that liquor has an entirely different effect on an Indian than on a white man but few comprehend the degree of that difference," he pontificated. "The jovial exhilaration we know and enjoy is forbidden to the Red man. Mayhem becomes the mildest of his desires."

Some modern anthropologists have rejected the notion that alcoholism among Indians stems from their physical and nervous systems being somehow void of immunity to liquor. Bruce Cox, a Carleton University anthropologist who specializes in the field, concluded that "Indians develop alcoholism at about the same rate as the rest of us, and (on average) drink no more than the general population. Indians *may* metabolize alcohol a little differently to the general population, but differences are not large and in any case this is a trait they share with other groups who are not known as alcohol abusers." ·A more complicated explanation is the theory set out in *Drunken Comportment* by two California anthropologists, Craig MacAndrew and Robert Edgerton. "Across a continent, the Indian observed the dramatic transformation that alcohol seemed to produce in the white man," they noted, ". . . and, reaching into his repertoire of available explanations, concluded that 'Brandy was the embodiment, or was the medium through which an evil supernatural agent worked.' Thus it was that the Indian came to see that changes-for-the-worse were to be expected during drunkenness, for at such times the drinker was temporarily inhabited by an evil supernatural agent. And from this, the Indian reached the entirely reasonable conclusion that since he was thus possessed, his actions when drunk were not his own and he was not responsible for them. After all, the Indians' precontact cultures already contained an ample array of *time out* ceremonies and supernatural agents (such as witchcraft, dreams, spirit possession, and so forth) under whose influence a man became less than strictly responsible for his actions. The notion that the state of drunkenness was excusing of those transgressions committed while 'under the influence' was entirely consonant with the model the white man provided."

Not all social scientists agree. Writing in a recent issue of the University of Saskatchewan's *Native Studies Review*, Lillian E. Dyck has made a strong case that the pattern of alcohol-metabolizing enzymes differs in Orientals and Caucasians, making the Japanese much more susceptible to the unpleasant effects of alcohol. "If it does turn out that some Indian peoples have a genetic aversion to becoming alcoholic, as does a large percentage of the Japanese race," she concludes, "and if the rates of alcoholism are higher amongst such Indians than in the Caucasian population, then one could speculate that these Indians are over-exposed to other factors which lead to alcoholism. Though a particular group of Indians may be resistant to developing alcoholism, perhaps they can still become alcoholic because of the presence of unusually high levels of environmental stress." Dyck also added the important proviso that "in White urban areas, Indians look different, are a minority and, therefore, are noticed and remembered. A Caucasian drunk who behaves in the same way will not be noticed to the same extent because he is not expected to behave in this manner and because he is considered to be the exception rather than the rule. Consequently, we do not mentally tally up the number of Caucasian drunks we see, but we do note and remember the drunken Indians we encounter."

The problem with this sensible thesis is the difficulty of substantiating the white man's drinking behaviour from historical records. While there is no shortage of descriptions of drunken Indians, there are few memoirs about equally crazed whites. It was only the occasional visiting outsider who commented on drinking orgies such as those that regularly took place at the meetings of Montreal's Beaver Club, for example.

One exception is the description by Daniel Harmon of a New Year's Day drinking spree in New Caledonia: "Some of the principal Indians of the place desired us to allow them to remain at the fort to see our people drink, but as soon as they (our people) began to be intoxicated and quarrel among themselves, the Natives were apprehensive that something unpleasant might befall them also, therefore they hid themselves under beds and elsewhere and said they thought the white people had become mad. [Later] I invited several of the Sicaany and Carrier Chiefs and most respectable men among them, to come and partake of what we had remaining—and I must acknowledge that I was surprised to see them behave with so much decency and even propriety as they did in drinking off a flaggon or two of rum and after their repast was over they smoked their pipes and conversed rationally on the great difference there is between the manners and customs of civilized people and those of savages."

Nearly every departure or arrival of brigades of traders and voyageurs at any terminus was enough to set off a drinking spree. A typical scene, involving the white inhabitants of the Fur Country, was caught in the journals of Alexander Ross, who visited Michilimackinac, the staging depot at the juncture of Lakes Huron and Michigan, in the early 1800s: "To see drunkenness and debauchery with all their concomitant vices, carried on systematically, it is necessary to see Mackinac . . . for in the morning they were found drinking, at noon drunk, in the evening dead drunk, and in the night seldom sober. Hogarth's drunkards in Gin Lane and Beer Alley were nothing compared to the drunkards of Mackinac at this time. Every nook and corner in the whole island swarmed, at all hours of the day and night, with motley groups of uproarious tipplers and whiskey hunters. Mackinac at this time resembled a great bedlam, the frantic inmates running to and fro in wild forgetfulness. . . ."

The alcohol problem on the frontier was bigger than either the NWC or the HBC—much more complicated and serious than its effect on the fur trade alone. The North West Mounted Police was established by the dominion government partly to counter the influence of American traders who came into southern Alberta to trade whisky with Blackfoot Indians for buffalo hides. Johnny Healy, the notorious Dubliner who went west with the U.S. Army and later founded the infamous Fort Whoop-up, the worst of the Canadian West's rotgut emporiums, once boasted to Isaac Gilbert Baker, a Montana liquor supplier, "I'll fix up 'coffin varnish' so strong, you'll be able to shoot an Injun through the heart, and he won't die till he's sobered up."

The Indian response to this decadence was not always passive. In the Athabasca Country, some Chipewyans quit the fur trade, retreating (as did many other bands across the Northwest) to their more tranquil, traditional tribal ways. But others, feeling they had been betrayed by the white man and his wicked brew, fought back.

In the summer of 1804, six Nor'Westers were killed during an Indian attack on Fond du Lac, a small fort near the eastern tip of Lake Athabasca, and four others were ambushed while hunting near Fort Chipewyan. Armed hostility on the prairies had begun as early as 1780 in the Eagle Hills of present-day Saskatchewan when an irresponsible Montrealer put an extra dose of opium into some trading rum. In the ensuing rumble there were serious casualties on both sides.

But the most vicious outbreak of violence was only partly due to liquor. As the fur trade moved west, guns became the decisive instruments for settling intertribal wars, and as a result, whichever fur company sold arms to any particular tribe's opponents would automatically be included among its enemies. During the 1790s the Gros Ventres, or Big Bellies (so named because of the sign language they used: the gesture for the tribe was a hand covering the solar plexus), had been defeated in several bloody encounters with the fur-rich—and therefore well-armed— Cree. The Gros Ventres had little to trade but wolf skins, which had tumbled in value on the London markets, prompting the companies to cut their standard price for the pelts in half. The Indians interpreted this as a hostile act and in 1793 raided the HBC's Manchester House on the North Saskatchewan, escaping with its store of rifles. The following summer, they rode out, a hundred strong, along the South Saskatchewan, eager for combat. While getting ready to attack an NWC installation on the river, they were spotted by a scout named Jacques Raphael, who, in the approved scenario of American Westerns, rode hell for leather to warn the post, was chased by menacing Indians and just made it inside the closing wooden gate. The ten-man garrison rushed to the barricades and maintained enough of a barrage to discourage a successful frontal attack. The Indians retreated when their war chief, L'Homme de Calumet, was killed. They then turned to a nearby HBC post. It was little more than a clutch of huts with no protection. Three of the resident traders were slaughtered where they stood. The fourth, John Cornelius Van Driel, hid under a rubbish heap and watched in horror as the tiny outpost's inhabitants were unceremoniously butchered. Having completed their carnage and appropriated what little booty there was, the Indians set the buildings ablaze. Forced from his hiding place, Van Driel waited until the conflagration was at its fiercest; then, using the smoke as a screen, he made a dash for the river, jumped into a canoe—and eventually reached safety with his grisly report.

THAT BLOODY ENCOUNTER was not typical of the fur trade, but during the decades straddling the turn of the century, the rivalry between the two main trading companies produced its own escalating violence. By 1806 the HBC's servants had opened five dozen inland stations, half of them within twenty miles of the already existing trading posts of their Montreal rivals.*

During the early stages of the struggle between the two companies, both had a common motivating force: to ship the maximum number of pelts to the London fur auctions. Other than that, the two coalitions of traders were so different it was hard to believe they were in the same business. The Hudson's Bay Company continued to rely on functionaries hired more because of their ability to cope with subsistence wages than for any excesses of imagination or courage. Their every move was directed by an overseas court whose members were so indifferent towards the territories they were administering that no HBC Governor visited Hudson Bay for an unconscionable 264 years after the Company's original incorporation in 1670. (Sir Patrick Ashley Cooper, the twenty-ninth man to hold the office, finally managed a fast-paced ceremonial tour in 1934.) In contrast, the senior Nor'Westers were in business for themselves. They dealt with the monopoly proclaimed in the HBC's vaunted charter by the simple stratagem of ignoring it, taking the not unreasonable position that the forests they had explored should be a hunting ground for *all* British subjects, Canada having been formally ceded to England by France in 1763. Since legal sanctions within the Fur Country were uncertain, the Nor'Westers—and eventually the Bay men as well—increasingly resorted to physical intimidation to achieve their aims.

The geographical odds in that wilderness decathlon decidedly favoured the HBC. The location of its posts in the centre of the continent meant the Bay men could get their furs to England in six to eight

---

*In typical bureaucratic fashion the Hudson's Bay Company installations were carefully graded by their functions, as:

Portage Posts – trans-shipment stations where natural obstacles blocked travel.

Wintering Posts – the basic trading units, located near Indian hunting grounds, manned only during the winter months. Frequently shifted, they were small and impermanent.

District Posts – local headquarters, each manned by a Chief Factor or Chief Trader, open the year round and in relatively fixed locations.

Provision Posts – mainly depots to produce or trade pemmican as sustenance for the canoe brigades.

Provision Depots – located at strategic points along the supply lines, most notably Bas-de-la-Rivière and Cumberland House, to store pemmican.

Main Depots – the major stations to which trade goods were sent for distribution to interior districts, and through which furs were shipped out of the Indian Country.

weeks, compared to the four months it took the Nor'Westers to lug the pelts from Athabasca to Montreal, and then another four weeks to London. With the variables of climate taken into account, the HBC could gather its furs and sell them within the same annual cycle, while the Montrealers faced a minimum two-year turnaround. This was a crucial difference.

Apart from that admittedly overwhelming advantage of location, most of the other natural benefits accrued to the Montrealers. The valleys of the St Lawrence basin were covered with forests that contained plenty of the splendid birch trees whose bark was essential for canoe building, but birch grows only around the most southern reaches of Hudson Bay. The parishes of Quebec provided a surplus of voyageurs jostling to enlist their skill and muscle in the fur trade, but the only white labourers at the bay were the dour Orkneymen who worked as "servants" to the factors in charge of the HBC posts. At ease navigating in the tempests that buffeted their home islands, they could not or would not handle a canoe or shoot a rapid. This left the Company with two choices—either to employ local Indian crews or try training the recalcitrant Orkneymen as canoeists. Neither option worked. The Indians had little intention of voluntarily surrendering their profitable middleman function by paddling the traders inland—and for the same reason refused to help the whites build canoes, even when the HBC moved far enough west to claim its own birch trees. (At the same time, the Company was not particularly keen to tie up too many Indians as paddlers or boatbuilders because that kept them away from their pursuit of beaver pelts.) The Orkneymen, most of whom were in the Fur Country on three-year hitches, demonstrated little initial inclination to become voyageurs; some eventually did learn to handle canoes, mainly because after 1793 the Company agreed to an incentive pay scheme pegged to the number of miles logged on trips inland.

The problem by then was how to attract *enough* new manpower into the HBC's service. During the half-century after the NWC's formation, England was at war for half the time, and throughout those harsh days, press-gangs roamed Britain's streets and docks, draining the labour market of healthy young men, and forcing the Company to hire dotards, cripples, dwarfs and teenage boys as temporary help.

Apart from these difficulties, the HBC's stumbling progress inland had become seriously disrupted by internal dissension among various Chief Factors, overeager to curry favour with their employers by producing larger catches at their posts than those of their neighbours on the bay. The major initial organizational shift recognizing the growing importance of the hinterland commerce was the appointment in 1786 of William Tomison, an energetic if temperamental Orkneyman, as the Company's first Chief Inland. This made him senior to Joseph Colen, a sophisticated and articulate Englishman then in charge at York Factory. The two men clashed not only about the parochial concerns of the imposing depot on the bay,* but about Tomison's obsession with organizing competition against the Montrealers along the Saskatchewan while ignoring the fur-rich ponds of the Athabasca. At the same time, the smaller brigades sent out by the HBC factories at Churchill, Moose and Albany were competing with one another for a thinning harvest of beaver. Overtrapping had dangerously depleted the animals, but when Colen suggested that the underpopulated areas be left temporarily idle to allow the rodents to propagate, he was roundly ridiculed.† The London Committee finally resolved the internecine warfare in 1799 by establishing clearly delineated routes inland and specific boundaries of jurisdiction for each of the bay forts. In the process, York Factory, once the Company's great tidewater trading centre, took on an important new role as an emporium, warehouse and distribution centre. By 1810, the post's business had become so routine that after the shipping season, its Chief Factor, William Hemmings Cook, could disappear into the bush to go hunting for three months, leaving his steward in charge.

The HBC as a whole was never that leisured; indeed, it was woefully undermanned and undersupplied. The Company's first hesitant probe westward, the setting up of Cumberland House at Pine Island Lake in 1774, was typical of the scale of its operations. The eight men assigned to the venture huddled in a low log bunker, thirty-eight by twenty-six feet, with moss as caulking and a leaky plank roof, while the nearby Montrealers, who had arrived half a decade before, were solidly entrenched, more than a hundred strong, in a fort worthy of the term. As late as 1811, when the Company became determined to move inland with a vengeance, it had 320 men in the field facing 1,200 Nor'Westers. A considerable portion of the HBC's trade goods was inferior: tobacco that wouldn't light despite attempts to improve it with

---

*For a history of York Factory, see *Company of Adventurers*, pages xvi-xxiii.

† Tim Ball, a professor of geography at the University of Winnipeg and a leading expert on northern Canadian climate, has argued that "Colen was right, but for the wrong reasons. A major cause of the lower beaver yields was the dramatic change in climate going on during these decades. The similar conditions that George Washington faced in his winter battles are described in his comments such as 'Indeed this winter has been so far the most remarkable for scarcity of provisions for neither Englishman or Indians can find anything to kill.'"

small doses of molasses, and guns that exploded in hunters' hands. William Auld, the Edinburgh surgeon who was in charge of Churchill and spent the winter of 1808–9 at Reindeer Lake, complained that the HBC post there was "the most miserable hovel that imagination can conceive. Surely such abominably disgraceful styes must affect the Natives. Dirty as they are, they must make shocking comparisons to our disadvantage. Such temporary shelter, infinitely below what an Ourang-Outang would have contented himself with, can only bespeak the glimmering dying lights of an expiring Commerce, not the residence of Britons, not the Settlements of the Adventurers of England."

At first, competition between the two camps was friendly enough that traders would get together for joint celebrations of St Andrew's Day, Christmas and Hogmanay, deliver each other's mail and, in some cases (as at Fort Vermilion and later Terre Blanche on the Saskatchewan), build rival posts within a common palisade. At Fort George on the Fraser, Angus Shaw invited the HBC's William Tomison to a typical homecoming ball, which *must* have been friendly, since seventy-two men, thirty-seven women and sixty-five children were entertained in his NWC trading hut that measured twenty-two by twenty-three feet. On May 7, 1805, Daniel Harmon of the NWC described a lively celebration he attended at Fort Alexandria: "When three-fourths of the people had drunk so much as to be incapable of walking straight the other fourth thought it was time to put an end to the ball, or rather bawl. This morning we were invited to breakfast at the Hudson's Bay House . . . and in the evening to a dance. This, however, ended more decently than the one of the preceding evening."

Such camaraderie was due partly to the natural brotherhood generated by the traders' being isolated together, but in their amicable overtures the Bay men, at least, were also obeying orders. In its annual message issued to Bay posts in 1806, the London Committee instructed its men "to avoid any discussion or disagreement with those people" and to "maintain the utmost peace and harmony with your opponents." The Company's directives went even further, absolving employees from trying to outdo the rambunctious Nor'Westers. "The great and first objective of our concerns," the lords of the HBC decreed, "is an increasing trade to counterbalance the very enormous and increasing Expences of it. We do not expect returns equal to those of our more powerful Opponents but we ought to receive such returns as are adequate to the quantity of goods you are annually supplied with."

That sensible-shoes policy may have impressed them on Fenchurch Street, but out in the trenches it did little but grant the North West Company licence to plunder. The Montrealers organized blockades to keep the Indians away from the HBC posts and, having few fixed standards of trade, often won their business, even when (or sometimes *because*) they already had credit outstanding with the HBC. In 1800 at a post near Nipigon, an NWC clerk named Frederick Schultz murdered one of his assistants for defecting to the HBC. Imperceptibly, the mood was changing. In the autumn of 1806, John Haldane broke into the English company's warehouse at Bad Lake, overpowered its manager, William Corrigal, and stole 480 beaver skins.

Three years later, Corrigal was in charge of the HBC post at Eagle Lake, east of Lake of the Woods, when a party of rowdy Nor'Westers, led by Aeneas Macdonell, pitched camp only forty yards away. On the gloomy evening of September 15, an Indian arrived to trade and settle his debts. Not being able to pay in full, he offered to leave his canoe—provided that he could borrow it back long enough to paddle his trade goods home. Next morning, the Indian was packing up his clothing and ammunition when he was accosted by the NWC's Macdonell, armed with a cutlass and a brace of pistols, claiming that since the Indian was still indebted to the NWC, his canoe and merchandise were being impounded on the spot. The HBC commander, watching the shouting match, sent two of his assistants—James Tate and John Corrigal—to prevent the confiscation. They ran down the hill to the shore and tried to calm the situation. Macdonell let out a whoop, drew his sword and lunged at Tate, aiming to cut his head open. The unarmed Bay man shielded himself with his hands and had his left wrist deeply slashed and part of his throat cut. Macdonell then took off after John Corrigal, who dived into the river. The Nor'Wester waded in after him and, following a brief tussle, drove home a sword thrust that laid Corrigal's arm above the elbow open to the bone. Macdonell took another broadsword swipe at the Bay man's head, aiming with such ferocity that a heavy canoe paddle used to ward off the blow was cut in two. The fight then moved towards the post, where several Bay men, including a labourer named John Mowat, were just arriving from a round of fishing. They dispersed at the sight of the blood-mad Macdonell charging up the hill after them—all except Mowat, who was lame and couldn't move fast enough. The Nor'Wester's first sword lunge came close enough to slash Mowat's waistcoat at his chest. Macdonell was winding up for a final killing blow when Mowat fired a pistol into his heart. The Nor'Wester staggered backward, stumbled down the incline, stuck his sword defiantly into the ground, and died.

"Then all our people came into the house, and us that was wounded got our wounds examined and tied up," James Tate calmly noted in his journal. "My handkerchief and the pad that was in the inside of it and the collar of my shirt was all cut through by the stroke that I got on my neck. Our floor was all over of blood from John Corrigal and me in such a manner that two of our people was nigh fainting at the sight. When the bustle was all over and everything quiet the Indian made his escape through the wood and we saw no more of him."

Mowat gave himself up when the surviving Montrealers surrounded the HBC post, angrily threatening to incite local Indians to slaughter them, even if it cost them a keg of rum for each HBC scalp. He was taken in irons to Rainy Lake for the winter and later to Fort William, where he languished in a windowless six-foot-square cell. Then he was moved to Montreal for trial before some obliging judges, relations of local NWC partners, who found the protesting Mowat guilty of manslaughter. Sentenced to six months in prison (and branded on the hand with a hot iron as a felon), he was offered a pardon but refused on the sensible grounds that he should never have been condemned for a clear act of self-defence in the first place.*

AN IMPORTANT NEW ELEMENT in the changing scene was the arrival, in the spring of 1806, of the first white woman to settle permanently in the West—Marie-Anne Gaboury of Maskinongé near Trois-Rivières, Quebec, who had married a free-trader named Jean-Baptiste Lagemodière. She had her first baby, Reine, at the HBC post at Pembina on January 6, 1807, but the occasion of her second delivery nineteen months later was more dramatic. "She was riding her horse, a spirited buffalo runner," wrote Sylvia Van Kirk in *"Many Tender Ties,"* "with young Reine tucked snugly in one of the saddle bags when she suddenly came upon a herd of buffalo. The horse immediately gave chase and the young mother could only cling desperately to the horse's neck until she was finally rescued by her husband. Later that night, Marie-Anne gave birth to a son, nicknamed La Prairie; within three days she was on her horse again riding back to Fort Edmonton. Marie-Anne† and her children were objects of much interest to the Indians; in fact one Blackfoot woman so coveted her little son that she reputedly tried to kidnap him."

---

*The unfortunate Mowat served his sentence and, disillusioned, decided to return home. He was drowned while crossing a river during freeze-up on his way to board a New York packet bound for England.

† Through her daughter Julie, Marie-Anne became Louis Riel's grandmother.

It was typical of the HBC's somnambulism that even though in 1754 Anthony Henday* had been the Company's first white employee to view the western mountains, having marched from York Factory to within forty miles of what would later be Rocky Mountain House, nothing was done to consolidate that discovery for more than half a century. Even then it was a puny affair that drew no follow-up for another decade. The sensitive son of a brazier, Joseph Howse, who was educated in Latin, French and Italian before he left England for Hudson Bay in 1795, had made a brief journey into the mountains from Edmonton House in 1809. The following season he spent a full year in the Rockies, crossing the continental divide and wintering near present-day Flathead Lake, Montana. Although Howse carried no instruments to prove where he had been, William Hemmings Cook, the York Factory chief, reported that he had "explored a Country European feet had never trod" and his ledger showed that the expedition, mounted at a cost of £576, had produced thirty-six packs of fur with a profit margin of 75 percent. Howse had many other adventures but was never assigned to the Rockies again, and the HBC blithely left that highly lucrative sphere of operations to be harvested by the Nor'Westers.†

This policy of retreating in the face of competition also initially held true for the fur-rich Athabasca Country. The Nor'Westers had developed a gainful trade there well before 1800, establishing posts westward along the Peace and northward down the Mackenzie, cutting the flow of pelts that had previously sustained the HBC post at Churchill. The first Bay man into Athabasca was Philip Turnor, the Company surveyor, who arrived in 1790 so ill-equipped he had to borrow a fishing net from the Nor'Westers, and so ill-provisioned that he survived mainly by shooting rabbits. But he did report back that the local Indians, remembering the fair way they had been treated on the bay, were friendly, while feeling "a settled dislike for the Canadians" who traded in the area, particularly because these Nor'Westers had the practice of seizing women as payment "for their Husbands or Fathers debts and then selling them to their [North West Company] men [for] from five hundred to two thousand Livres and if the Father or Husband or any of them resist the only satisfaction they get is a beating."

When Turnor arrived back at York Factory, he recommended that

---

*His journey is described in *Company of Adventurers*, pages 242–44.

†Howse himself retired from the Company in 1815 and devoted the next thirty years of his life to compiling the first published *Grammar of the Cree Language*, which became a standard text still cited by linguists.

the Company adopt the aggressive trading methods of the Nor'Westers and volunteered to march back to establish a permanent Athabasca trading post. No one paid any attention.

Turnor mapped many of the waterways running inland from Hudson Bay,* but his chief legacy to the HBC was his ability to spot and train promising newcomers. Besides teaching David Thompson the surveying skills that turned him into the NWC's greatest mapmaker, Turnor apprenticed Peter Fidler, a lesser known but also significant figure in the early probes of the western frontier. Fidler came to the western territory from Bolsover, Derbyshire, as a labourer in 1788, quickly rising to become a writer. He was stationed at Cumberland House just as Turnor was preparing to leave for Athabasca, and when Thompson broke his leg, the HBC surveyor took young Fidler with him instead. Turnor's main assignment was to prove that the Athabasca district could be reached by a river draining into Hudson Bay, which would have made it legally part of the original HBC grant. That proved impossible (because of a clearly defined watershed at Methy Portage), but this first incursion did provide the HBC with vital data and Fidler with valuable training. Not only did he become a qualified surveyor but he spent a full season living in a Chipewyan camp on the Slave River. There is a touching entry in his journal when, realizing how deeply assimilated into native life he has become, he marvels that for the first time he has dreamed in Chipewyan.

Finally, in 1802, Fidler was assigned to lead his own trading party into the Athabasca and establish a trading post near Fort Chipewyan known as Nottingham House. In its miniature "Big House," Fidler, his Swampy Cree wife, Mary, and sixteen Orcadian assistants spent the next four winters, living mainly on frozen fish, rarely daring to venture outside for fear of the wild, ravenous dogs roaming the snowdrifts. That first winter Fidler recorded, in his scientific way, the freezing temperatures of various substances: his English brandy froze at $-26°F$, rum at $-23°$, Holland gin at $-17°$ and "blood out of the body" at $25°F$. Fidler spent his time trading furs, studying French, operating a small hand-press and bindery—and jousting with Nor'Westers.

His first tormentor was a stout Highlander named Archibald Norman McLeod who flounced around Fort Chipewyan in a scarlet

---

*It was also Turnor who first propagated the notion that Canada could be usefully mapped if explorers went inland and then followed the great rivers downstream to the coast. In that way a traveller could avoid the always puzzling dilemma of which branch of a stream to follow, because rivers as they flow to the sea steadily increase in width and intensity.

military uniform of his own design, complete with sword and cocked hat. McLeod warned Fidler that he had no right to be in Athabasca and that "the proprietors of the NWC were resolutely determined that the servants of the HBC should walk over their bodies rather than they would allow an Indian to go into the Hudson's Bay Company House." McLeod's most effective tactic was to command one of his clerks, Samuel Black, to harass the HBC employees. Unlike most of his fellow Nor'Westers, who treated the Bay men with either respect or contempt, Black was a terrorist who took pleasure in his violent activities. He led raiding parties that plundered the Chipewyan camps trading with the HBC, slashed Fidler's fishing nets, set ablaze his winter reserves of firewood, uprooted his garden and personally moved into a tent pitched right at the Nottingham House gates to prevent any Indians from entering. The best description of this frontier brigand was provided by George Simpson, when he was making notes on the personalities of the men (including such former NWCers as Black) under his command to see who might—and might not—be suitable for promotion. Of Samuel Black, he wrote: "The strangest man I ever knew. So wary & suspicious that it is scarcely possible to get a direct answer from him on any point, and when he does speak or write on any subject so prolix that it is quite fatiguing to attempt following him. A perfectly honest man and his generosity might be considered indicative of a warmth of heart* if he was not known to be a cold blooded fellow who could be guilty of any Cruelty and would be a perfect Tyrant had he had power. Can never forget what he may consider a slight or insult, and fancies that every man has a design upon him. Very cool, resolute to desperation, and equal to the cutting of a throat with perfect deliberation: yet his word when he can be brought to the point may be depended on. A Don Quixote in appearance—ghastly, raw boned and lanthorn jawed, yet strong vigorous and active. Has not the talent of conciliating Indians by whom he is disliked, but who are ever in dread of him, and well they may be so, as he is ever on his guard against them and so suspicious that offensive and defensive preparation seem to be the study of his Life having Dirks, Knives and Loaded Pistols concealed about his Person and in all directions about his Establishment even under his Table cloth at meals and in his Bed. He would be admirably adapted for the Service of the North West coast where the Natives are so treacherous were it not that he cannot agree with his

---

*No matter what else he did, Black always sent some money home to his mother in Aberdeen.

colleagues which renders it necessary to give him a distinct charge. I should be sorry to see a man of such character at our Council board."*

Having to deal with Black's outrageous bullying tactics did nothing for Fidler's trading record, and he ended that first season with a disappointing total of only 253 skins. Ordered to stay where he was, he did even worse in the second season. Black had started trailing the Bay men's duck hunts; armed with a savage-looking cutlass, he would leap up to startle the birds at the crucial moment. He burned down the HBC watch-house near Fort Chipewyan and torched the lumber that had been collected to build another outstation. Still, enough Indians braved Black's blockade that Fidler grew determined to remain another season. That was a mistake.

Black declared psychological warfare at a more primitive level, denying the Bay men any sleep. Each night, he would pace outside their compound howling like a wolf and hurling rocks at their wooden walls. He once placed a heavy piece of bark atop the chimney, nearly asphyxiating the snoozing occupants, and even killed and ate their pet dog. He denied the Indians access to the English fort with the threat of shooting and so wore down Fidler and his crew that in June 1806 they decided to give up the venture and leave. But there was one more blow to come. Fidler had signed an agreement with an NWC winterer that in return for quitting the Athabasca district for two years, he would be given five hundred pelts and repaid the expenses incurred in establishing Nottingham House. Now that he was ready to depart, the Nor'Westers went back on their word and Fidler left empty-handed, lamenting in his journal: "We are so very few—they so numerous!"

Four years later, Fidler was posted back to the Athabasca gateway at Île-à-la-Crosse, only to be subjected once again to the guerrilla tactics of Black, aided this time by a young NWC recruit named Peter Skene Ogden, who swaggered about with two daggers in his belt. The Nor'Westers used the Company's flag and weather-vane for target practice, stole Fidler's fishnets, carried away his firewood, diverted Indians who arrived with furs and, finally, invaded his fort. "I told them both to return the same way they came and that they should not pass through our yard in the insulting manner they indicated," the Bay man dutifully noted in his journal. "I told one of our men to shut the west gates—which was at last done—they persevered in passing when

---

*Despite this devastating analysis, Simpson promoted Black, who in 1823 joined the HBC he had so hated, to Chief Trader and eventually to Chief Factor and placed him in charge of the Kamloops district, where he was killed by an Indian on Feb. 8, 1841.

I struck Mr. Black with a stick two or three times—Ogden immediately drew his dagger and cut two large holes in the side and back of my coat and pricked my body—but no further—Mr. Black then took up part of the stick I had broken over him and struck me on the thumb close at the upper end of the nail and smashed it to pieces—Ogden also struck me twice with a stick—all our men looking on the whole time without giving me any assistance—Mr. Black and Ogden yet followed me into my room with their guns and daggers and abused me very much while my thumb was dripping. . . ."

After that, the Nor'Westers (outnumbering the Bay men twenty-six to eight) forbade any of Fidler's men to leave their posts and shot at his twelve-year-old son, Charlie. Faced with circumstances so stressful that he feared outsiders would not believe him, Fidler logged in his diary on January 21, 1811: "Some people in reading this Journal might very naturally suppose, that many of the Ill actions that has been done was by people in a state of inebriety—but they are very sober people—it is a systematic plan that has been laid at the Grand Portage to harass and distress us and determine to expel us from these parts of the country where they get the greater part of their prime furs at very little expense. . . ."

Before Fidler left that unhappy post the following summer, Black and Ogden had one more torment in store. Because the post depended for its food on fishing, they induced an Orkneyman named Andrew Kirkness, who was the Company's best angler, to defect to the NWC. As bait they used his Indian wife, who had defected to the Montrealers' camp a few months earlier. Fidler had tried to get her back, having heard that she was unhappy. The Nor'Westers not only refused but threatened to cut off her ears if she left. Shortly after his desertion, Andrew Kirkness changed his mind and decided he wanted back into the HBC post, but according to Fidler's journal, Black told him that "if he offered to go to us, they would make every Canadian in their house ravish his woman before his eyes." Three days later, Kirkness deserted anyway, departing without his wife. As Fidler was leaving the post for the last time, the Indian woman tried running after the departing Bay man, but was yanked back inside the NWC post. "They have now given her to a Canadian," the hardened Fidler scribbled in his journal, adding, "Calm, hot weather."

When Fidler got back to Hudson Bay, William Auld, his superior, derided him for his "mean and spaniel-like behaviour." The surveyor remained with the Company until he died on December 17, 1822. During the last decade of his service, Fidler became the HBC's chief cartographer of the interior plains, drawing thirty-two invaluable maps of the area within the HBC's jurisdiction. After he retired at fifty-one, he was allowed to languish as a supernumerary clerk in the Swan River district of what is now western Manitoba. The last mention of this worthy geographer in HBC documents is a brief note describing him as "a faithful and interested old servant, now superannuated, [who] has had a recent paralitic affection [*sic*] and his resolution quite gone, is unfit for any charge." A typical Canadian hero.*

THE HBC'S DISPIRITING ATTEMPTS to compete with the Nor'Westers in the Athabasca—and everywhere else for that matter—led its London-based proprietors to the verge of taking the Company out of the fur trade altogether. During these years, administration of the Company's affairs had fallen into the flabby hands of a closed clique of interrelated and interconnected fiscal aristocrats whose idea of a truly daring act was to be the first among their circle to try out the new French restaurants then dotting London. Samuel Wegg, whose family connections with the HBC went back a century, was succeeded in the governorship in 1799 by Sir James Winter Lake, the last of the Lake family that had dominated the Company's board for most of eight decades. The only fresh voice among the Committeemen was that of George Hyde Wollaston, son of a theologian and brother of a mathematician, who produced a dispassionate analysis of the Company's prospects and

---

* Fidler's will had a curious wrinkle. In the document dated August 16, 1821, he bequeathed his journals and maps to the HBC and his library to the governor of the Red River Colony. His books are still available at the Legislative Library in Manitoba. Fidler also stipulated that his wife was to receive £15 in goods annually from the HBC for the rest of her life (she died in 1826) and that the interest on his investments was to be equally divided among his ten surviving children, until his youngest son, Peter, came of age. Then he added a strange codicil: "All my money in the funds and other personal property after the youngest child has attained twenty-one years, to be placed in the public funds, and the interest annually due to be added to the capital and continue so until August 16th, 1969 (I being born on that day two hundred years before), when the whole amount of the principal and interest so accumulated I will and desire to be then placed at the disposal of the next male child heir in direct descent from my son Peter Fidler. . . ." The estate was supposed to have been divided among Fidler's eleven children (the youngest, Harriet, was born in 1822, after the will was drawn up) and the document was not contested. But some of Fidler's modern descendants, business people in Portage la Prairie, Manitoba, claim that the HBC kept the geographer's savings and that no funds were passed on to the family. When asked about this possibility, Marian Wiggins, another Fidler descendant who now lives at Kinistino, Saskatchewan, replied: "I wouldn't be a darned bit surprised."

Colin Robertson

decided it had none—at least not in a fur trade by then overwhelmingly dominated by the Nor'Westers.

After studying the alternatives in April 1809, Wollaston presented his fellow directors with a bold initiative. Since the fur business had become prohibitively unprofitable and unsold pelts were piled high in the HBC's London warehouse while the supply of timber for Royal Navy masts, spars and decking was in dangerously short supply (because the Napoleonic wars were cutting off England's traditional Baltic sources), he proposed transforming the HBC into a timber company. The London-based plutocrats, never having visited the place, had no first-hand idea of how little usable wood grew around Hudson Bay. (In fact, York Factory had just used up a six years' accumulation of its precious spare timber merely to erect two tiny outhouses.) There were small forests twenty miles inland from Moose Factory, at the southern end of the adjoining James Bay, and Wollaston eventually arranged to have a steam engine shipped so that a sawmill could be built. The engine, manufactured by Boulton & Watt, was reassembled by Alexander

Christie, a Scotsman hired specifically by the Company to pursue timber sales. The trade never developed. Not only was the supply of raw materials inadequate but the Royal Navy was learning to evade Napoleon's blockades.

But something had to be done. By 1809, the Hudson's Bay Company's balance sheet was showing losses of £19,000. Dividends, which had declined to 4 percent, had to be eliminated, and the value of the Company's stock, which had sold for £250 a share, had declined to about £60. In 1808, the Committeemen had petitioned the British government for relief from custom duties. The Treasury granted a one-year reprieve, then looked the other way. Three Committee members had already lent the Company £25,000, and it was carrying a £50,000 overdraft with the Bank of England.

The quandary was resolved when Wollaston's negative influence on the HBC Committee was replaced by the drive of two remarkable men: Andrew Colvile and John Wedderburn Halkett.* They both purchased substantial share positions in the Company during 1809, and while Halkett did not become a member of the governing Committee for another two years, Colvile, who had previously been a successful London sugar broker, assumed a position of power almost immediately. He was determined to move the HBC away from his predecessor's counsel of despair. Colvile had the intellect and lively sense of resolve, but it was a renegade Nor'Wester named Colin Robertson who provided the winning idea. The same day Colvile took up his seat on the Committee, Robertson had made a forceful presentation to the board arguing that instead of cowering before the Nor'Westers the HBC should attack them, mainly by mounting an expedition from Montreal to conquer the Athabasca fur lands. He also advocated that the Company revise its compensation arrangements so that its senior traders would,

---

*The names of these animators require an explanation. At thirty-four, in 1814, Andrew Wedderburn assumed the surname Colvile because his mother, Isabella Blackburn, was the great-grandniece and heir of the last Lord Colvile of Ochiltree. Andrew and his father, James, had previously assumed the name Wedderburn-Colvile. He was a grandson of Sir John Wedderburn, 5th Baronet, who fought at Culloden in Lord Ogilvy's regiment, was subsequently taken prisoner and executed on Kennington Common in November 1746, when the baronetcy was forfeited. (A new baronetcy was created in 1803 for another grandson of Sir John Wedderburn.) Andrew's sister, Jean Wedderburn, married the Earl of Selkirk. Similarly, John Wedderburn, a cousin of Andrew's, assumed the surname Halkett in 1779 on the death of another cousin, Sir Peter Halkett. Aside from his interest in the HBC, Halkett served as governor of the Bahamas and later of Tobago. He married Lady Katherine Douglas, a sister of Lord Selkirk, and became his representative while Selkirk was in Canada.

much like the Nor'Westers, be paid as incentive-inspired partners. He was particularly vehement in his arguments on behalf of the Athabasca venture. "Good God! See the Canadians come thousands of miles beyond us to monopolize the most valuable part of your Territories," he told the Committee. Robertson was adamant in his view that the HBC's incumbents in the field were "drones and drivellers" who "may as well attempt to take hold of the moon with their teeth" as beat the Nor'Westers at their own game. But it was by enlisting Colvile's support for the new pay arrangements that Robertson won the day. Known as the Retrenching System, the scheme provided for setting aside half the profits for the officers in the fur trade, granting men in the field more incentives and greater freedom of action. What made this prospect so significant was its ultimate aim of allowing the HBC, for the first time, to stand on its own feet as a commercial trading corporation instead of remaining as it had started—a royally chartered and protected monopoly.

Robertson, who had served the NWC as a clerk and been fired the previous year after a fistfight with John McDonald of Garth, was a new kind of man in the service of the Hudson's Bay Company. His personal motto, "When you are among wolves, howl," accurately summed up his operating philosophy. He was a proud and combative Highlander and made the most of each new situation in which he found himself. The Committee expeditiously adopted his recommendations that the Company seek its future traders in Scotland's Western Isles, in the Shetlands and among the heather of the Highlands.

But the most essential recruit in that unexpected surge of newly found energy was Andrew Colvile's brother-in-law: a Scottish nobleman known as Thomas Douglas, 5th Earl of Selkirk.

Cold night camp on Lake Winipesi

Thomas Douglas, 5th Earl of Selkirk

CHAPTER 6

A FEARFUL INNOCENCE

Unable to bridge the gap between noble aspirations and distasteful realities, Lord Selkirk tarnished his cause and eventually succeeded in destroying himself.

HE WAS THAT MOST DANGEROUS OF COMBINATIONS: a blend of moral fastidiousness and spiritual intransigence. A frail Scottish earl with his lungs and soul on fire, Lord Selkirk recruited himself as an agent of destiny, determined to alter the course of history.

That he achieved. His actions triggered the demise of the North West Company, and the Highland settlers he brought to the Red River established Western Canada's founding community.

Yet there is an incomplete quality about his remarkable saga—an enduring uncertainty as to whether he was fool or saint that still haunts the descendants of his people. Cursed as a blight on the landscape by his many enemies and chided for being a misguided visionary by his few friends, Selkirk followed his self-imposed mission, blissfully ignorant of Newton's Third Law of Motion—that for every action there is an equal and opposite reaction. Unable to bridge the gap between noble aspirations and distasteful realities, Lord Selkirk tarnished his cause and eventually succeeded in destroying himself.

Selkirk was driven by his personal sense of guilt over the Scottish crofters' sufferings and by frustration at his own illness, that most falsely energizing of conditions, incurable tuberculosis. The disease racked his every breath during the last dozen years of his life. While devoting his whole being to the Red River Colony, he was trying to muffle in lace handkerchiefs the blood-coughs from his chest—and fighting to keep down the bile he felt at the chicanery of his opponents.

Although he became known mainly for his bold experiments at colonization, Selkirk's more important contribution was geographical. His relentless determination to settle the western lands extended Britain's tenuous hold on the northern half of the North American continent during a critical decade, drawing the attention of London's colonial authorities to a region that might otherwise have gone by default to the United States. The very fact of the Red River Colony's existence proclaimed Britain's transcontinental intentions by planting a vested interest in the path of expansion-minded politicians to the south.

The ragtag diaspora of approximately 270 displaced Highland crofters who settled on the Red River was the Prairie equivalent of the Pilgrims who had emigrated to the Plymouth colony aboard the *Mayflower* nearly two centuries earlier. Few contemporary maps noted Red River's location; no gazetteer listed its existence. Yet the tiny agricultural enclave at the junction of the Assiniboine and Red rivers developed into a pivotal community, quickly evolving its own social structures and home-grown middle class, its own tensions and pretensions and, eventually, a full-scale rebellion.

Selkirk himself visited Red River only once—in 1817, five years after its founding—and stayed for one fleeting summer. This was his one brief season as benevolent king of his personal domain. He spent the long prairie afternoons tramping the grasslands under the slanting sun, bestowing land on worthy recipients, planning roads and bridges, setting aside tracts for churches and schools, giving shape to his dream. Legend transmuted those thirteen weeks into a hallowed interlude, perpetuated in the community's still extant folklore as affirmation of its founder's compassion and his affinity for the land.

LAND HAD BEEN THE CHIEF PREOCCUPATION of the Douglases since the thirteenth century, and from 1300 to the Reformation no family had played a more conspicuous part in the affairs of Scotland. Its members, having intermarried eleven times with the Scots royal family (and once with that of England), had been involved in nearly every armed effort to guard and extend Scottish sovereignty.*

---

*The family's peerage is among the most complicated in the United Kingdom. The original Earl of Selkirk married Anne, Duchess of Hamilton in her own right, and by special arrangement was created Duke of Hamilton. The current head of the House of Douglas is the Duke of Hamilton, premier peer of Scotland, whose principal seat used

John Paul Jones

Thomas Douglas was born on June 20, 1771, at St Mary's Isle, his family's ancient seat in southwestern Scotland. He was still a youngster when he suffered the traumatic experience of having his home invaded by a raiding party under the command of John Paul Jones, the Scottish-born naval hero of the American War of Independence. Jones was determined to impress his potential for greatness on the noble family he felt had spurned him during his youth. The son of a maid and a gardener at nearby Kirkbean, Jones harboured a deep resentment of the Douglases based on more than the great family's master-servant relationship to his parents. Unlike those of his sisters, John's own name did not appear in the register of births at the parish of Kirkbean, and he believed himself to be an illegitimate and unacknowledged offspring of the Selkirks.

---

to be Hamilton Palace, southeast of Glasgow, one of the few non-royal residences called palace (another notable one is Blenheim, belonging to the Duke of Marlborough). Hamilton Palace was torn down in 1921 because the 13th Duke wanted to continue working the coalfield under his residence's grounds.

Apprenticed as a cabin boy on a merchantman at twelve, John Paul had become chief mate on a Jamaican slaver and in 1772 killed the ringleader of a mutiny aboard his vessel. To escape charges, he added the anonymous-sounding surname "Jones." When the 1775 revolutionary war broke out in the Thirteen Colonies, he joined the new Continental Navy. In command of the *Providence*, he swept the North Atlantic, capturing or sinking a dozen British ships. Later, in charge of the newly commissioned *Ranger*, he sailed to France, where Benjamin Franklin, then the American envoy to Versailles, ordered him to harass shipping off the British Isles and, if possible, kidnap a well-known personage who could be exchanged for American prisoners held in England. These assignments found the *Ranger* on April 23, 1778, nosing into Solway Firth to anchor off the Douglas mansion. Her captain, in full dress uniform, was nervously pacing the quarterdeck, planning an early morning landing party to kidnap Dunbar Hamilton Douglas, 4th Earl of Selkirk. His motive may have been deeply personal, but Jones's bold foray in plucking one of Scotland's leading aristocrats out of his own hall would have been a great coup for the future Republic.

Despite his elaborate preparations, Jones decided at the last moment not to lead the raid in person, assigning that delicate duty to his two chief lieutenants, Simpson and Wallingford. As the longboat landed at the family dock, a governess snatched young Thomas from where he was playing in the garden and whisked him to safety. When the two naval officers, leading their armed troop of disreputable-looking matelots, knocked on the mansion's great door, something akin to drawing-room comedy ensued. The family butler, Daniel, his professional sang-froid hardly ruffled, acidly pointed out that if the visitors were a Royal Navy press-gang, there was no one home to "press." The Americans huffily identified themselves, just as Lady Selkirk came out of the breakfast room to see what all the fuss was about.

With that genteel mixture of total calm and utter contempt that takes generations to cultivate, Lady Selkirk motioned the two officers into her drawing-room and demanded to know what they wanted. The explanation that they intended to kidnap her husband to be bargained for American prisoners was waved away with the curt comment that the Earl was not home—clearly implying that even if he were, he would hardly stoop to entrust himself to such uncouth colonials. When Lieutenant Wallingford cheerfully replied that it didn't really matter, they would kidnap instead the youngster they had passed in the garden, Lady Selkirk drew herself up to her full height and matter-of-factly declared they would have to take her life first. She then offered any *objects* in the house that appealed to them.

The discomfited officers looked around, spotted the silver service from which breakfast had so recently been served, and allowed that perhaps the tea and coffee pots and silver salver might be appropriate. Lady Selkirk ordered Daniel to pack the silver in a stout sack, then offered her visitors a glass of wine, asking the butler to pass some whisky to the crewmen waiting outside. The ever-faithful Daniel had no intention of surrendering all of the family's Georgian treasures to the ragamuffins from across the sea, and while packing some of the silver into the sack, substituted lumps of coal wrapped in paper, temporarily secreting a valuable urn beneath a maid's ample apron. The raiding party and Lady Selkirk were meanwhile proposing increasingly spirited toasts to one another's health. The visit came to an end when the waving sailors rowed off in their little boat, clutching the bag of silver—and coal.

Back aboard the *Ranger*, Jones was furious with his two officers. Instead of impressing the Douglases with his greatness, his subordinates had made him out to be a common thief. He decided to buy back the booty from the Navy, pay his crewmen their prize money and return the goods to Lady Selkirk. The following month, he sent her a flowery letter apologizing for the raid. "MADAM," it began, "it cannot be too much lamented that in the profession of arms the Officer of fine feelings, and of real responsibility, should be under the necessity of winking at any action of persons under his command, which his heart cannot approve. But the reflection is doubly severe when he finds himself obliged in appearance to countenance such Action by his authority. . . . Knowing Lord Selkirk's interest with his King, and esteeming as I do his private Character, I wished to make him the happy instrument of alleviating the horrors of hopeless captivity when the brave are overpowered and made Prisoners of War. It was perhaps fortunate for you, Madam, that he was from home, for it was my intention to have taken him on board the *Ranger* and to have detained him till thro' this means, a general and fair exchange of Prisoners as well in Europe as in America, had been effected . . . but some officers who were with me could not forbear expressing their discontent, observing that in America no delicacy was shown by the English, who took away all sorts of movable property. . . . I have gratified my men, and when the plate is sold, I shall become the purchaser, and I will gratify my own feelings by restoring it to you, in such conveyance as you shall be pleased to direct."

That bit of purple rationalizing should have been the end of the exchange, but Lord Selkirk haughtily sent word to Jones on the family's behalf that he could not possibly countenance return of his silver without consent of the Continental Congress. The objects, which had cost

Jones £50, became the issue of protracted legal negotiations before they were returned seven years later, the silver pot still containing dried tea-leaves from the interrupted breakfast.*

The harmless incident did much to spread the reputation for courage of Lady Selkirk (who wrote to a friend, ". . . I frankly acknowledge my composure to be constitutional"), but it had a lasting impact on the future Lord Selkirk. "This was a momentous event in my life," Thomas later confessed. "I was terribly frightened. . . . I developed an antipathy for the United States due almost solely to the buccaneering of John Paul." In his *Red River Valley*, John Perry Pritchett claims that the raid in fact had profound consequences: "Perhaps this may help to explain why the Earl, when considering possible sites in America for colonization projects, was decidedly in favour of districts lying in British territory rather than in the more temperate regions of the United States."

The young Thomas was educated in liberal arts at the University of Edinburgh, where he came under the influence of Dugald Stewart, a brilliant exponent of the Scottish "common sense" school of philosophy, which held that thought should flow from scientific evidence unfettered by metaphysical speculation. Stewart impressed on his youthful charges the notion that universal benevolence was the prime virtue, insisting that "only a man whose ruling or habitual principle of action is a sense of duty, or a regard for what is right, may be properly denominated virtuous." Counter to the prevailing tenet of the time, this system of beliefs demanded from its followers the active social involvement and aggressive individual initiation of good works that would become the hallmarks of Selkirk's life.

At university, Thomas also befriended Walter Scott (he later met and admired Lord Byron),† but the most romantic influences on his

---

*Jones went on to assume command of the *Bonhomme Richard*. He was on her quarterdeck when, in answer to a demand for surrender during an engagement with the Royal Navy's *Serapis* on September 23, 1779, he uttered his famous riposte: "I have not yet begun to fight!" He later became disillusioned with his adopted country and joined the Russian Navy (then fighting the Turks) as a rear-admiral but, plagued by discontented subordinates, returned to Paris. There he died a broken man in 1792.

†The Douglases also knew Robert Burns. It was in the Selkirk house at St Mary's Isle that he wrote the celebrated Selkirk Grace:

> *Some hae meat, and canna eat,*
> *And some wad eat that want it;*
> *But we hae meat and we can eat,*
> *And sae the Lord be thankit.*

youth were tales of his family's exploits, which stressed audacity above every other virtue. Sir James—the famous Black Douglas who had led Robert the Bruce's army into England—was an ancestor. A scarlet, crowned heart is still the centrepiece of the family's coat of arms, honouring James's vain attempt to carry out Bruce's dying wish to have his heart buried in the Holy Land. When he was outnumbered during an encounter in Spain with the Moors on his way to the Middle East, Douglas had thrown the silver chalice containing the organ into the advancing phalanx of his enemies, shouting, "Pass first in fight as thou wert wont to do and Douglas will follow thee or die!"—and fought his way towards his beloved friend's heart. He was slain just before he reached it.

Having seven centuries of fighting blood in his veins was not a heritage easy to live down, especially for young Thomas, who had no aggressive intentions for his own future. Unlike his elder brothers, he was not trained for the law or military service. But having been awakened to the new enlightenment sweeping continental Europe during his university years, he decided to visit France with his brother-in-law, Sir James Hall of Dunglass. That progressive baronet had many close links with some of the intellectuals behind the French Revolution, including the Marquis de Lafayette (a leader of the liberal aristocrats demanding restrictions on the absolute power of the French monarchy), Pierre-Samuel du Pont de Nemours (a reform-minded economist who advocated free trade) and Jacques-Pierre Brissot de Warville (the moderate reformer who took delivery of the keys to the Bastille after it was stormed in 1789). It was here in the sensitized salons of revolutionary France that the young man's social conscience took root. His humanitarian sensibilities were awakened to a realization of how urgent political imperatives can turn patrician intellectuals into effective men of action. At the same time, he became acutely aware that any society failing to alleviate the plight of the poor might suffer violent consequences *à la guillotine*. These two notions—that thoughtful aristocrats were not precluded from implementing social reform, and that *not* to initiate reform was by far the riskier course—became Thomas Douglas's motivating impulses.

After his return to Scotland, he astonished his father and brothers by choosing to work on the family farm, labouring from dawn to dusk as hard as any tenant, ploughing the black earth, scything the stalks of oats and barley. As part of his growing enthusiasm for improved land use, Selkirk began to take private journeys northward into the Highlands. There he came face to face with the notorious Clearances.

A DEAD HAND HAD LAIN on Scotland since the defeat of the clans at Culloden, that windswept moor of lost hope where the Jacobites under the Young Pretender were slaughtered by the English redcoats on April 16, 1746. Five thousand starving Highlanders equipped only with broadswords and stout hearts were confronted by a well-drilled cadre of professionals backed by cavalry and cannon. The odds were already uneven enough, but the Scots were also divided by internal jealousies. Many of the Macdonalds, for example, refused to fight because they had been placed on the left wing of the defending formation instead of on the right, which was considered the place of honour.

The battle lasted less than an hour, but 1,200 Scotsmen were killed (compared to 76 Englishmen) and once the fighting was done, the British decided not only to quell the Highland uprising but also to destroy the society that had given rise to it. The stragglers from Culloden were hunted down and killed, and the glens were invaded and occupied. The Highlanders' houses were burned, their herds appropriated, weapons banned, parish records destroyed; the powerful clan system was methodically dismantled. And then the British got serious: they outlawed wearing of the kilt and forbade playing of the bagpipes.

The traditional feudal bond between lords and followers broke under these measures, and Scottish society began to disintegrate. The clan chiefs, shorn of their authority, seemed to lose even the most basic concern for their own people. During the century after Culloden, the decision to disperse their crofters resulted in the glens and braes being turned into huge sheep farms. There was a ready market for mutton and wool—and sheep, unlike some of the poorer crofters, did not line up for a monthly dole. But clearing the land for pasturage meant driving out the men, women and children who had farmed it for generations. This was done with the help of police and soldiers or just by allowing flocks of Cheviot sheep to swarm over the Highlanders' crops.

The Clearances were a time out of joint. No one then (or now) could calculate exactly how many people were dispossessed in favour of sheep. According to one estimate, two-thirds of the Highlanders in the northern counties of Inverness, Caithness and Sutherland lost their homes. The forced evacuation was most vicious in Sutherlandshire. The Duke of Sutherland had landholdings of 1,332,000 acres, the largest in the realm. From 1811 to 1820, fifteen thousand people were evicted from Sutherland estates to make way for sheep. The valley of Strathnaver in northern Scotland, for example, was evacuated on one day's notice, leaving sixteen hundred people homeless. "The destruction was begun in the west at Grummore," reported British historian John Prebble. "Messengers were sent ahead to all the other townships warning the people that they had an hour in which to evacuate their homes and take away what furniture they could. 'I saw the townships set on fire,' recalled Roderick Macleod, who was a boy at the time. '... It was sad, the driving away of these people. The terrible remembrance of the burnings of Strathnaver will live as long as a root of the people remains in the country. ...' The timber of three hundred buildings burned in the thin May sunshine. The valley was filled again with terrible noise, the crying of women and children, the hysterical barking of the dogs the Northumbrian shepherds had brought with them. 'Nothing but the sword was wanting,' said Macleod, 'to make the scene one of as great barbarity as the earth ever witnessed.'"

The confiscated livestock of the evicted farmers was herded into large enclosures and left there to starve, with cows, goats and bulls goring and trampling one another. Some cattle were allowed to die by the roadsides, their eyes pecked out by ravens, still alive as they bellowed their final anguish.

Such were the scenes witnessed by the impressionable young Selkirk, and they created an obsession in him to find homes for the displaced crofters. His notion of sponsoring their exodus was hardly novel, since between 1760 and 1808 at least forty-two thousand people fled Scotland for sanctuaries overseas. Because he felt that too many Highlanders were being dispersed to lands where they were lost not only to their native country "but also to the British Empire," he decided to direct at least some of the migrants to British North America.

His prestige and ability to influence events were unexpectedly enhanced in 1799, when at his father's death, as the sole survivor among his brothers, he became the 5th Earl of Selkirk. The new lord used his inherited fortune and authority to purchase landholdings on Prince Edward Island, where in 1803 he successfully settled eight hundred Highlanders. The following year he shipped fifteen families to the twelve hundred acres he had bought at Baldoon in Upper Canada, but the experiment proved a failure; the land was poorly drained and during the War of 1812 the settlement was pillaged by the Americans.

THESE PRELIMINARY FORAYS brought Selkirk to Montreal, where he was treated to a lavish Beaver Club dinner by the nabobs of the North West Company and heard for the first time intriguing tales about North America's lucrative interior. He had read Alexander Mackenzie's recently published *Voyages* and was enthralled by its references to fertile lands owned by the HBC in the Red River Valley, with its 170-day growing season and plentiful buffalo herds to supply fresh meat. When

Mackenzie approached Selkirk with the idea of trying to gain control of the Hudson's Bay Company, the Earl readily agreed—though their unspoken aims were diametrically opposed. Mackenzie was the stalking horse for the Nor'Westers, who had by now determined that the only way they could be certain of gaining access to furs using the shorter route via Hudson Bay was to buy out the Company. To Selkirk, the fur trade seemed to provide an ideal entry-point for his colonization scheme at Red River.

The Earl was already interested in the HBC. In 1807, the year before Mackenzie approached him, he had married Jean Wedderburn, the vivacious twenty-one-year-old beauty whose family was about to make large investments in the Company. Her brother Andrew was named to the HBC's governing committee in 1809, and Selkirk had not long before obtained written opinions from London's leading legal firms indicating that Prince Rupert's original charter was not only valid but that it clearly assigned the right to grant parts of the Company's huge domain for the establishment of permanent colonies. By May 24, 1809, Selkirk had invested £4,087 in HBC stock, Andrew Colvile had purchased a further £4,454 and their kinsman John Halkett, £3,717. The price per share, which only two years before had been quoted at £250, was down to £50. The HBC at this point had a capitalization of £103,950, but there were only seventy-seven shareholding accounts in existence and fifteen of those were held by estates in names of the dead. Historian K.G. Davies, who referred to the HBC as "this dollhouse company," noted that "many of the shares were being held in chancery pending settlement of claims. One shareholder in 1802 was a lunatic; another, King George III, was intermittently mad. . . . [Neither] took an active part in the company's affairs."

As soon as Mackenzie realized Selkirk's true aims, he threatened a lawsuit but dropped it in favour of urging NWC partners William and Simon McGillivray to start buying stock on their own to thwart the Scottish peer's plans. He correctly estimated that it would take an investment of only £20,000 to capture control of the Company. At their 1811 conclave at Fort William, the Nor'Westers voted enough funds to achieve that total—but they did not move fast enough. Selkirk eventually purchased stock worth a further £15,000, which with his own and his relatives' previous holdings allowed them to dominate the HBC's affairs. Trade in HBC shares had been so inactive that the stock was not regularly quoted on the London Stock Exchange until 1820. The average number of shareholders who attended the Company's annual courts between 1801 and 1813 was eleven, which included each year's retiring Committeemen and their successors—very often the same individuals, voting to reappoint themselves.

Selkirk's motives in using the HBC charter as a means of establishing the Red River Colony were not entirely altruistic. Because he felt the Family Compact's hold over Upper Canada was so powerful that no large tracts of public land would be available to him,* he saw the charter as an ideal vehicle to further his colonization scheme. In that decision he weighed the possibility of ultimate profits, but wanted mainly to inaugurate a plan to benefit his countrymen. When he formally proposed to the HBC Committee that the Company establish an active colony at Red River, he was disappointed to find little support. Except for Colvile, the directors felt hesitant about investing funds of the cash-poor Company in such a risky venture. They were much more interested in restoring dividend payments, which had been halved in 1801 and done away with altogether in 1809. Most of the Committeemen were ready to dismiss Selkirk's idea as a nuisance proposition that would only add to the red ink already much too visible on the debit side of the Company's ledgers.

Instead of asking the Company to assume the operating risks of the venture, Selkirk decided to finance the new settlement himself, and on March 7, 1810, presented the HBC board with his revised proposal. Having been relieved of any obligation to back his colonization scheme with corporate funds, the Committeemen were quick to recognize the venture's advantages. It would affirm once and for all the validity of the HBC charter, at least in the sense that granting the land for colonization would clearly signify that the HBC had owned it in the first place. Existence of the colony would also neatly dovetail into Colvile's Retrenching System, which called for dramatically increased inland activity and the replacement of expensive imported food supplies with local provisions. Two other corporate reasons supported the colonial thrust: an indigenous settlement in the Fur Country would supply much-needed new recruits to the business and at the same time provide a welcome retirement community for the increasing number of HBC traders with Indian wives wishing to stay in the country at the end of their contracts.

After considering the details of Selkirk's request for nearly a year, the HBC Committee agreed to the terms of the land grant. The Scottish nobleman and his heirs would be responsible for settling a thousand

---

*The Family Compact consisted of the small group of self-appointed aristocrats who presided over Upper Canadian society until the 1830s. They were linked by Tory ideals, family connections, hostility towards the United States and patronage. They provided a governing elite so rigid that it prompted the rebellion that led to a more moderate form of politics.

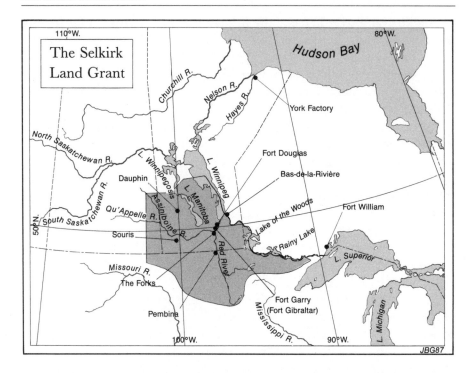

families in the Red River district within ten years; the colony would supply at least two hundred men each year to the Company's fur-trade operations; and HBC officers in the field would each be allocated two hundred acres in the settlement when they retired. In return for these hardly onerous conditions (and a nominal payment of ten shillings), Selkirk was granted a land empire of stunning proportions. Stretching over 116,000 square miles (the equivalent of 74,240,000 acres), the area covered territory four times the size of Scotland, or only about 5,000 square miles less than the combined land surfaces of the British Isles, including all of Ireland. The grant's borders (see accompanying map) extended into the present states of Minnesota, North Dakota and the northeast corner of South Dakota. Its western margin was deep in what is now Saskatchewan, almost to the source of the Assiniboine River. That bountiful domain contained what would later prove to be some of the earth's most fertile agricultural land with its self-contained waterways system, reaches of grass (for buffalo grazing) and the lush prospect of an inland empire. It was as magnificent a gift as was ever bestowed on a would-be colonizer. However dominant Selkirk's altruistic impulses, he must have known a bargain when he saw one, having already spent £10,000 on the soggy 1,200-acre settlement at Baldoon. He was now buying more than 74 million acres for ten shillings.

The understanding was accepted by the HBC board on March 6, 1811, with only the approval of the Company's annual Court on May 22 required to make it valid. The transaction quickly became a public issue. Protesting Nor'Westers toured London's coffee houses, whipping up support for their opposition. Pamphleteers published stories describing the Red River territory as a primeval solitude not suitable for human habitation, fit only as a breeding ground for wild animals. While walking in Pall Mall one afternoon, Selkirk was approached by an acquaintance who asked: "By God, Sir, if you are bent on doing something futile . . . why do you not plough the deserts of Sahara, which is so much nearer?"

At the shareholders' meeting, Sir Alexander Mackenzie delivered such a passionate objection to the Selkirk proposal that he won adjournment of the proceedings to May 30 and the Committee's undertaking that a recorded vote would be taken at that time. The Nor'Westers lobbied the Company's major shareholders and drew up a lengthy document detailing the dangers of the scheme to the Company's fur trade. But the following week, of the shareholders who made an appearance, twelve voted with Selkirk, five abstained, while only six were opposed—and three of those ballots were declared invalid because the stock they represented had been held less than six months. Amid loud complaints from the Nor'Westers that the land should have been offered at public sale and that the settlers would inevitably be exposed to slaughter by Indians, the meeting was adjourned, and thirteen days later Lord Selkirk received his grant.

The exasperated Nor'Westers reacted with barely contained fury. This silly anachronism called the Hudson's Bay Company was supposed to be dying, or dormant at best; what right did it have, they demanded, to reincarnate itself in vigorous new directions, especially in the very heart of the Fur Country? Simon McGillivray, one of the senior partners then in London to direct the attack, wrote to his wintering confrères: ". . . The Committee of the Hudson's Bay Company is at present a mere machine in the hands of Lord Selkirk, who appears to be so much wedded to his schemes of colonization in the interior of North America, that it will require some time, and I fear cause much expense to us, as well as to himself, before he is driven to abandon the project, yet *he must be driven to abandon it*, for his success would strike at the very existence of the [fur] trade." Other Selkirk critics attacked this peer who, they sneered, was "governed by the moon," and portrayed his colonizing initiative as "a cloak thrown over [his] avaricious designs to become a monopolizer of the fur trade."

The Nor'Westers' objections were easy enough to understand. At the most rudimentary level, the HBC had just handed over to Selkirk the land on which half a dozen of the Montreal company's most important trading forts were located (Pembina, Bas-de-la-Rivière, Dauphin, Gibraltar, Espérance and La Souris) and across which lay its main supply routes from Fort William westward. More important, the valleys of the Red River basin were the main source of the buffalo-based pemmican the NWC needed to feed its canoe brigades, and any inter-ference with that life-giving traffic would endanger the NWC's entire operation. Linked with these immediate concerns was the sinking feeling that nagged the more thoughtful Nor'Westers: that the long-term intention of the Bay men was to use Red River as a natural supply base to wedge themselves into the Athabasca Country, the NWC's most lucrative fur preserve.

Selkirk listened to the objections but was incapable of absorbing their content. To him, the Red River grant made eminent good sense, bringing together as it did his love of land, the crying need to relocate the Scottish crofters and timely reaffirmation of the HBC charter—thus furthering, in all its aspects, the imperialist ideal so popular among British aristocrats at the time. He shut his eyes and thought of England. "I really don't believe Selkirk realized what he was doing when he planted the Red River Colony right across the North West Company's main lines of communication," insists Dr W. Kaye Lamb, the internationally known fur-trade chronicler. "He just visualized a vast empty country and thought, 'Well, why can't they go five miles north or south of my colony?' never realizing he was cutting off the NWC's access to water-courses vital to their trade." Such naïveté was to haunt the Red River Colony's formative years. Selkirk could never bring himself to under-stand why his settlers could not simply be farmers without becoming pawns in the fur-trade wars. "It is a business," he wrote to Lady Selkirk about that commerce, "which I hate from the bottom of my heart."

Only four days after the HBC's dramatic shareholders' meeting, the Nor'Westers appeared at Hudson's Bay House with a new plan to prevent the bloodshed they could foresee if Selkirk received his grant. They suggested partitioning the Fur Country, permanently reserving Athabasca and the territory west of the Rocky Mountains for themselves, with the Red River Valley awarded to neither company. But having restored their self-confidence (by moving ahead with the Retrenching System) and their earnings (by 1811, profits were £57,860, compared with a loss of £19,000 for 1809), the HBC directors rejected the NWC offer without much thought or analysis. Accepting the NWC compromise might have prevented the tragic events that followed; turning it down meant moving beyond the possibility of averting the fatal consequences.

Miles Macdonell

SELKIRK'S FIRST EXPEDITION should have been a logistical and emotional triumph; instead, it was a misadventure of such proportions that the suffering of its participants became its dominant legacy. The crofters, recruited throughout Scotland, were asked to pay £10 per person for transportation to Red River and a year's provisions. Each head of family would then be granted a hundred acres at five shillings an acre, with Selkirk (through the HBC) responsible for marketing excess produce. The settlement was to have its own school and church with a Gaelic-speaking minister of the Presbyterian faith. The plan was to dispatch an advance party from Stornoway (that rocky burgh in the Outer Hebrides where Harris tweed originated) under the command of Miles Macdonell. A Scottish-born former captain in the Loyalist Royal Canadian Volunteers, Macdonell was hired by Selkirk to prepare the colony for permanent settlement. A high-strung martinet who had been frustrated in his army command, Macdonell suffered from the worst aspect of the military mentality: the notion that giving orders persistently and loudly enough can alter any annoying reality. If he had been hired as a double agent by the Nor'Westers to sabotage the project (which he was not—his loyalty to Selkirk was one of his few redeeming qualities), Macdonell could not have behaved much differently than he did. It was as if he were determined to make true the anti-settlement propaganda being spread throughout the Highlands by Simon McGillivray, writing under the pseudonym "The Highlander": "Even if the emigrants escape the scalping knife, they will be subject to constant alarm and terror. Their habitations, their crops, their cattle will be destroyed, and they will find it impossible to exist in the country."

Most of the ships serving the emigrant traffic out of Scotland at the time were little better than slave traders; a little worse, really, because the death of a slave in transit meant lower profits, while the unfortunate settlers paid their steerage fares in advance, and so their health and well-being upon arrival were of little concern to the agents and captains in charge. There is documentation of a brig that sailed for the Carolinas with 450 passengers crammed for eleven weeks into a hold measuring sixty by eighteen feet. Dysentery, typhus and scurvy claimed all but a handful. No wonder the departure of the ships was such a wrenching experience for those leaving and those who remained, as both groups instinctively realized they were likely never to see one another again. "The Highlanders were like children, uninhibited in their feelings and wildly demonstrative in their grief," wrote John Prebble. "Men and women wept without restraint. They flung themselves on the earth they were leaving, clinging to it so fiercely that sailors had to pry them free and carry them bodily to the boats. . . . Hands were wrung and wrung again, bumpers of whisky tossed wildly off amidst cheers and shouts; the women were forced almost fainting into the boats; and the crowd upon the shore burst into a long, loud cheer. Again and again that cheer was raised and responded to from a boat, while bonnets were thrown into the air, handkerchiefs were waved, and last words of adieu shouted to the receding shore, while, high above all, the wild notes of the pipes were heard pouring forth that by far the finest of pibroch tunes, *Cha till mi tuille*, We Shall Return No More!"

The scene at Stornoway in the summer of 1811 was no exception. If, indeed, these Scottish crofters were the Western Canadian equivalent of the Plymouth Pilgrims, their ship, the *Edward and Ann*, was a poor excuse for the *Mayflower*. Undermanned, with a crew of only sixteen boys, and commanded by a temperamental wharf-rat named Hanwell, she had been a derelict recommissioned especially for this journey, and there had been no visible upgrading from her former state of unseaworthiness. The grey sails were mottled with age, the rigging was loose and torn; the hull leaked and some of the caulking was coming off in large, dried chunks. The hold below decks was not divided into cabins, even though the three dozen regular HBC clerks who were being transported on the same ship to York Factory had been promised separate accommodation, as befitted their relatively exalted station.

The disorderly circumstances of the delayed departure were due in part to the fact that the Collector of Customs at Stornoway was John Reid, whose wife was an aunt of Sir Alexander Mackenzie—who had so recently been frustrated in his attempt to abort the Red River land grant to Selkirk. Reid did his best to postpone the ship's departure. During the embarkation process, his son-in-law, a roustabout who called himself "Captain" John McKenzie, circled the *Edward and Ann* in a bumboat, trying to recruit emigrants into the King's army. With windy promises of good treatment in the military he mixed lurid descriptions of the hellish conditions on the other side of the Atlantic.

On July 25, 1811, James Robertson, Reid's chief assistant, took his customs pilot boat out to the *Edward and Ann* to check the final muster. "Captain" McKenzie was at his usual station, yelling at the passengers, urging them to sign up for the army while simultaneously accusing those who had already accepted the King's Shilling of being deserters from His Majesty's forces. The HBC clerks were loudly voicing their dissatisfaction with their quarters, indignant that they were being forced to share the crowded lower deck with the emigrants, with only a stretched sail fastened to the bulkheads dividing their quarters.

The emigrants themselves at first seemed subdued, miserable at having to say their family farewells and feeling more than a little overwhelmed by the havoc. Then Robertson, the customs officer, following the practice of the day, announced to the assembled ship's company that, according to British Admiralty law, no one was obliged to depart against his will. That did it. Pandemonium. Half a dozen passengers rushed the rails and jumped overboard. Others commandeered one of the *Edward and Ann*'s lifeboats and rowed ashore. Several more escaped by crowding aboard Robertson's pilot boat and refusing to budge. Some of the deserters were recaptured, but early next morning Captain Hanwell, fed up with all the delays, weighed anchor and put out to sea, leaving at least 20 of the original 125 immigrants behind. It was July 26, the latest departure date for Hudson Bay ever recorded.

The nightmare voyage took sixty-one days, so that by the time the *Edward and Ann* dropped her rusty anchor at Five Fathom Hole off York Factory, it was far too late in the season to chance an overland journey to Red River. Because York Factory's food supplies were particularly strained that season and the incoming HBC employees were granted first

List of the men who founded the Selkirk Settlement

call on the post's limited accommodation, the Selkirk party was left huddling in makeshift quarters at Nelson Encampment, twenty-three miles to the west. The diet of deer and ptarmigan, limited in any event, could not prevent a bad outbreak of scurvy, and by breakup the next spring, fewer than half the men were mobile. When Macdonell finally departed on July 6, leading four crude boats up the Hayes River, his followers numbered only twenty-two.*

---

*The only reinforcements recruited along the way were Adam and Eve, a bull and a heifer purchased at Oxford House. They were a welcome addition to the first Red River Settlement but helped disprove Selkirk's theory that the buffalo might be persuaded to mate with domestic cattle to provide an uninterrupted supply of meat. Adam and Eve were not amused. There actually were successful crossbreeding experiments in the Carolinas and parts of Pennsylvania when buffalo calves were born to tame cattle, but this hybrid breed quickly disappeared because its bulls were sterile.

The move south, through wild unknown country along the boiling rivers and across moody Lake Winnipeg, took most of two months. Finally, on August 30, more than a year after leaving Scotland, the bewildered labourers arrived at the junction of the Assiniboine and Red rivers, traditionally a summer meeting place of local Indian bands and the very spot where, in 1738, Pierre Gaultier de Varennes, Sieur de La Vérendrye, had set up the advance depot he had named Fort Rouge. By 1810 there was a small HBC post in the district and the Nor'Westers had established Fort Gibraltar at the river junction under the command of Alexander Macdonell, Miles's cousin. The newly arrived Macdonell chose the west bank of the Red River, just below the Assiniboine and only a mile from the NWC post, as the site of Fort Douglas, which he hoped would soon be recognized as the new colony's headquarters. Guests from the establishments of both companies were invited to the formal ceremonies on September 4 at which Miles Macdonell officially took possession of the land on behalf of Lord Selkirk. A cannon was fired, flags were raised, and the usual "regale" of rum was offered to the Indians and Mixed Bloods watching the transfer of their lands with puzzled goodwill. After he was duly sworn in as governor, Macdonell acknowledged the seven-gun salute, then retired to his tent for snacks. Significantly, he spent his first evening celebrating the founding of the settlement at nearby Gibraltar, the NWC fort. The Nor'Westers not only tolerated but compassionately helped feed the newcomers during these early months, convinced that their venture was a foolish aberration that was bound to fail. A clerk named Willard Wentzel, the son of a Norwegian wool merchant, neatly summed up the Montreal company's attitude when he described the newcomers as "victims sacrificed to the sinister views of a noble imposter."

The ordeal endured by the Selkirk colonists during their first decade at Red River is usually tallied in terms of various armed confrontations with the Montrealers' local agents. But initially, the Nor'Westers did nothing to hamper the settlers. They didn't have to. Nature was a much more dependable enemy.

The newcomers may have been simple crofters from the Highlands, but they were men and women of inordinate fortitude and resourcefulness. They came not with ploughs but with hoes and spades to scratch the impervious surface of the great prairie; they boiled buffalo grease for soap and made starch from potatoes; they learned to pound pemmican, and flavoured it with sturgeon eggs. They survived, mainly because there was nowhere else for them to go.

When Sioux or Mixed Bloods attacked, the settlers hid their children under mats of sod or marsh grass; they knew that the nearest

The Red River, with Fort Douglas in the distance

possible source for significant reinforcements was York Factory, more than seven hundred miles away. It might as well have been seven thousand. Wolves, wild dogs and blizzards killed their few precious cattle; for two successive summers clattering plagues of grasshoppers destroyed every edible thing, plugging even the wells and chimneys. The Red River washed away what fragile crops had been planted on its flood plains, and drought withered the remainder of the valiantly rooted vegetation. Rats, wild pigeons, blackbirds, mites—the Red River settlers fought one after the other. When they survived the growing seasons (harvesting only two good crops in the first ten years), they were left to face the winters. Flesh shrivelled in the howling wind, and even the Clearances must at times have seemed more benign than staying alive in this frozen blankness. It was so cold, went the local legend, that you could shout outside in winter without being heard, because the sound of voices froze in the thick, frigid air—but come spring, the woods would be filled with an eerie hubbub as the preserved shouts thawed in the warming sun.

About two hundred and seventy settlers arrived in the first five years—Sutherlands, McKays, Gillespies, McLeods, McPhersons, Mathesons, Polsons, McBeaths, Campbells, Harpers, Bethunes, Isbisters, Finlays, McLeans, Johnstons, McKinnons, Malones, McDonalds, Mathewsons, Murrays, McBeths and Bannermans, among others—beating upstream from York Factory, sometimes led by a piper, always propelled by hope.

A Saulteaux Indian on the winter trail with his family

THE COLONY'S RELATIONSHIP with the Indians (except for occasional raids by the Sioux) was amicable, the local Saulteaux helping the people at every turn. Not so the Métis. The original settlers of these river banks, they quickly became the most distinctive element in the battles for tenure and supremacy that followed the arrival of the Scottish (and a few Irish) crofters. Métis, a word probably based on the Spanish *mestizo* (mixture), is an elusive term applying to anyone whose culture and genealogy combine the customs, living styles and values of their roots, European and aboriginal.* "It is, quite simply, the French expression for 'Mixed Blood' peoples," Don McLean of Regina's Gabriel Dumont Institute, which attempts to preserve their records, has noted. "The Mixed Blood people—French and Indian, mainly Cree—who acted as the original work force for the North West Company during the fur trade epoch were known as Les Métis. On the other hand, those mixed blood people who became the major element of the work force for the HBC were mainly Scots or English and Indian. They were known as 'Halfbreeds.' . . . Until recent times, the terms Métis and Halfbreed did denote the different European ethnicities of the Mixed Blood peoples, Métis indicating French, and Halfbreed English-Scots. Recently,

---

*Interestingly, the Cree word for Métis is *oteepaymsoowuk*, meaning "in charge of themselves." Although most Métis spoke French, they had a distinct language called Bungay, described by a traveller of that time as "polyglot jabber"—a mixture of broad Scots, a smattering of Gaelic and Irish brogue and rapidly uttered French.

however, Halfbreed has been seen as a pejorative term, and now all Mixed Blood people refer to themselves proudly as Métis."

A defiant people who prided themselves on being more than the sum of their bloodlines, the Métis enjoyed the natural grace of body proportion of their Indian ancestors, yet they rejected the traditional nomadic mode of life to become guardians of their own turf.* Their land, as it became an essential element in their identity, was one of the primary flashpoints between them and the newcomers. This was true especially after 1813, when HBC surveyor Peter Fidler arrived and, using the river-lot system common to Lower Canada, carefully laid out long narrow strips fronting on the river, the aim being to allow the Scottish families to live closer together and relatively near the protection of Fort Douglas. With the Métis linked to the fur-trading interests of the Nor'Westers just as firmly as the Highlanders were to the Hudson's Bay Company, the land tenure issue escalated the potential for conflict between them. "Lord Selkirk, philanthropist and humanitarian," wrote McLean, "seems to have been used as a tool by his more 'hard-nosed' business companions within the Hudson's Bay Company's London Board of Directors. Selkirk, wishing only to find a place to locate the destitute survivors of the Highland clans, was duped into founding the 'Selkirk settlement,' consisting of potential farmers and settlers who were to provide supplies for the Hudson's Bay Company. But this settlement was placed directly under the guns of Fort Gibraltar, in the heart of North West territory, where a trained paramilitary force of Métis cavalry held sway."

What had honed the Métis into a "paramilitary force" was the great semi-annual buffalo hunts. The shaggy beasts were just as vital to the fur trade as the beaver because their meat, pounded into pemmican, provided essential food for the voyageurs and traders criss-crossing the country. The Red River district had become the chief source of pemmican

---

*The social status of the Métis has fluctuated throughout Canadian history. There was a time, during the early part of the twentieth century, when many denied their Indian heritage. J.J. (Woody) Wood, an HBC trader who spent most of his career at Moose Factory on James Bay and who now lives in Victoria, tells how that conflict was resolved in one situation: "When I first went to Moose, Métis would almost always deny that they had Indian blood in them. I can remember old Métis women saying, 'Oh, *them* Indians,' with disdain in their voices. But while we were there, we saw the Métis become very proud of their Indian heritage. The first time it came out in the open was with Andy Faries, who was quite an aggressive fellow in the sense he was always taking on a new challenge in life. He was a good carpenter but decided there might be an opening for a barber. So he went to Toronto for barber school. The first thing they did when they got him in there was to lay out a bunch of tools he was going to have to buy, $125 worth. Andy hadn't thought about this part of it. So this fellow's trying to sell

for the Nor'Westers, and the livelihood of most Métis was based first on producing the edible tack, then taking it to the depot at Bas-de-la-Rivière on the Winnipeg River.*

Before the rise of the Métis, buffalo herds were the exclusive prey of the Plains Indians—the Assiniboine, Blackfoot, Cree, Gros Ventres, Peigan, Blood and Sarcee. By herding the animals over cliffs or funnelling them into pounds, the tribes increased the effectiveness of their hunts, but it was the introduction of horses in the first half of the eighteenth century that really multiplied the kill.

The buffalo was a walking emporium. Besides providing the meat that was its prime asset, it had a hide that could be used to make moccasins, leggings and tunics. When tanned, the hides became teepee covers; in the raw, they were cut into sleeping robes and winter coats. The inch-thick skin of a bull's neck could be toughened over a fire until it was strong enough to be a warrior's shield. The bladder made a fine waterproof carrying bag; the sinew was used for bowstrings; the long facial hairs were braided into rope. The animal's bones could be fashioned into cutting and scraping tools, the horns made perfect drinking cups and the tail, a handy flyswatter. The shorter body hairs could be stuffed into the saddle pads of warriors' horses. The buffalo's curved rib-cage yielded ideal sleigh runners; its incisor teeth could be strung into spectacular necklaces; and some of the spinal bones were polished and squared to make gambling dice. The greatest delicacies of all were buffalo tongues, which were salted and painted with molasses for shipment to the world's gourmet tables. Even the buffalo's dried dung was useful; it provided ideal fuel for fires. The hollows in the ground created by wallowing buffalos saved many lives by becoming small but essential reservoirs of water along the parched prairie. It was little wonder that with such a range of life-sustaining attributes these animals were thought to possess magical powers.

The Métis dominated the Red River hunts, which eventually spread southwestward into central Montana and later as far as the Cypress Hills in what are now Alberta and Saskatchewan. Hunting parties would rendezvous near present-day St Boniface, on the east bank of the

---

him all these tools, and Andy says, 'You know, my grandfather, he was a bit of a barber, but he only needed one tool.' And the teacher said, 'What do you mean? What did he have?' Andy replied, 'A tomahawk.' I thought that was a pretty good answer. That was the first joke I had ever heard a Métis person make about having an Indian heritage. From then on it became common."

*The boats used in this traffic were so roughly built that at the end of each voyage they were burned, with the handmade nails that had held them together carefully salvaged and carried back to the Red River to pin together the next fleet.

Métis on a buffalo hunt

Red River, and march sixty miles south to Pembina, where a tent city was erected. (The number of hunters swelled through the nineteenth century, reaching a peak of sixteen hundred, with four hundred horses and five hundred dogs, in 1840.) At Pembina, an overall chief and ten captains were elected to enforce the rules of the hunt. These regulations differed with each chase, but there were usually four points of conduct and the same number of precise punishments for disobeying them:

1. No buffalo to be run on the Sabbath.
2. No party to fork off, lag behind or go before without permission.
3. No person or party to run buffalo before the general order.
4. Every captain with his men, in turn, to patrol the camp and keep guard.
5. For a first offence against these laws, offender to have his saddle and bridle cut up.
6. For the second offence, the coat to be taken off the offender's back and be cut up.
7. For the third offence, the offender to be flogged.
8. Any person convicted of theft, even to the value of a sinew, to be brought to the middle of the camp and the crier to call out his or her name three times, adding the word "Thief!" each time.

Every morning the loaded carts fanned out from the encampment (during the 1840 hunt carrying 740 guns, 1,300 pounds of shot, 150 gallons of gunpowder and 6,240 spare flints) and followed the column of mounted riders until scouts had spotted a sizeable herd. The horsemen, four hundred abreast, would rein up in a long prancing line a mile or two from the peacefully grazing animals, waiting for the signal from the chief of the hunt. "*Commencez!*" came the command, and the horsemen approached the herd, slowly at first, then at a trot and finally at full gallop, thundering out of the sun. Too late, the bulls sensed danger, curving their tails and pawing the ground in gestures of magnificent if futile defiance. Flight was their only defence, and it usually came too late. The riders, their mouths filled with bullets, plunged into the mêlée of disoriented animals. Guiding their horses with their knees, the Métis kept their hands free to reach the loose gunpowder in the pockets of their buckskin jackets. After each shot, a palmful of powder was quickly poured down the barrel of the muzzle-loader and shaken home by hitting the gun butt against the saddle. Once he was riding alongside his chosen prey, the hunter would spit a bullet into the muzzle, the saliva making it adhere to the powder during the split second needed to depress the barrel, aim it just below and behind the buffalo's shaggy left shoulder, and puncture the animal's heart. Experienced hunters reloaded and fired fast enough to down three animals in the space of an

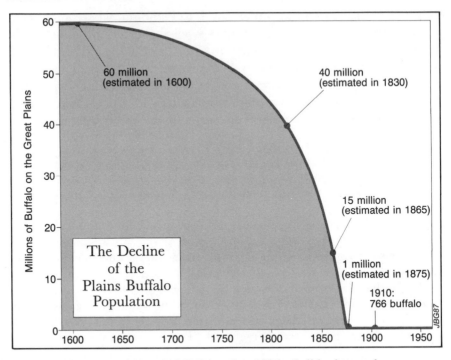

Between 1600 and 1910 the number of Plains buffalo plummeted
from 60 million to fewer than eight hundred animals.

acre's gallop. Each man threw a cap or scarf onto the body of his prey
to identify specific animals for the women, who would later skin the
carcasses. The kill seldom lasted more than an hour, with five hundred
or so dying buffalo strewn over six square miles of trampled prairie.
Some of the wounded animals stood stock-still in their tracks, with
fountains of blood pumping through their mouths and nostrils, dying
by ounces under the noonday sun. The hunters, their foam-flecked
mounts snorting with excitement, rode triumphantly among the mounds
of magnificent, expiring animals, boasting of their count.

Even the prolific buffalo could not long withstand massacre on this
scale. They had once covered the prairie (in fact, the entire pasture
region from Great Slave Lake down to Texas) like a sepia carpet.
Naturalist Ernest Thompson Seton estimated that in 1600 there were
sixty million in North America. Reports of herds fifty miles long and
half as wide taking days to pass a given point were common. Paul
Kane, the artist-explorer who toured the Canadian West in the 1840s,
described the rich profusion of the animals. "During the whole of the
three days it took us to reach Edmonton House," he wrote, "we saw
nothing else but these animals covering the plains as far as the eye

could reach, and so numerous were they, that at times they impeded our progress, filling the air with dust almost to suffocation. We killed one whenever we required a supply of food, selecting the fattest of the cows, taking only the tongue and boss, or hump, for our present meal, and not burdening ourselves unnecessarily with more."

As white men with their repeating rifles began to participate in the hunt, it degenerated into a blood sport; a million animals a year were killed, though often only their coats and many times only their tongues were utilized. (Buffalo Bill Cody, when he was employed to supply food to workers on the Kansas Pacific Railway, personally shot 4,280 of the animals in one seventeen-month period.) By 1889, only a meagre scattering of wild plains buffalo remained on the continent.* During the winter of 1886–87, starvation prevailed among Indian tribes who had only recently lived bountifully on the buffalo. "Owing to the destruction of game, the Indians, both last winter and last summer, have been in a state of starvation. They are now in a complete state of destitution, and are utterly unable to provide themselves with clothing, shelter, ammunition, or food for the coming winter," a petition to the Canadian government signed by local missionaries reported in 1888, going on to detail "consequent cannibalism" and how a party of twenty-nine Cree Indians had been reduced to three during the winter. The proud Plains Indians were soon forced to eat their horses and dogs, then beg for sustenance wherever they could.

Buffalo herds in the United States blocked early train travel, and passengers often shot the beasts for fun. The animals loved rubbing themselves on telegraph poles, destroying links in the communications system faster than they could be repaired. To avert the damage, sharp spikes called bradawls were installed, but the effect was not anticipated. According to one report published in Kansas after the earliest installations, "From the first time they came to scratch, they seemed to have felt a sensation in their thick hides that thrilled them from horn to tail.

---

*Paradoxically, the buffalo contributed to the welfare of their tormentors even after they vanished from the plains. Their bones (22,000 tons of them littering the Canadian West) were collected, processed into fertilizer and resold to nourish the soil of what had once been their dwelling place. When natural history museums learned how fast the buffalo were disappearing, there was a mad rush to collect specimens before they did become extinct. The descendants of the plains buffalo now number about 40,000; some are free-ranging, some are in parks and zoos. Some are raised commercially for their meat, and there are still places where they are hunted and shot as game. The largest concentration (5,000) is in Wood Buffalo National Park, straddling the border between Alberta and the Northwest Territories.

They would go fifteen miles to find a bradawl. They fought huge battles around the poles containing them, and the victor would proudly climb the mountainous heap of rump and hump of the fallen, and scratch himself into bliss until the bradawl broke, or the pole came down."

If the buffalo was the Métis equivalent of the fur trade's beaver, the Red River cart was its canoe. These creaky wooden conveyances were so important to their early way of life that the Métis were sometimes called "wagon-men" and in the Indian sign language of the time were described as being "half cart and half human." An integral part of the buffalo culture (there were 1,210 Red River carts employed in the 1840 hunt), the two-wheeled carts, like the birchbark canoe, had the advantage of being manufactured entirely out of locally available materials. Their wooden frames were held together with wooden pegs instead of nails or screws, and even the tires were made from buffalo hide, which had been stretched on the wheels when wet and allowed to shrink as it dried. The high, concave wheels could be removed and placed inside the main box of the cart, which, when enclosed in a buffalo-hide tarpaulin, could be paddled across lakes and rivers. The single axle was never greased because that would have attracted dust and grit, and the resultant noise was comparable to that of five thousand fingernails

The all-purpose Red River cart

drawn across a thousand blackboards. Pulled by oxen or over-the-hill horses, the Red River carts travelled in long, undulating caravans down to St Paul, over to Portage la Prairie and across to Fort Qu'Appelle.

The Red River carts, buffalo hunts and, above all, the land on which they had settled gave the Métis a sense of belonging—and that, in turn, meant that unlike the other non-Indian inhabitants of the Fur Country, they had a specific place of their own to defend. They were not, at least not yet, a "New Nation," as some of their more radical adherents maintained, but they were already a political force—Western Canada's first nationalists, a populist movement in search of a cause.

That cause was provided by the arrival of the Selkirk settlers. Here was a group of cast-offs from another continent insisting *they* had been granted title to the very land the Métis claimed by right of occupation— not to mention descent from Cree and Saulteaux ancestors who had been its original inhabitants.

Given the rallying cry of driving out the unwelcome intruders and the fact that the discipline of the buffalo hunts and their brushes with the Sioux had toughened the Métis into effective warriors, all they needed to launch Canada's first war of liberation was someone to command them.

The Battle of Seven Oaks, June 19, 1816

CHAPTER 7

SHOWDOWN

'If we are to be poor for three generations, we must absolutely fight this out."

—Lady Selkirk

THE LEADER WHO EMERGED to fill this pivotal role at the crucial moment was Cuthbert Grant, embodying in his person (and later in his actions) the coming together of the two pressures building up against the Selkirk settlers: the Métis's growing sense of nationhood, and the avowed strategy of the Nor'Westers to stop the Hudson's Bay Company from interfering with their trade by driving out the land-squatters threatening their supply lines. Grant may have been manipulated by one side or the other in this unusual melding of commercialism and chauvinism. But he didn't have to be. At that point in his life, he really was *both*, a Métis patriot and a loyal Nor'Wester.

The son of a Cree mother and a distinguished NWC wintering partner, also called Cuthbert, who had led the way to Great Slave Lake and become a leading member of the Beaver Club, Grant was baptized a Presbyterian at the Scotch Church on St Gabriel Street in Montreal and sent to school in Scotland. Orphaned when he was six, young Cuthbert grew up as a ward of the man appointed executor in his father's will—William McGillivray, who later became effective head of the NWC. That exalted sponsorship won him admittance to the inner circles of the Montreal trading concern virtually from childhood, so that Cuthbert was marked as special from the beginning. In 1812, at nineteen, after having spent eleven years in the apprenticing pursuits of a well-tended Scottish schoolboy, he was sent out to the Qu'Appelle

Métis leader Cuthbert Grant
The record of his baptism shows the signatures of
William McGillivray and Roderick McKenzie

River as an NWC clerk, destined for rapid advancement. His sister had married the current master of Fort Gibraltar, the NWC's installation at Red River, and shortly after he went west, Cuthbert fell in love with and married Elizabeth McKay, whose brother was head of a nearby HBC trading post known as Brandon House. These diverse kinship links and his demonstrated abilities as a hunter, horseman, organizer and warrior quickly moved him into a position of natural leadership. When the NWC decided to appoint him to the vague office of "Captain of the Métis," it was only confirmation of his already existing status as the recognized leader of his community. "He was able to identify himself with the new Métis nation, and stands at the beginning of their history, as Louis Riel stands at the end," concluded historians Margaret MacLeod and W.L. Morton.

It was the provocative tactics of Miles Macdonell, governor of the putative Selkirk Settlement, that united the Métis as never before. A Roman Catholic of Loyalist stock with the sublime faith that characterizes both, Macdonell had with one stroke removed any vestiges of doubt as to whether the settlers would interfere with the essential flow of pemmican from Red River to depots along the NWC trading routes. Two more boatloads of newcomers had arrived, and Macdonell didn't have enough horses to hunt his own buffalo. His puny farms were years from being self-sustaining; his people were hungry; yet pemmican by the ton was being shipped out of Red River to feed the NWC's distant brigades. Arguing that the life-sustaining food was being produced on land owned by Lord Selkirk, he issued the proclamations that would become opening shots in the Pemmican War: an edict forbidding further exports of the staple from Red River without his permission, and a prohibition against the hunting of buffalo from horseback within the Selkirk territories. He followed these foolhardy initiatives by confiscating four hundred bags of NWC pemmican and moving it under armed guard to Fort Douglas, boasting that he had force enough "to crush all the Nor'Westers . . . should they be so hardy as to resist . . . authority."

As if bent on self-destruction, Macdonell then escalated the antagonism. He sent notices to the commanders of NWC forts on Selkirk lands ordering them to evacuate their posts within six months. That was too much. At their annual council meeting in the Great Hall at Fort William, the Nor'Westers pledged to force the colony out of existence, first by weakening it with efforts to persuade the settlers to desert, and later by inciting the Indians and Métis against any who remained. As a third step, Miles Macdonell was to be arrested on charges of illegal seizure of pemmican and sent to Montreal for trial, leaving the survivors leaderless. The partner placed in charge of these tactics was Duncan Cameron, a veteran harasser of the HBC, who arrived at Red River

A utopian view of the Red River Colony, as sketched in 1817

resplendent in the scarlet uniform of a British army major, complete with epaulettes and dangling sword. That bit of theatre, with hints that he held the King's Commission, cowed the settlers whenever he arrived at their farms, accompanied by a restless retinue of Métis on wild-eyed horses, offering free transport and land in the balmy acreage of Lower and Upper Canada. (One of his aides-de-camp was Cuthbert Grant, wearing the uniform of an ensign in the Voyageurs Corps that had fought in the War of 1812.) Cameron's appeals, phrased in the Gaelic so dear to the settlers, often did the trick. His propaganda was aided by the nocturnal visits of hooting Métis firing shots in the air, riding over crops and occasionally burning a barn. Among the most active participants in these nightly missions was Grant, now clearly in charge of his people, convincing the Métis that they were the true lords of this rich soil and that their freedom depended on defying the settlers' legal pretence to ownership of the Red River Valley. From a camp at Frog Plain commanding a broad reach of the Red River, he participated in several shoot-outs, stealing the remaining settlers' implements and torching their houses. By summer's end of 1815, all but thirteen families had abandoned Red River, and their one cannon had been removed from Fort Douglas and mounted at Fort Gibraltar. Hoping to avert bloodshed, Macdonell surrendered to Cameron at the NWC fort and was promptly spirited away, first to Fort William and then to Montreal.

Disoriented and unprotected, the remaining straggle of settlers retreated by boat to temporary quarters near the north end of Lake Winnipeg. In the former colony, bands of Métis razed farms, burned buildings, attacked Fort Douglas and the small adjoining grist mill. The settlers' last sight of their utopia was smoke wafting in the soft summer breeze and the rampaging Métis spurring their buffalo-runners across the fields, trampling the precious wheat, barley and potatoes. For a while, the only sign of life left at the Selkirk Settlement was a salvage group of four Highlanders (John McLeod, Hugh McLean, Archibald Currie and James MacIntosh) who braved the taunts of the Métis to gather some of the abandoned tools and seed grains. Later, as if signalling some symbolic resurrection, the wheat, barley and potatoes did recover and ripen, unwatched, under the golden summer sun.

ON HIS WAY FROM MONTREAL to reopen the Athabasca Country trade, the HBC's Colin Robertson had by chance met the Red River refugees and persuaded them to return just in time to harvest the crops. That autumn another group of Scottish immigrants arrived, led by Robert Semple, the colony's new governor. Semple was a Boston-born Loyalist and popular travel writer whose innocence of cunning was matched by his overburden of self-importance. His commission provided dramatic proof of the Nor'Westers' and Métis's contention that the Selkirk Settlement was little more than an agency of the HBC, since he had been simultaneously appointed the colony's new governor and chief of the Company's Northern and Southern departments. That fall and winter, Colin Robertson took it upon himself to woo the Métis. A rogue with rusty sideburns and a long nose that swung around menacingly like a compass needle, Robertson was six feet tall and not afraid of any man's shadow. He had gained well-deserved notoriety as a scrapper but never uttered an oath stronger than "Oh for the love of beaver!" The Don

Robert Semple

Quixote of the Fur Country, he was one of the few traders who had read most of Shakespeare's works and could recite the main soliloquies. He had spent much of his energy—both in the Northwest and during his visits to England—trying to persuade the Bay men to drop their "slow, jog-trot manner" and adopt more of what he called "the glittering pomposity" of the Nor'Westers.

Robertson's entreaties to the Métis to remain neutral in the confrontation between the two fur companies worked mainly because Cuthbert Grant was not in residence at Red River, having moved to Qu'Appelle to be with the beloved Bethsy, as he called his wife, Elizabeth. Without him, there was no strong spokesman as a focus for their pride and heritage. On March 17, 1816, when Robertson attacked and temporarily captured Gibraltar, the NWC stronghold, and arrested Duncan Cameron, none of the Métis joined in the fort's defence. Inside Cameron's desk Robertson found documentary evidence that the Nor'Westers intended to engineer the final destruction of Selkirk's settlement that summer.

Robertson left the colony early in June, warning Semple to prepare for war. On the very day of his departure, the impulsive Semple ordered that the captured Fort Gibraltar be demolished. Some of the logs from its ramparts were rafted downstream to Fort Douglas, and whatever couldn't be moved was set ablaze. The Métis gathered in sullen clusters to watch the NWC stronghold burning. "The sight of the great fort in flames was too much," wrote Marjorie Wilkins Campbell, for "soon the fire which had been smouldering in every one of them also burst into flame. To each the destruction of the North West Company post was a warning of what might happen to his own small home. Like a prairie fire, news of the destruction of Fort Gibraltar raced from post to post, and from camp to camp wherever Métis and Indians gathered to hunt buffalo. The ancient war spirit of their Indian mothers, augmented by many a strain of fighting French and Highland Scots paternity, urged them to defend their existence; and the Nor'Westers were no longer in any mood to enforce restraint."

Here was the final, unforgivable act. Led by Cuthbert Grant, recently promoted by the NWC to be their "Captain-General," the Métis unfurled the New Nation's flag (blue with a horizontal figure 8 on its fly), cleaned their guns and waited.

Some friendly Saulteaux tried to warn Semple of the incipient dangers, but he would not listen. He did order one of his subordinates, the hard-drinking Lieutenant Ener Holte, late of the Swedish Navy,*

---

*Exactly how an alcoholic Swedish naval officer came to be stationed in the middle of the Canadian prairies at this crucial juncture is unclear.

to arm the cannon on the colony's schooner. The thirty-five-foot keel-boat, brought in from Norway House, was anchored at the mouth of the Red River to intercept incoming NWC canoes. In the tradition of his service, Holte saluted and delivered himself of a Nelsonian pledge: "I will be in my proper glory and will give the N.W. scoundrels a drubbing if I can!"

The target of Cuthbert Grant's first attack was the HBC installation at Brandon House, then commanded by Peter Fidler. After plundering the fort, Grant gathered his troops and, taking his orders from a group of Nor'Westers recently arrived from Fort William, decided to run Semple's blockade at the Red River junction. He had with him sixty-two men, most of them done up in war paint. Thus began the assault on Red River. This was no longer an informal bunching of malcontents out to make trouble; this was an army on the march.

INSIDE FORT DOUGLAS, Governor Semple had just received word of danger. Moustouche Boutino, a Métis who was on friendly terms with the settlers because Dr James White, the colony's doctor, had treated his recent wound, had arrived to warn that Grant and his armed band were on their way to capture the fort. The governor ignored the warning even when, late in the afternoon of June 19, 1816, a lookout spotted the advancing troops.

Still convinced that diplomacy might win the day, Semple decided to meet these marauders and read them a proclamation forbidding Métis to commit acts of violence against the colony. He ordered Lieutenant Holte and Captain John Rogers of the Royal Engineers, who was serving as his second-in-command, to round up two dozen men to accompany him. Asked whether they should take the fort's three-pound field-piece with them, Semple replied that it would not be necessary: his only intention was to discover what the intruders wanted.

Grant and his mounted men had reached a cluster of trees known locally as Seven Oaks. The two groups met there in the early twilight of the late spring day. The Métis halted in half-moon formation. Semple and his men advanced in single file. And then all grew quiet—a silence more intense than the absence of noise, with even the sweet sounds of nature temporarily stilled. A horse snorted. The Métis, reinforced by new arrivals at the edges of their formation, began to tighten their half-circle, pressing Semple's irregulars towards the river bank. Grant signalled one of his subalterns, a Métis named François Firmin Boucher, to order the governor and his men to lay down their arms or they would be shot. As Boucher urged his horse forward, Grant covered Semple with his gun. The stilted dialogue that followed caught the supercharged tensions of the moment:

"What do you want?" asked Boucher.

"What do *you* want?" demanded the affronted governor.

"We want our fort," was the spitting reply.

"Well, *go* to your fort!" Semple snapped back.

"Why have you destroyed our fort? You damned rascal!"

No Métis was going to call him, Governor of Rupert's Land, a rascal. Semple shouted something like "Scoundrel? Do *you* tell me so?" and made a grab for the stock of Boucher's gun while seizing the reins of his horse.

Cuthbert Grant pulled the trigger, wounding Semple in the thigh, and that shot set off the slaughter. Lieutenant Holte was the first to die. As if pulled by an invisible string, the Métis slid down behind their horses and levelled their guns across the animals' backs, while the Fort Douglas contingent milled in confusion around Semple to see if he was badly hurt. They were thus exposed to the full fury of the Métis cross-fire, and they began to die, returning random fire as best they could. When the Métis threw themselves on the ground to reload, the Semple survivors thought they had all been felled and with a cheer threw their hats in the air. Before those hats had landed, another multiple blast resounded. Rogers, the Royal Engineer, charged the Métis with his bayonet and was halted in his tracks, dying on his knees.

Within fifteen minutes, Semple had been killed by a Métis named François Deschamps, who placed his gun against the governor's chest and pulled the trigger. Twenty of his men lay dead at Seven Oaks.* Only one of the Métis had been killed and only one prisoner taken—John Pritchard, an NWC deserter now in Selkirk's service, who feigned death, then begged for mercy, and was used by Grant to deliver a surrender demand to Fort Douglas. The settlement gave in without resistance, terminating the Selkirk Settlement for the second time in two years as its inhabitants departed once again to their temporary shelters at the north end of Lake Winnipeg.

But the day's horror was not yet done. At Seven Oaks, the bodies of

---

*A plaque at the site of Seven Oaks (near Main Street and Rupertsland Avenue in the north end of modern-day Winnipeg) commemorates that encounter's victims: Robert Semple, James White, John Rogers, Laurence C. Wilkinson, Ener Holte, Alex McLean, Duncan McNaughton, Duncan McDonell, George Mackenzie, James Bruin, Daniel Donovan, Brian Gilligan, John Mihier, James Gardiner, Pat Maroony, James Moore, Sr., James Moore, Jr., Donald Sutherland, Adam Sutherland, Henry Sinclair and Reginald Green.

the dead were stripped and dismembered in an orgy of mutilation.* The best summing up of that chilling encounter is by Don McLean of the Gabriel Dumont Institute: "The nameless, faceless directors of the Hudson's Bay Company had placed the Highland Scots and Irish labourers into the mouth of a loaded gun; the Métis hunters, dupes of the North West Company, joyfully pulled the trigger."

THOSE FIFTEEN MINUTES AT SEVEN OAKS changed everything. No longer a commercial contest with the occasional skirmish and post-burning, the struggle between the Nor'Westers and Bay men had turned into a guerrilla war, fought along a four-thousand-mile front with unreliable troops and scheming generals. The Northwest became a land to flee across, as leaders of both sides gradually realized victory was impossible. Success would be determined by survival.

What changed most was that for the first time in the long rivalry between the two companies, the fur trade itself had become subordinate

---

*Many of the Métis and Indians involved were later to meet violent deaths. Historian Alexander Ross listed some of these strange coincidences: François Deschamps, who killed Semple, suddenly dropped dead while crossing a river near his home at Pembina a few weeks after the encounter; Ka-tee-tea-goose, one of the Indians at the affair, was scalped shortly afterwards by Gros Ventres near Brandon; Wa-ge-tan-me was struck by lightning; François Deschamps, Jr., was stabbed to death by a comrade, his wife was shot and killed and his children were burned to death near Fort Union on the Missouri River; La Grosse Tête was shot and killed by an Indian firing between the fence pickets of a trading post on the Missouri; Coutonahais suddenly dropped dead while dancing at a party at Grand Forks; Battosh was shot dead by an unknown hand in the Red River Colony; Lavigne drowned while crossing the Red River near Netley Creek; Frazer was run through with a sword by a French officer; Baptiste Morralle, in a drunken squabble on the Missouri River, was thrown into a fire and burned to death by his companions; La Certe died drunk on the high road along the Mississippi; Joseph Truttier was wounded by a gunshot and spent the rest of his life disabled in the Red River Colony; J. Baptiste Latour died a miserable death from infection; Duplicis was skewered by a wooden fork as he jumped from a haystack at Fort Carlton on the Saskatchewan River; J. Baptiste Parisien was shot dead by an unknown hand while running buffalo on the Pembina plains; Toussaint Voudre lost an arm by accident and was disabled for life at the Red River Colony; François Gardupie was shot and scalped in a fray with the Sioux on the banks of the Missouri; Bourassin was killed on the Saskatchewan River in mysterious circumstances; Louison Vallé was put to death by a band of Sioux on the Pembina plains; Ignace McKay was found dead on the public road at White Horse Plains; Thomas McKay died of intemperance at the Columbia River; Cha-ma-tan froze to death on the Pembina plains; and Ne-de-goose-ojeb-wan was gored to death by a buffalo during a hunt.

to their struggle for supremacy. No restraint or discipline was applied to the trapping of the beaver (even their sucklings were being skinned), to the distribution of rum and brandy (any excess was permissible) or to the tactics used in pillaging competitors' forts (at one point forty-two murder charges had been sworn out against Nor'Westers). Because the social contract had been so blatantly flouted, Lord Bathurst, the British colonial secretary, moved to appoint a commission to investigate the mass murders, and the Governor-in-Chief of Canada issued a royal proclamation on May 1, 1817, in the name of the Prince Regent, against "open warfare in the Indian Territories."*

Selkirk himself had meanwhile returned to Lower Canada during the autumn of 1815 to introduce Lady Selkirk to Montreal society. He hired a lawyer named Samuel Gale to protect his interests and had discussions about the fur trade with the NWC's William McGillivray. After preliminary negotiating postures, Selkirk was handed an astonishing proposal: the two companies should merge for a trial period of seven years, with the Montrealers supplying two-thirds of the goods and capital (and receiving two-thirds of the profits) while the Hudson's Bay Company retained the balance as a junior partner. The scheme was turned down because of the proportions being demanded and the NWC's reluctance to recognize the validity of the HBC charter, but the idea of amalgamation had been broached.

Having requested and been denied an official military escort for his intended inspection journey to Red River, Selkirk recruited instead four officers and a hundred members of the de Meuron and de Wattville regiments—Swiss, German and Middle European mercenaries who, after fighting in the Napoleonic battles, had been detoured to Malta and brought to Canada during the War of 1812. They accepted Selkirk's offer of free land at Red River in return for military service as it might be required, and the expedition moved west. Selkirk had himself sworn in as a justice of the peace, hired a hundred voyageurs, arranged for the canoes, and set off; he planned to bypass Fort William, hoping to reach his troubled settlement without provoking the Nor'Westers. He left Montreal in mid-June of 1816, and it was at Sault Ste Marie that news of the Seven Oaks killings reached his party. At this point Selkirk's tuberculosis was so far advanced that his accompanying physician, Dr John Allan, hesitated to pass on the gruesome details. But when Selkirk heard the facts, he vowed to lead his mercenary band against the very

---

*Even the weather was out of sorts: 1816 became known as "the year without a summer." At the time of Seven Oaks, snow fell as far south as 42° north and remained on the ground for as long as five days; Quebec City recorded below-freezing daytime temperatures.

Jean, Countess of Selkirk

heart of the villainous Montrealers' enterprise by capturing their great depot at Fort William.

On August 12, 1816, after most of the winterers had departed westward, Selkirk's armed flotilla swept out of Lake Superior and set up camp on the bank opposite the fort's main gate. Selkirk soon learned that William McGillivray himself was among the fifteen senior Montreal partners in residence and charged him with treason, conspiracy, and being an accessory to murder.

Hardly able to credit the outrageous message from Selkirk's emissary, McGillivray, accompanied by two of his senior lieutenants, Dr John McLoughlin and Kenneth McKenzie, decided to humour his visitors and pay what he imagined would be a routine courtesy call on this crazed aristocrat who seemed unaware of who ruled these woods. Selkirk promptly had the trio arrested. McGillivray submitted to the indignities, whispering loudly enough to be heard that it really was a dishonour to be fooled by this "piddling lord." Selkirk then ordered one of his assistants, John McNab, late of the Glengarry Fencibles, to arrest the twelve other partners still known to be at Fort William. McNab later remembered the ensuing events as follows: "We landed, and proceeded to the gate, as before, where several of the proprietors were standing and a number of men (their servants) and many Indians were assembled. The warrant was served on two of the gentlemen, but, on approaching the third, resistance was actually made, and a declaration uttered, that no further submission would be given to the execution of my duty, till Mister M'Gillivray was given up. In consequence I was nearly shut out of the fort by attempts to close one leaf of the gates.... At this moment I expressed the necessity of support to Captain D'Orsonnens [the de Meuron commander], who with much alacrity, aided by several of his men, instantly rushed in, and prevented the gate from being closed.... They ran forward, and, in a moment, took possession of two small cannons that were placed in the court within the gate."

The partners were herded into the Great Hall. They stood there beneath the bust of their patron saint, Simon McTavish, not quite sure whether to laugh or cry at the antics of this wearisome and apparently deranged Scottish earl. But Selkirk was in no mood to be gentle with anyone representing the North West Company. As far as he was concerned, these vicious woodsmen had murdered twenty-one of his people, and he was determined to "cut up by the roots one of the most abominable combinations that was ever suffered to exist in the British Dominions." He ordered the detainees to produce their papers, hoping to find evidence proving they had been responsible for ordering Cuthbert

Grant's attack. But weakened by his illness and the day's excitement, Selkirk could not continue the interrogation. He impounded the documents and had seals placed on their containers, naïvely admonishing these "agents of infamy" not to touch the files until next morning.

Barely was he out the door on his way to rest at his camp across from the fort when the Nor'Westers began to scurry around frantically gathering up the documents by the armload, pitching them into the oversized stove of the Great Hall's kitchen. All night the papers burned, shooting sparks into the starlit sky. "The news of Seven Oaks," John Morgan Gray, the best of the Selkirk historians, has speculated, "meant much more guilt than most were prepared to shoulder. The group seems to have behaved as if morality were a matter of being found out; judged on this basis, they were guilty of a great wrong." That night, the Nor'Westers stealthily placed guns in hidden caches on the property for a possible attack on the Selkirk camp.

Alexander Fraser, the NWC blacksmith who had spent such a pungent eternity in the fort's privy-like prison, deserted the next morning, crossed over to the enemy camp, and told Selkirk about the bonfire of documents and the hidden arms. The guns were soon discovered and confiscated, and a careful search of the partners' premises turned up an overlooked fragment of incriminating evidence in the form of a list of the rewards presented by the NWC to the Métis who had participated at Seven Oaks. After a desultory attempt to interrogate the Nor'Westers, Selkirk sent them back to Montreal under guard, with only one partner, a weak-kneed boozer named Daniel McKenzie, staying behind. The departing partners suspected him of being a turncoat, and as they were being pushed into the canoes, Kenneth McKenzie (no relation) whispered to Daniel McKenzie: "If ever I am acquitted [of murder], I'll blow out your brains!" (The threat was never carried out because Kenneth McKenzie and eight others were drowned on Lake Superior during the return trip to Montreal.)

Realizing that his ravaged colony at Red River could not hope to feed his accompanying army, Selkirk decided to winter at Fort William. He moved into the partners' suites adjoining the Great Hall and, walking about that alien fort, felt a long way from the elegant mansion at St Mary's Isle. His only consolation during that dreary winter was the correspondence he received from his beloved wife, Jean, in Montreal. "Everything in your expedition turns out for the best," she reported, cheerfully putting the best face on the situation, "and last of all the great armada, with all the warrants and constables, partners, clerks, Iroquois and guns and Congreve rockets, melts away and disappears, and a little canoe comes dropping in now and then, and one after

*During his illegal occupation of Fort William, Lord Selkirk
drew these two sketches, the upper one showing the front gates of the fort
as seen through the window that appears in the lower drawing.*

another of the partners return to Montreal looking very foolish, while all the world are laughing at them."

Using some fairly dubious tactics, Selkirk persuaded the faltering Daniel McKenzie to approve sale of the fort's food stores for £3,000, then dispatched his mercenaries westward to recapture Fort Douglas. This they accomplished in a surprise night attack without firing a shot, rushing the fort under the cloud-concealed moon and scaling its walls using pre-cut tree branches. The victorious troops captured several other NWC outposts, notifying the settlers who had scattered north towards Lake Winnipeg after the Seven Oaks débâcle that they could return to their land. By June they were joined by Lord Selkirk himself. Here at last, more than half a decade after he had first dreamed of providing a sanctuary for his beleaguered crofters, Selkirk was able to see for himself the hardship they had faced and the small promise their situation held out to them. Seized by the feverish exhilaration of his disease and the infectious beauty of the prairie summer, he walked among his people like a kilted messiah, granting freedom from further land payments to some two dozen of his most deserving disciples.*

By early autumn, knowing that he must deal with the barrage of charges and countercharges stemming from his illegal occupation of Fort William, Lord Selkirk returned eastward to face the uneven scales of Canadian justice.

THE TURMOIL AT RED RIVER had galvanized the Hudson's Bay Company into unaccustomed activity. Since the survival of the colony continued to menace the NWC's supply lines, this was the moment for the HBC to strike at Athabasca itself, the heart of the northwestern fur trade. Because that distant territory clearly lay beyond Prince Rupert's 1670 charter, the Nor'Westers had long regarded its fur-rich stretches as their own.

Selkirk's vivid exploits had demonstrated the vulnerability of the Montreal traders and instilled in the HBC officers and servants renewed vitality and pride of place. They felt ready at last to challenge their rivals in their home territory. Besides, a recent analysis of returns by

---

*They were James Sutherland, Alexander McBeath, John McBeath, John McLean, Alexander McLean, Martin Jordan, Hugh McLean, John Bannerman, Alexander Sutherland, William Sutherland, Jeremiah Sutherland, Angus Matheson, Alexander Polson, Alexander Matheson, John Matheson, Donald McKay, George McKay, William McKay, Robert McKay, William Bannerman, George Ross, Alexander Murray and John Flett. Selkirk also granted some free land for a new church.

individual posts had yielded the unexpected information that even those stations most fiercely competing with the NWC for a share of the catch were showing higher profits than the peaceful but fur-poor forts around Hudson Bay.

During the five years after Seven Oaks, the continent-wide rivalry between the NWC and HBC was nowhere contested more bitterly than within the Athabasca Country. Here the last violent clashes between the two companies determined the outcome of their protracted quarrel.

Athabasca became the Culloden of the fur-trade wars.

Infuriated by Selkirk's capture of Fort William, the Nor'Westers immediately seized the five tiny posts the Bay men had established in Athabasca during their tentative 1815 foray. That expedition, origi-nally led by Colin Robertson, who broke away to help lead the settlers back to Red River, ended in disaster. Command was assumed by John Clarke, a thirty-four-year-old Montrealer with the nasty habit of flicking specks of gunpowder into his opponents' eyes. He had served a decade in Athabasca as a clerk with the NWC, leaving it to join Astor's Pacific Fur Company, and had come within a hair's breadth of being scalped after he hanged an Indian for stealing a silver goblet in the Spokane River country and was attacked by the victim's brothers seeking revenge. He returned to Montreal, where Robertson hired him, mainly for his fighting ways. Nicknamed "Bon Garçon," Clarke loved swinging the diamond-studded cane given to him by John Jacob Astor—especially in the thick of a fight.

Clarke had launched the Company's return to Athabasca by build-ing Fort Wedderburn on Potato Island, right across the channel from the Nor'Westers' headquarters at Fort Chipewyan. It was moved when Samuel Black, the NWC bully who had so thoroughly tormented Peter Fidler, drew a line in the sand and dared any Bay man to cross it. Three did and were "fatally pricked in the body." Clarke constructed several other small trading outlets on Great Slave Lake and along the Athabasca River. Then he took fifty canoemen up the Peace to establish the Company's presence there. He carried no supplies, hoping to catch enough game along the way to keep them alive, but the Nor'Westers chased the animals from his route and threatened any Indians willing to help feed them. The embargo worked so well that sixteen Bay men eventually starved to death, bringing the Company's seasonal death toll in Athabasca to nineteen, close to the Seven Oaks total. By the time Clarke and his desperate survivors stumbled back to Fort Wedderburn, all the HBC posts had been captured and Black arrested the Bay men for theft. (Some Nor'Westers had planted small quantities of pemmican in the path of the starving men, and it was this food, which they had gobbled down, that provided the excuse for the arrests.) They were allowed to depart only when they took an oath to stay away from Athabasca for another two years. By the summer of 1818, the Athabasca venture had cost the HBC three dozen lives and £50,000. Yet the Company was barely able to retain one tiny fishing camp in the area.

Realizing that only a massive assault could turn the tide, the HBC commissioned Colin Robertson to lead an attack brigade of nearly two hundred armed men into the disputed territory. The flotilla was equipped to Robertson's extravagant tastes, with plenty of buffalo tongues and kegs of Madeira. "The lady with the ring in her nose is now holding a plum cake and with her delicate brown fingers is picking out the fruit," reads an enigmatic entry in the journal of his voyage west.

His determination (and Madeira) quickly proved effective in attracting the Indians; within weeks of his arrival, Robertson had restored Fort Wedderburn and was trading with four dozen Indian chiefs who had previously been loyal NWC customers. The Montrealers called in reinforcements, led by Simon McGillivray, Jr., the Mixed Blood son of that company's reigning grandee. But the day-to-day harassment was, as usual, left to the malevolent Samuel Black—though sometimes with mixed results. "Black the Nor'Wester is now in his glory leading his bullies," Robertson noted. "Every evening they come over to our fort in a body, calling on our men to come out and fight pitched battles. One of their hair-pulling bullies got his challenge accepted and an unmerciful thrashing to boot from a little Frenchman of ours—Boucher. . . . Our men are in high spirits. The Indians have regained confidence in us and boldly leave the Nor'Westers every day for the Hudson's Bay."

Then, on October 11, 1818, while Robertson was outside the HBC fort reading the funeral service for one of his men who had been drowned in a fishing accident, Black, accompanied by the young McGillivray, seized him at gunpoint and bundled him off into Fort Chipewyan. Robertson's diary vividly described his arrival inside the enemy camp: "Landing, I dashed for their Indian Hall and at once . . . called on the Indians, representing that the cowardly attack was an effort to reduce *them* to slavery; but Black rushed up to stop me. Seizing a fork on the hall table I kept the vagabond at bay. I loaded him with every abuse and evil name I could think of, then to the Indians: 'Do not abandon the Hudson's Bay on this account! There are brave men at our fort to protect you! That fellow was not brave enough to *seize* me; he *stole* me, and he would now rob you of your hunt if it were not for the young men I have left in my fort. Tell Clarke not to be discouraged. We will be revenged for this, but not like wolves prowling in the bushes. We will capture them as we captured them at Fort William, with the sun shining on our faces.' At this moment, the Indian chief came up and squeezing my hand, whispered, 'Never mind, white man, we are your friends.'"

Robertson was soon pinioned and confined inside a small shack next to the fort's privy. There he stayed for eight months. Apart from not having access to his Madeira (or ladies with rings in their noses), Robertson's main worry was that his troops had been left leaderless. Daily operational decisions had to be made to maintain and expand the HBC's beachhead. He persuaded his captors to allow him a keg of Madeira and devised a complex but literate code for sending out messages: "I began to arrange all our Posts, Gentlemen, Principal men with those of opponents in numbers, then all the monosyllables on which the meaning of a sentence rested, also sentences intimately connected with the affairs of this country ... untill my numerical figures amounted to 600. When the cypher was completed, the most difficult task remained, to convey the copy to my friends at Fort Wedderburn, which was effected by means of a small keg. First the cypher was written on long strips of paper having a pretty large margin on each side, then rolled up so tight as not to admit water beyond the first fold. Both ends were sealed; this finished, I perforated a small hole with a bent gun worm close by the bung, through which I passed a piece of holland twine, then hooked it up from the bunghole and attached to the end of the twine my Packet, repassed it through the bunghole, drew it up from the small aperture close to the stave of the keg. To fasten the letter I drove a small peg into the hole, over which I rubbed a little dust, that neither the hole nor the sound of paper could either be seen or heard."

That may have been ingenious, but there was no way for Robertson to inform his men how to locate the message—or to tell them there was a message there at all. The empty barrel was flushed out and put into storage without being examined for its hidden contents. Robertson next requested his personal volume of Shakespeare. He devised another code by annotating *King Henry IV*, and his men soon caught on. But he was eventually spotted scribbling out the coded instructions, and the Nor'Westers decided to pack him off to Montreal, still under arrest. On the way, the canoe in which he was travelling overturned in the rapids at Île-à-la-Crosse. No foul play was ever proved, but two of his NWC guards, both expert swimmers, mysteriously drowned, while a smiling Robertson bobbed out of the stream and waded to shore. He made his escape when they were passing Cumberland House by the simple stratagem of asking, on his word of honour, if he could step inside the HBC fort to say his farewells. Once inside, Robertson had the

William Williams, Governor of Rupert's Land

doors bolted and refused to come out. The angry Nor'Westers continued on without him.

In one of the messages he had managed to sneak past his guards during his imprisonment, Robertson had warned William Williams, the HBC's recently appointed Governor of Rupert's Land, that the Nor'West partners would probably be returning to Montreal loaded with furs and could be ambushed at Grand Rapids, the rendezvous near the juncture of the Saskatchewan River and Lake Winnipeg. This was a popular resting place for the NWC brigades heading east; while the voyageurs took the canoes through the rapids, the *bourgeois* could stroll down the portage trail swapping the tittle-tattle of the fur trade.

Williams, who had received the Robertson dispatch, was a new breed within the HBC's service. Because the Company was now engaged in war as much as in trade, it hired this truculent former East India Company sea captain to look after its affairs. As successor to the murdered Robert Semple, Williams required little motivation for the fight with the Nor'Westers. On the strength of Robertson's message, he left Red River aboard the colony's armed schooner with a detachment of twenty de Meuron soldiers, cannon loaded, and a sheaf of warrants. As the annual NWC brigades arrived at Grand Rapids, the accompanying *bourgeois* were apprehended by Williams's troopers. The trap netted five senior NWC partners, including Benjamin Frobisher, the son of an NWC founder. Each was spirited away to a temporary enclosure on a nearby mosquito-infested island. One of the partners, pleading a call of nature, disappeared in the bush. To thwart pursuit, he left a suicide note claiming he had drowned himself by jumping into the lake with a stone tied around his neck. That was not a brilliant improvisation because the lake at that point was only two feet deep, but no one went after him. The remaining prisoners were eventually taken to York Factory, but Frobisher, who escaped along the way, starved to death trying to get to the NWC post at Moose Lake.

The Grand Rapids affair (and the fact that along with the partners and the loads of fur, Williams captured documents incriminating the NWC in Seven Oaks and other incidents) seriously undermined the Montrealers' morale. "Our opponents," Robertson wrote to Williams, "have lowered their tone; they talk now of conducting their business on amicable principles. . . .The North West Company's servants have the old story of a junction in their heads . . . whatever their prospects may be, there is certainly a great change in their conduct; the affair of the Grand Rapids has not so much as produced a menace."

But the North West Company was not done yet. Outraged by Williams's behaviour, its partners promptly issued warrants for his arrest. During the following summer the Nor'Westers mounted their own ambush at Grand Rapids and were highly pleased when Colin Robertson, on his way east from a winter on the Peace River, fell into their hands. He was arrested and kept under close guard in preparation for shipment to Lower Canada.

Well aware that there were more warrants papering Montreal courtrooms calling for his arrest as soon as he stuck a foot into Lower Canada's jurisdiction, Robertson again mustered his natural talent for survival. He escaped by flinging a dish of biscuits in his captors' faces during a meal break and, after holding them off with a stolen gun, made a run for the U.S. border. Once in New York, he immediately sailed for London to participate in the negotiations rumoured to be leading towards amalgamation of the two fur-trading concerns. On his way across the Atlantic aboard the Western Ocean packet *Albion*, he found himself in the company of two arch-enemies, the NWC partners Dr John McLoughlin and Angus Bethune. As the ship was about to land and the passengers were lining up to sign chits for gratuities to the dining-room stewards, Robertson and his friend, a Roman Catholic monsignor, happened to be standing between Bethune and McLoughlin.

"Come, [Abbé]," chided the irrepressible Robertson, "put down your name; I don't like to sign between two North Westers."

"Never mind, Mr R.," came the reply. "Remember our Saviour was crucified between two thieves."

AT THE END OF HIS RED RIVER VISIT, Lord Selkirk, Robertson's hero, was struggling to extricate himself from the final and most traumatic episode of his Canadian misadventures. He had spent most of the interval since returning from that brief happy summer at Red River in stultifying courtrooms, first in Montreal and later at York (Toronto), pursuing the 170 charges he had preferred against the NWC and its partners. Characteristically, he entertained no doubts about their total guilt and his utter innocence, yet he was being forced to justify his own actions.

Selkirk spent, besides his time and the last of his energies, £100,000 out of his own pocket (and another £40,000 out of the HBC's) defending himself against a bewildering array of mischievously worded charges, trying to extract justice from a variety of contemptuous witnesses, corrupt judges and a colonial administration barely able to suppress its fervent wish to be rid of him. "If we are to be poor for three generations," the faithful Lady Selkirk wrote to her husband, "we must absolutely fight this out." Although the grand juries returned eighteen true bills against various NWC partners and associates, only one man was found guilty, and his sentence was never carried out. Not a single marksman from Seven Oaks was convicted of anything. Cuthbert Grant jumped bail and escaped by canoe back to Red River. All charges against him were later quietly dropped.

The bewildered Selkirk at first blamed the fact that most of the magistrates sitting in judgment over him were either associates or relatives of the Nor'Westers he had brought to trial, but other weighty factors were in play. Selkirk's quixotic idealism threatened the sanctity of Lower Canada's social and economic establishment, dominated as it was by the partners and agents of the North West Company. When the trial's venue was moved to York, Selkirk encountered the equally vehement opposition of the Family Compact, that self-perpetuating oligarchy of reactionary judges, bureaucrats, politicians and theologians. These unyielding clusters of privilege were abetted in their anti-Selkirk efforts by the Colonial Office in London. Its secretary, Lord Bathurst, and more particularly his influential Under-Secretary, Henry

Goulburn, openly favoured the NWC's claims, though both men tended to dismiss the feud as a routine commercial quarrel. One of Bathurst's dispatches, accidentally included in a sheaf of papers delivered to Selkirk, urged the attorney-general of Quebec to ensure the Scottish lord's prosecution and conviction.

Selkirk's London supporters took his case directly to the British prime minister, Lord Liverpool, hoping to bypass Bathurst and Goulburn, but the Family Compact's influence turned out to be too powerful. John Strachan, the rector of York's St James's Church, who also served on the colony's executive council and could claim the moral leadership of his circle, attacked Selkirk for being an irresponsible land speculator who had lured the poor Scottish settlers into a "polar region where even the minimal agriculture economy was impossible" since Red River was fit only as "a residence for uncivilized man." Strachan and his supporters saw in Selkirk's progressive views and colonial ambitions a threat to their own positions, believing that even if successful, the Red River Settlement "was so completely isolated from British civilization that, in the interests of mere survival, it would gravitate toward the southern republic." At the end of the lengthy litigation, Selkirk was assessed £2,000 for damages while not a single Nor'Wester was fined or imprisoned. Not waiting to hear this ludicrous verdict announced, Selkirk had returned to London, his health finally broken. "For pity's sake," Lady Selkirk begged her husband, "make up your mind to let the wicked flourish; they cannot take from us our own good conscience, and if we do not allow them to bereave us of health and tranquility, we can be happy without the right being proved."

But it was too late. His chronic consumption, seriously aggravated by the courtroom ordeal, had left her husband hardly able to breathe without retching blood. Following the practice of the day, doctors applied leeches to reduce his blood flow, but that only weakened him further. When his brother-in-law, James Wedderburn, objected that funds from his dangerously reduced estate were still flowing into Red River, Selkirk dictated a reply that might have been his valedictory: ". . . my honour is at stake in the contest with the North West Company and in the support of the settlement at Red River. Till that can be said to be fairly out of danger and till the infamous falsehoods of the North West Company are finally and fully exposed, expenses must be incurred which it is utterly impossible to avoid. . . . It is to be hoped that this state of things will soon be over, and when that is the case I will retire to St Mary's Isle and live on sixpence a day till I am out of debt."

His time was running out. Selkirk's illness was claiming so much of him that in September 1819 he was forced to leave England for the drier climate of Pau in the Pyrenees foothills of southwestern France, accompanied only by his doctor and the stalwart Jean. In the half-year remaining to him, Selkirk tried to reconstruct how the tumble of events had soured his generously motivated Red River venture.

He died on the morning of April 8, 1820, not yet forty-nine. Because Pau had no Protestant cemetery, he was buried in a plot at nearby Orthez, between two oak trees.* Probates revealed that his once-magnificent estate consisted of £160,000 in debts plus the bankrupt kingdom on the Red River.†

It had been Lord Selkirk's fate to juggle desirable ends with destructive means, and he had not always made the right judgments. Perhaps his greatest sin was that he believed too fervently in his difficult cause, and thus lost the objectivity to create the ameliorating circumstances that might have allowed it to flourish. In the end, he lost everything except the self-esteem that mattered more to him than life itself.

---

*The grave was restored in the mid-1970s through the efforts of Hubert G. Mayes of the French department at the University of Winnipeg.

†There was one more group expedition to Red River in this period organized by Captain Rudolf de May, one of Selkirk's former de Meuron subordinates. It numbered 165, mainly Swiss pastry cooks and clockmakers plus their families. Promised free land on which to grow bananas and other tropical fruits, they left Basle in 1821. After being barged down the Rhine to Rotterdam, they crossed the Atlantic and entered Hudson Strait, where they were trapped by ice. The young people danced on the icebergs by the light of the aurora borealis, but their parents may have begun to realize this was not citrus country.

II EMPIRE TRIUMPHANT

Rapids on the French River along George Simpson's route from Lachine to Fort Wedderburn

CHAPTER 8

A MARRIAGE OF GREAT CONVENIENCE

*The moribund feudalism of the HBC took on the rampaging
capitalism of the Nor'Westers and, in the process of winning,
transformed itself into a mirror image of the enterprise it was
trying to defeat.*

THE DEATH OF LORD SELKIRK and, only twenty-seven days earlier, the
passing of the bravest of his opponents, Sir Alexander Mackenzie,
combined to exert a liberating influence on the battle-weary fur trade.
Andrew Colvile, Selkirk's powerful brother-in-law, in his mourning
expressed the family's true feeling about the late earl's obsession when
he revealed to a friend how vehemently he wished the Red River
Colony "had been in the Red Sea twenty years ago."

Colvile and his fellow Committeemen were confronting a profound
problem in continuity of their operational management. William Williams, the overseas governor, was under threat of imminent arrest
following his allegedly illegal detention of the Nor'West partners at
Grand Rapids and, with no successor in place, the HBC's affairs in
Rupert's Land were in danger of floundering. The vacuum developed
at a particularly crucial moment. The tragedy at Seven Oaks had
temporarily exhausted the furies at Red River, but a final duel between
the two companies was in the wind, and, according to the prevailing
consensus, whichever side won the Athabasca fur-trade war would dictate
the terms of any amalgamation agreement. That required forceful leadership. To provide it, the HBC's governors made a startling decision.

Instead of entrusting the Company's overseas operations to yet
another professional warrior like Williams, or to a fur-trade veteran
such as Colin Robertson, they chose a youthful novice named George

Simpson. The selection of a man still in his early thirties, with no claim to background in the complexities of the fur trade or any demonstrable qualifications to assume such burdensome responsibilities, was audacious —and probably the most important appointment ever made by the London board. Simpson was chosen because he had not been tainted by the internecine warfare of the previous decade, because he could bring to the Company the counting-house mentality it needed, and because he carried himself with that manner of self-confident authority the circumstances demanded. That he had been London-trained but Scottish-bred was also significant, for if the HBC were to emerge dominant, it would have to deal quickly and effectively with the proud Highlanders in charge of the North West operations.

Simpson's heritage definitely had deep Highland roots, but its exact path was less certain. Born out of wedlock to an unknown mother and George, the wastrel son of a Calvinist minister named Thomas Simpson, he was raised mainly by his aunt Mary at Dingwall, a small port town in the northern county of Ross-shire. Having shown some promise in mathematics at the local school, the young George was offered an apprenticeship by his uncle, Geddes Mackenzie Simpson, at his London sugar brokerage, Graham & Simpson, a partnership that expanded in 1812 to include Andrew Colvile. Not much is known about the dozen years he spent in the counting-house at 73 Tower Street, but Simpson impressed his seniors enough that his nomination by Colvile in 1820 as locum tenens Governor-in-Chief of Rupert's Land and possible replacement for the embattled Williams was unanimously accepted. Thus began a lifelong alliance between two men of different backgrounds and generations. "To you," Simpson later wrote to Colvile in a confidential communication from York Factory, "I feel that I am solely indebted for my advancement in Life, and it will ever be my study that your good offices have not been misapplied." In other letters, Simpson confided some of his innermost and sometimes heretical thoughts to his mentor, such as his harsh dictum that "an enlightened Indian is good for nothing." Throughout his stewardship with the HBC, Simpson enjoyed the unparalleled benefit of having a man who felt (and acted) like a surrogate father dominating the Company's London head office. (Colvile served as the Hudson's Bay Company's Deputy Governor from 1839 to 1852 and Governor from 1852 to 1856.)

Ordered to leave for his new posting at only five days' notice, Simpson was entrusted by Colonial Secretary Lord Bathurst with two important messages. Identically worded, they required that both the NWC and the HBC strictly obey the 1817 proclamation that had been issued by Sir John Sherbrooke, Governor-in-Chief of Canada, requiring

The young George Simpson

that all parties in the fur-trade war refrain from hostilities and restore captured goods and forts. Simpson was charged with passing on this official communiqué to his own troops and specifically instructed to deliver its duplicate to the Nor'Westers' stronghold at Fort William.

On the thirty-one-day passage from Liverpool to New York, Simpson observed with interest the women passengers ("precious nymphs [who] were confined to their cabins the greater part of the Voyage, and if the Steward's [word] be true, solaced themselves with copious brandy draughts to the downfall of the House of Bourbon") and became irritated with the arrogance of his American dining companions, haughtily assuring them that "John Bull merely wanted the opportunity to chastise them for their presumption and insolence."

His trek from New York to Montreal was a portent of many journeys to come. Spring thaw had turned the rutted trail between the two cities into a syrupy quagmire, slowing ordinary travellers to a careful crawl. Not Simpson. He rented an open horse-drawn cart and drove himself nineteen hours at a stretch, enduring with impatience at least fifty spills, to arrive at the southern shore of the St Lawrence in only seven days. Dodging floating ice and other debris of spring breakup, he was among the first across the river that season.

As an HBC executive obviously on the rise, Simpson was immediately accepted by Montreal society, and fêted by the resident mavens of Mount Royal as an important personage, and a vibrant bachelor to boot. The lightning transformation from counting-house clerk to courted celebrity at the nightly masquerade balls and theatre parties tilted his equilibrium. With unbridled bravado that sounded like a declamation more fit for *Boy's Own Annual*, Simpson wrote to friends in England vowing that once in the wilderness he was determined to "show my Governors that I am not wanting of courage if necessity puts it to the test. There is a possibility that I may be obstructed in my route as the N.W.Coy, a band of unprincipled Lawless Marauders, stick at nothing however desperate to gain their ends; I am however armed to the teeth, will sell my Life if in danger as dear as possible and never allow a North-Wester come within reach of my rifle, if flint steel and bullet can keep him off."

His introduction to the North American hinterland was the journey along the voyageur route from Lachine to Fort William. While delivering Lord Bathurst's admonition he was able to assess first hand the Nor'Westers' impressive physical facilities and size up their fragile morale. The fort was in a state of high excitement because just a few days before, a party of sixty armed men had been dispatched to harass the HBC at Grand Rapids. Camouflaging his intense curiosity and behaving as if he were little more than an interested traveller, Simpson left the fort and headed north. At Norway House, he met Governor Williams, and while delivering the HBC's copy of Lord Bathurst's message was apprised of the recent capture by the Nor'Westers of the elusive Colin Robertson. That left the Athabasca brigade, due to depart at any moment for that distant territory, without a leader. Having little choice, Williams accepted Simpson's offer to take charge himself.

The transformation in the tyro was instantaneous. Not only did Simpson assume the partisan abhorrence of the Nor'Westers that had become every local Bay man's second nature but he quickly entered into the spirit of the occasion by taking a country wife.* Placed in command of a grand brigade of sixty-eight, Simpson issued each man a musket, a

---

*On his way west, Simpson camped at Cedar Lake on the lower Saskatchewan close to the memorial erected for Benjamin Frobisher, the Nor'Wester who had starved to death attempting to escape HBC detainment at York Factory. The tablet bearing the inscription was missing after Simpson left the area, and the Nor'Westers never forgave him that act of desecration.

bayonet and ten rounds, pledging to "maintain the rights and interests of the Honourable Company, and defend their property and our persons" by every means within his power. He set a gruelling pace, shaking his voyageurs awake long before sun-up and keeping them at their paddles well past sundown. By September 20, 1820, having passed several NWC canoe flotillas en route, he arrived at tiny Fort Wedderburn, a mile and a half from the imposing quarters of the Nor'Westers at Fort Chipewyan. His Athabasca adventure was about to begin.

SIMPSON PLUNGED INTO THE FRACAS of the Athabasca fur trade with boyish enthusiasm. Observing his rush to learn, some of the curious Nor'Westers mistook his eagerness as the mark of a naïve and ineffective novice. "Mr Simpson, a gentleman from England, last Spring . . . being a stranger and reputed a gentlemanly man, will not create much alarm," was the initial assessment of the NWC clerk Willard Wentzel.

His assessment of Simpson could not have been more wrong. The "gentleman from England" quickly proved to be just as determined as the redoubtable Colin Robertson had been—but unlike that worthy renegade, he managed to garner the respect of the Nor'Westers while beating them at their own game. His first task was to gain the respect of his own crew. This he achieved by absorbing their knowledge and experience, then assimilating it into his own very precise set of priorities. Instead of concentrating only on enlarging the post's fur catch (which he increased that first season by £726), he imposed severe cost-cutting measures (saving £1,054), which he labelled "OEconomy." Fish, not meat, became the daily ration, and every customary extravagance was curtailed or eliminated. Local Indians, for example, had kept the price of sled dogs high by eating them after every trapping season, forcing the HBC to purchase new teams each autumn. Simpson ordered that bitches be kept in Company kennels with an eye to producing his own cut-rate dog teams. (His experiment to domesticate the passing caribou as handy beasts of burden was a dismal failure.) He travelled eighteen hours a day, poking his Scottish nose into every aspect of his territory's commerce, busily imposing his version of proper discipline. Whenever flattery or reprimands failed, he had no hesitation about placing defiant underlings on short rations or handcuffing them until they came around to his way of doing things. When one of his post managers, Joseph Greill at Berens House, was found to be drinking too much, Simpson sent him a pointed rebuke: "It has been hinted that you are rather addicted to the Bottle; this report I cannot believe until it is substantiated on conclusive evidence, and I trust your conduct will

Fort Chipewyan on Lake Athabasca

be so perfectly correct as to challenge the strictest examination; a Drunkard you are aware is an object of contempt even in the eyes of the Savage race with whom we have to deal in this country."

Despite such advice, at this novice stage of his experience in the fur trade, Simpson's method of dealing with Indian traders was to ply them with liquor—and cajole them with words. He boasted in his journal about being in top form during one of his orations to a group of elders ("they look upon me as the greatest man who ever came into the Country"), cynically noting that "a little rum operates like a charm on the Indians. They cannot resist the temptation, and if the bait is properly managed, every skin may be had from them." With remarkable success he persuaded at least some local natives that he could cast magic spells and that he would *know* if they surreptitiously traded pelts with the Nor'Westers. He gained this reputation in part by casting a spell on the unfaithful wife of a Chipewyan who had eloped with a fellow tribesman. When she was recaptured, the husband demanded guarantees from Simpson that she would remain faithful during the forthcoming winter. Simpson assured him that she would be—and she was. (He achieved this bit of magic by taking the lady aside and assuring her she would turn into a dog if she strayed.)

Samuel Black, the veteran nemesis of every HBC trader in the Athabasca since Peter Fidler, soon appeared on the scene, and when they met again on the Pacific Coast three years later, Simpson noted in his journal: "Black could at first scarcely look me in the face, he recollected my Athabasca Campaign, and never will forget the terrors in which he was kept that Winter. . . ." The rivalry between the two companies in that faraway outpost of empire centred on the line of demarcation between two particular forts. The Nor'Westers had built a small raised blockhouse on Potato Island only a dozen yards from Fort Wedderburn's main gate and had angled its back window so that they could observe the comings and goings at the rival post, taking careful note of which Indians were trading there in order to harass them later. Simpson decided to erect a palisade that would shield his post from the Nor'Westers' spies. When his men were set to the task, the younger Simon McGillivray, son of the NWC's chief executive officer and then in command at the company's Fort Chipewyan, decided to retaliate by moving the NWC blockhouse even closer to the HBC fort. As soon as Simpson noticed that McGillivray had trespassed twenty-four inches inside HBC property, he stormed out to protest.

His Scottish terrier, Boxer, waddled across the dividing line, and Simpson, pretending exasperation, ostentatiously ordered the animal to repent its sins: "Come here, Boxer, you do not seem to be aware that you are committing a trespass!"

"We have no intention to molest your dog, Sir," retorted the proud McGillivray.

"Nor shall you his Master with impunity," Simpson hissed over his shoulder, and walked away.

Shortly afterwards, Amable Grignon, an HBC clerk, arrived at Fort Wedderburn, bearing a Montreal warrant for McGillivray's arrest that he grandly intended to exercise. Simpson read it over, suspecting that it was really meant for the elder Simon McGillivray (his Athabasca opponent's uncle) but limited himself to an unctuous promise that he would, of course, never think of interfering with the law of the land. Promising Grignon armed support if McGillivray resisted arrest, Simpson pushed two loaded pistols under his belt and called out: "Mr. McGillivray, I should be glad to have some further explanation with you on the subject of this boundary line."

As soon as McGillivray was within grabbing distance, Grignon collared him, shouting: "I arrest you in the King's name!"

The Nor'Westers were furious, threatening reprisal, but the armed Bay men stared them down. McGillivray was beside himself, cursing in turn Grignon, Simpson, the HBC and his fate. He reluctantly settled into his imprisonment, made easier when Simpson allowed his country wife and children to join him. The Nor'Wester was permitted to dispatch letters back to his post, but they were censored by Simpson, who was not averse to enclosing his own version of the events being described before forwarding them. He often supped with McGillivray, hoping to learn more about the Nor'Westers' mentality, and the two men grew, if not friendly, at least mutually respectful. Then, early on the morning of December 4, 1820, while Simpson was falling asleep, congratulating himself on having "got to the blind side of these Argus-eyed Gentlemen," McGillivray made his escape.

Simpson had been abruptly alerted at one o'clock by a guard who reported a great commotion at Chipewyan and that Nor'Westers bearing torches were running back and forth from the NWC fort to their bastion outside Wedderburn. Expecting an attack, Simpson roused his men, armed them and fortified them against the bitter cold with a dram of rum. But no attack came. It seemed to be a false alarm. An HBC interpreter named Joseph Bouché was sent on a secret mission to reconnoitre the enemy bastion.

"The English are up," he heard one of the armed Nor'Westers whisper to his partner.

"Yes," was the reply, "and one of them is now listening close to the Port Hole of the Bastion."

Bouché tiptoed home. Fast.

Simpson served another dram of rum and ordered the post fiddler to lead the assembled troops in a reel to keep toes from frostbite. But nothing seemed to be happening. Next morning, when a tired duo of HBC servants went to the lake for a bucket of water, an NWC clerk inquired mischievously whether Mr McGillivray had danced to the music he had heard coming from the HBC fort. When he received a confused reply, the Nor'Wester exploded with the gleeful news that Simon McGillivray was back among his friends at Fort Chipewyan.

McGillivray's country wife at first insisted that he had vanished up the chimney, but it was too small for human passage. She then confessed that McGillivray had bribed his HBC guard, a former de Meuron soldier named Johann Knipe, and had escaped disguised in her nightgown. The recalcitrant guard was interrogated in English, French, Italian and Spanish—languages he had previously been heard speaking —but all he would say was that unfortunately he could answer questions only in German, which happened to be beyond the range of everyone else at the post.

That bloodless episode was more of an occasion for laughter than reprisal, and for the next seven months the traders of both companies concentrated on gathering pelts from the Indians. Simpson left Wedderburn on May 23, satisfied that his personal star was in the ascendancy. He had, in effect, won his field commission, having dealt effectively with Indians as well as Nor'Westers and, of more importance, having won the confidence of his own men. When he arrived at the foot of Grand Rapids a month after leaving Athabasca, rumours reached him that the London negotiations between the HBC and the North West Company had been completed. Instead of being elated that he was now heir apparent to their combined operations, he complained that the Nor'Westers could have been beaten in the field, presumably by himself, in a fight to the finish.

IN MOST WARS based on differing value systems, opposing armies tend to dissolve into composites of the causes driving the individuals who fight them. But if hostilities continue long enough, and if they are being waged in a region isolated from outside influences, the participants tend to become interchangeable, employing one another's strategies and ethics and gradually losing sight of the aggressive impulses that originally stirred them. The feud between the North West and Hudson's Bay companies was no exception. Professor K.G. Davies compared their struggle to the English Civil War that drove Charles I from the throne: "On one side were the North Westers, the Cavaliers of the fur trade, flamboyant, extravagant, preoccupied with the 'honor of the concern,' dashing but defeated. On the other side stood the Hudson's Bay Company, the Roundheads: sober, persistent, concerned above all with their own rightness and winning the charge at the end of the day." Davies made the telling observation that the Roundheads beat the Cavaliers "not by being right but with better cavalry; and as the competition for the fur trade proceeded to climax, the Hudson's Bay Company threw some of its traditions overboard and fought the Nor'Westers with their own weapons."

This was what decided the bitter contest's outcome: the moribund feudalism of the HBC took on the rampaging capitalism of the Nor'Westers and, in the process of winning, transformed itself into a mirror image of the enterprise it was trying to defeat. The HBC lost most of the battles but won the war, partly because it eventually recruited the quality Highlanders previously sought out only by the North West Company, and because it adopted the Montrealers' field tactics. With the escalation of hostilities, the London Governors expanded their inland facilities and incurred expenses with a momentum that had hitherto been the exclusive trait of their opponents. They also established an aggressive policy to drive their rivals out of competing fur areas by deliberately setting their barter exchange rates with the Indians at levels ruinous to the Nor'Westers. As the long fight wore on, the once-quiescent royally chartered company emerged in the guise of a band of merry adventurers determined to surpass the derring-do of the Montrealers. "By 1821," concluded Davies, "the Hudson's Bay Company had become an organization the North Westers could join."

Conversely, the Montrealers were ultimately defeated because the metamorphosis did not, indeed *could* not, work both ways. Their British rivals could adopt the Nor'Westers' methods and ethics simply by altering their strategy and personnel, never losing the sustaining advantages of access to long-term credit from the Bank of England, a supportive bulwark of highly placed politicians willing to respect the monopoly bestowed by an antique charter—and, above all, a management committee whose members, awash in alternative sources of income, could afford to skip dividends and, if necessary, help tide the Company over with personal loans. These were privileges more easily envied than copied. Even at the height of its power, when the North West Company's domain extended from Lachine to the Arctic, over to the Pacific and back again, it lacked secure long-term financing. When the grandiloquent Marquis, Simon McTavish, had been in charge, no British prime minister would lift a finger in response to his entreaties that the HBC's monopolistic privileges be abrogated. Neither McTavish nor his successors enjoyed any significant claims to British money at a time when most investment funds emanated from London.

To outsiders observing the pride and the arrogance, the fight and the flux of the Nor'Westers the impression was one of omnipotence; the reality was much closer to frailty. The same qualities that had made the North West Company great inexorably drove it to the wall.

The Montrealers could never overcome the handicap of their pathetically overextended transportation network—the interminable and prohibitively expensive hauls in and out of the heart of the continent in which the HBC was already entrenched. Here was ultimate proof of the animating notion propounded by those original caesars of the wilderness, Pierre-Esprit Radisson and Médard Chouart, Sieur Des Groseilliers. They had first ventured into this wild country in 1659 and then sped to England to persuade the British they should bypass the French fur buyers on the St Lawrence by trading directly into Hudson Bay.* The commercial enterprise spawned by this daring idea had survived pitched battles and every kind of challenge—frost and starvation, parliamentary plots and coupon-clipping neglect—through the simple stratagem of keeping a keen and undistracted eye on profit margins and fiscal stability. Because the Governors and Committeemen were not owners, they could afford the tight-fisted policy of keeping dividends at a minimum—or not paying any at all (as between 1691 and 1717, or 1809 and 1815) even while maintaining reserves and credit facilities against the inevitable down cycles in fur sales.

The North West Company operated on the opposite principle. Because its managers were also its proprietors and their extravagant style of living depended on their dividend income, ever larger payouts *had* to be made, year after year, and that drained most of the NWC's working capital at the end of each season. Maintaining this quixotic situation required multiplying profits annually, which in turn demanded constant territorial expansion. But once the Nor'Westers' march westward was stopped short by the Pacific Ocean, and once the Bay men began to respond with their own brand of vigour and trading panache, the Montreal company faltered. And having faltered, it cracked.

By the autumn of 1820, the companies had reached an impasse that a merger alone could resolve. Beyond their commercial imperatives was the pressure being applied by the Colonial Office for an extension of British influence across the North American continent. Such an objective could be achieved only by a single, financially sound trading company.

---

*See *Company of Adventurers*, Chapter 4.

That was why, not long after Selkirk's death, Lord Bathurst assured representatives of both firms that if they could hammer out the financial details, he would sponsor an Act of Parliament approving their amalgamation. And there was a further inducement to the union promised by the Colonial Secretary: the new, amalgamated company would be granted exclusive trading privileges west of Rupert's Land all the way to the Pacific Coast. To promote such a merger, Bathurst enlisted one of Britain's most successful power brokers, the enigmatic Edward ("Bear") Ellice.

A PARAGON OF MERCANTILE PRAGMATISM, Ellice had earned his nickname, not out of any predisposition to ferocity, but because, like a bear, he was considered well greased in his dealings with friend and foe alike. He appeared playful—his cherry-cheerful face grooved by the laugh lines of inner self-confidence—but he could be deadly if crossed. Although he was a pivotal influence within the governing Whig party for half a century, Ellice's main function was to act as an honest or at least expedient broker between men, ideas and money on both sides of the Atlantic. Not much happened within Britain's governing circles without his unofficial blessing, which led an associate, the diarist Charles Greville, to label him as a "very serviceable man." Ellice had more wit than irony, acted as everybody's mercenary and nobody's intimate, and was grand master of that penchant peculiar to the British upper classes for looking down one's nose while talking through it. His capacity for moral suasion prompted more than occasional resentment, such as this complaint from the acid-tongued social observer Emily Eden to a member of the Clarendon set: "I never could see why the Bear was not only allowed to assume that he advised and managed and thwarted and assisted all the distinguished men of the age, but was also the authority by which every assertion was to be met and refuted. 'The Bear says the country does not like it'; 'the Bear thinks Lord Grey a fool'; 'the Bear says the Queen is unpopular,' etc., etc."

As well as depending on his innate sense of occasion, his solid background and family fortune, Ellice used his two marriages to advance his social standing—the first, to Lady Hannah Althea Bettesworth, the widow of a gallant sea captain and sister of Prime Minister Earl Grey; the second, to Anne Amelia, Dowager Countess of Leicester and daughter of the 4th Earl of Albemarle. Elected Whig member of Parliament for Coventry in 1818, Ellice served as an MP for all but four of the next forty-five years, rising to Secretary of the Treasury and, later, Secretary of War in the Earl Grey government.

Almost as if he led a double life, the Bear was at the same time deeply involved in the Canadian fur trade. His father owned the quarter-million-acre Beauharnois seigneury in the St Lawrence Valley, his two brothers had served in the Canadian Fencibles and he had himself spent much time in Montreal, becoming a senior NWC partner as well as the company's chief London agent. Five months before Selkirk's death, Ellice had approached the HBC's Andrew Colvile, offering to buy the consumptive earl's shares at his own valuation, while pledging to maintain all existing obligations to the Red River settlers. Selkirk dismissed this option as "all bunkum," but it wasn't. What was left unmentioned in this flash exchange—although Ellice and Colvile may or may not have been aware of it—was that the North West Company's bargaining status had been grievously undermined at its 1820 conclave in Fort William—and that it would soon either have to buy out the HBC or be bought out instead.

By this time, two generations of NWC winterers had expended their lives fighting the Hudson's Bay Company. Even though the Royal Adventurers seemed to stumble from one defeat to the next, they were often cowed but never vanquished. Although the Nor'Westers had endured all the hardships of the trade, they had not become its chief beneficiaries. Now they were being asked to renew for another decade the partnership agreements signed in 1802 and 1804 that were due to expire on November 30, 1822. Aware that their company was in perilous financial condition, worried about their own futures and those of their country families, weary of the violence and debauchery that had become such easy riders of the fur trade, they took out their resentment on the Montreal agents. William McGillivray tried to hold the mutineers in check, but for the first time in the NWC's reign, the country partners would not listen. Instead, eighteen of the most senior winterers voted their proxies to two of their own, Dr John McLoughlin and Angus Bethune, charging them with a momentous mission: to sign a peace treaty with the Hudson's Bay Company—in effect, replacing McGillivray and his London agent with the Royal Adventurers. It was this rebellion of the wintering partners more than any other catalyst that swung the ensuing negotiations in favour of the HBC.

Of the duo chosen for this delicate task, one lacked impressive credentials. Angus Bethune, who had been marginally involved in the NWC's takeover at Astoria and was briefly in the company's China trade, was later characterized by George Simpson as "a very poor creature, vain, self sufficient and trifling, who makes his own comfort his principal study; possessing little Nerve and no decision in anything: of a snarling vindictive disposition, and neither liked nor respected by

Edward ("Bear") Ellice,
a major player in the amalgamation
agreement . . . and William and
Simon McGillivray, who stood up for
the Nor'Westers

his associates, Servants or Indians. His Services would be overpaid by the victuals himself and Family consume."

But McLoughlin was a man of very different composition. The son of an Irish subsistence farmer at Rivière-du-Loup in Lower Canada, he completed his Quebec City medical studies in 1803 and became a Nor'Wester under unusual circumstances. McLoughlin and his lady friend, the story goes, had been walking up a narrow Quebec street when they came to a plank lying across a puddle. Midway across, they met a drunken British officer in full regalia who was trying to balance himself as if he were walking a tightrope. He rudely ordered them off the narrow plank. When they refused to move, the officer shoved McLoughlin's companion into the mud. With a yelp of fury, the young doctor picked up the startled redcoat, lifted him over his head and threw him into the mud face down—epaulettes, sword, shiny boots and all. McLoughlin left town that evening to join the NWC. After a brief apprenticeship in the fur trade, he was appointed resident physician at Fort William during the summer rendezvous. Named a partner in 1814 and the next year placed in charge of the fort, McLoughlin quickly emerged as a natural leader.

Bent on their covert mission to London on behalf of the winterers, McLoughlin and Bethune first stopped in Montreal, where they contacted Samuel Gale, Selkirk's legal counsel, to inquire whether the HBC might enter into a new partnership with them. Gale expeditiously communicated the offer to London, so that Andrew Colvile was aware of the Nor'Westers' internal dissension before serious and more public negotiations on amalgamation got under way. The arrival in London of the two hot-eyed wintering partners accelerated everyone's timetable. Ellice and the McGillivrays knew this was the last available moment

if they wanted the HBC to negotiate with them instead of with the envoys of the mutineers. Colvile, who had been charged with formulating the union on behalf of the HBC, also realized there would never be a better time to strike a deal.

As they moved among the classical Georgian façades of the City, London's financial district, the negotiators were determined to hammer out an agreement, figuratively looking over their shoulders at the looming shadows of Dr McLoughlin and his sidekick, who were prepared to throw the winterers' support to whichever side would give them most leverage. Ellice chaired the crucial discussions, but it was Simon McGillivray and Colvile who cut the final deal. "Simon Pure and I," exulted the triumphant Bay Committeeman, "settled it in a quarter of an hour.... We retain the power of management and get paid for our stolen goods, and they kiss the rod."

The twelve-thousand-word contract, signed March 26, 1821, was a complex and sophisticated document, but its effect was simple. When one of the NWC winterers finished reading it, he looked up from its convoluted clauses and exclaimed: "Amalgamation? This isn't amalgamation but submersion. We are drowned men!" Certainly, the HBC's seventy-seven shareholders had little to complain about—particularly since their stock moved up 100 percent on news of the merger.

The contract was to be effective for twenty-one years, commencing in 1821; its multiple provisions provided for amalgamation of the Hudson's Bay Company and North West Company assets, each valued at £200,000. The new business would clearly be operating under the HBC name and charter. A joint board established to advise on management of the fur trade included Ellice and Simon McGillivray, but it was dominated by Bay Committeemen, and the stock split guaranteed control by the HBC. Profits were to be divided into a hundred shares, with a block of twenty going to the HBC directors and the same size of holding going to the Montreal partners, five to the Selkirk estate and two and a half each to Ellice and McGillivray. Ten more were to be invested by the HBC as a floating reserve. The remaining forty shares were subdivided into eighty-five equal parts, two of which were dealt out to each Chief Factor in the reorganized Company, one to each Chief Trader and seven to eminent retirees. Because the new partners were chosen on the basis of ability rather than seniority, fifteen of the twenty-five Chief Factors selected were Nor'Westers, as were seventeen of the twenty-eight Chief Traders. "The union of the North West and Hudson's Bay companies created an enterprise of power unequalled in the history of the fur trade," concluded John S. Galbraith, the pre-eminent American scholar of British Empire history. "The resources, experience and business acumen of the Hudson's Bay Company blended with the energy of the Nor'Westers to give unusual vitality to the monopoly that came into being in 1821."

That monopoly was legally strengthened and geographically expanded by Lord Bathurst, as his promised reward for the merger, through an Act of Parliament passed on July 2, 1821. For an annual token payment of five shillings, the new organization was granted monopoly control, renewable in twenty-one years, over the whole of British North America except for the colonies already occupying the Atlantic shore and the St Lawrence–Lower Great Lakes area. The empire-sized grant extended the Company's territorial domain beyond Rupert's Land into Athabasca, across the Rocky and Coast mountains to the edge of the Pacific and well into the Oregon Country—although trading rights below the 49th parallel were held jointly with the Americans.* Sir Alexander Mackenzie's twenty-year-old dream of a transcontinental trading empire had finally come true.

Because the parliamentary grant was made jointly to the McGillivrays and Edward Ellice, as well as to "the Company of Adventurers of England Tradeing into Hudsons Bay," it seemed at least theoretically possible that a rival coalition of frustrated interests might find an opening to enter the trade. Ellice, who immediately upon the amalgamation

---

*To ensure order and good government, the Act's provisions included extension of the jurisdiction of Upper Canada's courts to the Pacific, and servants of the Company were commissioned as justices of the peace and charged with administering all but the most severe infractions of the law. The Act also recognized, for the first time, the parliamentary validity of the HBC's royal charter, since it specifically stated that none of its provisions should affect the existing rights of the Company of Adventurers.

had characteristically transmogrified himself into a rabidly loyal Bay man, feared that those Nor'West winterers who had been excluded from the new concern might be tempted to fight the grand coalition. In the interests of a peaceful changeover, the new HBC Committee made an unprecedented decision: it would send one of its British members on tour of the most important posts of its overseas territories. The candidate, selected mainly because he was the only bachelor on the board and any journey into "Indian Territory" was taken at the individual's own risk, was Nicholas Garry. A former Baltic timber merchant fluent in German, French and Russian, Garry was a sensitive soul, perfectly attuned to the touchy nature of his mission. He left London, accompanied by the two McGillivrays, only three days after the coalition agreement had been signed, bound for the crucial 1821 gathering of wintering partners at Fort William. After being appropriately lionized in Montreal, he was paddled to the head of Lake Superior, and vividly recorded his impressions along the way. "At the [foot] of this magnificent fall," he wrote about one nocturnal stopover, "we dined and a power of imagination and description might picture it in the most enchanting colours. Indeed to my feelings there is something very animating and inspiring in the life of a voyageur. In Nature's wilds all is independence, all your luxuries and comforts are within yourself and all that is pleasurable within your own minds; and after all this is happiness, if there is such a thing in the world; which no mortal can say. Indeed there is no reasoning unhappiness. Our whole life is spent on wishing for something which, when we acquire it, often becomes insipid and new objects and new views crowd upon the mind, producing dissatisfaction with the present and a longing or desire for something in the future."

For both Garry and William McGillivray, this would be more of a pilgrimage than mere passage through the wilderness. For the HBC Committeeman, whose health had never been robust, it was to be his last great adventure. Declared to be of unsound mind in 1835, he would spend the last twenty-one years of his life confined to an asylum. For McGillivray, it meant the end of his dream of empire. He had been transported this way for most of two decades, to be feasted and hailed at Fort William as king of all he surveyed, haranguing his freebooting battalions against the British intruders. Now, he was making his final journey to the scene of his former triumphs—if not physically a prisoner certainly feeling like one. The express canoe in which they were travelling arrived at the dock of Fort William just eighteen days after leaving Lachine, and it was Nicholas Garry, not one of the McGillivrays, who was lodged in the senior partner's quarters.

There was no dancing or coquetry in the Great Hall now. On July 10, the grim-faced winterers filed in to be told their fate. The reading of the documents of amalgamation was met with shouts of protest. Why should they surrender the territory they had fought so hard to claim? How could the McGillivrays have agreed to the substitution of York Factory on bleak Hudson Bay for this magnificent fort as the centre of the continent's fur trade? What about the men not specifically named in the Deed Poll that listed those Nor'Westers being retained by the new organization? Many good questions; not many good answers.

As the McGillivrays and winterers glared at one another in that one-sided debate, each group was aware of what the other was thinking: we could have struck a better deal if only we had remained united. It had been the mutiny, staged in this very place only thirteen months before, that had triggered the NWC's collapse. Then another thought began to dominate the gathering. As the dour farewells were exchanged and claimants set out to fill their new postings, they were struck by the chilly realization that they would never meet here again. Fort William's glory days as the great entrepôt of the Canadian fur trade were done.*

Setting off for York Factory via the Red River Settlement, Garry noted that he had never in his life left a place with less regret. But William McGillivray, in one final gesture of defiance, made a presentation to the fiercest of the HBC's enemies, Samuel Black. It was a ring, bearing the telling inscription: "To the most worthy of the Northwesters." His point made, McGillivray decided he was too exhausted spiritually to journey any farther with the victorious Bay executive and asked his brother Simon to go in his stead. He then sat down and wrote a long letter to his friend the Reverend John Strachan of muddy York, who had fought so hard against Lord Selkirk in the Upper Canadian courts. That epistle, penned in the ghostly confines of the Great Hall after his once-loyal legions had dispersed for the last time, was a touching valedictory not only for a man but for his time:

"I avail myself of the opportunity of Mr. Alexr McDonell going down by York, to tender you my devoirs.—I have been at this place since the 1st inst: settling a most important Business—the carrying

---

*Relegated to the status of an ordinary supply depot within the new HBC's trading system, Fort William lingered in a state of accelerating decay until it was closed in 1878. Five years later, the derelict structures were flattened to make way for the Canadian Pacific Railway's lakehead freight yard. The reconstruction carried out under the sponsorship of Ontario Premier John Robarts in the early 1970s has produced a thoroughly authentic monument to the early Canadian fur trade, seven miles upriver from the original site.

into effect the various Deeds and Covenants entered into on the part of the North West Company in London with the Hudson Bay Company; —these arrangements are happily completed, and I part with my old troops—to meet them no more in discussions on the Indian trade— this parting I confess does not cause me much regret—I have worked hard & honestly for them, and I am satisfied that I have at least done my duty. I have been an Agent or Director, since 1794—and Chief Superintendent since 1799, the management has not been easy, for we had too many storms to weather from without, and some derangement in the Household. But thank God! the whole is closed with honour— and the trade will be productive if well managed, after the Country shall have been restored to order, which it will require a couple of years to effect,—thus the Fur trade is forever lost to Canada! the Treaty of Ghent destroyed the Southern trade—still the Capital and exertions of a few individuals supported the Northern trade, under many disadvantages, against a Chartered Company, who brought their goods to the Indian Country at less than one half the Expense that ours cost us— but it would have been worse than folly, to have continued the contest further. We have made no submission—we met & negotiated on equal terms—and rating the N.W. Co. collectively—they hold now 55 out of 100 shares. . . . My own fortunes have been singular as connected with the N W Fur trade—I was the first English Clerk engaged in the Service of the N.W. Co., on its first Establishment in 1784, and I have put my Hand and Seal to the Instrument which closes its career—and name in 1821. . . ."

During a short stopover at Red River, Garry and Simon McGillivray noted that the colony was still clinging to existence, numbering 419 people, 221 of them the original Selkirk settlers. Along the way, at Slave Falls on the Winnipeg River, Garry had recorded another of his moody epiphanies. "Our dinner table," he scribbled in his journal about a particularly beautiful campsite, "was a hard rock, no table cloth could be cleaner, and the surrounding plants and beautiful flowers sweetening the board. Before us the waterfall, wild, romantic, bold. The River Winnipic here, impeded by mountainous rocks, appears to have found a passage through the rocks, and these, as if still disputing the power of water, show their heads, adding to the rude wildness of the scene, producing whirlpools, foam, loud noise, and crystal whiteness beautifully contrasted with the black pine. This again is softened by the freshness and rich foliage of the ash, maple, elm, red willow and occasionally the oak bringing to the mind England and all the delightful recollections this happy country produces, and showing in fact all the folly of my opening phantasy of a want of happiness in this life."

The meeting at Norway House* near the foot of Lake Winnipeg was even more crucial than that at Fort William for the new coalition because in its customary diplomatic wisdom, the company had allocated the most coveted assignments to the best of the Nor'Westers, and Garry would now have to convince the gathered traders that such an arrangement was worthwhile. This he achieved, mainly by making it clear that executive direction would remain firmly in HBC hands. The trading system was divided into a Southern Department based at Moose Factory, under the continuing stewardship of William Williams, and the much more significant Northern Department placed under the command of the newly promoted George Simpson. His mission successfully completed, Garry sailed back to England from York Factory aboard the *Prince of Wales*, noting in the final entry of his diary: "I was not insensible to the kind, flattering manner in which the gentlemen of York Fort took leave of me. . . . Thus has terminated my mission to Rupert's Land, the last gun fired from the Fort. . . . All parties satisfied except those who have sinister & sordid views."

THE HARD-WON TERMS OF AMALGAMATION stayed in place for barely three years. In 1824 the original profit-sharing agreement was abrogated and under the new arrangement the former NWC agency partners were

---

* So called because in 1814 eight Norwegian axemen had been brought in to cut a winter road to York Factory. Originally Lord Selkirk's idea, the mode of transport along a trail winding beside the Hayes River was to be large sleds drawn by reindeer. Parts of the road were completed, and the scheme was not entirely abandoned until the 1840s, but it was never used. With the downgrading of Fort William, Norway House became the main inland distribution depot and base camp for the Athabasca brigades. (Its original warehouse and powder magazine are still standing.) The post's best-remembered character is a Wesleyan minister named James Evans, stationed there in the 1840s. Realizing while he was at York Factory that local Cree would never better their circumstances unless they could read and write, he demanded that the HBC import a printing-press. But the Company, preferring to keep the Indians illiterate, refused to send him into the territory. Fed up with waiting, Evans taught himself metalworking, built a tin canoe and paddled up to Norway House, taking along a soldering iron to repair any punctures. Indians along the shore were awed by the spectacle and named his craft the "Island of Light." Once at his missionary post, he fashioned a printing-press. Using carved oak moulds, he cast type from melted musket balls and tea-chest foil. Natural fish oil mixed with soot was his ink, birchbark his paper, and an unused beaver-fur press his duplicating machine. He codified the Cree language into a syllabic alphabet with nine main symbols and laboriously produced a hundred copies of a hymn book that he bound in deerskin and distributed to local bands. His alphabet remains in

issued common stock instead.* They thus lost their votes and influence in the HBC's affairs and, worse, had to put up a bond of £50,000 to meet the many legal claims being made on their former partnership. Their financial affairs had reached crisis proportions. The McGillivrays' firm, which had been appointed the HBC's Montreal agency, was in such fiscal chaos that Thomas Thain, their accounting partner, who was also a vice-president of the Bank of Montreal, was spending all his time trying to balance the books. He finally gave up, locked the records in his private office, placed the key in his pocket and fled across the Atlantic to seek permanent and presumably more peaceful sanctuary at a Scottish insane asylum.

William McGillivray died suddenly on October 16, 1825, while on a visit to London, leaving instructions in his will that Simon satisfy the family's mounting debts. The surviving brother, who had been in England trying to raise money by selling his art collection, rushed back to Montreal, discovered the company's records in Thain's locked office and declared bankruptcy. The McGillivrays' creditors eventually received only ten shillings on the pound, and to make even that settlement possible, Ellice had to contribute £110,000. William McGillivray's daughters remained in London, living out their days in destitute circumstances, while the penniless Simon fled to Mexico, where he found employment as a "gold commissioner."

---

use today. Evans was eventually forced to leave his wilderness manse because of a sex scandal (being falsely accused of living immorally with a Cree woman) and the obdurate opposition of George Simpson. Once back in England, he was blackballed, and his name was not even included among the 167 Evanses listed in the *Dictionary of Welsh Biography*. When he died in 1846, his last recorded words were: "Heaven is as near England as Norway House."

*The occasion of the 1824 agreement was also used to straighten out the Company's accounts with royalty. Stock had originally been granted to the Duke of York, the HBC's second governor, who had become King James II of England in 1685. Dividends were paid only until 1764; after an 1812 claim for back payments by financial advisers to the royal household was disallowed, no further action was taken. An 1824 resolution of the HBC Committee placed the King's stock permanently in an unclaimed account.

Rumour persists that the royal family retains holdings in the Hudson's Bay Company. In a 1980 interview Lord Adeane, then financial adviser to Queen Elizabeth II, confirmed this fact to the author but refused to divulge details. The HBC's own registry of stockholders shows no entry for the royal family, but many shares are held in "street names" or through surrogates such as British merchant banks. Possibly the best clue to the true status of the monarch's shareholders was a brief exchange between Prince Philip and HBC Governor Don McGiverin during the 1977 Canadian royal tour. At a noisy reception in Winnipeg, Philip sidled over to McGiverin and whispered in his ear: "How are *we* doing?"

True to form, of all the Nor'West agents, only Edward Ellice prospered following the union. He gained a seat on the HBC's Committee after the 1824 reorganization and remained as one of its senior members until his death in 1863. The Bear became so influential within HBC affairs that in 1858, when Simpson suggested that trade goods be sent into Red River through St Paul, Minnesota, instead of via York Factory, approval of the current Governor and his Committee was contingent on consent of the seventy-five-year-old Ellice.

The so-called amalgamation, which had now been clearly revealed as the takeover it always was, launched the Hudson's Bay Company's golden age. By the summer of 1821, the HBC was chartering clipper ships to supply its newly won bases on the Columbia and farther up the Pacific Coast. "For another quarter of a century," noted the Canadian historian Chester Martin, "the commercial empire of Hudson Bay remained a marvel of lucrative fortune and efficiency."

Not so the empire on the St Lawrence. When McGillivray lamented that "the fur trade is forever lost to Canada," he had in mind the century-old route stretching from Montreal westward. Not only was Fort William downgraded and allowed to rot but the main artery of the fur trade—the voyageur trail to Lake Superior—was left largely unused, not to be revived for another sixty years, when parts of it were traversed by the Canadian Pacific Railway.

The North West Company, that defiant alliance of voyageurs and Highlanders whose audacity had established Canada's first indigenous national enterprise, vanished almost overnight. Instead of spawning dynasties, the NWC partners left their few heirs deep in debt, and the capricious castles at the foot of Mount Royal turned out to be only monuments to their self-indulgence. They had set down the matrix of a country and had been its uncrowned rulers but were brought down by overextending their reach. "The feudal state of Fort William," elegized Washington Irving, "is at an end; its council chamber is silent and desolate; its banquet-hall no longer echoes to the auld-world ditty; the lords of the lakes and the forests are all passed away."

Penetanguishene Harbour

Governor George Simpson on a tour of inspection

CHAPTER 9

THE BIRCHBARK NAPOLEON

A bastard by birth and by persuasion, George Simpson dominated the HBC during four crucial decades, the agent of a muscular corporate ethic that overwhelmed friend and foe alike.

THEY CAME FROM EVERY QUADRANT of the recently amalgamated Hudson's Bay empire. Deep in the summer of 1821, the triumphant traders of the Company of Adventurers and the vanquished wintering partners of the now-defunct North West Company, both freshly transformed into Chief Factors and Chief Traders of the newly created Northern Department of the HBC, converged on York Factory.

They were there to attend a banquet arranged by their untested governor, George Simpson. Most of the traders of the two recently warring concerns would be meeting face to face for the first time, although they might have seen each other previously while sighting down rifles and cannon.

As the brightly decorated express canoes rounded the final downstream curve of the Hayes River, the Nor'Westers caught their first glimpse of the three dozen whitewashed structures that made up the HBC's tidewater headquarters on Hudson Bay.* In the distance, beyond the hexagonal cupola of the great depot building, they could see the London supply ship riding impatiently on its anchor chain, apt symbol of the direct sea link so crucial to the Company's supremacy.

The paddlers and retinues of the various regional power barons gathered on York Factory's broad foreshore—Cree, Iroquois and Métis, serving different white masters but bound together by the brotherhood

---

*For a description and history of York Factory, see *Company of Adventurers*, pages xvi–xxiii.

of the rivers. They were soon tending bonfires, singing, arm-wrestling, setting off the occasional fireworks, drinking and playing cards long into the starry night, gradually melding into an amicable unit.

Inside the walls, there was as yet no parallel sociability. The two groups eyed each other with suspicion, the gaunt cast of their weather-ravaged faces and their self-conscious gestures reflecting the tensions of the occasion. Even though many of the former Nor'West winterers had retained command of the richest and most extensive fur districts—New Caledonia, Columbia, Athabasca and the Mackenzie River basin—they stood about glaring defensively at the Bay men who were taking over most of the fiercely defended Saskatchewan River posts. However favourable the transitional arrangements might be, the HBC men were now in charge, and the fact that this victory celebration was taking place on Hudson Bay rather than at Fort William underlined that galling fact. Among the banquet guests was John Tod,* a young HBC clerk whose notes provide eyewitness evidence of what happened after the dinner bell rang and the two groups filed into the mess hall. Conspicuously silent and looking appropriately grave, the assembled dinner guests initially showed not the slightest inclination to mix with those who had once been their enemies.

"Evidently uncertain how they would seat themselves at the table," the observant clerk reported, "I eyed them with close attention from a remote corner of the room, and to my mind the scene formed no bad representation of that incongruous animal seen by the King of Babylon in one of his dreams, one part iron, another of clay; though joined together [they] would not amalgamate, for the Nor'Westers in one compact body kept together and evidently had no inclination at first to mix with their old rivals in trade." It was George Simpson, appearing "all bows and smiles," who acted as social director and great conciliator, getting them to shake hands and even eliciting the occasional ghost of a smile from the dour Highland countenances. There were some highly awkward moments. A volatile old Nor'Wester named Allan McDonell found himself seated directly opposite his mortal foe, Alexander Kennedy, the HBC Chief Factor with whom he had crossed swords in a bloody duel only months before over control of the Swan River fur

---

*A native of Glasgow, Tod spent forty years with the HBC, in charge of several important northern and western outposts. When he left the service in 1849, he became the first person to choose Victoria as his retirement home and brought with him a teenage bride from Kamloops (his fourth wife) named Sophia Lolo, who gave birth to the last seven of his ten children. His one-time residence at Oak Bay is still reported to be haunted by the most assertive of his former spouses.

catches. "One of them," noted Tod, "still bore the marks of a cut on his face, the other it was said on some less conspicuous part of the body. I shall never forget the look of scorn and utter defiance with which they regarded each other the moment their eyes met. The Highlander's nostrils actually seemed to expand, he snorted, squirted, spat, not on the table, but between his legs and was as restless as if he had been seated on a hillock of ants; the other looked equally defiant, but less uneasy and upon the whole, more cool. I thought it fortunate that they were without arms . . . it seemed not improbable they might yet renew the combat, which probably was only prevented in time by a side movement from the upper end of the table, where sat that plausible and most accomplished gentleman Simon McGillivray who used to talk of the 'glorious uncertainty of the law' and the 'nullity of the H.B.C. Charter.' He, seeing the state of affairs near my quarter, sent a request couched in the most gracious terms to [McDonell] to be allowed to take wine with him, which bye the bye had to be repeated more than once before the latter could be induced to remove the glare of his fierce eye from the person of his adversary. . . . Kennedy too, by similar means, put in operation by one of his friends at hand, was also induced to adopt the appearance of peace and tranquility."

The lavish courses of venison pie, roast partridge, basted wild duck and grilled Arctic char washed down with generous refills of sherry and old port soon had their mellowing effect. The feast, so carefully choreographed by the wily Simpson, developed into a garrulous mutual admiration society. They began to compare notes, laughing at how they might have bested each other in this or that confrontation. By dawn both groups were swearing allegiance to one another—and to George Simpson, now their acknowledged leader.

A BASTARD BY BIRTH and by persuasion, George Simpson dominated the HBC during four crucial decades, the agent of a muscular corporate ethic that overwhelmed friend and foe alike. "To dare and dare again" might have been his motto—though his family coat of arms bore the enigmatic inscription, *Avis nutrior* ("I am fed by birds"). He was one of the few men who lived up to his own Napoleonic pretensions.

The Bonaparte tag was no mere historical allusion. Simpson had triumphed over the Nor'Westers in Athabasca by employing a battlefield dictum followed by the Corsican: One must never interfere with the enemy while he is in the process of destroying himself. He went on to rule an empire larger than any in Napoleon's most fanciful dreams. A painting of the French Emperor decorated the anteroom of Simpson's office. Like his idol, the wilderness autocrat laid claim to uncommon privilege that was nurtured by the obsequiousness of lieutenants in the field, deferring to his certitude. In height and bearing he even resembled the "Little Emperor."

Simpson's small, darting eyes betrayed the tensions of a setter constantly on point; his hair curled tightly against the back of his neck like fleece. John Henry Lefroy, who toured the Canadian Northwest in 1843–44 making magnetic observations for the British army, noted that Simpson was the toughest-looking man he had ever seen, "built upon the Egyptian model, height two diameters, or like one of those short, square massy pillars one sees in an old country church. . . . He is a fellow whom nothing will kill." His critics reviled George Simpson as a malevolent wraith—ruthless, chauvinistic and petty. Yet if the history of countries and great institutions flows from an interplay between character and circumstance, he was strictly the right man in exactly the right place at precisely the right time.

His style of buccaneering capitalism belonged less to an age than to a system. At a time when the Hudson's Bay Company's counterparts, the once-glorious East India Company, for example, were collapsing beneath administrative overloads, the HBC under Simpson's whip hand was transformed into an ornament of Empire. Its outriders carried the Union Jack (with its qualifying HB.C. initials in the fly) across the North American continent. While the early patriots of a nascent Canada in the old fiefdoms of the St Lawrence basin were struggling for responsible government, Simpson became an engine of manifest destiny, surging across the boundless reaches of his domain.

The most capable field marshal the HBC ever had, Simpson achieved the daunting task of re-establishing the Company's monopoly after four decades of fierce competition with the Nor'Westers. He did this by sending search-and-destroy teams of his most ruthless traders into the outer reaches of his empire with orders to eliminate putative rivals. The territories south and east of the Columbia River, which Simpson realized might one day be claimed by the United States, were trapped clean in a deliberate scorched-earth tactic meant to confound the American mountain men. Where encroachment by other activities, such as lumbering in the Ottawa Valley or fishing in the Great Lakes, already existed, the HBC launched itself into these enterprises, absorbing such sizeable deficits to capture the market that its opponents retreated in disarray. In the southern extremities of the HBC holdings, Simpson licensed independent trappers to carry their trade into the forests dominated by the American Fur Company, eventually forcing it to abandon the field. On the Pacific Coast, the Governor negotiated an agreement with the Russian-

American Company for trapping and maritime rights, displacing the Yanks and then the Russians themselves. When nothing else worked, the HBC distributed liquor on the frontiers of its territories to attract the Indian trade, although alcohol was gradually proscribed elsewhere.

To diversify the Company's holdings to the full, Simpson traded lumber, cranberries and frozen salmon with Hawaii, started the first factory farms on North America's West Coast and even sold ice to Californians. In the 1850s, when San Francisco's population was swollen by the Gold Rush and ice had to be shipped around Cape Horn, the HBC leased some of its glaciers in the northern Pacific to American entrepreneurs, who cut and shipped the ice south. It proved such a success for meat preservation that at one time six large ships were participating in the trade.

By protecting the flanks of his empire, Simpson was able to regenerate the HBC's fur monopoly inside the Rupert's Land boundaries, jealously guarding it from intruders. Except for the traffic in and out of the Red River Settlement, during Simpson's long reign few outsiders were allowed to visit his magic kingdom. Those who did receive permission were mostly artists bent on glorifying the Governor's deeds, members of the British aristocracy engaging in a spot of buffalo hunting, botanists and other natural scientists sent out on behalf of the Royal Society, or land surveyors confirming the full extent of the HBC's impressive holdings.

During Simpson's stewardship, the Company's dividends reached unprecedented levels, rising from 4 percent in 1824 to 10 percent the following year, 20 percent by 1828 and 25 percent a decade later. In the process, the Company's capitalization was increased from £103,950 to £400,000, yielding inordinate capital gains to its stockholders. "Simpson represented in purest distillation the zeal for efficiency which dominated the managers of British industrial life in the early nineteenth century," concluded John S. Galbraith, the Little Emperor's biographer. "He became a nearly perfect instrument of Company policies . . . preoccupied with the life of the Company with which he fully identified his own."

While it was certainly true that within the galaxy of his personal universe the Company meant everything, Simpson's psyche was more complicated than that. Like some red-headed magpie with quivering beak and glittery eye, he hoarded private grievances against anyone brave enough to question his iron will. He was a masterly politician, picking his surrogates and underlings with a view to advancing the Company's interests—and perpetuating the personality feuds that would leave him in place as the one indispensable presence. He played his associates off against one another and, like most charismatic leaders, maintained a luminous distance between himself and lesser men. He was so determined to retain this aura of mystery that even in 1841 when he was knighted and the editor of Dod's *Peerage, Baronetage and Knightage* requested the usual personal details required for publication, Sir George refused to supply anything beyond his name, position and address.*

The small arts of popularity found little place in Simpson's business make-up. He was in charge of a wilderness empire under siege by jealous competitors and would-be settlers; his officers were mostly Highland-bred Nor'Westers who regarded any form of corporate discipline as something good only for spayed weaklings. His servants—and few occupied territories have ever been held by such a thinly spread garrison—were mostly stolid Orkneymen, Métis on short-term contracts and ambitious but inexperienced apprentice clerks. To parlay such a corporal's guard into an effective work and occupation force was a magnificent achievement. Simpson drove himself and his men mercilessly, expecting flawless performance and hardly ever taking into account human fallibility. His audacity, his compulsive work habits and the brute force of his manner when he was riled left lesser men gasping for forgiveness, but it was seldom forthcoming. He had little patience with underlings brazen enough to suggest that considerations other than the maximization of profit (such as the welfare of the Indians) might govern the conduct of the fur trade. "It had occurred to me," he wrote to one would-be emancipator, his quill pen dripping with sarcasm, "that philanthropy is not the exclusive object of our visits to these Northern regions." On another occasion, justifying a harsh personnel decision, he noted that "nine out of ten men are captivated with the phantom, Popularity"—and pointedly added that he was not one of them.

His own cousin Thomas Simpson, who left a brilliant academic career at King's College in Aberdeen to join the HBC and later became a

---

*The precise date of Simpson's birth remains a mystery, with estimates ranging between 1786 and 1796 and no parish records at Loch Broom in Ross-shire available to provide the correct data. In the Canadian census of 1851, his age was given as fifty-five (making 1796 the year of his birth), but since he was in England when it was taken, he was not the data's source; a register from the paddle steamer *Caledonia*, when she docked at Boston in 1841, listed him as a passenger and gave his age as fifty (which would mean he was born in 1791), but that information is believed to have come from his secretary, E.M. Hopkins. *The Times* of London, in its 1860 obituary, gave Simpson's age as sixty-nine, but his gravestone in Montreal's Mount Royal cemetery states that he was seventy-three when he died. Having studied the available evidence, Galbraith concluded that 1787 was most likely Simpson's birth date.

noted Canadian explorer,* recorded one of the harshest contemporary assessments of his senior kinsman: "His Excellency miscalculates when he expects to get more out of people by sheer driving. By assuming a harsh manner towards me, he should have known . . . that the necessary effect on a young and generous mind would be a reciprocal repulsiveness, perhaps hatred; but I know his real sentiments and forgive his apparent, though unnecessary, unkindness. . . . On a nearer view of his character than I before had I lost much of that internal respect I entertained towards him. His firmness and decision of mind are much impaired: both in great and small matters he has become wavering, capricious and changeable. . . . He has grown painfully nervous and crabbed, and is guilty of many little meannesses at the table which are quite beneath a gentleman and, I might add, are indicative of his birth."

Even more telling—though the source was suspect because the Governor had refused its author a promotion—was John McLean's *Notes of a Twenty-Five Years' Service in the Hudson's Bay Territory*. "In no colony subject to the British Crown," complained the disappointed Chief Trader, "is there to be found an authority so despotic as is at this day exercised in the mercantile Colony of Rupert's Land; an authority combining the despotism of military rule with the strict surveillance and mean parsimony of the avaricious trader. From Labrador to Nootka Sound the unchecked, uncontrolled will of a single individual gives law to the land. . . . Clothed with a power so unlimited, it is not to be wondered at that a man who rose from a humble situation should in the end forget what he was and play the tyrant."

McLean also issued a more general warning to any future recruits contemplating service with the HBC: "They may learn that from the moment they embark in the Company's canoes at Lachine or in their ships at Gravesend, they bid adieu to all that civilized man most values on earth. They bid adieu to their families and friends, probably forever, for if they remain long enough to attain the promotion that allows them the privilege of revisiting their native land (twenty or twenty-five years), what changes does not this life exhibit in a much shorter time? They bid adieu to all the comforts and conveniences of civilization to vegetate at some solitary post, hundreds of miles perhaps from any other human habitation, save the wigwam of the savage, without any society other than that of their own thoughts or of the two or three humble persons who share their exile. They bid adieu to all refinement and cultivation,

---

*For details of Thomas Simpson's exploits and his subsequent murder, see *Company of Adventurers*, pages 299–300.

not infrequently becoming semi-barbarians, so altered in habits and sentiments that they not only become attached to savage life, but lose all relish for any other."

George Simpson's career and personality left few observers neutral—even in retrospect. Many historians have praised his accomplishments as the man who rescued the HBC from its fragile status following amalgamation and turned it into a profitable enterprise and an effective instrument of empire. But Alan Cooke, the head of Montreal's Hochelaga Research Institute, roundly condemns the Little Emperor for his money-grubbing single-mindedness: "Simpson must have been one of the best-hated men in North America. . . . He existed only as a man of business. More than any Indian, he was a slave—a willing slave—of the exploitive machinery of nineteenth-century mercantile capitalism. Although he achieved power, prestige and wealth, his only satisfaction came from work and his only pleasure was in incessant rapid travel. . . . He is an outstanding example of an immature ego possessed by personal complexes, which he projected onto his colleagues, and by an archetype he did not understand. He had unrivalled opportunities for personal growth but did not seize them."

THE MAIN REASON SIMPSON AROUSED so much loathing among some of his contemporaries was his obsession with "OEconomy"—his Draconian version of cost-cutting—which was precisely what was needed to get the business back on track and thus earned him such high esteem among the Company's London proprietors.

At the time of the 1821 merger, the HBC had seventy-six trading posts and the NWC ninety-seven. Within the next half-decade, the geography of the trade was completely reorganized. Norway House, not far from the foot of Lake Winnipeg, became the main distribution depot, its Chief Factor acting as continental dispatcher for the floating brigades that left in their various directions with the precision of express trains. Trading posts were strung at logical intervals along the North Saskatchewan River, with pemmican depots positioned at strategic crossings. Cumberland House was the transit point from the Saskatchewan north to the Churchill River. From Edmonton House, the Athabasca brigades swept on to the Mackenzie and the Peace, while packhorses carried furs and trade goods back and forth through the Okanagan Valley to Fort Vancouver on the Columbia and, later, by other routes, to Fort Langley on the Fraser.

This proved to be such an efficient system that during the four years after amalgamation, the number of HBC employees was reduced

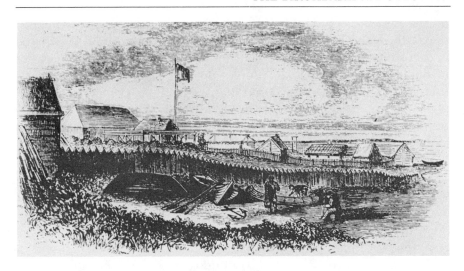

Cumberland House

from 1,983 to 827. Although the London Committee initiated the economy drive, Simpson stretched its directives to extremes, reducing wages one-quarter below the official requests and methodically eliminating most of the perquisites and European imports the Chief Factors and Traders had come to regard as their due. He fired many of the trade's veterans and instituted such meticulous cost accounting that he knew to the smallest item the contents of every fur-storage room and larder at each post. An example of the trivia that occupied Simpson was the following provision concerning protocol passed at one of his northern councils: "That all Chief Factors and Chief Traders for whom no special provision is made, accompany their loaded craft from the Depot inland, and all Chief Factors coming out to Depot, be allowed to precede their loaded Craft, thither for the purpose of attending Council, provided no loss of Freight is sustained thereby, and provided measures are concerted to enable two or more to embark in the same Craft." Willard Wentzel, the former NWC clerk who had once welcomed Simpson into the country as a gentleman who would not cause much alarm, now reversed his opinion. "The Northwest," he lamented, "is beginning to be ruled with an iron rod."

No detail seemed to escape Simpson's attention. Leaky boats, the proper manner of observing the Sabbath, declining buffalo tongue harvests, the going rate for Mexican silver dollars, how much mustard should (or should not) be used at each post, tea rations, even cutlery were dealt with in minutest fashion. In a typical missive, he ruled what must constitute a proper set of meal utensils: "The Table Appointments throughout the Country have hitherto been upon much too large a scale, far exceeding the consumption of most respectable families in the civilized world, and I think you may safely reduce the usual supplies by 50 p Cent—the descriptions to be of the cheapest, vizt. Tin plates: ... no table cloths, which with Towels are considered private property. No [earthenware] Dishes: a few Tumblers which answer for Wine glasses. Knives and Forks ought to last at least half a dozen years—in private families they sometimes last 20."

The most significant effect of Simpson's omnipresent OEconomy was felt by the Indians. They were essential to the fur trade, since they did nearly all the work, trapping and skinning the animals and bringing the pelts to the trading posts. But Simpson viewed them as immature creatures, fortunate beneficiaries of the Company's peculiar brand of paternalism.* In an 1822 letter to London explaining the effect on the Indians of the NWC/HBC merger, Simpson set down the tenets he would follow during his governorship: "The late arrangements [absorption of the North West Company] have given mortal offence to Indians .... Their immediate wants have been supplied, but of course the scenes of extravagance are at an end, and it will be a work of time to reconcile them to the new order of things. I have made it my study to examine the nature and character of the Indians and however repugnant it may be to our feelings, *I am convinced they must be ruled with a rod of iron, to bring and to keep them in a proper state of subordination, and the most certain way to effect this is by letting them feel their dependence upon us.* In the woods and Northern barren grounds this measure ought to be pursued rigidly next year if they do not improve, and no credit, not so much as a load of ammunition, given them until they exhibit an inclination to renew their habits of industry." At times, Simpson's condescension got the better of him. In 1825, during his first tour to the Pacific Coast, he noted in his journal: "Two Nez Percés Chiefs arrived to see me from a distance of between [200 and] 300 miles; my fame has spread far and Wide and my speeches are handed from Camp to Camp throughout the Country; some of them have it that I am one of the 'Master of Life's Sons' sent to see 'if their hearts are good' and others that I am his 'War Chief' with bad Medicine if their hearts are bad. On the whole I think my presence and lectures will [do] some good."

---

*To impress the Indians, Simpson had a tiny music box attached to his dog's neck in such a way that when it was wound up, music seemed to come from the animal's throat. Generations later, the Carrier were still referring to George Simpson as "the great chief whose dog sings."

During the commercial war between the NWC and HBC, Indian trappers had become adept at playing off one company against the other, often arranging for credit at one post and later bartering their season's catch at another. They developed a sophisticated business network complete with well-connected middlemen, but once Simpson took over, that seesaw technique was diluted as more detailed accounts were kept, reducing the Indians' nomadic preferences. Simpson also did away with the granting of presents, which had become an accepted tradition during the annual trading ceremony.* The Company reduced and eventually eliminated the use of rum and brandy for inland trading.†
While this was a long-term benefit, the changes tended to colonialize the relationship between trader and trapper—breaking down the sense of mutual exploitation that had once characterized their dealings.

The most contentious ruling by the HBC's Governing Council for the Northern Department was passed at its 1841 meeting: a strict limit was imposed on the beaver catch. This was meant as a sensible conservation measure aimed at allowing the doughty animal to rebuild its lodges and supply of offspring, but native trappers construed it as unwarranted interference with their way of life. Traders at individual posts enforced the regulations with a vengeance. George Gladman, then stationed at Norway House, proudly wrote to the Governor: ". . . an Indian brought me a Beaver skin the other day. The animal being recently killed, this being against the rule, I slapped his face with it!"
To ensure obedience from some of the less enthusiastic subscribers to his creed, Simpson issued one of his typical no-nonsense edicts: "[If] it be found that gentlemen disregard this instruction, as they have done many others issued from time to time for the same object, it is [resolved] That the Governor and Committee be respectfully advised to give

---

*For an explanation of how the Indian–HBC system worked, see *Company of Adventurers*, Chapter 10.

†The HBC could not be accused of acting with indecent haste in winding down the liquor trade that had caused such havoc during the competition with the NWC. The final anti-liquor regulation was approved by a council meeting at Red River on June 17, 1843—twenty-two years after amalgamation: "RESOLVED that the Indians be treated with kindness and indulgence and mild and conciliatory means resorted to in order to encourage industry, repress vice, and inculcate morality; that the use of spirituous liquor be gradually discontinued in the very few districts in which it is yet indispensable and that the Indians be liberally supplied with requisite necessaries particularly with articles of ammunition, whether they have the means of paying for it or not, and that no gentleman in charge of district or post be at liberty to alter or vary the standard or usual mode of trade with the Indians except by special permission of Council."

The York boat could carry three times the payload of the canot du nord.

notice of retirement from the Service to such Gentlemen as may not give effect to the Spirit and the letter of the resolution now passed for the preservation of Beaver."

SIMPSON KNEW THAT THE MOST EFFECTIVE operational economies must eventually mean replacing canoes because of their relatively puny payloads. He substituted the sturdy York boats on all possible routes, although primitive versions of the craft had been in use for many seasons. Based on an age-old Orkney design, which in turn was derived from the shape of Viking longships, the vessels had been built from time to time at Fort Albany since the 1740s. Called York boats because York Factory was initially their most frequent destination, the reliable craft were capable of carrying three times the payload of the *canot du nord*. They could run most rapids, were more stable in rough lake-crossings than canoes and were resistant to floating ice during spring breakup. Their raised bow and stern posts, mounted with a 45-degree rake, allowed them to be easily backwatered off sandbars. Along portages, the little ships had to be rolled on pre-cleared paths of logs, but this proved to be not an impossible task.

Crewing these larger craft, far less finicky than canoes, required more muscle than skill. Six or eight oarsmen would man the twenty-foot sweep-like oars, rising in their seats to get a purchase on the water, then, bracing themselves with one foot, falling back onto their thwarts—a series of movements that if elegantly executed was not dissimilar to the cadence of Venetian gondoliers. The bowsman would fend off rocks, the stern man steer. A large sail, used as a tent at night, could be hauled up a makeshift mast in following winds. The flat-bottomed vessels were strengthened by being clinker-built, with the overlaps of spruce planking dispersing the impact of steep waves and rocky outcrops.

A York boat, which took two skilled men only two weeks to build, would last three seasons with minimum maintenance. The trickiest part of the construction process was to find the proper piece of spruce or tamarack for a seaworthy keel. Samples were tested by being placed on stocks and a pocket watch held against the butt at one end. The builder listened for the tick at the other. Only if the ticking resonated loudly and clearly through the wood was it judged suitable to withstand the stresses of being carved into a keel. Little effort was expended on aesthetics; outside surfaces were tarred, interiors left unpainted.

As the West began to be settled, the York boats were used for general traffic as well as for the fur trade. The bells in the St Boniface cathedral at Red River arrived by York boat, for example, as did the settlement's first piano.*

These boats may have been fine for everyday traders, but they were not nearly fast enough for George Simpson himself. He did accompany a brigade of the pudgy craft to the Athabasca Country in 1822 to demonstrate their utility along northern routes, but most of his travel time was spent in his own express canoes manned by a praetorian guard of Iroquois boatmen from the Caughnawaga (Kahnawake) band across the St Lawrence from Lachine. A dozen men paddling at speeds up to sixty strokes a minute could propel the boat, measuring thirty-three feet with a five-foot-three beam, ninety to a hundred miles a day.†

The Governor's travels were legendary. During all but three of the thirty-nine years he spent in charge of the HBC's northern fur trade,

---

*The final York boat brigade arrived at York Factory in 1871, though York boats continued to be used at isolated posts for many years after that. The last commercial York boat was built at Norway House in 1924; several are still there for summer races on nearby Little Playgreen Lake.

†In 1889, the *Rob Roy* was discovered at Fort Timiskaming. Measuring a full seven fathoms (forty-two feet) long, it was authenticated as one of Simpson's personal craft and would have been one of the largest birchbark canoes ever built.

Simpson ranged across the continent in furiously paced forays, inspecting his posts, hectoring discouraged Factors, preaching the doctrine of cost efficiency and loving every minute of it. He was constantly in motion. He crossed the Rockies at three latitudes, completed twelve transatlantic round trips, eight visits to Boston and New York, and three great journeys to forts on the Columbia River in the Oregon Country. His most trying trek was by snowshoe during the winter of 1822–23, when he went from Lake Athabasca to Great Slave Lake and back, up the Peace River to Fort Dunvegan and across Lesser Slave Lake to Edmonton House. Simpson loved being on the move, wafting through the melodious forests of the great Northwest, dictating memoranda to his accompanying secretaries and being treated everywhere like a resplendent emperor on an imperial progress. "It is strange," Simpson once wrote to his friend John George McTavish, "that all my ailments vanish as soon as I seat myself in a canoe."

Simpson drove his crews sixteen hours or more a day, determined to demonstrate his own immunity to human weakness and demanding by example that they do the same. *"Levez! Levez! Levez nos gens!"* he would call out at two or three o'clock in the morning before plunging into some nearby lake or river to flaunt his own *joie de vivre*. After that morning dip and half a dozen hours of hard paddling, he would call a brief halt for breakfast and, three or four hours later, another for a quick lunch stop, his crewmen munching pemmican while he sat back and allowed his manservant to present him with tidbits and wine. The Governor had a habit of dozing off between meals but his crews were never allowed to relax. While he appeared to be asleep he would trail the fingers of one hand over the gunwale, testing the cruising speed by noting how high the water splashed up his wrist. The killing pace never let up. One steersman became so exasperated on one of the longer stretches that he picked the Governor up by the collar, lifted him over his head and pitched him into the river—then, with immediate remorse, dove in to help him out. Paradoxically, Simpson never had any trouble recruiting crews of men proud to test their endurance.

He set speed records that have never been beaten (or even attempted), and when he ran out of challenges in North America, he embarked on a voyage around the world. He was the first man to circle the earth by what was then called the "overland route"—and may have been a model for the hero of Jules Verne's *Around the World in Eighty Days*.

Simpson's travels were relieved by many diversions. He once took a sauna during a quick visit to Alaska, and his description of that "castigation" is a classic example of his humour and unexpected self-depreciation: "While at Sitka, I took a bath, which might be a very good thing for those that liked it. On entering the building, I was much oppressed with the steam and heat, while an ill-looking, long-legged, stark-naked fellow was waiting to officiate, as master of the ceremonies. Having undressed in an antechamber, so far as decency would permit, I made my way into the bathroom, which was heated almost to suffocation. Having thus got me into his power, the gaunt attendant threw some water on the iron furnace, while, to avoid, as far as possible, the clouds of steam that were thus raised, I squatted myself down on the floor, perspiring profusely at every pore. I next seated myself on a bench, while bucket after bucket of hot water was thrown on my head; and then, making me stretch myself out, my tormentor soaped me all over, from head to foot, rubbing and lathering me with a handful of pine-tops. . . . Once more taking his bucket, the horrid operator kept drenching me, the successive pailfuls descending gradually from nearly a boiling heat to the temperature of fifty degrees. The whole process occupied about an hour. I then returned to the antechamber, where, after being dried with hot towels, I was very glad to put on dry clothes. It was impossible, however, to make my escape immediately, for I was so relaxed as to be obliged to recline on a sofa for a quarter of an hour; and then I withdrew, inwardly resolved never again to undergo such another castigation."

One reason for his whirling-dervish approach was that Simpson wanted to catch his post managers off guard so he could check up on the efficacy of their daily rounds. He relocated posts, opened a few and closed many more. To heighten the patrician impact of his cavalcade on the woebegone little forts, Simpson arrived at each major stop with a sequence of punctilious flourishes worthy of a pope presuming worship. The pomp nearly always outdid the circumstance. Simpson's party, which usually included an escorting canoe or two, would put in to shore just before entering any settlement to give the Governor time to don his beaver topper and his paddlers a moment to spruce up in their best shirts. Ready and set, they would sweep towards the fort's tiny log dock at top speed. Once they were within sight and sound of the HBC fort, the performance would begin. A bugler, an occasional bagpiper and the voices of his chanting paddlers would meld into an impressive orchestration. This was how Chief Trader Archibald McDonald, who accompanied Simpson in his own canoe during the 1828 inspection tour to the Columbia, described the spectacle: "As we wafted along under easy sail, the men with a clean change and mounting new feathers, the Highland bagpipes in the Governor's canoe, was echoed by the bugle in mine; then these were laid aside on nearer approach to port, to give free scope to the vocal organs of about eighteen Canadians to chant one of those voyageur airs peculiar to them, and always so perfectly rendered. . . . On the signal hill of rock, from a tall Norway Pine shaft, floated the 'grand old Flag'. From the 'hollow rocks'—the world of rocks—all around us, awoke the wild echoes, by 'the bugle', 'set flying'. Then the grand thunder—skirrl of 'the bag pipes', with their 'Campbell's are coming, hourray! hourray!' or some such 'music of our mountain land', loud droned out to the very vault of heaven. And then—as a cadenza of soothing, gladdening, exquisite charm—the deep and soft and so joyously toned voices of those full throated voyageurs, timed with a stroke—so quick—of glittering paddle blade, singing with such heart their 'La Claire Fontaine', or some such loved air of their native land—our own land, let us say . . . when the Governor's canoe, with its grand high prow rounded, and brightly painted, flashed out of the dark rock 'at the point' into our full view, and gracefully turned into the little 'port' at our feet, the heart seemed to swell with admiration and delight at the sight. Never; never, had anything so grand and splendid, and delightful withal, been seen in those primitive wilds!"

Flags flying, cannon blasting, his piper leading the way, the Governor would step ashore in his theatrical Royal Stuart tartan cloak with collar of soft Genoa velvet. Simpson's insistence on being convoyed by a piper was only partly vanity. What better, what more emotional way to reach the hearts and souls of his men in these lonely huts than with the mantra of the glens? Those eerie wailings must have been the equivalent of the trumpet flourishes that paced Giuseppe Garibaldi's march on Naples—their sound described by British historian G.M. Trevelyan as ringing "through the noonday stillness like a summons to the soul of Italy." Simpson's piper was Colin Fraser, who arrived in 1827 at York Factory from Kirkton, in Sutherlandshire. To win the £30-a-year job, he was asked to walk in front of a carriage the twenty miles to the point of embarkation, playing all the way; Fraser was the only one of three candidates who made it.

The bagpipes may have wowed the Highlanders, but Simpson's caravan left behind many puzzled Indians. According to one anonymous and quite possibly apocryphal story, a Cree who heard Colin Fraser play at Norway House reported to his chief: "One white man was dressed like a woman, in a skirt of funny color. He had whiskers growing from his belt and fancy leggings. He carried a black swan which had many legs with ribbons tied to them. The swan's body he put under his arm upside down, then he put its head in his mouth and bit it. At the same time he pinched its neck with his fingers and squeezed the body under his arm until it made a terrible noise."

BY 1824, SIMPSON'S ENERGY and singleminded dedication to reforming the fur trade within the confines of Rupert's Land was paying dividends, but on the other side of the Rockies and to the south along the West Coast, the so-called Columbia Department was still showing serious losses. It was in part a problem of sovereignty: Alaska was Russian, California remained Spanish, and the territories in between, jointly administered by the United States and Great Britain, were loosely occupied by the Hudson's Bay Company.

To reorganize and invigorate that Pacific operation, Simpson appointed as Chief Factor Dr John McLoughlin, the former Nor'Wester who had led the wintering partners' rebellion prior to amalgamation. McLoughlin left York Factory for his new assignment at Astoria on July 26, 1824, vowing that despite the Governor's reputation for speed, he would be first to reach the Columbia. Simpson had decided to await the arrival of the annual supply ship so that he could catch the season's incoming mail from the London Committee. He waited three full weeks, and when the vessel had still not arrived, he set off accompanied by a Chief Trader named James McMillan to teach the proud McLoughlin a lesson.

Instead of following the good doctor up the Hayes River, he chose the much more difficult but shorter route up the Nelson, setting daily speed records along the way. Less than five days out of York Factory, he exulted in his journal: "I believe there is nothing known in the annals of Rupert's Land travelling, equal to our journey so far." Six weeks later on the banks of a shallow river, at seven o'clock one dewy morning, McLoughlin and his party were still trying to stretch themselves awake when the Governor's canoes hove triumphantly into view. Despite his twenty-day head start, McLoughlin had been beaten, and he was anything but pleased by the speedy Governor. Simpson's description of the hulking wilderness doctor was appropriately unsentimental: "He was such a figure as I should not like to meet on a dark Night in one of the bye lanes in the neighbourhood of London dressed in Clothes that had once been fashionable, but now covered with a thousand patches of different Colors, his beard would do honor to the chin of a Grizzly Bear, his face and hands evidently Shewing that he had not lost much time at the Toilette, loaded with Arms and his own herculean dimensions forming a tout ensemble that would convey a good idea of the highwaymen of former days." The joint party reached the Pacific in eighty-four days' travel time, cutting three weeks off previous records, though Simpson complained all the way that he had been forced to slow down "to give the Dr. an opportunity of keeping up with us."

Simpson's return journey was even more dramatic. Although he realized that he was due to preside at a Northern Council meeting in Norway House during early June, he did not leave the Columbia until late April 1825—and that meant fighting his way against spring flood waters. Because some prearranged horses did not show up, he and his party had to walk through the tortuous Athabasca Pass in the Rocky Mountains, crossing the rushing Wood River seventeen times. "Some of the people were so numbed with the cold," he dispassionately observed, "that on getting out of the water, they actually could not stand." After a second such nightmare tumble down the range's eastern slope (crossing the icy Whirlpool River twenty-seven times), he finally clambered into a waiting canoe and sped down the North Saskatchewan to Fort Carlton, an old HBC post on the boundary of the Plains Indians' hunting grounds. The Indians were on the warpath, and his retinue was too frightened and physically spent to continue. Not Simpson. He commandeered some horses and, with half a dozen volunteers, rode off over the hostile prairie. They eventually reached the juncture of the Qu'Appelle and Assiniboine rivers. Both were in full flood and there seemed no way across. "The water was too wide; there was no wood of any kind to make a Raft; several of our people could not swim. . . . I however being more at home in the Water than any of my fellow travellers and anxious to save the lives of the poor animals [horses], stripped and Swam across with a few things; three others followed my example and by making several crossings in this way we got the whole of our little Baggage over; the Horses were driven across, those people who could not Swim holding on by their Tails. . . . In like manner we got across the Assiniboine River."

His personal servant, Thomas Taylor, and a trader named George Bird got lost while hunting for food. Simpson coolly noted that if they were to meet any hostile Indians along the way, "they will lose their scalps as a matter of course." (Taylor and Bird did eventually stumble into an HBC post.) By the time the Simpson party reached White Horse Plain, sixteen miles from Fort Garry at the Red River Settlement, none of the Governor's companions could continue. His melodramatic final dash is best described in his own journal entry: "I got on my old charger 'Jonathan,' gave him the Rein with a smart cut across the haunches and commenced a furious attack on the Gates of Fort Garry at 12 midnight, was immediately answered by a most hearty welcome from Mr. McKenzie and every person at the Garrison and here I purpose taking a rest for Eight Days after having performed one of the most dangerous and harassing Journeys ever undertaken in the Country through which, thank God, I have got with no injury or inconvenience worthy of Notice."

At the Norway House meeting that followed this exploit, Simpson was rewarded by tangible evidence of the London board's esteem—a raise in pay of £200 to £1,200 a year, plus a £500 bonus. At the same time, he received a resounding vote of confidence from the assembled Chief Factors, who praised his "unremitting exertion ... masterly arrangements and decisive measures." Significantly, the testimonial was signed by such hard cases as the former Nor'Wester Samuel Black.*

Simpson's next venture to the Pacific three years later was even more rushed, covering the 3,261 miles from York Factory to Fort Langley near the mouth of the Fraser in a breathtaking sixty-five days. Accompanied by Chief Trader Archibald McDonald and Dr Richard Hamlyn, Simpson embarked to the (compulsory) three cheers of York Factory's permanent staff and a seven-gun salute at one o'clock in the morning of July 12. The two passengers were assigned the duty of waking up the crews at precisely two each morning, and since there were no alarm clocks, that meant each could sleep only on alternate nights. For the first time, Simpson was also accompanied by his country wife, Margaret, the Mixed Blood sister of his servant, Thomas Taylor. "The commodity has been a great consolation to me," was the chauvinistic tribute to his female companion in a letter he sent from Stuart Lake, along the way, to his friend McTavish.

Except for its furious pace, the journey was uneventful until they crossed the Rocky Mountains. Because Simpson realized that the Company could not hold on forever to its trading rights in the Oregon Country and would therefore lose the access to the Pacific afforded by the Columbia River, he was set on discovering an alternative route. He thus decided to explore the Fraser River and its great tributary, the Thompson, both of which their discoverer, Simon Fraser, had so eloquently declared to be unnavigable only twenty years previously. Simpson had also been warned by local traders that he would never descend those rocky torrents alive. That, of course, ensured he would make the attempt. After facing the terrors of the Thompson, which he admitted "made whitened countenances of the boldest among us," he tackled the relentless Fraser with its perpendicular canyons and deadly

---

* Black in fact became just as loyal to the HBC as he had once been to the NWC. Placed in charge of various posts in the Columbia Department from 1825 to 1841, he was promoted to Chief Factor's rank in 1837. When the visiting botanist David Douglas proclaimed that in his view there was not an officer in the Hudson's Bay Company with a soul above a beaver's, Black immediately challenged him to a duel. It was too dark for the encounter that evening, and by next morning when Black showed up, Douglas was nowhere in sight.

whitewater shoots. Though Simpson praised his Iroquois bowman for being "nearly amphibious," even he was forced to concede that passage down that river of hell was certain death and disappointedly ruled it out as a trade route. That also eliminated Fort Langley as the HBC's future Pacific terminus, though it remained an important regional trading post well into the 1880s.

DURING THESE AND OTHER EXCURSIONS, Simpson devoted most of his time to assessing the strengths and weaknesses of his men in the field. He could be occasionally compassionate and frequently cruel. As in James Thurber's celebrated metaphor, Simpson knew how to cut off a man's head so that he didn't realize it was severed until he tried to sneeze. He displayed little sympathy for the Company's veterans. In a confidential letter he wrote to the London Committee's Andrew Colvile in 1826, he explained: "Many of our principal Clerks are nearly worn out and I should not consider it good policy to allow them to have commissions as the step from a Chief Tradership to a Chief Factorship I think ought to be gained by important active services which none except such as are in the prime and vigour of Life should be qualified or required to perform. I consider it highly injurious to the general interests to have old worn out men in our councils, they are timid, indolent and helpless and would be of no manner of use in cases of difficulty danger or emergency. Worn out Indian Traders are the most useless helpless class of men I ever knew and the sooner the Company can get rid of them after their days of activity and labor are over the better; but that will always be a difficult matter as they become attached to the Country to the half savage Life they have been accustomed to lead and to their women and Families and will not move unless actually forced away."

Still, Company morale during most of the Little Emperor's reign was high, partly because service with the HBC had become something of a family affair. Youngsters had been following fathers and uncles into the Company for five or more generations. Out of touch with their extended families in Scotland, many of the more isolated traders nurtured a filial relationship with Simpson, seeking him out for advice about their lives, personal as well as corporate. They asked for his help in finding wives, lost children or new postings; they turned their savings over to him for investment and often named him executor of their wills. Loved or hated, he was the great patriarch of the clan.

Among his closest associates were John George McTavish, the former Nor'Wester in charge of Fort William at amalgamation, who was transferred to similar responsibilities at York Factory; Alexander

John Rowand

Christie, who lasted forty-two years in the HBC; Duncan Finlayson, a talented veteran who spent his last three years with the HBC as a member of its London Committee; James Hargrave, a crusty fur trader also remembered because of his hospitable and literary wife, Letitia; and Angus Cameron, the Fort Timiskaming Chief Factor, who received what was probably the Governor's highest compliment: "From what I have seen of you, I consider you worthy of whatever can be done for you, command me therefore when you may think I can be useful."

But Simpson's favourite fur trader was John Rowand, son of a Montreal doctor, who had joined the North West Company as a fourteen-year-old apprentice and for thirty years ruled the HBC's key Saskatchewan district with something close to inspired tyranny. Simpson promoted him to Chief Factor at Edmonton House in 1823, took him along for part of his round-the-world tour and treated him as a confidant rather than an employee.

Edmonton House and its NWC counterpart were relocated on several occasions, sometimes as much as 125 miles at a time, from the original 1794 site. It became a key post because the old canoe route to the Athabasca and Pacific via the Churchill River and Methy Portage was abandoned after 1824 in favour of the North Saskatchewan water route and later along the Carlton Trail. Pioneered by Simpson on his dramatic return journey from the Columbia in 1825, this land route became a major artery, eventually worn clear by more than three hundred Red River carts making round trips at eighty-day intervals.

Aside from being a key conduit, Edmonton under Rowand's direction quickly became the most productive fort in the territories, in terms both of its impressive fur catch and as a production centre for York boats and bags of pemmican. Rowand developed the West's first horse-breeding spread, complete with a two-mile racetrack, and his sixteen-hand chestnut hunter was the object of much envy. A vital trading centre for tribes in the Plains group (the Assiniboine, Cree, Blackfoot, Sarcee, Gros Ventre, Peigan and Blood), the hexagon-shaped enclosure at Edmonton soon sprouted a dozen warehouses, residences and workshops. All were smeared with the red earth found in the neighbourhood, which, when mixed with oil, produced a shade called "durable brown."

The most imposing structure of all was Rowand's own "Big House," his residence and office, which boasted the Northwest's first glass windows. (They had been shipped from England in barrels of molasses to minimize breakage.) Known to the locals as Rowand's Folly, the three-storey extravaganza had an outside gallery running the length of the building where the resident piper could tread his measured path, wheezing the call of the Highlands to the fort's population of 130. Off the second-storey gallery was a gentlemen's mess on one side and the Northwest's only ballroom on the other. Under the high-pitched roof were the bedrooms and on the ground floor the armoury, kitchen and stewards' quarters. Rowand used the ballroom mainly to hold court and impress visiting Indian chiefs, but at Christmas he could entertain 150 at a single sitting for dinner and dancing. Itinerant artist Paul Kane, who was there to enjoy the 1847 repast, wrote glowingly of a meal that included boiled premature buffalo calves, dried moose noses, wild goose, and whitefish delicately browned in buffalo marrow. "The walls and ceiling," he reported, "are painted in a style of the most startling, barbaric gaudiness, and the ceiling filled with centre pieces of fantastic gilt scrolls, making altogether a saloon which no white man would enter without a start and which the Indians always looked upon with awe and wonder." Although Rowand forbade most Indian and Mixed Blood women from dining with "the gentlemen," they were welcomed in for the dances that followed, enjoying mightily the famous Red River jig and toe-tapping theatrics of the local fiddler. *Harper's Magazine* described a typical Métis dance of the period in its October 1860 issue: "Jigs, reels, and quadrilles were danced in rapid succession

Fort Edmonton in the 1840s

... fresh dancers taking the place of those on the floor every two or three moments. The men were stripped to shirt, trousers, belt and moccasins; and the women wore gowns which had no hoops ... a black-eyed beauty in blue calico, and a strapping Bois Brûlé, would jump up from the floor and outdo their predecessors in vigor and velocity—the lights and shadows chasing each other faster and faster over the rafters; the flame, too, swaying wildly hither and thither; and above the thumps of the dancers' heels, and the frequent 'Ho! Ho!' and the laughter ... rose the monomaniac fiddle-shrieks, forced out of the trembling strings, as if a devil was at the bow."

The fountainhead for all this merriment, John Rowand, stood even shorter than Simpson but was known as the Big Mountain for good reason, his ample girth* being supported by equally outrageous quantities of bombast and bluster. His temper made even Simpson seem a bit of a milquetoast. When several of his servants came down with a serious malady, Rowand accused them of shirking their duty and decreed that "... any man who is not dead within three days' illness is not sick at all." His operating philosophy was summed up in the terse credo: "We know only two powers—God and the Company!" On one occasion, when he and the well-known Catholic missionary Albert Lacombe were out riding across the plains, they were resting at a campfire when they suddenly found themselves surrounded by two hundred Blackfoot, clearly on the warpath. Rowand marched up to the chief and roared, "*Stop, you villains!*"—then turned his back and resumed his meal. Recognizing his opponent, the chief not only called off the raiding party but was so abject in his apologies that according to the piper Colin Fraser, who reported the incident, many of the Indians "actually cried with vexation."

That was an obvious exaggeration, but Rowand's influence did help keep the Prairies free of antagonistic incidents at a time when the American Plains ran with the blood of Indian wars. Rowand's affinity for his region's inhabitants was no doubt influenced by his romantic first encounter with Louise Umphreville, his Mixed Blood country wife. As a young man he had gone buffalo hunting one morning,

---

*It was a family affair. His wife weighed in at only 322 pounds, but Rowand's daughter Margaret reached 336 pounds, while his son John, Jr., was an even 350. When Margaret married an HBC trader named James McKay (364 pounds), an observant guest at the wedding noted that the moment the four of them got up to jig, 1,372 pounds hit the dance floor. McKay, later a Manitoba minister of agriculture, was so huge that when he and his bride went for rides in their hackney carriage, they had to sit one behind the other.

riding out alone through the gates of Fort des Prairies, where he was then stationed. She had noticed his departure, and when his horse returned riderless, she became alarmed and jumped on a pony and followed the horse to where Rowand, who had been thrown by his mount, was lying immobilized with a broken leg. She set his limb, binding the splints with strips from her leather garments. They fell in love while she was nursing him back to health, and although their marriage was never officially consecrated, they stayed together for thirty-nine years, and Louise became the proud chatelaine of their wilderness chateau.

In the spring of 1854, Rowand was leading the Edmonton brigade down the Saskatchewan, planning to take a year's furlough prior to retirement. While at Fort Pitt, where his son was Chief Trader, he noticed two Métis crewmen having a fight. He stepped between them, his face flushed, temper rising. Without warning, he clutched his chest and dropped dead of a heart attack. His bereaved son and members of the little outpost's garrison buried the staunch trader with full honours.

Then the fun began. Rowand had stipulated in his will that his bones should rest in Montreal, his birthplace, and George Simpson was not about to ignore his friend's final request. In the spring of 1855, Rowand's body was disinterred and an elderly Indian was instructed to boil the flesh off the bones, which were then stored inside a keg that was carefully filled with rum as a preservative. (The women at Fort Pitt utilized the considerable amount of residual fat to make soap.) Simpson sent his own canoe to bring the remains to Red River, but the superstitious crew threw the keg over the side of the express canoe during a storm on Lake Winnipeg, believing that the dead man's unrequited rage had caused a tempest to swamp them. The barrel was eventually recovered and trundled onward to York Factory.

Since there was no direct link between Hudson Bay and Montreal, the makeshift coffin was loaded on a supply ship heading for London. There, the HBC Committeemen tendered the battered barrel a magnificent funeral service, complete with muffled drums and standardbearers. The keg was then taken to Liverpool, where it was for a time lost in a storage shed but ultimately loaded on a Montreal-bound steamer.

Nearly four years to the day after his death, John Rowand's remains were ready to be buried at Mount Royal cemetery. When the peripatetic barrel was finally pried open, it was full not of rum but of water.

Sir George Simpson in the late 1850s

CHAPTER 10

THE VICEROY

Under George Simpson, the HBC tacitly agreed to serve as an informal territorial agency of the British Empire, ensuring that there existed a modicum of law and order in this far corner of Queen Victoria's globe.

MASTERMINDING THE THIN VANGUARD of Bay functionaries holding together a territory ten times the size of the Holy Roman Empire, George Simpson acted with the lordly hauteur of a man in charge of his private universe. But he was in fact a viceroy—one who ruled his province as the representative of an external sovereign power and exercised his authority in its name.

Every summer while the trade was slack and the rivers were flowing wide, the Council of the Northern Department of Rupert's Land met either at York Factory or, more often, at Norway House. Unlike the bonny reunions of the Nor'Westers at Fort William, which were as much excuses for great parties as discussions of policy, these HBC conclaves were sonorous business sessions, with the gathered Chief Factors and Traders exchanging views and auguries, but being very much guided by the Governor's every word and gesture.

The most practical advice on how to deal with Simpson was tendered by a veteran Chief Factor named John Stuart, who told Donald Smith, his newly arrived Scottish nephew (who would one day hold Simpson's office), that there was only one way to cultivate the Governor's sponsorship: "No man is more appreciative of downright hard work coupled with intelligence. . . . It is his foible to exact not only strict obedience, but deference to the point of humility. As long as you pay him in that coin you will quickly get on his sunny side and find yourself in a few years a trader at a congenial post, with promotion in sight."

Even though many of the Chief Factors who sat pondering around the conference tables at the Northern Department Council meetings were formerly high-spirited Nor'Westers who had come within a breath of beating the HBC at its own game, they realized only too well they were no longer "lords of the lakes and forests"; they had become integral cogs in an efficient transcontinental fur-gathering machine. Members of the Council had the right to nominate their own successors, but it was Simpson and the London Committee who made the final selections. "They could outvote me, but it has never been so," Simpson wrote, referring to the Council as "my own government." He presided at these gatherings flanked by his recording clerks and listened to the debates with ill-concealed, foot-tapping boredom. Although it was not true, as alleged by his critic John McLean, that he wrote the minutes of the meetings *before* they took place, the renegade trader's verdict on how much power the Council actually had was chillingly accurate: "The few individuals who compose it know better than to offer advice where none would be accepted; they know full well that the Governor has already determined on his own measures before one of them appears in his presence. Their assent is all that is expected of them, and that they never hesitate to give."

Simpson was much too wise to make it appear that he was not heeding the advice of his pastoral parliament. When he asked John George McTavish to substitute for him at one of the meetings, the Governor explained the secret of his approach. "Keep your temper," he advised, "and do not allow yourself [to] be drawn into altercation with any of those who may be there; you can gain neither honour nor glory by quarrelling with them, but can twist them around your finger by setting about it properly." Despite his deftness in dealing with his troops and scattered lieutenants, Simpson came under heavy criticism for playing favourites and bypassing established procedures. (Chief Traders were supposed to be appointed only after nine years as clerks, while to become a Chief Factor required at least sixteen years in the service.) But he had many more claimants for preference than he could possibly satisfy, and even at their worst, Simpson's personal likes and dislikes did little to prejudice the profitable conduct of the trade.

Like everything else he did, Simpson judged the character of the Highlanders under his command in a methodical manner that revealed as much about himself as it did about them. In a secret Character Book, he analysed with absolute candour the personalities and motivations of his senior people. The pocket notebook's entries, which delved into his subalterns' lives both private and professional, was strictly for his own use. It was not listed as being in the HBC's Archives until 1923, and its code (he numbered each entry instead of using names) was found separately on a piece of scrap paper by an archivist named K.E. Pincock. Professor Glyndwr Williams of Queen Mary College, London, who edited the document for publication, noted that "as a feat of memory and sustained reportage the Character Book is a *tour de force*. . . . The men who helped the Hudson's Bay Company to its period of greatest dominance in the North American fur trade . . . emerge not as names in an official letter or signatures at the end of a formal report, but as human beings, usually fallible, sometimes frail and inconsequent. Many are shown in a harsh, ungenerous light which magnifies the imperfections and deepens the shadows."

Even Simpson's friends received objective reviews. John George McTavish was one of the Governor's closest companions, sharing personal as well as professional concerns. Yet in his Character Book, the Governor pointed out that McTavish was "generous to extravagance . . . unnecessarily dignified and high minded which leads to frequent difficulties with his associates by whom he is considered a 'Shylock' and upon many of whom he looks down . . . has of late Years become very heavy unwieldy and inactive; over fond of good living and I much fear is getting into habits of conviviality and intemperance." Not even John Rowand escaped criticism. Simpson extolled his boldness and added that he "will not tell a lie (which is very uncommon in this Country) but has sufficient address to evade the truth when it suits his purpose . . . ."

A sampling of Simpson's little red book leaves open the question of how he managed to run an empire with such an emotionally crippled crew. These are a few typical examples of his more negative assessments:

Antoine Hamel: . . . A stout strong illiterate common kind of fellow who was employed during the opposition in River St Maurice because he could walk well on Snow Shoes and had the name of being a tolerable bruiser. Can drink, tell lies and Swear.

Charles Ross: . . . A good classical scholar and a man of very correct conduct but so nervous at times that it is quite painful to see him. Very Slovenly both in business and in his appearance. . . . I have often thought that he was not quite of Sound Mind and am much mistaken if he has not shown decided symptoms of Madness although it has been carefully concealed by those about him.

Thomas Dears: . . . A flippant, superficial, trifling creature—who lies more frequently than he speaks the truth, can take a Glass of Grog and I strongly suspect is given to pilfering: altogether a low scampish fellow, but active, can make himself useful either at a Trading Post or Depot and has a facility in acquiring a smattering of the Indian Languages. Was picked up in Canada during the opposition when character was not much enquired into and I suspect him a Gentleman's Servant "out of place."

Leslie Bryson: An Irishman. . . . Was attached to the Commissariat in the Peninsular War, but I should think in one of the lowest capacities . . . is evidently a fellow who has been accustomed to live from hand to mouth by his Wits. Deals in the Marvellous but his fiction is harmless.

Francis Ermatinger: . . . A stout active boisterous fellow who is a tolerable clerk and trader and qualified to be useful where bustle and activity without any great exercise of judgment are necessary. Talks a little at random but will not descend to a deliberate falsehood. Got into disgrace lately in consequence of having employed one of the Company's Servants in cutting off the Ears of an Indian who had had an intrigue with his Woman, but which would not have been thought so much of, had it been done by himself in the heat of passion or as a punishment for Horse Stealing.

It was when he harboured a personal dislike for one of his officers that Simpson's sarcasm really struck home. Characteristic entries dealt with two of the most distinguished pre-amalgamation Bay men, John Clarke and Colin Robertson.

John Clarke: A boasting, ignorant low fellow who rarely speaks the truth and is strongly suspected of dishonesty; his commanding appearance and pompous manner, however, give him a good deal of influence over Indians and Servants; and his total want of every principle or feeling, allied to fair dealing, honour and integrity, together with his cruel and Tyrannical disposition render him eminently qualified for playing the lawless, cold blooded Bravo in opposition. He is in short a disgrace to the "Fur Trade."

Colin Robertson: A frothy trifling conceited man, who would starve in any other Country and is perfectly useless here: fancies, or rather attempts to pass himself off as a clever fellow, a man of taste, of talents and of refinement; to none of which I need scarcely say he has the smallest pretension. He was bred to his Father's Trade an operative Weaver in the Town of Perth, but was too lazy to live by his Loom, read Novels, became Sentimental and fancied himself the hero of every tale of Romance that passed through his hands. Ran away from his master, found employment for a few months as a Grocer's Shopman at New York, but had not sufficient steadiness to retain his Situation. Pushed his way into Canada and was at the Age of 25 engaged as *Apprentice* Clerk by the N W Co for whom he came to the interior, but found so useless that he was dismissed from the Service. His age about 55 and his person of which he is exceedingly vain, large, soft, loosely thrown together inactive and helpless to infirmity. He is full of silly boasting and Egotism, rarely deals in plain matter of fact and his integrity is very questionable. To the Fur trade he is quite a

Burden, and a heavy burden too, being a compound of folly and extravagance, and disarranging and throwing into confusion whatsoever he puts his hand to in the shape of business. The concern would gain materially by allowing him to enjoy his situation a thousand Miles distant from the scene of operations instead of being taxed with his nominal Services in the Country.

This last was the most ill-considered of Simpson's entries, jumping as it does from Robertson's early NWC days to his later, somewhat tarnished years without taking into account his magnificent contributions to the HBC's survival in between. Simpson shunted Robertson aside by giving him insignificant assignments such as the Chief Factorship of New Brunswick. He was retired in 1840 after thirty-seven years' service and a year later was elected member for the Lake of Two Mountains riding in the Legislative Assembly of Canada.

The Character Book was an important if covert guide to Simpson's decisions because once an entry had been made, the Governor seldom altered his view of officers and clerks, no matter how their performance might improve or deteriorate. The real source of his authority flowed from the fact that he was the London Committee's man in North America. He held a tight grip over the HBC's Northern Department from 1821 onwards, but it was another five years before he supplanted Governor Williams of the Southern Department to head both districts, and he was officially accorded the grand title of Governor-in-Chief of Rupert's Land only in 1839. By then he was running the company's everyday affairs, although as late as 1846 the London board vetoed his request that he be allowed to appoint clerks in the Montreal Department without their approval.

The overseas Governor's most important leverage in his struggle for expanded authority was the slowness of the communications system with London—the days of transatlantic cable transmissions still being well in the future, conveniently after his time. As it was, a letter forwarded aboard the Company's spring supply ship to Hudson Bay was delivered in late summer, duly answered, and the reply received in England only by late autumn—to be acted upon the following spring in time for the vessel's return to York Factory, a full year after the original inquiry. By the time this annual cycle had run its course, most operational decisions had already been taken. At that, Simpson had few substantive arguments with his corporate parent, except that he wanted to exercise greater daring than the London Committee could stomach. He was also a more enthusiastic British Imperialist (and devout anti-revolutionary), urging London in 1824, for example, on no account to give up any Oregon territory north of the Columbia River.

In his dealings with London, Simpson enjoyed the incalculable advantage of having in his corner his original mentor, Andrew Colvile, that most influential of the HBC's Committeemen. For the first thirty years of Simpson's term, the London Governor in charge was Sir John Henry Pelly, who had already spent more than a decade on the HBC's board. He served simultaneously as a director and ultimately Governor of the Bank of England. Cultivated, clever and cordial, Pelly viewed the making of money as something of an intellectual tumbling exercise. His father, grandfather and great-grandfather had all been skippers in the service of the East India Company, and he himself enjoyed four years in command of his own ship. He insisted on being called Captain Pelly ever afterwards, and his official portrait shows him wearing the gold-braided Royal Navy jacket of Nelson's vintage, posing beside the model of a lighthouse. The beacon's presence was more authentic than his assumed RN captaincy, since Pelly was Deputy Master of Trinity House, Britain's pilotage and principal lighthouse authority.*

Pelly's lengthy tenure conveniently consolidated the Hudson's Bay Company's status within the British financial establishment. The reticent and largely self-perpetuating oligarchy that controlled most of its stock operated out of the Company's headquarters at Numbers 3 and 4 Fenchurch Street, near the corner of Gracechurch. Corinthian columns flanked the red brick building's arched front gate; inside, the height of the hall's white ceilings was set off by tall mahogany doors, brass lamps and velvet swags up the staircases. Each Wednesday at high noon the Governor, Deputy Governor and half a dozen Committeemen would gather to consider the Company's affairs, exchange City gossip and speculate on the government's evolving policies towards North America.

Herman Merivale, the Colonial Office's permanent undersecretary, voiced no objection to the HBC's occupation of the Prairie region on condition that the Company improve the social and economic situation of the native peoples within its purview. Under George Simpson, the HBC tacitly agreed to serve as an informal territorial agency of the British Empire, ensuring that there existed a modicum of law and order in this far corner of Queen Victoria's globe. In return, it was understood that the British government would help keep out settlers and prevent free trade in furs. Either incursion would have weakened

---

*Master of Trinity House at this time was the Duke of Wellington, a close friend and associate of Sir John's. During Pelly's term at the Bank of England, the nation's credit position grew so precarious that £2,000,000 had to be borrowed from the Bank of France. In the ensuing riots, Pelly (as the bank's former governor) invited Wellington to inspect the building's paramilitary defences, including the gun positions on its roof, in case there was a run on the bank. They knew how to deal with creditors in those days.

Sir John Henry Pelly

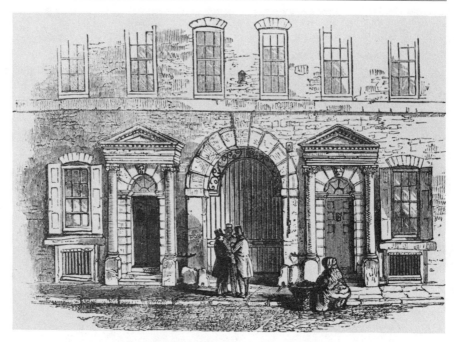

*Headquarters of the Hudson's Bay Company at
Numbers 3 and 4 Fenchurch Street, London*

or destroyed the HBC's monopoly, which the London bureaucrats recognized as being an essential deterrent if the territory in question was not to degenerate into a killing ground similar to the American West. "The reason for this situation was clear," commented historian David McNab. "If the Company did not treat its skilled native labour humanely, then there was always a distinct possibility that the Company's supply of furs would be either disrupted or curtailed altogether in any particular region. Using this reasoning, Merivale marshalled his arguments and concluded that, for the circumstances existing in Rupert's Land in the mid-nineteenth century, the best ruler was the Hudson's Bay Company." This practical attitude was of necessity based on third-hand information, with the Colonial Office dependent on reports from the HBC's London headquarters about what was really happening west of Lake Ontario.

One plaintive countervailing voice of protest was that of Alexander Kennedy Isbister. The articulate son of an HBC clerk and a Cree mother, he had joined the Company and served with distinction at Fort McPherson, then its northernmost outpost, which he had helped establish. Angered by what he considered Simpson's reluctance to promote Mixed Bloods, he resigned. After spending some years at Red River, he enrolled in the University of Aberdeen, was admitted to the bar, and eventually became dean of an important British teachers' college. He used his prestigious position to lobby Westminster and the Colonial Office on granting free trade to the Red River Métis, but his speeches, articles and books went unnoticed. His petition remains one of the most eloquent and unanswerable indictments of the Hudson's Bay Company's treatment of the Indian peoples: "When we assert that they are steeped in ignorance, debased in mind, and crushed in spirit, that by the exercise of an illegal claim over the country of their forefathers, they are deprived of the natural rights and privileges of free born men, that they are virtually slaves, as absolutely as the unredeemed negro population of the slave states of America—that by a barbarous and selfish policy, founded on a love of lucre, their affections are alienated from the British name and government, and they themselves shut out from civilisation, and debarred from every incentive thereto—that the same heinous system is gradually effacing whole tribes from the soil on which they were born and nurtured, so that a few years hence not one man among them will be left to point out where the bones of his ancestors repose—when we assert all this in honest, simple truth, does it not behoove every Christian man to demand that the British legislature should not continue to incur the fearful responsibility of permitting the extinction of these helpless, forlorn thousands of their fellow creatures, by lending its countenance to a monopoly engendering so huge a mountain of human misery? For the honour of this great country, we pray it will not be; and, sincerely trust we, some few voices will respond earnestly, Amen."

The native peoples had succumbed in dramatic numbers to the 1837 smallpox epidemic. That summer, the dreaded infection spread up the Missouri from St Louis, carried by crewmen of an American Fur Company supply ship who spread the virus at every stop. The Indians who went south to trade brought the disease back into Rupert's Land, and the virulent plague wiped out about three-quarters of the Plains people in one wave. A frightened traveller noticed there was no smoke rising from the Indian lodges. "Not a sound can be heard to break the awful stillness, save the ominous croak of the ravens, and mournful howl of wolves fattening on the human carcasses that lie strewed around. It seems as if the very genius of desolation had stalked through the prairies, and wreaked his vengeance on everything bearing the shape of humanity."

IN 1838, THE BRITISH GOVERNMENT had renewed the Company's licensed monopoly for a further twenty-one years, and during the next three years Queen Victoria had rewarded John Pelly with a baronetcy and

George Simpson with a knighthood—ostensibly for their support of Arctic exploration.

It was an auspicious moment. The young Queen was restoring the popular splendour of the monarchy, and although there is no firsthand record of Simpson's visit to Buckingham Palace, it would have been a grand occasion. The past triumphs of Lord Nelson and the Duke of Wellington, followed by its magnanimous treatment of France, had made England the pre-eminent leader among nations; the Royal Navy patrolled three oceans, ready to sink unbelievers at a moment's notice. The Empire was already being touted as an instrument of Christian destiny, and burgeoning London was the arbiter of world commerce and culture. It was a splendid time to be a member of the British gentry, and Simpson had just been initiated into its golden circle. He might be only the viceroy of an empty land, but he was still a worthy field marshal in the imperial obsession of Anglicizing the outer reaches of what was condescendingly defined as "the civilized world."

The Hudson's Bay Company was in a similar state of euphoria. Its Rupert's Land monopoly had been successfully extended in every direction; no significant rivals had replaced the Nor'Westers; American settlers had not yet captured the Oregon Country; the monetary returns of the Company's operations had never been higher; its Governor and his Committeemen had Britain's leading politicians in their pockets; and even if changing fashions were depressing the price of beaver hats, the Company's commercial prospects were sound. Sir George was being accorded most of the credit for this halcyon state of affairs. The Northern Department Council's forty-three Chief Factors and Traders presented Simpson with an ornate sterling silver trophy weighed down with scampering beavers and naked dancers. That spontaneous vote of confidence, and his freshly minted knighthood, permanently altered Simpson's outlook. Gone was the wilderness administrator; the Governor now ranked himself a diplomat and international financier.

His first venture into diplomacy had occurred three years before, when, along with Pelly, Simpson had visited St Petersburg to negotiate a new Alaskan fur-trade treaty with the Russian fur company. The dispute had lengthy historical roots. The commerce had its start in 1742 when the handful of starving survivors of Vitus Jonassen Bering's doomed expedition reached Petropavlovsk with valuable sea-otter pelts. After three decades of private trading, the largest operators in the region, the Shelikhov-Golikov Company and the Mylnikov Company, united in 1797 to form the Russian-American Company, which was granted a twenty-year monopoly of the North Pacific fur trade. Under its energetic resident governor, Alexander Baranov, an abundance of

*Sitka in 1805: headquarters of
the Russian-American Company*

seal skins was harvested and the company's operations were extended north and south along the Alaskan coastline. Its headquarters was built on the west coast of the Alexander Archipelago at Novo Arkhangelsk, now Sitka. So far from home base and operating in an agriculturally inhospitable climate, Baranov was forced to purchase food and trade goods from visiting Boston skippers. As an imaginative alternative, he sent an expedition southward to establish a factory farm near Bodega Bay, California. Some of the field crops did well and the company herds numbered fifteen hundred sheep and three thousand head of cattle. But the farm was not productive enough and too far away to be a dependable field kitchen.

By 1821, the combination of American privateers and Russian trappers had so depleted the quality and quantity of the Alaskan maritime fur catch that Tsar Alexander I issued his famous ukase unilaterally decreeing the North Pacific Coast, down to 51° north (just north of the tip of Vancouver Island), Russian territory. No foreign ships were to be allowed shore access within that boundary. Few paid much attention to this grand proclamation, least of all the Russians on the spot, who still needed what food they could get from the holds of visiting Yankee trading ships. It was at this point that the HBC entered the negotiations, boldly demanding that the Russians retreat northward beyond the 60th parallel of latitude. Eventually the border was set at

54°40′N, and the HBC gained the right to navigate international rivers across the Alaska Panhandle to its inland posts in what is now British Columbia. The uneasy peace was broken by the appointment of a charismatic naval officer, Baron Ferdinand Petrovich von Wrangell, to the post of Russian-American Company governor,* where he reigned with his nineteen-year-old bride, the Baroness Elizabeth Rossillon. Wrangell expanded the California farms, encouraged the detailed exploration of his territory, sponsored the first significant ethnological studies of Alaskan natives—and forced a confrontation with the HBC.

In 1834, Simpson dispatched one of his toughest traders, Peter Skene Ogden, to establish a Company post up the Stikine River. Aware that the attempt would be made, Wrangell hastily set up a blockade at the river mouth, fortifying a nearby Indian village (which he grandly renamed the Redoubt of St Dionysius) and anchoring the fourteen-gun *Chichagoff* under the command of a ferocious captain named Zarembo at a strategic turn in the channel. When Ogden appeared aboard his little brig, the *Dryad*, Zarembo fired a shot across her bow and ordered the HBC ship back into the Pacific. Ogden and the Russian captain argued their respective positions ever more loudly for eleven days. Characteristically, the HBC beat a strategic retreat, only to win by diplomacy what it dared not take in open combat.

The ambassadors chosen for this touchy assignment were Simpson and the HBC's British Governor, John Pelly. They left London in the summer of 1838, bound for St Petersburg, but detoured briefly to Copenhagen where Simpson challenged a local swimming champion to a race in the harbour, and won. "Few," he boasted, "can overmatch me in the water." They toured Pelly's Scandinavian timber estate, which Simpson was surprised to learn provided most of the wooden blocks used to pave London streets at the time. During a state dinner at Christiania (Oslo), Simpson purred when he heard himself described as "head of the most extended Dominions in the known world, the Emperor of Russia, the Queen of England and the President of the United States excepted." But his vanity was a bit deflated later that evening when he had to spend an hour in his hotel room mending his clothes: ". . . retired at 11, occupied till 12 Sewing Buttons on my Shirts and mending my breeches and Waistcoat. Damned bad Needles, worse thread and Villainous Sewing!"

During his journey Simpson complained about the homeliness of

---

*The Baron's best-known modern kinsman was George Wrangell, the debonair fellow with the patch over one eye who posed as the Man in the Hathaway Shirt for advertising campaigns during the 1950s.

European women. "Indeed," he noted, "I have not observed what I should call a pretty looking woman in the course of my travels through these northern Regions: our Canadian and half breed women of North America are angels compared with them." At St Petersburg, Simpson and Wrangell met for the first time, and they immediately recognized each other as kindred spirits. "An extraordinary-looking, ferret-eyed, red-whiskered little creature in full regimentals," was Simpson's comment on his negotiating opponent, adding, "Wrangell and I are very thick ... a nice, intelligent clever little man." The arrangement they signed allowed the HBC trading rights across the Alaska Panhandle in return for supplying fresh produce from its farms in Oregon and paying an annual rental of two thousand prime sea-otter skins. The pact, which endured until Alaska was sold to the United States in 1867, was so mutually beneficial it survived hostilities between the two companies' parent governments that broke out as the vicious Crimean War in 1854.

The impressive results of that initial foray into statesmanship fed Simpson's already substantial sense of self-importance. Feeling that his bush empire was no longer a stage significant enough for his airs and graces, he set his mind on becoming the first man to circle the world via British North America, Hawaii, Alaska and Siberia, through Europe and back to Canada. He even hired a ghost writer to record his progress across the continents. Only two months after he had been knighted and appropriately fêted in London, Simpson was ready to begin the first lap. Accompanied by two young British aristocrats (Lords Caledon and Mulgrave) who were headed west on a buffalo hunt, he intended to leave dockside at Lachine in grand style. The two dozen Iroquois paddling his two canoes were each supplied with specially dyed red feathers for their caps and the Company boat flags were to have been unfurled simultaneously. But a spring snowstorm came up, and they barely managed to get across Lake St Louis without being swamped.

Up the Ottawa-Mattawa route the canoes rushed, across the upper reaches of Georgian Bay and along the northern shore of Superior— the old voyageur journey—reaching Fort Garry in record time. There his two companions disembarked and Simpson set off on a breakneck ride across the Prairies. He covered at least fifty miles a day, using relays of horses to save time. The description of his caravan's departure from Fort Garry, at five in the morning on July 3, 1841, is typical of the overblown sense of drama attached to Simpson's journey by Adam Thom, his ghost writer: "While we defiled through the gates into the open plain with an horizon before us as well defined as that of the blue ocean, the scene resembling the moving of an eastern caravan in the boundless sands of Arabia—a medley of pots and pans and kettles, in our single vehicle, the unruly pack horses prancing under their loads, and every cavalier armed to the teeth, assisting his steed to neigh and caper with bit and spur. The effect was not a little heightened by a brilliant sunrise, the firing of cannon, the streaming of flags and the shouts of spectators."

Getting across the western mountains and down to the Columbia River had taken six weeks and five days of hard riding. Although Simpson was well into his fifties by then, he was never in the saddle less than eleven hours a day. He inspected all the posts en route, reorganized his Company's Pacific fur trade, and took an unexpected detour to the Company's southernmost station. Yerba Buena, named for the Spanish mint plants that covered the area, had a population of fewer than fifty, and the area (renamed San Francisco in 1847) did not really flourish until after the mid-century gold rush. But there were furs to be traded, so the HBC had opened a small outpost and put William Glen Rae in charge of it.

Brigades of Bay men had actually been venturing into the area for most of a decade but had been run out of the country for buying mustangs from Indian horse thieves. Rae, who was the son-in-law of Dr John McLoughlin, Chief Factor at Fort Vancouver on the Columbia, arrived at the post six months earlier than his wife, Eloisa, and almost immediately got into personal and political trouble. The local government at the time was in debt to London financiers for the equivalent of about $50 million, and the sudden appearance of the HBC on what was still Mexican territory alarmed local citizens, who feared it might be a plot to turn California over to the British bondholders instead of repaying the loan. These rumours were fanned by Rae's support of the revolutionary leaders, Juan Bautista Alvarado and José Castro. When they were defeated in 1842 by General Manuel Micheltorena, who remained in California as governor for three years until driven out by the rebels, they were carrying arms and ammunition worth the equivalent of $15,000, advanced for future considerations by Rae's HBC outlet. At the same time, Rae was known to be drinking too much and indulging in a torrid affair with a Spanish woman; he had also been overheard boasting that while it had cost £75,000 to drive Yankee traders from the Columbia, the Hudson's Bay Company would drive them out of California if it cost a million. Worst of all, the rebels did not honour their debts, and his little post began to show serious financial losses.

When Simpson arrived at Yerba Buena in December 1841, he accused Rae of departing from Company policies by granting credit too easily and was so unhappy about the manager's various misadventures that he ordered the outpost closed. Wishing to give his son-in-law another chance, McLoughlin delayed implementing the order for a few seasons, but on January 19, 1845, Rae short-circuited the dilemma by blowing his brains out. When his servant, William Sinclair, rushed in at the sound of the shot, he found a swooning Eloisa, an empty pistol, a bottle of opium potion and a note explaining that the victim had fallen into difficulties through the malice and intrigue of others.*

Simpson did not tarry long in California but sailed off aboard the HBC brig *Cowlitz* to Hawaii, then still known as the Sandwich Islands.† France had already colonized Tahiti; New Zealand had come under British control; and Hawaii was attracting the ambitious attention of the United States, France and Britain because of its relatively prosperous economy. Once merely a provisioning way station for whalers and a fur-trade trans-shipment point between London and the Columbia River, Hawaii had begun to export sugar, molasses, salt and arrowroot in return for imports of flour, lumber and machinery. As the island's economy became more sophisticated, the once semi-clad women were evangelized by New England missionaries, and their muumuus became the voluminous badge of their conversion.

The HBC had maintained an agency on the islands since the early 1830s, manned by George Pelly, the British Governor's cousin, mainly as an outlet for the sale of salted salmon and timber from the Pacific Northwest. Located at the corner of Honolulu's Fort and Queen streets, the Hudson's Bay post was yielding a significant profit. Simpson's arrival coincided with an alteration in status of the Hawaiian king, Kamehameha III, who had recently surrendered some of his personal power by voluntarily signing the islands' first constitution. After looking over the situation, the HBC Governor emerged as a militant champion of Hawaiian independence, mainly because he recognized that the most likely alternatives—French or American occupation—would be bad for business. Although he became an energetic spokesman on

---

*The HBC post, which was on the west side of what is now Montgomery Street, between Sacramento and Clay, was permanently closed in 1849. Nine years later, when workmen were excavating for sewers on nearby Commercial Street, they found a glass-covered coffin containing Rae's headless remains.

†The name was given to the beautiful archipelago by Captain James Cook in honour of his patron, the 4th Earl of Sandwich, who had served as First Lord of the Admiralty during the American Revolution. An inveterate gambler, the Earl would spend twenty-four hours at a time playing games of chance and invented the sandwich so he wouldn't have to lose time leaving the room to eat.

The port of Honolulu, 1857

behalf of Hawaiian freedom, in his private correspondence with London, Simpson speculated about buying the island nation's territory and reselling it (at enormous profit) to the Russians, who were intently seeking a warm-water port in the Pacific. In his consultations with Hawaii's royal circles, Simpson made a particularly strong impression on the Reverend William Richards, a Congregational missionary who had wormed himself into the islands' prime ministership. He arranged for Richards to meet him back in London, where he promised to help argue the case for Hawaiian independence and even negotiated an HBC loan of £10,000 to back the cause of liberty—at 12 percent interest, of course. Once back in England, Simpson did in fact prove genuinely helpful to the Hawaiian cause, accompanying the islanders' delegation to Paris and Brussels. Britain, France and Belgium committed themselves to recognizing Hawaii's independence, but the islands were eventually annexed by the Americans.

After his Sandwich sojourn, Simpson sailed back to Alaska. Then he crossed over to Siberia and, accompanied by an escort of Cossacks, rode by horse and carriage across seven thousand miles of inhospitable terrain, the momentum broken only by sumptuous banquets along the way tendered by local governors. When they fed him pyramids of caviar he reciprocated with a delicacy of his own: hors-d'oeuvre· of travel-weary pemmican. Simpson arrived in St Petersburg too exhausted to participate in the Tsarist court's piquant social scene and was back in London nineteen months and nineteen days after leaving on his round-the-world adventure. The final page of his diary records no more substantial conclusion about his momentous voyage than the fact that the prettiest girl he had seen along the way was in Gotland, a Swedish island in the Baltic.

GEORGE SIMPSON'S RELATIONS with women were legendary. When he was referred to as "the father of the fur trade" it was sometimes with a nudge and a knowing wink. Grant MacEwan, a former lieutenant-governor of Alberta and a popular Western Canadian historian, claimed the Governor had "fathered seventy sons between the Red River and the Rocky Mountains." That is an unlikely if mathematically possible proposition, but he did spend ten years in the Fur Country and certainly made the most of his bachelorhood. After he had married his eighteen-year-old cousin Frances in 1830, there was no indication that Simpson was anything but a faithful husband. But before he joined the HBC, Simpson had already acknowledged two children born out of wedlock in Britain,* and during the decade between his arrival in Canada and his marriage, he had at least five other children by four women.

His derisive references to Indian Country women as "bits of brown" are only the best known of what are now considered sexist comments. In a letter to his friend McTavish from Île-à-la-Crosse, where three babies were born during his brief visit, he remarked that "the White Fish diet of the district seems to be favourable to procreation, and had I a good pimp in my suite I might have been inclined to deposit a little of my Spawn. . . ." His lechery, not uncommon for the times, was unabashedly rampant.

In the same letter to McTavish at York Factory, in which he asked him to arrange a "private or separate entrance to my apartments" to make it easier for his nocturnal female companions to come and go, he instructed his friend to "turn off" Betsey Sinclair, the first of his wilderness loves. The daughter of Chief Factor William Sinclair and his native wife, Margaret Nahoway, she had borne him a child. "Simpson continually violated the custom of the country, creating confusion and anguish. Fur-trade society thought it appropriate, for example, to consider Betsey Sinclair as 'Mrs. Simpson', but to Simpson she was just a mistress of whom he soon tired," Sylvia Van Kirk, the University of Toronto historian who is a specialist in social aspects of the fur trade, has noted. ". . . He never really served an apprenticeship in the country which might have conditioned him to the 'custom of the country' and his attitude coincided with the first missionaries' attacks on country marriages." Once he wanted to be rid of her, his instructions to McTavish were crude and precise: "My Family concerns I leave entirely to your kind management, if you can dispose of the Lady it will be satisfactory as she is an unnecessary and expensive appendage. I see no fun in keeping a Woman, without enjoying her charms which my present rambling life does not enable me to do; but if she is unmarketable I have no wish that she should be a general accommodation shop to all the young bucks at the Factory and in addition to her own chastity a padlock may be useful; Andrew is a neat handed Fellow and having been in China may perhaps know the pattern of those used in that part of the World."

Simpson's longest-lasting country relationship was with Margaret, the daughter of George Taylor, York Factory's sloop master. She

---

*One of those daughters, Isabella, married James Cook Gordon, a Scottish solicitor; the other, Maria, became the wife of Donald MacTavish in Inverness and, later, of Donald Campbell from Grafton, Ontario.

accompanied him on his 1828 Pacific adventures. When he left her pregnant on Hudson Bay during another journey, he gave these curt instructions to McTavish: "Pray keep an Eye on the commodity and if she bring forth anything in proper time and of the right color let them be taken care of but if any thing be amiss let the whole be bundled about their business. . . ." Simpson had two sons by Margaret, referred to her brother Tom as his brother-in-law and treated her family with special consideration. He also had at least two other simultaneous affairs (and a child each), one with Mary Keith, the daughter of Chief Factor James Keith, the other with a Montreal mistress named Ann Foster. "He was utterly ruthless, and introduced the regency-buck approach to women into Western Canada," the fur-trade historian Irene Spry has concluded. "His sex-object attitude to women was largely responsible for the breakdown of marriage *à la façon du pays*, which was a humanly decent type of relationship. He created a total dislocation in what had been a perfectly valid type of society."

Unlike the American West, where the so-called squaw men living with Indian women were regarded as inferior, in the Canadian Northwest, country marriages were respectable liaisons, many lasting their partners' lifetimes. Even the courts occasionally recognized the special status of such unions. William Connolly had married a native woman called Suzanne Pas-de-Nom in a country ceremony; they were together thirty years and had six children. But when Connolly retired to Montreal, he officially married a white woman, his cousin Julia Woolrich. On his death his eldest Mixed Blood son sued for a share of his father's estate. The courts ruled that the marriage was valid and declared the son a legal heir. John Macdonell, who retired in 1814, took his country wife, Magdeleine Poitras, out of the Fur Country and married her in a church ceremony forty-six years after she had joined him at the age of twelve on the Qu'Appelle River. When the wife of Chief Trader Nicol Finlayson died of dropsy, he penned this moving obituary: "I have not got over the shock of my severe bereavement. My hearth is desolate. I have not even a domestic animal to caress me when I enter my house from a journey. . . . I feel greatly the loss of her prattle, as it beguiled me for many a solitary hour."

In the absence of officiating clergy, these country weddings were an accepted and lasting phenomenon that had evolved within fur-trade society. In effect, they were a form of civil marriage. Besides being the Bay men's sexual partners, the women, proficient in comfort and survival skills, gave meaning to life in the raw land.

As with most other aspects of daily existence in the bush, the Nor'Westers had been more progressive about recognizing the benefits of these domestic arrangements in terms of furthering trade, particularly if a local chief's daughter were involved and kinship connections came into play. After initially attempting to outlaw such relationships, the HBC Governors relented, heeding the advice Simpson sent to London in a report dated May 18, 1821, from Fort Wedderburn in Athabasca. "Connubial alliances are the best security we can have of the goodwill of the Natives," he wrote. "I have therefore commended the Gentlemen to form connections with the principal Families immediately on their arrival, which is no difficult matter as the offer of their Wives and Daughters is the first token of their Friendship and hospitality."

To discourage transferred or retired traders from leaving families across the Northwest to be nourished at Company expense, the HBC at its 1821 council meeting adopted a tough (if unenforceable) resolution stating that "all officers or servants of the company having women or children and wishing to leave the same in the Country on their retirement therefore be required to make such provision for their future maintenance, more particularly for that of the Children as circumstances may reasonably warrant and the means of the individual permit . . . all those desirous of withdrawing the same from the country be allowed every facility for that purpose and none be allowed hereafter to take a woman without binding himself down to leave 1/10 of his annual wages in the hands of the Company as a provision for his family in event of Death or retirement from the country. . . ."

One of Simpson's peeves was those country wives who insisted on advising his resident officers on how to deal with the Company. He lamented the influence of "petty coat politicians" and was particularly incensed with Mrs McDonald, wife of the Chief Trader at Fort Qu'Appelle, whom he described as "a stout good looking Dame" but condemned for trying to run the post with her backstage "persuasion and cunning."

Most of the country marriages worked well, even if the women had fewer rights than church-wedded wives of the time. After 1823, their HBC husbands had to sign marriage contracts and whenever a Bay man left his country wife, besides supporting their children, he had to find her another suitable provider.

It was Simpson himself who disrupted this cosy arrangement by marrying a white woman and importing her into the Fur Country as his consort. "[He] led the stampede among the active and retired officers for a European marriage with a British-born white wife," noted John E. Foster, the University of Alberta historian. "It was no longer acceptable to have a grandmother, let alone a mother or wife, who smoked a pipe as she strung snowshoes." The fact that it was the Governor—their role model—who had irrevocably altered the pattern

After Simpson's marriage to Frances it became
unfashionable to have an Indian wife

of what had become an accepted practice had cataclysmic consequences. Once the Bay men began to marry in Scotland and England, Indian women, on whose kindness and energy the vast fortunes of the fur trade had largely been built, were relegated to inferior status as either workhorses or mistresses. "The coming of white women to the Indian Country," argues Sylvia Van Kirk, "brought into disrepute indigenous social customs of the fur trade. Marriage *à la façon du pays* was no longer acceptable, especially with the presence of missionaries intolerant of any deviation. The presence of white women underlined the cultural shortcomings of mixed-blood wives, particularly in more settled areas where their native skills were no longer required. Unfortunately, European ladies themselves, by zealously guarding what they considered to be their intrinsically superior status, actively fostered an increasing stratification of fur-trade society."

When Simpson decided to visit England in hopes of finding a suitable bride, he sent his country wife, Margaret Taylor (then with child), to Bas-de-la-Rivière at the mouth of the Winnipeg River, presided over by Chief Factor John Stuart, whose own country wife was

Lady Frances Simpson

Margaret's sister. Simpson told them nothing of his plans, and by the time he received a letter from Stuart telling him the news of his newly born, bonny wee son, the Governor was within two weeks of marrying his beautiful cousin Frances, twenty-six years his junior.

THE WOOING OF FRANCES by the middle-aged Governor had to be sandwiched between business meetings with his London principals. At one point he asked his faithful sidekick McTavish, who was in Britain at the same time and bent upon a similar mission, "Let me know if you have any fair cousin likely to suit an invalid like me," noting, "I see you are something like myself, shy with the fair, we should not be so much so with the Browns. . . ." Within weeks of the writing of this missive, both men had chosen their loves and married—McTavish in Edinburgh to Catherine Turner, the Governor in a suburban London church (Bromley St Leonard's) to Frances, the daughter of Geddes Mackenzie

Simpson, who two decades earlier had given the young George a first job with his London sugar company. The two happy couples decided to sail across the Atlantic and spend their honeymoons together proceeding inland by canoe.

Their lighthearted mood was shattered in a dramatic domestic confrontation when they reached Montreal. McTavish had also abruptly abandoned a country wife, but his relationship had been much longer and seemed more solid than Simpson's. He had lived with Nancy McKenzie, the Mixed Blood daughter of a distinguished Nor'Wester, for seventeen years, and they were the parents of six living children. When he sailed away from York Factory on his British courting venture, he took one of his daughters with him and left all his personal effects behind, which must have reassured Nancy that he intended to return. McTavish allowed others to break the news of his overseas marriage and had his personal possessions shipped to Moose Factory, where the sympathetic Governor had found a good posting for him. "I owe it all to Geordy," he breezily confided to a friend.

McTavish finally did pay a lump-sum dowry of £200 to an HBC veteran named Pierre Leblanc willing to marry his Nancy. The prospective bridegroom was even granted a week's leave of absence by the Company for courtship duty. Margaret Taylor, the Governor's last country wife, was similarly "placed" with an HBC employee, Amable Hogue by name. Simpson took great trouble to hide his previous brood from his new wife—although Frances later confessed she "was always terrified to look about her, in case of seeing something disagreeable." Most Chief Factors, themselves devoted to their country wives, felt bitter about what had happened and, afraid of criticizing the Governor, turned their scorn on McTavish. "What could be your aim in discarding her whom you clasped to your bosom in virgin purity and had for seventeen years with you?" demanded John Stuart, who had known Nancy McKenzie from childhood. "She was the wife of your choice and has borne you seven children, now stigmatized with ignominy . . . if with a view of domestic happiness you have thus acted, I fear the aim has been missed and that remorse will be your portion for life . . . I think it is well our correspondence may cease."

When the newlyweds arrived in Montreal, McTavish's thirteen-year-old daughter, Mary, who was attending school nearby, surprised them one evening by being ushered unexpectedly into their private dining quarters. According to the only report of the scene that followed, McTavish introduced her to his new wife, "who got stupid, but shook hands with the Miss who was very pretty and mighty impudent. . . . [Mrs McTavish] got white and red and at last rose and left the room, all the party looking very uncomfortable except [her husband] and the girl. [Mrs Simpson] followed and found her in a violent fit of crying, she said she knew the child was to have been home that night, but thought she would have been spared such a public introduction."

These awkward unpleasantnesses behind them, the quartet set out from Lachine on May 2, 1830, for their wilderness honeymoon. Only George Simpson would have chosen a departure time of 4 A.M., but he did allow a brief breakfast pause five hours later, the gentlemen being carried ashore on the backs of the Iroquois paddlers and the ladies being cradled carefully in their brawny arms. At Lake of Two Mountains a deputation of Algonquin chiefs gathered to pay the Governor homage, and an eight-year-old girl presented Frances with a bouquet of cherry blossoms.

They were later entertained at Bytown by the wife of Lieutenant-Colonel John By, who was busy building the Rideau Canal between the Ottawa and St Lawrence rivers. After leaving the Ottawa, the two canoes turned west along the Mattawa, and Frances recorded her impressions of the passing panorama: "On either side are stupendous rocks of the most fantastic forms. Some bear the appearance of Gothic castles, others exhibit rows of the most regular and beautifully carved corinthian pillars; deep caverns are formed in some, while others present a smooth level surface, crowned with tufts of pines and cedars. From the upper end of the portage is seen a beautiful waterfall, which dashes over immense masses of rocks thro' which it had worn itself many a channel foaming and roaring to a considerable distance, the spray glittering in the sun with all the varied hues of the rainbow."

Through Georgian Bay, across the North Channel of Huron and along Superior they went, and after a brief stopover at Fort William (where they changed to smaller canoes), they reached what Frances described as "the Savage World." Three of the paddlers had deserted by then, worn out by Simpson's relentlessness. The portages were getting tougher. At one half-mile crossing rendered all but impassable by fallen trees and slippery rocks, the water was waist-deep in places. "To cross this," noted the exasperated Frances, "baffled the skill both of Mrs. McTavish and Myself (good walkers as we flattered ourselves to be) and accordingly after mature deliberation, it was agreed that each should be carried by a man chosen for the purpose. Tomma Felix took me up in his arms, and Nicholas Monique, an old Indian, volunteered his services in transporting my companion across the miry portion of road which lay before us. Tomma pushed on, despite of every difficulty making however many stumbles and false steps—but

Nicholas' load being rather heavier, he absolutely came to a stand still, in the midst of a bog, and declared he could not take the Lady a step farther in his arms, but if she would get on his back, he thought he might accomplish the journey. Mr. Simpson who was coming on after us, persuaded Mrs. McTavish (with some difficulty) as a last resource to do as Nicholas recommended, which she at length agreed to, and on the back of Nicholas accordingly mounted: the scene however was so ludicrous that the by-standers could not resist a laugh, in which Mrs. McTavish joined so heartily, that poor Nicholas was thrown off his equilibrium, stumbled forwards, fell on his face, and gave his unfortunate rider a summerset over his head, into the mud: throwing her into a situation the most awkward, and ridiculous that ever a poor Lady was placed in."

At one encampment, having slogged the entire day through a succession of rain squalls, members of the bedraggled little expedition were awake until eleven at night drying their clothes—only to be rudely roused by the hated shout "*Levez! Levez!*" a few minutes after midnight. Honeymoon or not, Sir George was determined to break yet another speed record.

Along the way, Frances Simpson was paid a personal honour. At the far end of the aptly named Rainy Lake at a trading post then known as Fort Lac la Pluie, she made such a luminous impression on its drenched inhabitants that they decided to rename their community Fort Frances. The Governor's lady later recalled her guided tour of the lilliputian settlement by Chief Trader Thomas McMurray: "... old and weather beaten as he was, he surpassed all the Gentlemen I had met with in these Wilds, as a Lady's Man but altho' our walk did not occupy an hour, it quite exhausted all his fine speeches, and the poor man seemed as much relieved when we returned to the house ... as if he had just been freed from an attack of the Night-Mare."

On the final lap into Fort Garry, they travelled the clock round and arrived at midnight. Riders had spotted the Governor's party and had warned the settlers of his coming, so there was a lively torchlight parade mustered to meet them. "The reception I here met with," Frances recalled, "convinced me that if the inhabitants of this remote region were plain and homely in their manners, they did not want for kindness of heart, and the desire of making every thing appear favorable, and pleasing, to the eye and mind of a stranger."

When the Simpsons eventually settled there, it turned out to be a far from happy experience. Instead of trying to repair the existing Fort Garry at the juncture of the Red and Assiniboine rivers, which had been devastated by the flood of 1826,* the Governor built himself a new official residence above the flood plain, nineteen miles to the north. Known as Lower Fort Garry, it covered thirteen choice acres and took eight years to complete. Its limestone bastions were erected by the best masons in the territory. No expense was spared during construction, and the Governor uncharacteristically tried to hide the expenditures from London, not reporting any disbursements for a whole year and then claiming the cost had really amounted to little more than the provisions consumed by the workmen. The grandeur of the imposing buildings was enhanced by the installation of an elegant pianoforte, provision of sets of monogrammed cutlery, and all the most fashionable furnishings worthy of turning the new fort into the community's social as well as economic centre. The Simpsons moved into the Stone Fort (as it quickly became known) in 1832, but it was soon clear that the *beau monde* pretensions of the Governor and his lady would never be realized.

Their first child, George Geddes, was so frail at birth that he survived only seven months, and both parents suffered serious depression and subsequent maladies. Simpson talked vaguely about quitting the fur trade but could not afford to retire because he had lost £4,000 in a bad investment. His oversupply of energy found so few outlets that he expended most of it picking quarrels with the fort's cook. He spent his time at Red River brooding about why a Governor of his repute and accomplishments should have to count his days in such godforsaken outskirts of empire. He refused to accept the Mixed Bloods of the settlement as appropriate company for himself or Frances, and was particularly insulting to HBC officers for living with and loving country wives—even though he had himself been an ardent champion of the practice for most of the preceding decade. When Colin Robertson tried to visit the Stone Fort with his Mixed Blood wife, Theresa Chalifoux, Simpson was enraged at such impropriety. "Robertson brought his bit of Brown with him to the Settlement this Spring in hopes she would pick up a few English manners before visiting the civilized world," he noted with disdain, "but it would not do—I told him distinctly the thing was impossible, which mortified him exceedingly." Only two country-born women, both maids, were allowed into Mrs Simpson's

---

*The last of several forts built at or near this location, it remained the HBC's inland administrative headquarters for thirty-five years, becoming the seat of the Métis Provisional Government during the Red River Rebellion. Everything but its north gate was demolished in 1882 to permit the straightening of Winnipeg's Main Street.

*The Reverend William Cockran, who once came to dine
at the Simpsons' riding a cow*

sanctified presence. (Ironically, one of these servants was Nancy Leblanc, McTavish's former country wife.)

Having rebuffed the idea of social intercourse with most of the colony's population, the Simpsons were thrown upon the company of the few white settlers, mainly the missionaries' wives, who suited the Governor's temperament even less. "I am most heartily tired of Red River," he wrote to McTavish, complaining that his bride had made no friendships there and recounting peevishly the social shortcomings of the local clerics' wives. "Mrs. Jones is a good unmeaning Woman whom we merely see for half an hour occasionally," he wrote, "and Mrs. Cockrane [Cockran] whose assumed puritanism but ill conceals the vixen, shines only when talking of elbow Grease and the scouring of pots and pans."*

---

*Simpson was especially miffed when the Reverend William Cockran arrived late at a formal dinner riding a cow, with the lame explanation that his horse was snowbound.

By 1833, it had become obvious that the Simpsons would have to move away from their wilderness fort.* The Governor transferred his management operations permanently to Lachine and took Frances back to England where she remained for the next dozen years, seeing her husband only occasionally while raising their four children, Frances Webster (Fanny), Augusta D'Este (Gussy), Margaret Mackenzie (Maggie) and John Henry Pelly (Moses). Within the limitations of Simpson's expedient boorishness towards women, theirs was a workable and occasionally loving relationship.

Simpson treated Frances as a prized but almost inanimate possession, seldom allowing her to express any will or view of her own. After she returned to live with him at Lachine in 1845, she continued to be heartsick for London, enduring her chatelaineship of the Canadian fur trade with well-trained grace but no enthusiasm. Her husband was impatient with the formalities of the times, even with such simple rituals as reciting grace before meals, and at one formal dinner, when Frances insisted he do so, Simpson embarrassed her by abruptly blurting, "Lord have mercy on what is now before us," then immediately digging into the first course.

Their mansion on the north flank of the old Lachine Canal (large enough that it had once been an inn) became the Company's overseas headquarters, although most commerce still flowed in and out of York Factory. By moving to Lachine, Simpson for the first time tied the Hudson's Bay Company into Montreal's commercial mainstream. Here at last he found an outlet for his social aspirations, quickly earning his place as a key member of the fledgling metropolis's Establishment. To exploit that function to the full, he converted his house into a showplace, permanently exhibiting paintings and objects from the continent's hinterland. Besides the portrait of Napoleon in his antechamber, the house was filled with a dozen oil portraits from the Indian Country by Paul Kane and other artists, Indian bark boxes with porcupine quill embroidery, ornamental canoe paddles, a model Indian bark tent, buffalo robes and glass cases brimming with stuffed birds.

---

*Lower Fort Garry served as a barracks for British soldiers stationed at Red River in the mid-1840s and later became the residence of Eden Colvile when he was associate governor of Rupert's Land. The fort languished as a minor trading centre, a North West Mounted Police training depot, a prison and an asylum until 1911. Two years later it was leased to the Manitoba Motor League and became known as the Manitoba Motor Country Club. Lower Fort Garry was later transferred to the government as a National Historic Park; its restored quarters are open to the public.

From a large office overlooking Lake St Louis on the main floor of the magnificent residence, the aging Sir George ruled his empire. He entertained visiting dignitaries, dispensed rough justice and, in calm possession of authority, comforted himself with the certainty that his tenure was fulfilling heaven's command.

Return of a war party with Fort Victoria in the background

CHAPTER 11

GALAHADS OF THE PACIFIC

"Necessity has no laws."
—Peter Skene Ogden

THE WILDEST SHORES OF GEORGE SIMPSON'S TRADING ESTATE were the HBC's Columbia and New Caledonia departments, stretching from the Gulf of California to the southern edge of Alaska. Separated from the U.S. eastern seaboard and the Company's main sphere of influence across British North America, the people of these mountain valleys and jagged coasts obeyed their own laws.

Within a few decades the two satrapies were transformed from Indian hunting grounds into HBC fur-trapping preserves. The Americans, driven by the gravitational pull of their manifest destiny, were bent on extending their Union westward to encompass the continent; the British stepped in to claim Vancouver Island and mainland British Columbia. "An imperial tide lapped the shores of the Northwest Coast," wrote historian Barry M. Gough, "and in doing so changed the character of human occupation, and it brought with it at the flood new political, legal and social institutions whose legacies are still apparent." For the two countries destined to share the upper part of the North American continent, the takeover of these westernmost lands meant having to confront the Hudson's Bay Company. For Great Britain, which initially claimed both regions, the process strengthened the conviction of its wiser statesmen that trade, not dominion, constituted the wealth of nations.

The Company's Pacific affairs, while ultimately governed by the whims and dictates of George Simpson acting on behalf of the HBC's London Committee, were in the hands of a defiant triumvirate of Galahads: Dr John McLoughlin, Peter Skene Ogden and Sir James Douglas, former Nor'Westers all, who ruled their distant provinces with unorthodox methods and astounding results.

ONE OF SEVERAL ELEMENTS making the Pacific fur trade different from that of the rest of the continent was its use of horses instead of canoes, because of the difficult topography and formidable river systems. The animals became essential to the trapping outfits, lugging in trade goods and provisions, carrying out the pelts, finding their own forage along the way—and, in the last resort, being themselves a handy food supply for starving trappers. Burdened with wood-frame packs, the horses had a tough time of it. To thwart nocturnal thieves, the animals were tethered so close to their sleeping owners that they could rarely reach enough grazing ground to regain their strength from the day's exertions. The steep, rocky trails and absence of inland smithies to provide new shoes meant that their battered hooves were soon worn away, curtailing their usefulness as beasts of burden. Because every trapper required three or four animals each season, the Indians realized that the horse trade could be at least as profitable as the bartering of fur, and made the most of the situation by selling the white man their culls—wild-tempered mustangs or nags more suitable for the boneyard.

Nor were Indian-HBC relations nearly as peaceful as in other Company territories. The Oregon Country's American mountain men had introduced the violent tradition of their breed, competing directly with the Indians for furs and treating them as a species less worthy than beaver. Violence and murder were so common that Senator Thomas Hart Benton, who championed westward expansion during his three decades in Congress, estimated that by the end of the 1820s at least five hundred of the American trappers had been killed in skirmishes with Rocky Mountain tribes.

The Northwest Coast Indians were ruled by an elite of slave-owning chiefs with a highly developed culture and powerful brigades of war canoes. Relieved of having to expend most of their energies in the daily hunt for food that hampered the evolution of inland Indian societies, the Haida, Nootka, Bella Coola, Tsimshian, Kwakiutl and Coast Salish geared their year to the rush of salmon swarming up Pacific inlets. One early explorer claimed the fish filled the rivers, so that "you could walk across on their backs."

At first, the coastal and inland peoples viewed the white invaders as very strange indeed: they were all males and carried "magic sticks," as muskets were first described. But once the newcomers and their demands became known, they were treated as envoys from distant tribes—in other words, as potential enemies, especially when they began interfering with the traditional slave trade. Many of the Northwest Coast Indian tribes kept slaves, valued at from eight to fifteen blankets for a healthy male and more for an agreeable female. Regular slave auctions were held not only in Oregon but in what is now Canadian territory near Fort Simpson on the Nass River of British Columbia. Yankee skippers regularly bought slaves at Cape Classet, the present-day Cape Flattery, at the northwest tip of Washington State, and at Nahwitti, near the northern end of Vancouver Island, trading them to the Haida of the Queen Charlotte Islands for sea otter skins. Driven by their Company's paternalistic impulses, HBC traders did their best to eradicate such practices, granting protection to runaway slaves and treating all Indians as British subjects. But George Simpson was not above manipulating personal lives in an effort to develop trade. In April 1825 he instructed John Work, one of his Columbia Department officers, to marry the daughter of a chief of the Cayuse, uncharacteristically promising that the ceremony would be at Company expense, because its traders would be travelling through Cayuse territory and the lady (whom Simpson ordered taken along on every journey) might afford protection to the Company's brigades.

Unlike the Cree, who provided most of the pelts at the posts around Hudson Bay, Pacific Coast Indians were rarely lured into the fur trade. In the Oregon Country, their places were taken by so-called Freemen, usually discharged or retired HBC servants who wanted to remain in the wilds. Most of them had Mixed Blood backgrounds, but they missed the permanent home base of the Red River Colony that provided the Métis with personal stability and communal support. Simpson described them as "the very scum of the country and generally outcasts from the Service for misconduct . . . the most unruly and troublesome gang to deal with in this or perhaps any other part of the World." He was not far wrong. They were impossible to control, fought constantly among themselves, abandoned their trapping parties on impulse to go hunting on their own and accumulated debts at Company stores they had no intention of paying—simply trading their next catch to the competition.

That competition was American, based in St Louis on the Mississippi River; the Missouri route to the west coast tracked by Lewis and Clark was too circuitous and dangerous for easy trade. Originally held back by sheer distance, the disruptions of the War of 1812 and the fury of the rampaging Blackfoot, the Americans by the mid–1820s began moving into the HBC's domain, seriously undermining the Company's commerce. Simpson regarded this intrusion as highly dangerous, not only in terms of daily trade but because he saw the mountain men as the inevitable precursors of colonization. As it turned out, the more significant forerunners of the U.S. claim on Oregon were the missionaries who started arriving in the mid–1830s and immediately recognized the country's economic potential; they soon became effective evangelists for its emancipation into the waiting arms of the American Union.

The vast expanse of the Oregon Country had been officially declared open to joint occupation by the 1818 Convention between Britain and the United States, a policy that was expediently renewed in 1827. Because these accords provided only for equal freedom to occupy, both the American and British governments were anxious to strengthen their claims to more enduring possession. Washington felt its case was particularly strong because the Columbia River had been discovered by the Boston trader Captain Robert Gray in 1792 and first explored by Lewis and Clark a dozen years later. The first permanent settlement in the region had been the trading post established by John Jacob Astor's Pacific Fur Company at Astoria. In its counter-claim, London pointed out that while Gray might have discovered the mouth of the Columbia, Captain George Vancouver's men had ascended the river and mapped it and that even if Astoria had been there first, the North West Company had captured it. Besides, the territory was currently occupied by the Hudson's Bay Company with its growing chain of trading posts—and possession was nine points of the law. Ironically the Americans were determined to seize British Columbia's coast, while most British jingoists felt more strongly about claiming and holding Oregon. Although ambassadors on both sides lacked any realistic idea about the character of the land in dispute, their multiplying claims made diplomatic compromise difficult to negotiate.

The stage was set for an escalating conflict not only between the Company and the American free traders but also between two irreconcilable views of the world. The American frontier ethic was highly individualistic, disinclined to collective, corporate or governmental solutions—stressing instead the virtue of challenging authority at every turn. The Yanks felt they were entitled to all the pelts they could nab on any given day, especially on what they considered to be their home turf, and dared anyone to show them otherwise. The Hudson's Bay Company represented a very different set of values, being a bureaucratic monopoly run by absentee landlords employing mostly wage-earning functionaries. Its traders were all too aware that they were stewards in a foreign land. Discouraged from being too blatantly aggressive, they were seeking comfortable survival rather than self-motivated adventure.

AT THE 1821 AMALGAMATION, the Hudson's Bay Company was not entirely certain it wanted to keep the half-dozen posts south of the 49th parallel it had inherited from the North West Company. They were known to be difficult and expensive to maintain and had been producing little if any profit. But the Company's London Committeemen, well aware of the

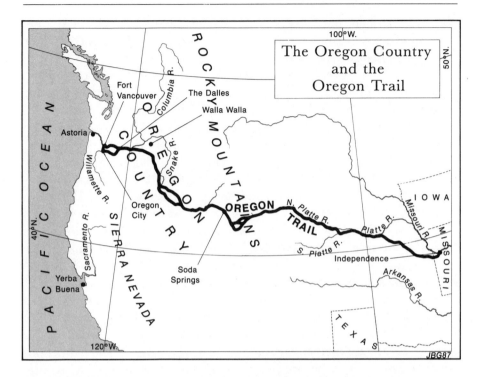

American craving for the desirable New Caledonia Department north of the disputed territory, decided that the Oregon Country—stretching north from California to include the present-day states of Oregon, Washington and Idaho, southeast into Nevada and across Utah all the way to Wyoming and north to Montana—was potentially too lucrative to surrender without a fight. At worst, its tenure would act as a buffer against Washington's ambitions to extend the United States' territorial reach northward. Simpson was ordered to survey the district, cut its expenses and reorganize its trade, keeping in mind that the international boundary would most likely be eventually fixed at the 46th parallel— which happened to coincide with the line of the Columbia River's westward flow.

When the HBC Governor arrived at Astoria on November 8, 1824, accompanied by Dr John McLoughlin, his designated commander of the Columbia Department, he found that the peculiar stories he had been hearing about the self-indulgent habits of its occupants were all too true. The warehouses held not only the standard fur-trade items but such luxuries as silk stockings, umbrellas, ostrich plumes and jewellery. Seating at dinner was strictly by rank, and the hierarchical protocol was carried to such ridiculous extremes that three grades of tea were poured, sweetened with three grades of sugar—refined loaf, common crushed and inferior brown. At Spokane House, the traders had built themselves a ballroom that fit well into the decadence of their daily—and nocturnal—pursuits.

Noting that "everything appears to me on the Columbia on too extended a scale *except the Trade*," Simpson not only jolted the local fur society into an abrupt appreciation of his OEconomy but cut the staff by half and ordered the Company's headquarters moved about a hundred miles inland to a pastoral plateau on the Columbia River's north shore, six miles past the mouth of the Willamette. The site, more easily defensible, offered opportunity for growing local food crops, thus saving the funds that had been spent supplying Astoria with European delicacies. At sunrise on March 19, 1825, Simpson broke a bottle of rum on the fledgling post's flagstaff and portentously declared: "In behalf of the Honourable Hudson's Bay Company I hereby name this establishment Fort Vancouver. God Save King George the Fourth!" That evening he noted in his journal that the object of naming the post after the distinguished British navigator was "to identify our claim to the soil and trade with his discovery of the river and coast on behalf of Great Britain." During his visit Simpson also devised a daring plan to keep the mountain men at bay south of the Columbia. He left instructions that the area was to be trapped bare of every last beaver kit, so that there would be little incentive for the Americans to occupy it. This scorched-earth policy would produce short-term profit and neatly fit the Company's strategic master plan. The area in question consisted mainly of the Snake River's immense drainage basin, a convoluted pattern of unclimbed mountains and torrential streams stretching from Wyoming (its source) into the northwest corner of Utah, northeastern Nevada, much of Idaho and slices of what are now the states of Oregon and Washington.

One of the Company's first traders assigned to the Snake was Finan McDonald, a six-foot-four Highlander with a bushy red beard whose first (and, some swore, only) language was Gaelic. At the end of his 1823 venture, which had included running battles with Blackfoot war parties (McDonald's men killed sixty-eight Indians, while sustaining half a dozen casualties), the weary Bay man wrote to a friend: "I got home safe from the Snake Cuntre, thank God, and when that Cuntre will see me agane, the beaver will have gould skin." To head up the methodical destruction of animal life that would create the fur desert he had in mind, Simpson appointed Peter Skene Ogden as Chief Trader in charge of the Snake River campaign.

An odd character to find in the fur trade, Ogden was the son of a prominent Montreal jurist who had joined the North West Company out of a sense of adventure.* In 1810, while stationed at Île-à-la-Crosse with Samuel Black, he had tormented the HBC trader Peter Fidler and was later involved in the murder of an Indian suspected of trading with the HBC. To place him beyond reach of the criminal indictment that followed the incident, he was transferred to the Pacific and spent the last three years before the NWC's absorption as one of its Oregon agents. Left off the original list of transfer appointments because of his violent anti-Bay activities, Ogden was eventually rehired as a Chief Clerk and soon promoted to Chief Trader. The reason for plucking this relatively obscure daredevil for the key assignment on the Snake was revealed in the secret assessment of Ogden in Simpson's Character Book: "A keen, sharp, off hand fellow of superior abilities to most of his colleagues, very handy and active and not sparing of his personal labour. . . . Has been very Wild & thoughtless and is still fond of coarse practical jokes, but with all this appearance of thoughtlessness he is a very cool calculating fellow who is capable of doing anything to gain his own ends. His ambition knows no bounds and his conduct and actions are not influenced or governed by any good or honorable principle. In fact, I consider him one of the most unprincipled men in the Indian Country, who would soon get into habits of dissipation if he were not restrained by the fear of their operating against his interests, and if he does indulge in that way madness to which he has a predisposition will follow as a matter of course. A man likely to be exceedingly troublesome if advanced to the 1st Class as the Trade is now constituted, but his Services have been so conspicuous for several years past, that I think he has strong claims to advancement."

During the course of his six forays into the Snake River basin between 1824 and 1830, Ogden had plenty of opportunity to put into practice his personal credo: "Necessity has no laws." Bolstered by his combative nature, he faced brutal challenges and survived them all. Besides trapping beaver,† he became the first white man to explore

---

*Ogden's voice never changed from its pre-puberty soprano, so that even though he completed some legal training before leaving Montreal, he accepted the fact that he could never be a convincing court advocate.

†Ogden was one of the few HBC traders who demonstrated even momentary consternation at the indiscriminate slaughter of the animals, noting in his journal on April 28, 1829, while camped on Bull Run Creek in southeastern Oregon: "It is scarcely credible what a destruction of beaver by trapping there has been at this season; within the last few days upwards of fifty females have been taken and on an average each with four young ready to litter. Did not we hold this country by so slight a tenure it would be most to our interest to trap only in the fall, and by this mode it would take many years to ruin it."

Peter Skene Ogden

parts of Idaho, California, Nevada, Utah and Wyoming, outwitting the rampaging mountain men and hostile Indians along the way. He judged each tribe on its merits, forming attachments with the Nez Percés and Cayuse but having nothing but contempt for the Blackfoot and especially the Snakes of Oregon. In the winter of 1828, when the Americans offered to join the British in a punitive war against the troublesome Snakes, he confessed to his journal: "I would most willingly sacrifice a year and even two to exterminate the whole Snake tribe, and in so doing I am of opinion could justify myself before God and man."

In his personal life, Ogden married, country-style, first a Cree woman and later the legendary "Nymph of Spokane," Julia Mary Rivet, the stepdaughter of a French-Canadian trapper. Ogden nick-named her his Princess Julia (she called him M'sieu Pete) and they became inseparable for the rest of their lives. Julia's exploits, such as the time she dove into a turbulent river to retrieve a runaway raft loaded with furs, were the talk of the Oregon Country. When the Ogden expedition's horses were stampeded by marauding American mountain men led by Joe Meek, she was horrified to discover that one of the vanishing mounts was carrying her first-born son in a moss satchel dangling from its saddle straps. She jumped on another horse, rode straight into the enemy camp, found the missing horse with baby attached, leaped from one saddle into the other and galloped off to her home base—leading a stolen Company nag loaded with furs behind her for good measure.

Peter Skene Ogden commanded his Snake River platoons, which numbered as many as 75 men and 372 horses, as if they were military units, with rotating rosters of night watches, advance and retreat strat-egies worked out beforehand and Spartan discipline. When one of his men got lost in the wintery bush, Ogden went up a hillside to fire rifle shots and built a large fire to guide the missing trapper home. But when the stray finally showed up the following morning without his outfit, suffering from exhaustion and frostbite, Ogden fed him a cup of hot broth and sent him right back out again to recover his missing horse, blanket and furs.

Ogden's most humiliating brush with his American competitors occurred at Deserter Point on the Weber River in Utah on May 25, 1825, when a group of mountain men, led by Johnson Gardner, a member of William Ashley's Rocky Mountain Fur Company, per-suaded a dozen of Ogden's Freemen to desert (along with their horseloads of furs) by telling them they were in U.S. territory and would be freed of their debts to the Hudson's Bay Company. Gardner and Ogden got into a heated argument, with the American claiming that the expedition was violating U.S. territorial sovereignty and the Bay man insisting

A Nez Percé Indian

that the fate of the Oregon Country had yet to be determined, and at present was mutually occupied by Great Britain.*

Apart from being constantly harassed by the Americans and hostile Indians, Ogden and his men suffered from a strange malady peculiar to the area. Like all trappers they ate beaver meat after the animals had been skinned but now they found themselves afflicted with racking pain that immobilized their limbs. The beaver, it turned out, had been feeding on poison parsnip (water hemlock) and even though they grew fat on the plants, humans consuming their meat became violently ill.†

---

*They were both wrong. Being south of the 42nd parallel, they were in Mexican territory. Under a treaty concluded between the United States and Spain on February 22, 1819, and proclaimed two years later, that parallel of latitude (the present northern boundary of California, Nevada and the western part of Utah) from midway across what is now southern Wyoming to the Pacific Ocean was declared to be the dividing line between the two countries in North America.

†The remedy was equally violent. Ogden discovered that he could obtain relief only by drinking liberal doses of a cocktail with the ultimate kick: pepper and gunpowder mixed in creek water.

Joe Meek, American mountain man

Ogden's final Snake River expedition in 1829–30 was marred by tragedy, when nine men drowned and five hundred beaver skins were lost in the turbulent cascades of The Dalles on the Columbia River. "This life makes a young man sixty in a few years," he complained in the privacy of his journal. "A convict at Botany Bay is a gentleman at ease compared to my trappers. Still they are happy. A roving life suits them. They would regard it as a punishment to be sent to Canada." The toll on his followers was appalling. When Joseph Paul, a youthful companion from his earliest forays, died at twenty-nine of the beaver disease, Ogden lamented, "There remains now only one man living of all the Snake men of 1819 and rather extraordinarily all have been killed, with the exception of two who died a natural death." He summed up his feelings for the country whose exploration became his monument, while suffering from heat prostration, camped near Goose Lake (California) where the only available drink was liquid mud: "This is certainly a most horrid life . . . without exaggeration Man in this country is deprived of every comfort that can tend to make existence desirable."

Dr John McLoughlin

THE TRADER IN CHARGE of the troublesome Columbia Department for twenty-two years was John McLoughlin, the former North West Company doctor who had impressed Simpson as a man of integrity able to get things done. Although he had privately criticized McLoughlin for being far too conscious of social rank and for believing too firmly in his own incorruptibility, the Governor realized that to run the Company's outposts in the potentially explosive Oregon Country he would have to hire no ordinary fur trader. What he needed was a Chief Factor capable of attracting other men to his own and the Company's cause. McLoughlin, who had by this time spent more than two decades in the fur trade, not only fit the part but looked it. A six-foot-four mountain of a man with a mane of loose-flowing, prematurely white hair, he resembled a born-again Elijah. His stern jaw, the disciplined set of his face and eyes, his grace of movement and careful speech—all lent his presence natural authority.

Fort Vancouver, where McLoughlin ruled with such benevolent effectiveness that he was posthumously accorded the title "Father of Oregon," was a community of forty wooden houses inside a twenty-foot-high stockade, including a two-storey lodging for the Chief Factor's family. Because he recognized that fur was a finite resource, McLoughlin also set up sawmills and flour mills and established large farming and fishing operations manned by servants who lived in a sizeable village outside the fort's gates. The day's work was run with shipboard exactness, the clanging of bells marking changes of shift and activities. Workmen were issued weekly rations of eight gallons of potatoes and eight salted salmon plus bread, and occasionally meat. The lives of the officers were considerably more gracious. Nightly, the Company's traders and visiting dignitaries of varying ranks and purposes gathered at the Fort Vancouver officers' mess to trade tall tales in the warm light of candelabra, lolling at tables laden with crested cutlery, crystal glasses and blue earthenware dishes. Roast beef and pork, boiled mutton, baked salmon, beets, carrots and turnips were the fare, plentifully and elegantly served, with McLoughlin leading spirited exchanges of ideas that spun on long into the convivial nights.

What impressed the Indian chiefs who came to call was McLoughlin's sense of justice. Anyone—white or Indian—caught breaking the Chief Factor's concept of permissible behaviour was sentenced to be lashed while tied to the fort's cannon. Flogging was common in those days, but few Chief Factors were even-handed enough to mete out the same punishment regardless of the culprit's skin colour. That did not mean McLoughlin was soft on Indians. On the contrary: when provoked, he could be brutal. In 1828, after the Clallam Indians on Puget Sound had

*In the officers' mess, John McLoughlin presided
over sumptuous feasts and entertainments.*

murdered HBC clerk Alexander MacKenzie, McLoughlin dispatched his men on a series of punitive expeditions. Twenty-three Indians were killed and their camps at Port Townsend and New Dungeness burned before the assassins were executed by their own families to placate the Company's death squads. A year later, the HBC's supply ship *William and Ann* was wrecked on the Columbia River bar, and Clatsop Indians appropriated the salvageable trade goods. When McLoughlin demanded restoration of the stolen property, the local chief insolently sent back a used ship's broom and an old scoop. An armed schooner was sent to teach him a lesson, and three Indians died in the mêlée that followed. Throughout these and other incidents, McLoughlin managed to retain the Indians' respect, becoming known far and wide as The White-Headed Eagle.

His relationship with the Americans arriving in growing numbers was more ambivalent. The HBC's presence acted as a deterrent to their territorial aspirations while at the same time providing the only available support system for lost or hungry mountain men and would-be settlers. McLoughlin was too good a Christian to turn anyone away from his fort, even those who had come specifically intending to drive the British intruders into the sea. Acting against orders from his own principals in London and Lachine, who saw no good reason to extend succour to enemies, McLoughlin not only welcomed all comers but granted them supplies on extended credit terms, thus encouraging the very settlements that inevitably strengthened the American hand in the Oregon Country's eventual disposition.

One of McLoughlin's favourite visitors was Jedediah Smith, a bible-quoting mountain man of extraordinary endurance and sagacity who confessed to having "a bump of curiosity the size of a goose head" for exploring the outer reaches of the Oregon Country. Only thirty-two when he died at the point of a Comanche lance near the Cimarron River, during his eight years in the fur trade Smith became the first white man to reach California by land from the east and the first to cross the Sierra Nevada and Siskiyou Mountains. Although a Methodist teetotaller, he was one of the founding organizers of the annual Rocky Mountain Rendezvous, the combination trade fair and debauchathon where mountain men met to trade gossip, merchandise and women. When Smith was attacked by Umpqua Indians, who killed all but two of his companions, McLoughlin not only gave Smith and the other survivors shelter but sent out an HBC party to recapture their purloined furs. They were purchased by the Company at a fair price and Smith spent the winter of 1828–29 enjoying McLoughlin's hospitality. Ironically, Smith's reports home about McLoughlin's ability

The annual Rocky Mountain Rendezvous

to handle Indians and successful agricultural ventures were so glowing they prompted a succession of independent backers to mount expeditions to share Oregon's bounty.

One of Fort Vancouver's more eccentric visitors was a near-sighted Boston schoolteacher named Hall Jackson Kelley, who arrived via Mexico, dressed in a white slouch hat, blanket capote and leather pants with a red stripe down the seam—"rather *outré*, even for Vancouver," McLoughlin noted in his journal, with raised eyebrows, no doubt. Kelley (who boasted of having ruined his eyesight as a young man reading all of Virgil by moonlight) claimed to have experienced a heavenly vision that had assigned him the task of colonizing the Oregon shore. For reasons that were then (and remain) obscure, McLoughlin viewed Kelley as a common horse thief and treated him shabbily during his four-month sojourn at Fort Vancouver, ostracizing him to a hut used to gut fish. Ever afterwards, Kelley blamed the HBC for most of the many mishaps in his misspent life, claiming at one point that he had been thrown into debtors' prison at the instigation of "an unscrupulous hireling of the Hudson's Bay Company in the shape of a lawyer, living in a dark alley in the City of Boston." When his wife left him, Kelley plaintively observed that she "probably felt sad, though her affectionate regards had been somewhat alienated by deceiving monsters."

One of the few Kelley disciples who eventually reached Oregon was Nathaniel Wyeth, a handsome Boston merchant who had made a small fortune ferrying ice around Cape Horn to tropical ports. McLoughlin was delighted with his company but when Wyeth built his own trading posts on Sauvie Island, west of Fort Vancouver, and at Fort Hall on the Upper Snake, the HBC Chief Factor organized a boycott among the Indians and paid them extra until the intruder gave up and sold out to the Company in 1837. There followed troops of missionaries. The best known of them was the remarkable Marcus Whitman, a scholarly and courageous medical cleric who arrived with seven companions, including his bride, the beautiful Narcissa, aboard the first wagon to cross the ranges from Wyoming. McLoughlin was enchanted by the pair, giving them extended credit at the Company store, and free horses and cattle to start a settlement in the Willamette Valley. The Whitmans ignored McLoughlin's advice and decided to move deeper inland, into the domain of the volatile Nez Percés.

The preachers sent messages back East, and their description of the idyllic life in Oregon aroused so much attention that President Andrew Jackson decided to send a secret agent disguised as "a private gentleman" to gather firsthand observations of the area. Captain William Slacum arrived at Fort Vancouver aboard the U.S. brig *Loriot* in late December 1836. It didn't take McLoughlin long to detect Slacum's real motives, but he entertained the visitor anyway and lent the American a canoe to make a brief tour of the surrounding territory. Slacum's subsequent report described Oregon as the world's finest grazing country and accused the HBC of having established an immense foreign monopoly that supplied arms to the Indians to perpetuate the institution of slavery. Slacum recommended that Washington take firm and immediate action to possess the territory once and for all.

THESE INCURSIONS WERE ONLY THE MOST VISIBLE manifestations of John McLoughlin's increasingly difficult tenure at Fort Vancouver. His real battle was within his own ranks. The combination of his generous treatment of potential American settlers, his diversification into non-fur enterprises and several other simmering issues had roused George Simpson's ire. The main problems were based on personality, distance and the peculiar circumstances of the Oregon trade.

Unlike Simpson, who regarded himself primarily as a colonial administrator, tough and efficient but only marginally concerned with the welfare of the people and land where the HBC operated, McLoughlin felt he was in the process of founding a new society. Given the choice between fattening the Company's balance sheets and acting according to the dictates of his conscience, he opted for the latter. Not that he was disloyal to the HBC's interests, but he viewed them as part of a much more extended horizon, certain that the Company's future would be best served by his sometimes costly efforts to treat the growing influx of settlers as potential customers rather than unwanted pests. He was constantly expanding his influence—building a new sawmill on the Willamette River and setting up trading posts inland, as well as establishing a major farming community on Puget Sound and a string of coastal depots north towards Alaska. These actions suggest McLoughlin had in mind the possibility that the tentative British claim to the territory would lapse and that only a reservoir of goodwill would permit continuation of the Company's impressive revenue flow. Instead of measuring these efforts within the context of the Company's eventual benefits, Simpson regarded McLoughlin as a self-centred and vainglorious rival busy erecting foundations for an American republic on the Pacific—a Chief Factor bent on creating his own constituency so that he might slip beyond the Governor's authority.

Both men's assessments were awry, and the lack of rapid communication over the immense distances involved meant that their differences grew ever deeper. Simpson was certainly correct in maintaining the position that none of his Chief Factors would act on his own in what appeared to be a deliberate flouting of corporate edicts. But he was uncharacteristically myopic in refusing to recognize that no matter how unorthodox McLoughlin's methods appeared, they worked. Within a decade of Fort Vancouver's founding, both the Missouri Fur Company and the Rocky Mountain Fur Company, which had been the HBC's main American rivals, were bankrupt, and the Snake River basin had been swept clean not only of beaver but of mountain men.

One reason there was so little understanding between the two men was that they hardly ever saw each other. McLoughlin so closely identified his physical presence with Oregon's welfare that he could not bear to leave even on a brief furlough, and interrupted his twenty-two-year stewardship with only one journey to England. Similarly, during his nearly forty years in charge of the HBC's North American operations, Simpson visited Fort Vancouver only three times, and his initial foray hardly counted, because the post was barely established and none of the subsequently divisive issues were yet in train. His longest stay was during 1828, when he lingered at Fort Vancouver for five months and thoroughly inspected every aspect of McLoughlin's operations. He lavishly praised the good doctor's efforts, noting with satisfaction that "eatables and drinkables no longer fill the precious space in the holds of the supply ships arriving from England," concluding that "never did a change of system and a change of management, produce such obvious advantages in any part of the Indian country, as those which the present state of this Establishment in particular, and of the Columbia Department as a whole, at this moment exhibits."

But there were already signs of strain. The main burr of irritation was whether emphasis was to be placed on ships or trading posts in developing the Company's business along the Pacific Coast. During the early 1820s, that area had been dominated by intrepid skippers sailing out of New England in late summer, their holds crammed with trade goods and casks of rum. Rounding the Horn in December (the Antarctic's summer), they would touch at Hawaii to replenish their food supplies before setting sail for the Alaskan coast in spring. There they would spend the summer bartering with the Indians for pelts, then set off for Canton, stopping once again at Hawaii to load up with sandalwood. In China, their precious fur and lumber cargo would be exchanged for tea, silk and nankeen (a buff-coloured cloth used in making work clothes) bound for markets in Boston or New York.

At its zenith, more than a dozen ships were engaged in this risky transoceanic commerce and McLoughlin was determined to compete —or, better yet, to drive them out of the trade—by establishing permanent posts that would monopolize pelt supplies the year round. Langley was well placed near the mouth of the Fraser; other forts were added: Nisqually, Simpson, McLoughlin, Rupert, Taku and Stikine. Governor Simpson, on the other hand, insisted that an expanded fleet of Company trading ships would be more effective, even when McLoughlin produced figures showing he could maintain four small land forts for the cost of one vessel. His pleading could not dint Simpson's determination to build up the Company's Pacific flotilla. The Governor appointed his kinsman Aemilius Simpson head of a new marine department and this fur-trade "Admiral" had under his command a formidable armada, consisting at various times of the *Vancouver* (324 tons, 6 guns, 24 men), the *Cadboro* (71 tons, 4 guns, 12 men), the *Dryad, Eagle, Isabella* and *Broughton*.*

McLoughlin was disillusioned not only with having to account for this disproportionately powerful fleet but with having to mollycoddle the restive crews and drunken captains. In that regard, at least, George Simpson agreed with him. "Captain Davidson's talent as a Navigator I know nothing about," he noted, "but his talent as a Grog drinker I understand is without parallel and I shall be agreeably surprised if he and his ship ever reach the Port of Destination."

The nautical squabble between the two men reached its crescendo over the acquisition in 1835 of the *Beaver*, the first steamship to be

---

*This reckoning does not include the HBC supply ships that arrived annually from London, including the 310-ton *Columbia* and the 10-gun *Nereide*. The most famous of these flyers was the clipper *Titania*, which once made the passage from London to Fort Vancouver in a record 105 days.

The SS Beaver

commissioned under HBC colours. Launched at a Thames shipyard in the presence of a crowd of cheering onlookers, the 101-foot paddle-wheeler had gone by sail around the Horn (her Boulton & Watt engines safely stored in the hold) to arrive 227 days later at Fort Vancouver. Simpson recognized two advantages in adding the steamer to the HBC's fleet: unlike other Company sailing vessels, the *Beaver* could move into tiny coves even when there was no favouring wind, thus stealing a march on American skippers bidding for the same cache of furs, and its novelty would, as he put it, have the effect of "overawing the natives."* McLoughlin saw the whole enterprise as a waste of money and suggested that if the main purpose was to impress Indians, the *Beaver* ought to be treated as a travelling circus, steaming from post to post to hoot its

---

*At least one group of Indians, the Bella Bella, was so taken by the ship that they told John Dunn, an HBC clerk, they intended to build their own version of the *Beaver*. A few days after this boast, a thirty-foot contraption, black with painted white portholes, hove into the Bay man's view, apparently propelled by red wooden paddles at each side. The copy had been built atop a hollow log, inside which crouched panting Indians frantically turning a crank that moved the paddles, producing a respectable cruising speed of three knots.

whistle and belch smoke—that she was far too ungainly and expensive to be involved in the serious business of the fur trade. The crusty Chief Factor certainly had a point in terms of the little ship's wood consumption: it took about ten cords of wood a day to keep the *Beaver* under way, and she had to carry thirteen woodcutters and four stokers to chop and haul the fuel for her insatiable boilers.* Despite these and other quirks (or perhaps because of them) the *Beaver* became a symbol of the Hudson's Bay Company's early dominance on the Pacific Coast. After thirty-one years in its service, and twenty-one as a survey vessel, *ad hoc* tug and log-boom towboat, she went aground in 1888 at Prospect Point near the entrance to Vancouver Harbour.†

McLoughlin could never see the *Beaver*'s brave prow without being reminded that the presence of the belching little paddle-wheeler represented Simpson's repudiation of the authority originally delegated to him. These feelings came to a head during the Governor's next (and final) visit to the Oregon Country in 1841, as part of his whirlwind world tour. Only a week after arriving at Fort Vancouver in late August, he went north to satisfy himself that the Americans had been driven out of the Alaska fur trade. Scrutinizing the southern tip of Vancouver Island along the way, Simpson appraised its excellent harbours, abundance of timber and moderate climate, carefully noting that it would be worth colonizing.

When he returned from his coastal sidetrip, Simpson had devastating news for McLoughlin. The Chief Factor was peremptorily ordered to dismantle most of the northern forts. The trade was to be conducted from the decks of the *Beaver* instead. The doctor was beside himself. The successful trading system he had created was to be wiped out on the strength of an apparently wilful gesture based on one superficial tour. Not only had Simpson made his momentous policy decision without consulting McLoughlin but he had already announced it to the various subordinates stationed in the posts he had visited along the way. "I am not aware that these subjects have been discussed," McLoughlin complained to the Governor, "as it is perfectly out of the

---

*A cord is a pile of wood 4 feet high, 8 feet long and 4 feet wide; by that measure, ten cords would amount to 1,280 cubic feet—a harvest that would take two men chopping two full days to produce.

†After half a century's service, she was still sturdy enough to survive four years of battering by the sea on her involuntary rocky perch. The *Beaver* was finally sunk in 1892 by the wash of a passing HBC freighter; her remains have recently been discovered near the Lions Gate Bridge by divers from Vancouver's Underwater Archeological Society.

question, to talk of discussion, when there are only two persons at the discussion, and one has the power to decide as he pleases and does."

Having delivered himself of his kangaroo verdict and dismissed McLoughlin's objections as based on nothing more substantial than the Chief Factor's regret that he had not originated these "reforms," Simpson set out for Alaska once again, this time on his way to Siberia for the longest leg of his round-the-world odyssey. When he arrived at Fort Stikine, Simpson found the Company flag at half-mast and was told that four nights earlier its commanding officer, John McLoughlin, Jr., the Chief Factor's son, had been killed by one of his men during a drunken orgy. Instead of investigating the tragedy properly, the Governor dismissed the affair as "justifiable homicide" and turned the actual murderer, a tripman named Urbain Heroux, over to the Russian authorities at Sitka. Because he felt that any further inquiries would only embarrass the Hudson's Bay Company, he wrote a heartless letter to the dead man's father condemning the son's behaviour and strongly advising the elder McLoughlin not to press charges.

The distraught father, already shell-shocked by Simpson's destruction of his trading system, vowed to clear his son's name. "Instead of conducting the examination so as to endeavour to find out what had led to the murder," he wrote to Simpson in one of his milder missives, "you conducted it as if it had been an investigation into the moral conduct of the Deceased, and as if you were desirous to justify the conduct of the murderers." Evidence that young McLoughlin had in fact not been drunk on the night of his death began to mount, with several visitors to Fort Stikine swearing affidavits that he had hardly touched a glass in their presence. His personal liquor ration was found to be untouched. Pierre Kanaquassé, an HBC servant who shortly afterwards visited Fort Vancouver, matter-of-factly explained that the youthful McLoughlin had been murdered because he would not allow his traders to have Indian women in their rooms overnight and because he punished those of his men who stole Company goods to give their mistresses. The assassination had been no spur-of-the-moment crime but a long-standing plot by frustrated employees to rid themselves of their commanding officer, who seems to have been guilty of nothing more than defending the Company's interests. Kanaquassé coolly outlined how he himself had made three attempts on McLoughlin's life and produced a written pact, signed by all but one of Fort Stikine's staff members, swearing to murder McLoughlin and cover up the crime.

When an independent investigation confirmed that the murder was premeditated, the elder McLoughlin expected some form of vindication or apology. What he got was further abuse. Simpson ignored the incontrovertible evidence that his snap verdict had been wrong and instead berated McLoughlin for allowing his judgment to be sacrificed to his feelings. When the aggrieved father finally managed to have the real murderers extradited to York Factory, he was censured for sending them so far without permission, then told they could be tried only in England at a cost of at least £10,000, which he personally would have to pay.

The resulting impasse forced McLoughlin to drop the case, but it solidified his bitterness. He was by then facing trouble from another quarter. On May 2, 1843, during a meeting at Champoeg, the Oregon missionaries and settlers decided to organize a provisional government, an idea secretly planned at so-called "wolf meetings"—informal get-togethers, ostensibly convened to discuss the threat of predators to their flocks of sheep and herds of cattle. The following season fourteen hundred new settlers arrived, and by 1845 the Willamette Valley boasted a permanent population of more than six thousand. The tentative rivulet of immigrants into the Oregon Country from the eastern United States had become a torrent. Trains of covered wagons, after gathering at Independence on the Missouri, lurched two thousand miles across the arid midlands towards the mountain ranges, along the Oregon Trail, carrying bright-eyed pioneers anxious to share the bounty of the new land.

The election of James K. Polk (the original "dark horse" candidate) who came out of the backwoods of Tennessee politics to win the U.S. presidency in 1844 on the slogan "Fifty-four forty or fight!" served to hurry the process. By thus setting the southern tip of Alaska as their territorial target, the Americans forced Westminster to reach a workable compromise on Oregon. Britain was by this time much more interested in maintaining good trading relations with Washington than in arguing about rights to a faraway colony on behalf of an already prosperous trading monopoly. The issue came up for decision at a time when the British government was facing many more significant questions, including strained relations with France and a threat that repeal of the Corn Laws would destroy its political base. These and other internal strains prompted the London politicians to negotiate a relatively quick agreement. The Oregon Treaty, signed on June 15, 1846, salvaged for the HBC the mainland territory north of the 49th parallel plus Vancouver Island, but the Company lost its rights in Oregon.*

---

*Despite the treaty, the Company did not immediately abandon its Oregon-based operations. The last of its American trading posts was closed in 1871. Legal proceedings to compensate the HBC for its original rights of possession dragged on for most of another decade after that, but the U.S. Government eventually paid the Company $650,000 (including $200,000 for the agricultural lands on Puget Sound) in gold bullion.

For John McLoughlin, these political manoeuvres had become academic. By the spring of 1844, the London Committee had decided to be rid of the old-timer by terminating his superintendency of the Columbia Department, demoting him to temporary membership in a trio of HBC officers who would take over management of Fort Vancouver and Oregon's fur trade. The Committeemen had anticipated the effect on the Chief Factor's pride correctly. Deeply offended by their treatment of him, McLoughlin resigned. "Gentlemen," he wrote, with laudable understatement, "I will serve you no longer."

He retired to Oregon City at the falls of the Willamette River and applied for U.S. citizenship, but the Americans didn't treat him any better than his former employers. Suspicious because he was British, a Catholic and a former Bay man, the settlers whom he had helped now turned on him and arranged to have his property confiscated. At the same time, Simpson insisted that McLoughlin pay back out of his own pocket the balances outstanding for the goods he had sold on credit to help the incoming settlers. They refused to honour their debts, dismissing their former benefactor as a traitor. "By British demagogues," McLoughlin lamented in one of the justifiably bitter epistles of his last dozen years in exile, "I have been represented as a traitor. What for? Because I acted as a Christian, saved American citizens, men, women and children, from the Indian tomahawk. . . . American demagogues have been base enough to assert that I had caused American citizens to be massacred by hundreds of savages—I who saved all I could. . . . I founded this settlement and prevented a war."

The unheralded "Father of Oregon" died on September 3, 1857, bitterly indignant to the end. "I might better have been shot forty years ago," he wrote to a friend shortly before his death, "than to have lived here and tried to build up a family and an estate."

BEFORE THE HBC FADED from Oregon's history, a dramatic event shook the new settlement's tranquility. The Reverend Dr Marcus Whitman and his wife, Narcissa, had been living at Waiilatpu, in the dangerous Walla Walla country, for eleven years, trying to minister to their charges' spiritual lives but finding themselves dealing more and more with their physical ailments. According to Indian belief of the day, medicine men were only as good as their latest cures; occasionally their own shamans were put to death if a chief died following unsuccessful treatment. The Whitmans had lost several native patients of high station, and the young men from a nearby Indian village were angry with the missionaries for larding the melons in their garden with laxative to discourage theft. Years before, Indian-white relations in Oregon had been poisoned by the stupid boast of former Nor'Wester Duncan McDougall, who had tried to disarm an unruly mob of Indians by playing on their understandable fear of smallpox. He had shown their leaders a small black bottle, claiming that it contained the dreaded smallpox virus, and threatened to pull the stopper. After a family of newcomers arrived in the Whitmans' precinct afflicted with measles and several Indians caught the disease, their chiefs planned a war party against the mission.

Early in the morning of November 29, 1847, as the doctor and Narcissa were starting on their rounds, an unusually large number of Indians gathered on the premises, hiding weapons under their blankets. As one of the chiefs engaged Whitman in animated conversation, another tomahawked him from behind, and the massacre was on. In the next hour, Narcissa and twelve other white people were killed and forty-seven women and children taken prisoner.

A week later, a Métis reported the massacre to Fort Vancouver, then co-commanded by Peter Skene Ogden, late of the Snake River expeditions. Ogden had spent most of the intervening years on HBC duty in Alaska as well as New Caledonia, and was now in the process of settling the Company's affairs before its forced move out of Oregon. Although the territory's provisional government was already in place and the HBC had no authority or responsibility in the situation, Ogden set off at dawn the next morning, determined to free the hostages. He went unarmed with sixteen paddlers up the Columbia, travelling light to gain time. When he reached Walla Walla, he realized that a full Indian uprising was brewing. The white captives had been dispersed to several Indian camps, so he sent a message to the chiefs of the Nez Percés and Cayuses that he wished to meet them for a parley. When they were assembled, he entered their longhouse alone and spoke in their own tongues. "The Hudson's Bay Company has been with you more than thirty years without bloodshed," he began, in what was to unroll as an all-day oration. "We are traders, and of a different nation than the Americans. But we are of the same colour, speak the same language, and worship the same God. Their cruel fate causes our hearts to bleed. Besides this massacre, you have robbed the Americans passing through your country, and you have insulted their women. We have made you chiefs, but you say that you cannot control your young men. They are cowards, and you are responsible for their deeds. If the Americans begin war, you will have cause to regret, for you will be exterminated. I know that many Indians have died; so have white people. Dr Whitman did not poison those Indians who died. You now have the opportunity to make some reparation. I advise you, but I promise you nothing should war be declared against you. The Hudson's Bay Company has nothing to do with your actions in this trouble. Deliver to me these captives and I will give you a ransom. That is all."

The Cayuse chief Tiloukaikt gave a long and dignified reply, concluding with this promise: "Your words are weighty. Your hairs are grey. We have known you a long time. You have had an unpleasant journey to this place. I cannot therefore keep the captives back. I make them over to you, which I would not do to another younger than yourself." The prisoners were delivered unharmed six days later, and Ogden paid the ransom of sixty-two blankets, sixty-three cotton shirts, twelve muskets, six hundred loads of ammunition, thirty-seven pounds of tobacco and twelve flints.

The suspected murderers of the Whitmans were eventually captured by a posse and taken to Fort Vancouver, which had become a U.S. Army camp. Five of the Cayuse tribesmen who were thought to have killed the missionaries were lined up on makeshift gallows, and Joe Meek, the former mountain man since promoted to U.S. marshal, released each drop with a tomahawk blow. Thus Oregon's time as a "Company town" came to a bloody and abrupt end.

Source of the Columbia River

Sir James Douglas

CHAPTER 12

BRITISH COLUMBIA'S MULATTO KING

James Douglas turned parsimony into an art form.

THE COMPANY'S WEST COAST PURSUITS now passed into the hands of James Douglas, a mulatto of elegant mien whose character was a perplexing combination of endearing romanticism and glacial tenacity. In his actions and person, he guided British Columbia's metamorphosis from savage fur farm to British colony to Canadian province—and played a dominant role in all three incarnations.

He was imperious, penny-pinching, obsessed by detail and ritual; his swarthy complexion would cloud over dangerously if subordinates failed to jump at his many commands. Decribed by one contemporary as "a cold brave man . . . with a wooden hard face, which said very plainly, I am not afraid," Douglas had been in the fur trade since before his seventeenth birthday and knew all its tricks and subtleties.

Paternal despotism was his operational code, though his devotion to duty (as he defined it) made him seem more pompous than he really was. He could (and did) make a terrible fuss to ensure that his family's croquet lawn was laid out precisely thus and so, yet in 1853 at Cowichan he sat stock-still on a camp-stool for most of a day, staring down two hundred armed and angry Indians. On that occasion, he smoked his pipe, a pile of gifts ready at one hand, his cutlass firmly grasped in the other, impassively waiting for the band to surrender one of their kin who had murdered an HBC shepherd. When they gave in, he walked away with his prisoner, making a mental note to order a more service-able sword for future confrontations. He was so stiff and formal that his men referred to him behind his back as "Old Square-Toes," yet he was sentimental enough to retain in his watchcase a shilling given him by a grandchild as a birthday gift to "spend as he liked," and at the age of sixty-nine could still be seen nearly every morning skipping rope on his veranda.

Self-possessed and self-serving, he moved so carefully within the reefy confines of the HBC's internal politics that *both* sides on any given issue usually praised his behaviour and his decisions. Perhaps because he was so far removed from any countervailing authority and thought himself to be the personification of almost kingly powers, he practised a policy of social superiority that suited neither his background nor his circumstances. Joseph Watt, an Oregon immigrant who had met him, noted: "Douglas ... would step around in a way as much as to say: 'you are not as good as I am, I don't belong to your class.' " He was so taken with postures and titles that at one point he was signing official documents over the self-composed description: "His Excellency, James Douglas, Governor of Vancouver Island and its Dependencies, Commander-in-Chief and Vice-Admiral of the same."

James Douglas turned parsimony into an art form. He was so obsessed with money that when he was receiving handsome salaries while serving as both the local head of the Hudson's Bay Company and Governor of Vancouver Island, he requested additional payment for acting as Lieutenant-Governor of the Queen Charlotte Islands—though that function involved no duties. A few years later, when he was far and away the richest man in British Columbia, he wrote a long letter to his London outfitters instructing them to ship his clothes in as small a package as possible because local customs officers judged parcels by size rather than by weight. In the same letter, he asked the British company to subtract his 5 percent rebate for prompt cash payment from the total cost in advance because that way he could save a fraction on the 20 percent *ad valorem* duty.

Despite such microscopic attention to mundane matters, Douglas could also be a visionary. He was the first man to urge the building of a trans-Canada highway, for example, advocating as early as 1862 a cross-country route that would have "the peculiar advantage of being ... remote from the U.S. frontier and traversing a country exclusively British, which from its position, and general resources can hardly fail ... to become the seat of a large population." Douglas was literate, seldom spending a night without dipping into his prized leather-bound forty-five-volume set of English classics, and could be poetic in his insights. Reminiscing about the departure of the annual express from Fort Vancouver to York Factory, he wrote in his journal: "A day highly suggestive of the past, of fresh scenes, of perilous travel, of fatigues, excitement and of adventures by mountain and flood; the retrospect is full of charms; images of the morning breezes, the bright sky, the glowing sunrise, the rushing waters, the roaring cataract—the dark forest, the flowery plains, the impressive mountains in their pure white covering of snow, rise before me, at this moment, as vividly as ever and old as I am, my heart bounds at the bare recollection of scenes I loved so well . . . I can recall nothing more delightful than our bivouac on a clear moonlit May night, near the Punch Bowls—the highest point of the Jasper Pass. The atmosphere was bright, sharp and bracing, the sun set in gorgeous splendour, bringing out the towering peaks and fantastic pinnacles dressed in purest white, into bold relief. Our camp was laid and our fire built, on the firm hard snow which was about 20 feet deep. As the daylight faded away, and the shades of night gathered over the Pass, a milder light shot up from behind the nearest Peak, with gradually encreasing brilliancy until at last the full orbed moon rose in silent majesty from the mass of mountains shedding a mild radiance over the whole valley beneath."

Born out of wedlock to John Douglas, a Glasgow merchant who owned sugar estates in Demerara, British Guiana, and Martha Ritchie, the daughter of a black freewoman from Barbados, the young James was taken to Scotland, where he passed his preparatory grades at Lanark and was later sent to a boarding school at Chester in England. He joined the North West Company in 1819 as an apprentice and two years later went over to the HBC, eventually being assigned to Fort St James in the New Caledonia Department. There he served as a clerk under William Connolly, whose fifteen-year-old Mixed Blood daughter Amelia he married in 1824. The posting was almost his last. A pair of Carrier Indians had killed two HBC employees at nearby Fort George some time before, and the employees' bodies had been eaten by dogs. When one of the murderers arrived back at a camp near Fort St James, Douglas and a group of Bay men set out to apprehend him. He was discovered hiding in a sick woman's tent under a pile of pelts and, while attempting to escape, stabbed Douglas with an arrow. In the fracas that followed, the Indian was hanged on the spot and his body fed to wolves.

When Kwah, the local Carrier chief, returned from a hunt and discovered what had happened, he marched into Fort St James at the head of a war party. Connolly was away, and Douglas was quickly overpowered and pinned down on a table. Tloeng, the Indian chief's assistant, held a knife to the HBC clerk's throat, ready to pierce the jugular. At this precise moment, Douglas's wife, Amelia, who had

Lady Douglas

been hiding in an upstairs storeroom, began to throw tobacco, blankets and other goods at the Indians' feet, the customary compensation for an Indian death, begging for her husband's life. Chief Kwah accepted the offer, waved the dagger away from Douglas's neck and, suitably placated, retreated from the fort. Later in his HBC career, Douglas enjoyed fairly good relations with local tribes, so much so that some Vancouver Islanders resented it. "Though the Governor is a wonderfully clever man among the Indians, he does not seem to be governing a white population at all," complained Lieutenant Charles William Wilson, a visiting Royal Navy officer.

Transferred to Fort Vancouver in 1830 as an accountant, Douglas was promoted to Chief Trader in 1834 and Chief Factor in 1839. If McLoughlin was the Oregon Country's king, Douglas was its prime minister, having served the Company's interests in the Columbia Department faithfully for nearly twenty years before being placed in charge of its relocated headquarters on Vancouver Island. "The place itself appears to be a perfect 'Eden,' in the midst of the dreary wilderness of the North west coast," he wrote to a friend when he first reconnoitred the new territory in 1842, "and so different is its general aspect, from the wooded, rugged regions around, that one might be pardoned for supposing it had dropped from the clouds into its present position."

The new HBC installation was first named Fort Camosun, then very briefly Fort Albert, but after December 12, 1843, it was known as Fort Victoria in honour of the young queen of England. With its tiara of mountains reflected in a jade sea, the island's unspoiled beauty astonished most newcomers, especially those who ventured along its west coast, where rugged slashes of rock elbowing into the Pacific surf etch some of the earth's most spectacular landforms. But not everyone was impressed. When the Honourable John Gordon, brother of the Earl of Aberdeen, the British Foreign Secretary, arrived as captain of the fifty-gun HMS *America*, he took a look around and concluded that he would "not give one of the bleakest knolls of all the bleak hills of Scotland for twenty islands like this arrayed in barbaric splendor."

Fort Victoria was planned with its future significance in mind. Its quadrangle, more than three hundred feet on a side and surrounded by a stockade of pointed eighteen-foot pickets, enclosed a dozen buildings including an octagonal bastion three storeys high mounting nine-pound guns. To forestall the possibility of invasion by American settlers from the Oregon Country, Vancouver Island was granted to the HBC by the British government in 1849—the Company thus being utilized as a colonizing agent by the Crown. The Mormons of Utah had already been in touch with London seeking to claim the island and James

Edward Fitzgerald, a private British entrepreneur, had submitted a detailed proposal to Westminster for exploiting the colony at its southernmost tip. The HBC did not particularly wish to take on the responsibilities of colonization, but it certainly had no intention of allowing anyone else to grab its advantageous new Pacific site. The Royal Adventurers were charged by the government with establishing "settlements of resident colonists, emigrants from Our United Kingdom of Great Britain and Ireland, or from other Our Dominions . . ." and disposing of "the land there as may be necessary for the purposes of colonization." Although the Company agreed it would sell land to settlers at a fair price, they had to purchase at least twenty acres at a time, and anyone buying larger spreads had to bring out five single men or three married couples at his own expense, for each hundred acres under cultivation. Land costs were set at £1 an acre. These stringent regulations, ostensibly meant to discourage squatters and land speculators, were in truth designed to perpetuate Britain's agricultural class system, so that the new colony would attract gentleman farmers and not fall prey to the populist agitations that had shaken the established orders of Lower and Upper Canada during the 1830s.

Although its grant specifically stated that the HBC would lose jurisdiction over Vancouver Island at the end of five years if it had not fostered a successful colony, the Company showed little enthusiasm for its assigned task, treating the outpost as little more than an ideally located bulwark for its mainland fur preserves. At the end of that period, only seventy men, women and children had arrived and no more than five hundred acres had been settled. Typical of those early pioneers was Captain Walter Colquhoun Grant, son of Wellington's chief intelligence officer at Waterloo and late of the Scots Greys, who arrived aboard the *Harpooner* in the summer of 1849, preceded by eight workmen. Bankrupted by a bank failure, he secured his passage from the Company by claiming to be a competent land surveyor. He brought few instruments with him but managed to supply himself with the necessities of a gentleman travelling to the colonies: a fancy carriage harness, a large library, two small brass cannon and a plentiful supply of cricket wickets. He chose to settle at Sooke, twenty-five miles west of Fort Victoria, and on his thirty-five-acre estate erected a log manor house complete with circular driveway. His duties as the Company's land surveyor were considerably hampered by the fact that he lacked all sense of direction, and once got lost for five days trying to make it from Sooke to Fort Victoria. Although he was the life of many a party at the officers' mess (on one notable occasion he challenged anyone to a duel after demonstrating his skill by snuffing out a candle with one swipe of his cutlass and splitting it in half with another), he soon grew peevish and by the winter of 1851 was contemplating suicide. To cheer himself up (and to escape James Douglas's well-founded suspicion that he was a hopelessly incompetent surveyor), Captain Grant hopped on a Company ship and spent two winter months in Hawaii. It was there that he made his most lasting contribution to Vancouver Island. He brought back with him seeds of the broom plant (given to him by the local British consul) and broadcast them around his estate, thus introducing the yellow-flowered shrub that now blooms profusely throughout the island's southern parts.*

To govern its new island colony, the British Cabinet appointed Richard Blanshard, an ambitious thirty-two-year-old barrister who had already seen service in the West Indies and was eager for further experience that might lead to higher government appointments. He left England under the impression that he would receive a grant of a thousand acres of free land, occupy a suitable governor's mansion and generally be able to exercise the considerable power then vested in colonial officials. When he arrived aboard HMS *Driver*, Blanshard discovered that he was slated for no land and no residence and that James Douglas had no intention of sharing his authority with the newcomer. The only recognition of his exalted station Blanshard ever received was a seventeen-gun salute from Fort Victoria on his arrival. After that there was silence. He submitted regular dispatches about his increasingly futile daily rounds, twitched his walrus moustache in frustration, diverting himself with lonely horseback rides and cursing his solitary fate. Douglas made certain that he had no advisers, no budget, no proper accommodation and no prospects. When Blanshard finally unearthed from the regulations something that he felt even a governor with his restricted mandate could do—clear ships officially in and out of Victoria Harbour—he was flattened when Douglas himself pointedly gave clearance to the HBC trading vessel *Cadboro*. Blanshard promptly took Douglas to court and tried to jail him inside Fort Victoria. This proved awkward because Blanshard commanded no law enforcement facilities and Douglas was the fort's commanding officer. In weary desperation, Blanshard bound Douglas over to appear for sentencing at some indeterminate future date and sent in his resignation. The poor fellow even had to pay his own passage home.

---

*Grant left Vancouver Island permanently a few months later, found work in San Francisco as a longshoreman, sailed back to England and rejoined his regiment. He fought with distinction in the Crimean War and died at thirty-nine of dysentery contracted during the Indian Mutiny.

Blanshard's tenure had the makings of a minor Gilbert and Sullivan operetta, but he did leave behind one important legacy. When a group of settlers headed by Captain James Cooper, a retired HBC skipper and cranberry broker who had been put out of business by the Company, petitioned him to set up an executive council, he agreed. Blanshard appointed Cooper, the retired HBC trader John Tod, plus Douglas, to the newly instituted council in what was the first, however feeble, step in the colony's evolution to representative government. That trend seemed to reverse itself a few weeks after Blanshard's departure, when Douglas became Vancouver Island's Governor—without being asked to give up his HBC appointment. The potential for conflict of interest was so obvious that the British government insisted he establish a functioning elected assembly. Douglas went through the motions, but by allowing absentee landlords to vote through their locally appointed agents, he made certain that loyal HBC men held the balance of power. The Speaker of the new House was John Sebastian Helmcken, the Company doctor, and, not incidentally, Douglas's son-in-law; the colony's collector of customs was a retired HBC Chief Trader; the colony's chief justice was Douglas's brother-in-law, David Cameron; and so forth. All revenues from the sale of lands, timber and minerals went straight into Company coffers, with only the fees from licensed taverns being directed towards general expenditures. That was a source of revenues hardly liable to dry up, but it was not enough to provide a counterweight to the HBC's continued dominance of the island's affairs.

A more profitable venture proved to be mining. Coal had been discovered at Beaver Harbour (later renamed Fort Rupert) on the northeast coast, but when Scottish miners were brought in, they dug seventy feet down and found the seam no more than eight inches wide. Then an elderly chief from a Nanaimo Indian band arrived at Fort Victoria one winter day to have his gun repaired. While watching the blacksmith at his forge, he noticed the coal and mentioned that there was plenty of such black rock up his way. Offered a bottle of rum and no charge for the gun repairs, he arrived back a few months later, his canoe filled with coal — and the rush was on. A major coal deposit was soon outlined at Nanaimo, and the miners, Robert Dunsmuir among them, were ferried back from Fort Rupert. Coal was mined at Nanaimo for most of the next century, first by the HBC and later by the Dunsmuir family. (The pits employed three thousand miners at the height of their productivity.)

The colonists' attention was soon diverted northward to the ethereal Queen Charlotte Islands, a scimitar-shaped archipelago visited by James Cook in 1778. An Indian woman had found a gold nugget on a local beach in 1850 and when it was traded at Fort Victoria, Douglas dispatched an HBC ship to Mitchell Harbour on Moresby Island to investigate. A quartz vein, said to be a quarter pure gold, was pinpointed, and thirty miners were sent to work the lode, but the Haida strenuously protested the removal of their heritage. "They arrived in large numbers, say thirty canoes," reported Chief Trader W.H. McNeill, a former captain of the *Beaver* in charge of the expedition. "When they saw us blasting and turning out the gold in such large quantities, they became excited and commenced depredations on us, stealing the tools, and taking at least one-half of the gold that was thrown out by the blast. They would lie concealed until the report was heard, and then make a rush for the gold; a regular scramble between them and our men would then take place; they would take our men by the legs, and hold them away from the gold. Some blows were struck on these occasions. The Indians drew their knives on our men often. The men who were at work on the vein became completely tired and disgusted at these proceedings, and came to me on three different occasions and told me that they would not remain any longer to work the gold; that their time was lost to them, as the natives took one-half of the gold thrown out by the blast, and blood would be shed if they continued to work at the digging; that our force was not strong or large enough to work and fight also. They were aware they could not work on shore after hostility had commenced, therefore I made up my mind to leave the place."

Not enough gold was found on the Queen Charlottes to make mining ventures worthwhile, but the fever was in the air. More nuggets were spotted along the Thompson River near its junction with the Fraser and by 1858 a full-scale rush had started, with California's Forty-Niners leaving behind their worked-out claims and scurrying north. Because Victoria was the only supply depot in the region, the California miners headed for Vancouver Island. On Sunday, April 25, 1858, the fort's citizens emerged from church to find an American paddle-wheeler disgorging half a hundred red-shirted men lugging pickaxes, panning equipment and tent poles. The little settlement's population doubled in one afternoon, and the ensuing building boom irremediably altered its character. That year thirty thousand impatient miners passed through the streets of Victoria. On one July morning two San Francisco steamers landed twenty-eight hundred men. Land values rose a hundredfold almost overnight; gambling saloons, opium dens and brothels promptly opened for business. All was set for one of history's most frenetic gold rushes. "The entire population of San Francisco—merchants, capitalists, businessmen of all descriptions, as well as the ever-present gamblers—were alike seized by the insane

Victoria, about 1860

desire to sell out their businesses, their homes and any other property they were possessed of, for any sum that would bring them and their outfit to the golden banks of the Fraser," American journalist H.B. Hobson reported in his description of these hectic times. "Pieces of valuable real estate on Kearney and Montgomery streets, and in other desirable locations in San Francisco, were sold for less than the cost of the improvements by the excited people in their haste to get to the new gold fields. It is needless to dwell upon the many trials and hardships of these pioneers of British Columbia. A comparatively small number reached their goal and succeeded beyond their most sanguine expectations; many fell by the wayside, and many more returned to their deserted homes in California—sadder, poorer, but wiser men."

For those who got as far as Victoria, the most daunting problem was to find transportation across the Strait of Georgia's tide rips to the Fraser River delta and beyond. Since few sailing vessels were available, the crossing was attempted in commandeered skiffs and even canoes, often with fatal results. The miners' knowledge of local geography was so sketchy that some of them navigated strictly by tasting the water to see how salty it was—the theory being that it would get sweeter as they approached the mouth of the Fraser River.

By the end of 1859, the sandbars of the Fraser had been panned clean for two hundred miles and the rush subsided as suddenly as it had started—until the late autumn of 1860 when word came from the high interior that even richer deposits had been found in the Cariboo Country,

Boomtown Barkerville

far to the north. There, as it turned out, the yellow metal had been deposited in highly concentrated form. One miner named J.C. Bryant retrieved an incredible ninety-six ounces out of one pan.* The miners worked their way up the Fraser, eventually taking out gold then worth $50 million, using the more complicated sluice boxes and rockers instead of the rudimentary pans. The instant city of Barkerville (named after a Cornish sailor who struck it rich there) soon boasted every civilized facility, including thirteen saloons—and the largest population north of San Francisco and west of Chicago.

Because Simon Fraser's river was as impassable as ever, alternative transportation arteries had to be created, the most sophisticated of them being the Cariboo Road built under James Douglas's sponsorship from Yale to Barkerville by Royal Engineers imported from Britain. Mule teams were the customary beasts of burden, but a group of imaginative trail-blazers imported two dozen camels from Manchuria via San Francisco, probably because they thought the animals were sure-footed and would not require much food. The odd thing was that the theory proved true, and several camel trains eventually swayed their way into Barkerville. The problem was smell. The spoor of the animals spooked every horse and mule in the district, setting off many a stampede. The camels also had unforeseen feeding habits. Contemptuously

---

*An 83.2-ounce nugget was later found on Spruce Creek, east of Atlin near the Yukon.

refusing the hay and other forage offered by their keepers, they seemed to hunger only for miners' shirts and socks, preferably unwashed. The animals were eventually set free and vanished into the wilds, with only the occasional sighting (one as late as 1905) to indicate any had survived.

Throughout the gold-rush period, the Hudson's Bay Company represented the only form of law enforcement on or near the Fraser, and even though Douglas had no authority on the mainland, he decreed that miners would require licences to be allowed into the diggings—and that he was the only source of such permits, obtainable at twenty-one shillings a month, payable in advance. This was partly a revenue-raising device, but it also served as a practical way to exert British sovereignty over the suddenly valuable territory. It was Douglas's further insistence that all supplies had to be purchased at Fort Victoria, Fort Langley or from HBC ships anchored off the Fraser River that prompted the British government to intervene. (The last straw was when Douglas ordered the seizure of any ships selling non-HBC goods.) On August 2, 1858, British Columbia was declared a Crown colony and the Company's exclusive trading licence in New Caledonia was permanently revoked.* The boundaries of the new colony stretched from over the summits of the Rocky Mountains to the Pacific and from the Finlay branch of the Peace River in the north to the 49th parallel in the south, with the Queen Charlottes but not Vancouver Island included for the moment.

The administration of the new colony was to be headed by a governor with wide powers—and no one seemed better qualified to wield them than James Douglas. "I trust and think he is a safe and sensible man, barring his too close connection with the Company," wrote Herman Merivale, the British Undersecretary of State for the Colonies, in an internal memorandum. "If he is, detailed instructions will only hamper him. If he is not, they will do him no good." Douglas was appointed for

---

*When a name was chosen for the new colony, the territory's HBC label, New Caledonia, was rejected because there was already an island of that name (owned by France) in the South Pacific. "British Columbia" was picked by Queen Victoria herself. In a letter to the Colonial Secretary, she explained (writing of herself in the third person) her reasons: "If the name of New Caledonia is objected to as being already borne by another colony or island claimed by the French, it may be better to give the new colony west of the Rocky Mountains another name. New Hanover, New Cornwall, and New Georgia appear from the maps to be the names of the subdivisions of that country, but do not appear on all maps. The only name which is given to the whole territory in every map the Queen has consulted is 'Columbia,' but as there exists a Columbia [Colombia] in South America, and the citizens of the United States call their country also Columbia, at least in poetry, 'British Columbia' might be, in the Queen's opinion, the best name."

For a short time, Manchurian camels were used on the Cariboo Road.

a six-year term (at £1,000 per annum) but was ordered to sever his ties with the Hudson's Bay Company and required to organize a Council and eventually to hold elections for an Assembly.

But first the new Crown colony had to be officially proclaimed. On one of those rainy days when the sky appears painted permanently gunmetal-grey, Douglas and his retinue (Rear-Admiral R.L. Baynes, Commander of Her Majesty's naval forces, Pacific Station; David Cameron, the Chief Justice of Vancouver Island; Matthew Baillie Begbie, judge designate of British Columbia; plus a naval guard of honour) boarded HMS *Satellite* for the trip across the Strait of Georgia to Point Roberts, where they transferred to the HBC ship *Otter* and later set course for Fort Langley aboard the *Beaver*. The next day (November 19, 1858) Douglas disembarked at the post's muddy shore to the tune of an eighteen-gun salute, and before an audience of a hundred cheering, if drenched, spectators administered the oath of office to Begbie, who in turn read aloud Queen Victoria's commission appointing him British Columbia's first Governor.

Begbie, who became known for his fairness on the bench and never really earned his sobriquet, "The Hanging Judge," helped Douglas administer the fledgling colony, as did a detachment of 150 Royal Engineers under the command of Colonel Richard Moody, sent out by the British Government to survey the land and pick a new capital.

Moody promptly chose New Westminster, a freshwater port on the north bank of the Fraser; that site found little favour with Douglas, who much preferred Victoria and seldom visited the mainland. By 1860, settlement had spread to Cowichan and Chemainus and to Saltspring, the most luxuriant of the Gulf Islands. Douglas's administration erected lighthouses and built bridges and roads, providing the new colony with everything except democracy. The Governor insisted on legislating by proclamation, so that he could keep control of the government firmly in his grasp. That rigid attitude fed ammunition to his critics, chief among them being Amor de Cosmos, publisher first of the *British Colonist* and later of the Victoria *Daily Standard*.

Born William Smith, at Windsor, Nova Scotia, the crusading journalist had changed his name by California edict to "Lover of the Universe" as being a more appropriate reflection of his aspirations. After arriving in Victoria from California, he established the *British Colonist* to promulgate his emphatic views.* In the newspaper's first issue, dated December 11, 1858, he attacked the Governor's record: "He wanted to serve his country with honor and at the same time preserve the grasping interests of the Hudson's Bay Company inviolate. In trying to serve two masters he was unsuccessful as a statesman. His administration was never marked by those broad and comprehensive views of government, which were necessary to the times and to the foundation of a great colony. It appeared sordid; as exclusive and anti-British and belonged to a past age. A wily diplomacy shrouded all. . . . The great mistake of the administration occurred early. Instead of taking the responsibility to throw the country open to free trade and colonization; instead of sinking all sordid considerations for the public good, we fear our Executive gave honeyed words to those whom he would partially prohibit; made his policy approximate to 'masterly inactivity', published obstructive proclamations for acts; and excused all by a doubtful claim to exclusive trade and navigation."

By late 1863, the pressures from England for Douglas to summon a legislative assembly had grown irresistible and the Governor was ordered to organize an election. The opening session of British Columbia's first Legislative Council sat at New Westminster on January 22, 1864, but

---

*He was premier of British Columbia for fourteen months in 1872–74 while holding down an MP's seat in Ottawa, where he sat as a Liberal from 1871 to 1882. A firebrand for responsible government and later a pro-Confederationist, he was described by George Walkem, his successor as premier, as having "all the eccentricities of a comet without any of its brilliance."

Douglas felt allergic to all that populism. He resigned a few weeks later and huffily retired from public life. He had been knighted by Queen Victoria the previous year and now decided to indulge himself with the fortune he had built up during his half-century in the fur trade. He led his family on the grand tour of Europe and, on his return, settled down at James Bay as Vancouver Island's wealthiest citizen. Formal to the end, he decreed that only male guests could attend his retirement dinner; the ladies were allowed merely to "look on."

His HBC associate John Tod, who came to call on the former Governor during that final period (Douglas died on August 2, 1877), reported in a letter to his friend Edward Ermatinger: "You probably think me unjustly severe on our old friend, but it is with sorrow I say it, that to all those who have known him for years, he has even appeared cold, crafty and selfish; and justly merits the reward he now reaps of isolation and desertion of all who have known him from early times."

By 1862, the Crown had taken back all rights over Vancouver Island, so that the Hudson's Bay Company was reduced to the status of any other enterprise, its only enduring advantage being long tenure and physical presence. The Pacific empire forged by Peter Skene Ogden, John McLoughlin and James Douglas had come to a peaceful end, which is more than can be said of most empires. Their legacy was to maintain the British presence on North America's western shore just long enough to ensure that Canada would one day stretch eastward and westward from coast to coast.

III END OF EMPIRE

Steamship on the Assinboine River

CHAPTER 13

UNRAVELLING THE FUR MONOPOLY

George Simpson's opinion of missionaries verged on the benign, but he could never concede that there might exist a presence within his empire claiming allegiance to any authority higher than himself.

BY THE MIDDLE OF THE NINETEENTH CENTURY, precise knowledge of Canada's hinterland had scarcely moved beyond the "HERE BE DRAGONS" inscriptions on early exploration charts. The navigable lakes and rivers were familiar, but much of the rolling prairie and most of the tundra to the north had been viewed only in passing.

Fort Edmonton was the largest settlement west of Red River; the postage-stamp farms comprising Fort Langley, near the mouth of the Fraser River, and Fort Victoria on Vancouver Island were the only communities of any consequence on the Pacific. Known as the "Great Lone Land," the fertile prairie was cut off from Upper Canada (renamed Canada West in 1841) by eight hundred miles of wilderness. The famed voyageur route from Lachine to Lake Superior had been abandoned, its portages overgrown with weeds, being used mainly by George Simpson's express canoes on his annual dashes to inspect the inland posts. The grandiosely named North West Transportation, Navigation and Railway Company obtained a government contract to deliver mail to Red River at $1,000 a trip, but on its first run between Collingwood on Georgian Bay and Fort William, the company's steamer carried only fourteen letters. Red River residents were so unimpressed they consigned only two letters to the vessel's return journey, and the service folded soon afterwards.*

---

*To test the reliability of the service's claimed rapid delivery, Simpson mailed two letters from Lachine on October 12, 1858—one by way of the U.S. railway route, the other via the North West Transportation, Navigation and Railway Company. The former arrived on November 10, 1858; the latter on March 2, 1859—141 days after it was mailed.

The most dangerous threat to the HBC's monopoly should in theory have been the agitation for annexation of its lands by leaders of public opinion in the Canadian provinces. There was no shortage of windy political rhetoric on the issue, and George Brown, the founding editor of the Toronto *Globe*, wrote thunderous editorials claiming that only the extension of Canada's borders westward to the Pacific would revive the colony's stagnant economy. But there was little initial response. The politicians were all too aware of the inadequacy of their treasuries; taking on the administrative cost of the huge HBC territories seemed neither desirable nor realistic.

Then, with the suddenness of a summer storm, this standoffish attitude changed. The realization struck home that if nothing was done, Red River and what would someday become the Canadian heartland might be annexed by the United States. American expansionists had been mobilized by their discovery that steam was about to redraw the map of the continent. Although a few short "portage" rail lines were built in the Canadian provinces during the 1830s and 1840s, the first really major rail project was the Grand Trunk, completed between Lévis and Sarnia in 1859. In contrast, American entrepreneurs had been pushing steel across their country at a much faster pace; by 1860, thirty thousand route-miles of track had been laid. Whatever territory was not made accessible by snorting locomotives had been or was being exploited by steamboats, the belching paddle-wheelers that were turning the Missouri and Mississippi into riverine freeways. By 1858, Minnesota, just south of the original Selkirk grant, had attained statehood and was a nest of 150,000 expansion-minded citizens.*

These and other stirrings prompted the nationalists of Canada West to rally against the possibility of Red River annexation and eventually against the monopoly of the Hudson's Bay Company itself. The early Canadian capitalists, especially the competition-conscious owners of the lumber and grist mills, began to express their revulsion at this foreign, feudal and forbidding enterprise, which, as a petition from the Toronto Board of Trade complained, "assumed the power to enact tariffs, collect custom dues, and levy taxes against British subjects, and has enforced unjust and arbitrary laws in defiance of every principle of right and justice."

---

*There is a documented instance of an ingenious American, during the 1862 Sioux uprising at Mankato, Minnesota, hoisting a British flag. He was the sole white man to escape the massacre alive—and the only possible explanation was that the Indians, having become familiar with the Red Ensign through their connections with the HBC, considered him to have kindlier designs and spared his life.

After nearly two centuries of having taken its mandate for granted, the HBC was facing a fierce and widespread challenge to its hegemony: a wave of populist sentiment that viewed its monopoly as the chief obstacle to dreams of free trade, settlement and transcontinental nationhood.

AT RED RIVER ITSELF, a much more subtle undercurrent touching racial, social and religious confrontation was changing the character of the settlement and its people. The most jarring disruption to the Colony's stability had been the arrival of Frances, Simpson's British bride. Distinctions of class and parentage that had largely been ignored over a generation of HBC and NWC occupancy suddenly surfaced to upend family and community equilibrium. "There is a strange revolution in the manners of the country," James Douglas noted later. "Indian wives were at one time the vogue, the half breed supplanted these, and now we have the lovely tender exotic torn from its parent bed. . . ."

This shift in the pattern of sexual liaisons and marital unions was fundamental. It did much more than alter the lives of the specific men and women involved. It meant that the status of the country marriage, which had proved to be such an integral and essential element of the fur trade, was permanently downgraded, disrupting what had been considered the natural order of things.

Worse still, the arrival of well-meaning but narrow-minded missionaries in Rupert's Land led to imposition of a moral code on fur-trade society that branded most of its traditions, including the honourable custom of country marriage, as not only wrong but sinful. According to the earnest tenets of these righteous ranters, native women had to be indoctrinated with what they considered to be the proper wifely attitudes. "A good wife must be clean and industrious in her habits and docile and obedient to her husband," wrote Sylvia Van Kirk, outlining the rigid value system missionary wives tried to inculcate in the schools they established at Red River. "Above all she must be sexually pure. Every vestige of the sexual freedom to which Indian women had been accustomed was to be stamped out; chastity, it was impressed upon young mixed-blood women, was their greatest virtue and responsibility. According to contemporary British sentiment: 'A woman who has once lost chastity has lost every good quality. She has from that moment all the vices.' "

Although such a state of vestal purity was presumably difficult to attain retroactively, the missionaries insisted on sanctifying by formal church service the informal unions of HBC traders and their country wives. In some instances this proved a happy arrangement, but some

The Reverend John West visiting an Indian encampment at Red River

Chief Factors and Traders seized the moment as an excuse to "turn off" their native partners and marry younger overseas brides instead.

To compound the complexities, the missionaries also insisted on identifying Christian conduct with their own vision of civilized behaviour. While agricultural pursuits fell within their reckoning of acceptable conduct, hunting did not. They equated the Indians' nomadic life with barbarism. Their culture and struggle for survival were disparaged as distractions from opportunities to contemplate the nature of existence and the eternal mysteries of Christianity's God. Proud hunters who had survived unimaginable hardships by following their own ancient codes were told that worshipping the white man's God, handling a fork correctly and using handkerchiefs would save their souls. What these opinionated parsons really meant when they railed about converting "the heathen savages" was that they were determined to make Indians not quite so outrageously un-British. "They struggled to recreate the English rural parish," wrote the historian Frits Pannekoek, describing the itinerant clerics' aspirations, "a little Britain in the wilderness, with the parson as a major landowner, teacher, custodian of charities, and law giver. They saw themselves as sharing these tasks with the other members of the elite: the squirearchy, the Company's officers and the settlement's Governor. The Anglican clergy's plans for this society placed them at the helm and made outcasts of all who did not comply. Firm in their conviction that 'civilization must go hand in hand with Christianity,' they preached what they assumed were the virtues of nineteenth-century England as fervently as the Gospel."

Except for an occasional visit, such as the solitary season spent at York Factory by the Reverend Thomas Anderson in 1693, the HBC had historically welcomed few evangelical diversions within its territories. As late as 1815 there was not a single church in Rupert's Land, but Lord Selkirk invited Father (later Bishop) Joseph Norbert Provencher to establish a Catholic mission in 1818 and had arranged for the dispatch to Red River of a Church of England chaplain named John West two years later. Since nearly all the colony's Protestant settlers were staunch Presbyterians, West's brief stay was not a happy one. He felt over-whelmed by the size and nature of his mandate and established little empathy with his parishioners. But he did build a small school and a chapel, performed a grand total of sixty-five marriages and inaugurated an auxiliary of the British and Foreign Bible Society for Rupert's Land at York Factory. There he welcomed his successor, the Reverend David Jones. That worthy was an even harder-shell divine who would not baptize country wives before their church weddings and refused to marry them if they were not baptized, insisting that it would be sacrilege to pronounce "our excellent Liturgy" over such "heathens." Officially, Jones worked under the auspices of Britain's Church Missionary Society, but his real sponsor was Benjamin Harrison, brother-in-law of the HBC's long-time Governor John Pelly. Harrison himself served as an HBC Committeeman from 1807 to 1854, including a four-year stint as Deputy Governor. A member of the Clapham Sect, a group of Evangelicals within the Church of England,* Harrison sent more than three dozen missionaries to Rupert's Land. By the mid-1850s, Red River alone boasted eight churches, and there were forty-two missionary stations within the HBC lands, a dozen of them Catholic, five Wesleyan, one Presbyterian and the rest Church of England.

George Simpson's opinion of missionaries verged on the benign, but he could never concede that there might exist a presence within his empire claiming allegiance to any authority higher than himself.† Besides, the nosy parkers favoured free trade in furs and diverted the Indians from trapping. In his mind, that categorized the lot of them as necessary evils at best. In a letter to London, he complained that the diffusion of Christian doctrine within Rupert's Land really did little good other "than filling the pockets and bellies of some hungry missionaries and rearing the Indians in habits of indolence."

The most troublesome man of the cloth called to the Fur Country was the appropriately named Herbert Beaver, who arrived with his wife, Jane, at Fort Vancouver in 1836. He was a creature of fathomless rectitude whose idea of imposing his rigid ethics on the wilderness fort was not helped by an awkward personality, a squeaky voice and pretensions of grandeur that exceeded spiritual boundaries. The clash between Beaver and Dr John McLoughlin, the post's Chief Factor, was not long in coming. At first it concerned trivialities: Jane Beaver wanted boiled salmon, though the resident cook usually baked it, and

---

*The Claphamites, led by William Wilberforce, campaigned for prison reform and against slavery, gambling and blood-sports. Mostly well-connected Anglicans, they were politically conservative, convinced that public morality should be imposed from above, namely, by them. Firmly committed to preserving the existing social order, they believed that what the poor needed above all else was religious instruction and better table manners. Their more outspoken members were frequently lampooned as "Saints," yet it was the Clapham Sect that was mainly responsible for turning British public opinion against the slave trade.

†Frits Pannekoek has documented the fact that most of the missionaries who came to Red River were mediocre representatives of their churches. "What was most remarkable about these clergy was the rise in status that their move to Rupert's Land signified. Where before they had had marginal livings, and their wives had been considered nothing more than 'Dollymops' or barmaids, they now hobnobbed with the fur trade's gentlemen; indeed they often set the social pace for the entire settlement."

the room assigned to the parson and his wife was enclosed only by a thin partition. Beaver complained that he had not been assigned proper servants (having rejected the Sandwich Islander and his wife who had been offered by the HBC) and snivelled about the liquor rations he had been allocated—yet fort records showed that from August to October 1838 alone he had been issued 143¾ gallons of brandy, port, sherry and porter. What drove Beaver to self-righteous frenzy was the idea that men and women could live together without benefit of a church ceremony. His sermons, delivered in a high-pitched whine, disparaged women partners in country marriages as little better than concubines and condemned their men as fornicators. This doctrine was inappropriate enough while he was apportioning damnation indiscriminately among the fort's residents, but when Beaver deliberately homed in on McLoughlin and Marguerite McKay, his country wife of twenty-six years, that was a fighting matter. In a report to the HBC Committee in London that fell into McLoughlin's hands, Beaver referred to the respected chatelaine of Fort Vancouver as "a female of notoriously loose character" and the "kept Mistress of the highest personage at this station"—charging that the fort's officers were practising concubinage. That was too much for the good doctor. When the two men met in the yard, McLoughlin demanded an explanation.

"Sire," replied Beaver, "if you wish to know why a cow's tail grows downward I cannot tell you; I can only cite the fact."

The enraged Chief Factor delivered a hard right to the reverend gentleman's jaw, then grabbed his walking stick and thrashed him with it, roaring: "You scoundrel! I'll have your life!"

Only the hysterical intercession of Mrs Beaver prevented her husband from being seriously injured. McLoughlin later apologized for his outburst, but the parson would not be quieted. He threatened to sue the Company and wrote the draft of a book exposing the iniquities of its employees. Beaver's crusade ended when he was fired and paid £110 in compensation for his claims of mistreatment.

The incident was not important in itself—particularly because, unbeknownst to the eager Beaver, McLoughlin and Marguerite had actually been formally married at that time. (Because McLoughlin was a Catholic and wanted no part of the clergyman's militant brand of Protestantism, the ceremony was performed by Fort Vancouver's second-in-command, James Douglas, in his capacity of Justice of the Peace.) A later episode at Red River, which also involved the conflict between Victorian morality and indigenous culture, had deeper and more enduring consequences. The old familiarity of the Fur Country, the sense of belonging, of sharing a prevailing sense of values, was threatened by the Foss-Pelly sex scandal of 1850. It threw into doubt the position of Mixed Bloods among the Red River elite of the mid-nineteenth century. The cast of this wilderness soap opera was almost too stereotyped to be real, and its denouement seems less appropriate to the historical record than to the purple-plot purveyors of supermarket romance novels. Yet it served to underline the racial prejudices tethered within the respectable society of Red River.

John Ballenden, the Chief Factor at Fort Garry, had married Sarah, the exquisitely beautiful Mixed Blood daughter of Chief Trader Alexander McLeod. Her striking appearance and natural vivacity were so compelling that her social achievements easily eclipsed those of the local white women. As the Chief Factor's wife, Sarah gave dinner parties and organized masked balls; she presided over the Upper Fort Garry officers' mess, and quickly became the object of intense male attention and even more intense female buzz. When Mrs Robert Logan, a school teacher, remarked that Mrs Ballenden was the type who "must always have a sweetheart as well as a husband," everybody at Red River knew which lover she had in mind. According to the settlement's gossips, Sarah had repelled the ardent advances of A.E. Pelly, the fort's accountant, but was rumoured to have found more pleasant accommodation with Captain Christopher Vaughan Foss, a rambunctious Irishman who had arrived in Red River two years earlier as part of the British garrison. Local tattlers were maliciously pleased to whisper that Foss was parking his boots under Sarah's bed.

The breezes of innuendo turned into a gale when Anne Clouston, daughter of the HBC agent in the Orkneys, arrived at Red River as the wife of Mr. Pelly, Sarah's rejected admirer. Since Pelly was a member of one of the HBC's most distinguished families, the bride assumed that her mere presence would catapult her to the top of the colony's social register. She dressed the part, bringing with her from Scotland five new bonnets and other finery. But her aristocratic pretensions and tendency to protest each imagined slight by carefully choreographed fainting spells soon made her a figure of fun at the Red River officers' mess. In retaliation, the Pellys withdrew from that circle and Anne began to interrogate Sarah Ballenden's German maid, Catherine Winegart, about her mistress's rumoured adventures. Convinced that she had valid evidence of Sarah's dalliances, Mrs Pelly petitioned Major William Caldwell, governor of the colony, to take action. Caldwell, who had been Foss's commanding officer, was stymied. He had a high regard for John Ballenden, was fond of Foss, yet feared the Pellys' powerful London connections and hoped that the whole tempest would be forgotten. But Sarah and Captain Foss were determined to strike back. Mrs Ballenden obtained a sworn affidavit from her maid confirming that she, Catherine Winegart, had in fact no evidence of her mistress's immorality. Foss for his part posted a public notice on the door of the fort's general store denouncing Anne Pelly and proclaiming his intention of suing her for defamation of character.

John Ballenden himself, who never doubted his wife's public denials of unfaithfulness but spent a lot of time away on company business, was forced to resign as Chief Factor after Anne Pelly obtained a sworn deposition from the Fort Garry mess cooks, John Davidson and his wife, implicating Sarah and Foss. The issue became a *cause célèbre* when the persistent Pellys repeated the charges in front of George Simpson during one of the Governor's visits, and Captain Foss promptly launched his threatened lawsuit.

The three-day trial, which started on July 16, 1850, became the sensation of the territories. According to Alexander Ross, the best of the contemporary fur-trade historians: "Writs were carried to every hole and corner of the colony, in high and low life: Knights, Squires, Judges, Sheriffs, Counsellors, Medical men, all the Nabobs of the Co., the Clergy, Ladies and Gentlemen, down to the humblest pauper were summoned, a glorious turn out. I happened to meet one of the officials, and he alone had no less than 52 summonses! . . . A special court was summoned and 50 jurors were in attendance. A Jury was impanelled, and The Court, and same Jury sat . . . three solemn days. The bible in the hands of the Clerk of the court might well be hot!"

The trial itself was more farce than formality. The resident clerics' wives pursed their lips in well-practised disgust as they testified against the aggrieved couple, presenting billows of rumour but little hard evidence. At one point, Adam Thom, the presiding judge (who was godfather to one of Sarah's children), stepped down from the bench, walked over to the witness box and spoke glowingly about her honesty and strength of character. The twelve Anglophone Métis who made up the jury found the defendants guilty of defamation of character, and Judge Thom awarded Foss damages from the Pellys of £300. That should have ended the drama, but instead it only helped fan the embers of racial prejudice. Sarah Ballenden continued to be ostracized by the white women. Most of the settlement polarized into opposing factions. "All the inhabitants," Simpson noted with considerable dismay, "thought it proper to espouse one side or the other and to regard the verdict as a personal triumph or a personal injury."

When Eden Colvile arrived to take Red River Governor Caldwell's place, he found himself trapped into playing straight man in the ongoing skit. "Today," he wrote to Simpson about a visit from the Right Reverend David Anderson, "the Bishop and his sister were calling on us, & in the middle of the visit I heard a knock at the door and suspecting who it was rushed out & found Mr. and Mrs. Ballenden. I had to cram them into another room till the Bishop's visit was over, but as he was then going to see the Pellys he had to pass through this room, so that I had to bolt out and put them into a third room. It was altogether like a scene in a farce."

Colvile reinstated the Ballendens in Red River's good graces, and when John Ballenden had to visit Scotland for medical treatment, Colvile allowed Sarah to move in with his family at Upper Fort Garry. Shortly afterwards, an unsigned letter believed to be in Sarah's handwriting inviting "darling Christopher" to visit her turned up anonymously. She later went alone to his lodgings for an afternoon's visit. At this point, Thom and some of her other supporters deserted Sarah, but her husband did not, later writing to Simpson: "I entreat you, for my sake, if not for hers, to cease and let her rest in peace—if that is now possible."

It wasn't. When Ballenden was posted to Fort Vancouver, Sarah's deteriorating mental and physical health kept her from following him. Alexander Ross lamented that "if there is such a thing as dying of a broken heart, she cannot live long." Sarah died of consumption at thirty-five, only three years after the trial, but not before she and her John (who had been invalided home) met in a tearful, final reunion at Edinburgh. Sarah Ballenden's gothic tale exposed the tensions and pretensions of the pioneer community. The affair had pitted white against Mixed Blood, clergy against laity and placed the HBC—as the defender of established authority—uncomfortably in the middle.

THE ROOTS OF THESE CONFLICTS had been planted long before. After the death of Lord Selkirk, the colony had languished. Its presence provided living proof of the HBC's charter rights, yet nearly every active Bay man resented Red River's intrusive influence on the fur trade. In 1836, the Selkirk family had moved to rid itself of the unhappy land asset by selling it back to the HBC for stock worth £84,000, which eventually brought returns many times the late Earl's losses. Despite the severe flood of 1826,* the settlement had grown, with imported livestock, new grist mills and the continued buffalo hunt providing the chief economic mainstays. Its population had mushroomed from less than 300 in 1818 to 4,369 by 1840, but by mid-century less than 12,000 acres had been settled, although land was priced at only five shillings an acre.

Red River continued to expand not only geographically but socially, sprouting five distinct communities. There were the Scots of Kildonan,

---

*The floodwaters are estimated to have been three times larger in volume than they were during the devastating inundation of 1950.

the brave remnants of the original Selkirk immigrants, who eschewed the buffalo hunt and the fur trade. They concentrated on farming, conversed in the Gaelic and whispered to their own God under Presbyterian auspices. They had become isolated, like the stranded inhabitants of an island within an island, feeling morally superior but too proud to acknowledge their declining influence and numbers. Nearby lived the retired Hudson's Bay factors and their families, who treated Red River as a fur-trading post over which they claimed natural managerial rights, living out old glories and supporting the influx of Anglican missionaries. They quickly became the settlement's self-appointed leaders, sharing, in W.L. Morton's wonderful phrase, "neither the Ishmaelite wildness of the Métis nor the careful poverty of the Kildonan Scots." To the south and west of the river junction lived the Métis of the Upper Settlement and White Horse Plain, the most dynamic element in the region; their way of life focused on the seasonal buffalo hunts and fostered increasingly militant aspirations to control their own destinies. Finally, there were the villages of Swampy Cree in St Peter's, above the Red River Delta, and the band of Saulteaux at Baie St Paul up the Assiniboine. The census of 1849 also listed one Pole, one Dane, one Norwegian and a Dutchman.

Nearly all the would-be Swiss settlers who had come to the Selkirk Settlement in 1821 had left Red River soon after arriving and taking a good look around. They moved to Fort Snelling, near modern-day St Paul, Minnesota, as did most of the De Meurons. The mercenaries' departure was hastened by the fact that immediately after the 1826 floods had scattered local dairy herds, the De Meurons suddenly had quantities of beef and hides for sale, while the Scottish settlers never did locate their lost animals. Thirteen families came out from Lincolnshire in 1836 to work the HBC's experimental farm, but the colonization of Red River did not become a mass movement. This minimal inflow meant that it was the indigenous population of Mixed Bloods who assumed natural dominance within the settlement.

The problem with Red River as a farming community seemed at times extra-terrestrial, as if a committee of vengeful archangels had decided to twist the indifferent forces of nature into a malignant conspiracy to prevent agriculture from flourishing there. Thirty crop failures, resulting from early frosts, locusts and alternations of drought and flood, blighted the land between 1813 and 1870.

The Selkirk colony shared with many other Canadian communities the problem that at least one of the rivers on which it was located flows north, from a harsh climate into one even more severe. This means that spring breakup occurs on the upper parts of the stream first, with the thawing waters, impounded behind the ice of still-frozen river mouths, flooding the lower banks. The 1811 spring flood on the Red, just above its junction with the Assiniboine, for example, raised water levels by fifty feet. (One of the few men known to have taken advantage of this phenomenon was Alexander Griggs, captain of the river steamer *International*, en route to Fort Garry from the United States with a load of liquor destined for the Hudson's Bay Company. On May 10, 1873, a new tariff that would have cost the Company extra duty was due to come into effect. The skipper was having trouble manoeuvring his vessel along the flooded river because he couldn't see the usual shorelines. According to a report in the *Manitoban*, he turned the ship "out of the bed of the river and made a short cut over the prairie ... thereby reducing the distance materially and gaining the Customs House" before the midnight tax deadline.

Apart from natural hazards, the Red River economy was difficult to sustain because nearly everything had to be imported. Most goods and provisions brought from England were subject to mark-ups of 110 percent—33 percent for ocean freight, 20 percent for land transport from York Factory and 57 percent for HBC profit. Yet the Company could purchase locally produced grain at almost any price (usually as low as two shillings sixpence a bushel) because there were no other buyers. The farmers could not engage in the fur trade, which was an HBC monopoly, and were excluded from the settlement's main cash crop—production of pemmican for export into the Fur Country—since that was the preserve of the Métis.

Simpson launched a series of experiments, hoping to diversify Red River's revenue base, but none worked. The Buffalo Wool Company of 1822 was supposed to process the animal hair for export to British textile mills, but the harvesting expenditures and transportation charges raised the manufacturing cost to $12.50 a yard for cloth that sold at only $1.10. The HBC then tried to start an export business in tallow— the hard fat rendered from butchered cattle, widely used in making candles and soap. Two particularly tough winters and an invasion of predator wolves reinforced by the colony's wild dogs killed the hundred cows allocated to that enterprise, and Simpson turned his attention back to the wool industry. This time he planned to raise sheep, dispatching two HBC traders to purchase 1,471 of the animals at St Louis or in Kentucky. The duo was more familiar with the habits of beaver, and so many of their charges died along the fifteen-hundred-mile journey that by the time the two unlucky shepherds returned to Red River, only 241 sheep were trotting after them.

These and other equally disastrous ventures proved to the settlers that their only economic salvation lay in precisely the option the Hudson's Bay Company was bound to resist most fiercely: free trade in furs with the United States.

THE HBC HAD NEVER GENERATED MUCH LOYALTY from its employees at Red River. Because Simpson preferred to recruit his new officers in Scotland, he promoted few if any Métis. The York boat crews were hired locally on a per-trip basis to take the pemmican from Red River to Norway House. The trade goods (brought in from York Factory) were then shipped to Athabasca, where pelts were loaded for the return journey. The four-month round trips were joyless excursions, and the tripmen developed little affinity for the Company.

Simpson had no mixed emotions about Red River. He hated it. Dealing with the settlers, he complained, was like training what he called a "Libyan tiger"—the more you try to tame it, the more savage it becomes. "[They] are a distinct sort of beings," he groused, "somewhere between the half Indians and overgrown children. At times they need caressing and not unfrequently the discipline of the birch, in other words the iron rod of retribution. But in the present instance the latter not being within our reach, it behooves us to attempt by stratagem what we cannot compass by force."

Paradoxically, his choice of agent to defend the Company's interests was none other than Cuthbert Grant, leader of the death squad that had savaged the HBC's settlers at Seven Oaks a decade earlier.* After that bloody episode, Grant had been part of the NWC contingent dispatched to guard Grand Rapids and at a nearby rendezvous had

---

*Simpson's description of Cuthbert Grant in his confidential Character Book gave the rationale for his decision. "A halfbreed whose name must long recall to mind some horrible Scenes which in former Days took place at Red River Settlement in which he was the principal actor," went the entry. "A generous Warm hearted Man who would not have been guilty of the Crimes laid to his charge had he not been driven into them by designing Men—A very stout powerful fellow of great nerve & resolution but now getting unwieldy and inactive. Drinks ardent spirits in large quantities, thinks nothing of a Bottle of Rum at a Sitting but is so well Seasoned that he is seldom intoxicated altho it undermines his constitution rapidly—A sensible clear headed man of good conduct except in reference to the unfortunate habits of intemperance he has fallen into. Entirely under the influence of the Catholic Mission and quite a Bigot. The American Traders have made several liberal offers to him, but he has rejected them all being now a staunch Hudsons Bay Man and we allow him a Saly. of £200 P. Annum as 'Warden of the Plains' which is a Sinecure afforded him intirely from political motives and not from any feeling of liberality or partiality. The appointment prevents him from interfering with the Trade on his own account which he would otherwise do in all probability; it moreover affords us the benefit of his great influence over the half breeds and Indians of the neighbourhood which is convenient inasmuch as it exempts us from many difficulties with them. He resides at the White Horse plain about 16 miles up the Assiniboine River where he has a Farm and only visits the Establishment [Fort Garry] on business or by Invitation; but is always ready to obey our command and is very effective when employed as a Constable among the half breeds or Indians—is perfectly satisfied with what has been done for him which is quite Sufficient and has no prospect of advancement."

become involved in the killing of the HBC's Owen Keveny, leader of the second group of Selkirk settlers. Following amalgamation of the two companies, Grant spent eleven months in disgrace before Simpson invited him back into the fur trade as a constable-clerk at Fort Garry.

With a group of followers Grant founded the village of Grantown (now Saint-François-Xavier, Manitoba) at White Horse Plain on the Assiniboine. Promoted by Simpson in 1828 to Warden of the Plains, Grant was eventually sworn in as a justice of the peace and was later also named a magistrate and sheriff. He became an influential voice on Company matters within the Council of Assiniboia, the HBC's puppet colonial administration. Grant's official assignment was to police the border with his volunteer cavalry units against free traders, but his real function was to co-opt the rebellious spirit of the Métis. This he achieved, at least temporarily, but neither Simpson nor Grant could long hold back the forces gathering to engulf the settlement.

The edgy situation at Red River attracted its share of freebooters and soldiers of misfortune, none more bizarre than "General" James Dickson (who also called himself Montezuma II), whose self-imposed mission was to recruit a Métis army for a march on Santa Fé, where he intended to free the Indians and establish his own kingdom. He first materialized in Montreal during the spring of 1836, equipped with the gold-inlaid sword of a British general and exquisitely tailored uniform to match. He wore a fierce-looking false beard (which he frequently switched from a suitcase filled with spare vandykes and moustaches) and carried with him a coat of mail in which he presumably intended to mount his Santa Fé throne. Dickson had enough money to recruit a sixty-man advance guard and promptly set off for Red River to sign up his invasion force. By the time the General and his party arrived at Red River, Simpson had formulated a strategy to prevent the exodus of Métis who might be tempted to follow him. The HBC store refused to honour the General's drafts, thus depriving him of funds, and the Company hired away most of his saner lieutenants.

The frustrated Dickson stomped around Red River during the winter of 1836–37, changing beards and uniforms to suit his darkening mood. He made friends with Cuthbert Grant, and that spring the Métis leader arranged for a guide to start Dickson on his way to Santa Fé. The General had the last word. "You are the great soldier and leader," Dickson told Grant. "I am a failure. These belong to you. . . ." With that, he took off his epaulettes, fastened them to Grant's shoulders, handed over his sword and rode away into the sunset, never to be heard from again.

On a more serious level, Simpson decided to meet the mounting challenge of competition by realigning the Assiniboia trading system, allowing settlers to barter furs with the Indians under Company licence. His hope was that he could defuse some of the resentment of the HBC's monopoly and thus gather pelts that might otherwise be smuggled across the border. The theory was valid, but in practice, giving outsiders a taste of the mark-ups to be gained only drove them to the conclusion that they would benefit most by going into the fur business for themselves. Donald MacKenzie, the HBC's Chief Factor at Upper Fort Garry, tried his best to halt the fur pirates, arresting the worst offenders, searching the Red River carts heading south and, in summer, poking sticks up the chimneys of settlers' cabins in search of secret pelt caches.

The free traders soon began to move both ways across the international boundary. A Mixed Blood named Alexis Bailly, employed by the American Fur Company, had driven a herd of cattle to Red River as early as 1821 and sold the animals at great profit. Even the HBC's general store at Fort Garry had competition—Andrew McDermot, an ambitious former HBC clerk, claimed his newly opened shop could supply anything except second-hand coffins. The most articulate leader of Red River's free-trade movement was James Sinclair, the British-educated son of an HBC Chief Factor, whose sister Betsey had been abandoned by George Simpson.

The fragile equilibrium of the situation changed dramatically in 1843 when Norman Wolfred Kittson, an emigrant Lower Canadian serving with the American Fur Company, opened a trading post at Pembina in North Dakota, about seventy miles south of Fort Garry. His instructions were to capture the Red River fur trade, and he set about it with energy and cunning. He drew Sinclair, McDermot and many other independent traders, including an outspoken Mixed Blood named Pierre-Guillaume Sayer (son of a former NWC winterer), into his orbit. By the late 1840s, free traders had infiltrated so much of the commerce that Simpson realized the continued existence of the Red River Colony was at stake. Using the threat of American incursion as their fulcrum and lever, the London Committee persuaded the British government to dispatch three companies (340 men) of the 6th Regiment of Foot (the Royal Warwickshires) to maintain the peace. They arrived by way of York Factory and hacked their way to Red River, dragging a nine-pound cannon and three six-pounders behind them.

The presence of the soldiers provided a deterrent to free trade, but there was little in the colony to allay their own sense of ennui. The 6th had been at Fort Garry only three months when Wemyss Simpson, the Governor's brother-in-law, reported: "They are not too fond of the country, as they have so very little amusement and so little occupation.

Free-trade movement leader James Sinclair

They tried to get up races, but did not succeed. Mr. Mosse, one of the ensigns, walked from the Upper to the Lower Fort in three hours, 39 minutes, for £5 sterling. The men are very orderly, and there have only been a few rows. One man was stabbed by a half-breed, who was jealous of him. Two others were tried and flogged, one 100 lashes, the other 50. They did not say a word during the whole time of the punishment, and therefore saved themselves from being laughed at. The people in the settlement were never so well off, as the Government spends about £30 per day, and the Company also spends a great deal, buying all the cattle, pigs, sheep and grain. McDermot and the Scotch settlers are making fortunes. The soldiers buy great quantities of beer, and give any price for it, and there are few houses in the settlement where they cannot get it."

After two years, their place was taken by a dubious rabble of fifty-six British Army pensioners under the command of Major William Caldwell, who was also appointed Governor of Assiniboia. Each man was promised twenty free acres if he made the journey, and though they were not so much an occupying army as policemen, the Red River resident who condemned them as worse than useless was overly generous in his assessment. The only distinction any contemporary observer

Jean-Louis Riel, "the miller of the Seine"

could attach to Major Caldwell was the fact that he was unusually tall. The agitation for free trade, which had languished during the pacifying interlude of the Warwickshires, now came alive with a vengeance. Kittson's take of furs, greater than ever, was threatening to dominate the trade. Using the flimsy excuse that Caldwell's appointment had separated local governing authority from the Company's orbit of influence, HBC Chief Factor John Ballenden arrested Pierre-Guillaume Sayer and three other Métis on charges of illegal trafficking in pelts. Ballenden never questioned that a proper verdict would be returned, reinstating the Company's monopoly.

The Métis harboured no such illusions. The trial was set for May 17, 1849 (the Feast of the Ascension, their priests carefully noted), and neither the hunters nor the tripmen went out that day. Their protests were organized by a Committee of the New Nation. One leader of that militant confederacy was Jean-Louis Riel, known as "the miller of the Seine" because he had dug a nine-mile channel from the Red River to increase the flow over his mill wheel on a little river named for the local custom of seining fish. An ardent Métis nationalist (whose first-born and namesake would become the patron saint of French Canadian rebels), Riel *père* had dreamed of establishing a wool factory in the region, but his efforts had been frustrated by the HBC's monopoly. The Sunday before the trial, the Métis leader had read a public letter urging every man in the church to attend the proceedings armed and prepared to assert his rights.

On the day of the trial, Riel addressed the three hundred Métis gathered near the steps of St Boniface Cathedral, exhorting them to liberate Sayer and assert freedom of trade for the New Nation. Riel then led the armed buffalo hunters across the river to the courthouse presided over by Adam Thom, the recorder of Assiniboia, who had a well-earned reputation for being both anti-French and anti-Catholic. Some of Riel's more militant sharpshooters threatened to pick off the judge on his bench. Inside the courtroom, James Sinclair, acting as Sayer's counsel, was following a carefully plotted legal course. Members of the empanelled jury—seven English and five French—settled into their seats with powder horns and shot pouches at their belts and guns on their knees.

The testimony droned on into the long afternoon, with various witnesses contradicting one another on the extent of Sayer's free-trading habits. When Donald Gunn, the jury foreman, finally delivered the verdict, it was divided into two parts. Sayer was found guilty of trading furs, but the jurors also recommended mercy "as it appeared that he thought he had a right to trade as he and others were under the impression that there was a free trade." Ballenden committed the strategic error of unthinkingly accepting this mixed verdict and compounded his mistake by setting Sayer and his co-defendants free on the spot.

As the doors of the courtroom opened and Sayer stepped into the sunshine, Riel and his troops came to the instant (and as it turned out, irrevocable) conclusion that their fellow Métis had been acquitted— and that the fur trade had officially been set free. "*Vive la Liberté! Le commerce est libre!*" went the victory shouts. Musket-fire exploded skyward as the exhilarated Métis rode out to spread the news—the HBC's monopoly had been broken at last.

Maybe. In line with its usual strategy, the Hudson's Bay Company simply switched horses. Instead of trying to defend its trading rights, which had been ended by popular reaction if not yet by invalidation of its legal position, the Company immediately started undercutting the free traders by offering higher prices for furs (eventually putting Kittson out of business) and by agreeing to most of the Métis' political demands. Simpson removed Adam Thom from his post as recorder even though the controversial Scottish-born lawyer had acted as a good HBC man, merely following orders. Use of the French language in the settlement's courtrooms was allowed, and the first independent Métis representatives were appointed to the Council of Assiniboia.

The Anson Northup

One inadvertent victim of the Sayer trial was Cuthbert Grant. He no longer commanded the loyalty of the Métis, who had pointedly ignored his presence on the Council when demanding representation. They noted with dismay that he had been on the bench during the Sayer trial as one of the associate magistrates. With Grant's usefulness to the Company exhausted, Simpson fired him as Warden of the Plains after twenty-one years of faithful HBC service. Grant spent the half-decade before his death (from injuries sustained falling off a horse) as a token totem, entertaining gentleman buffalo hunters.

Although the Company maintained a dominant share of the business, free traders were now swarming across its territories and had defiantly built a storehouse on the banks of the Red within sight of Fort Garry. By 1858, six hundred Red River carts were running a commuter line between Red River and St Paul, Minnesota. That ambitious city's newly formed Chamber of Commerce offered a $1,000 prize to anyone daring enough to run a steamboat into Fort Garry.

A nautical daredevil named Anson Northup first persuaded the Chamber to double the reward, then bought a derelict stern-wheeler that had been beached at St Anthony Falls on the Mississippi River and floated her up to Crow Wing just before freeze-up. To drag the hull and 11,000-pound boiler the 160 miles to the Red River, Northup put together a land caravan consisting of thirty teamsters to drive the seventeen span of horses and thirteen yoke of oxen through snowdrifts and over makeshift bridges. The vessel, reassembled in six spring weeks, was christened after her owner, and the little thumper set off merrily down the Red River, past Grand Forks and Pembina and across the border towards Assiniboia. Ninety feet long, twenty-two feet wide, with a draft of only fourteen inches, the ungainly contraption could carry fifty tons of cargo; passengers slept in open berths that extended along the main saloon. The ship's silhouette resembled nothing so much as a log cabin mounted on a washbasin, with a smokestack sticking up its middle. One of the vessel's later captains, C.P.V. Lull, described her as "a lumbering old pine-basket, which you have to handle as gingerly as a hamper of eggs."

Without advance warning, the *Anson Northup* pulled into Fort Garry on June 10, 1859. "Within moments there was pandemonium," reported Theodore Barris in *Fire Canoe*, his wonderful book on prairie steamboats. "Panic-stricken Indians fleeing to the river forks cried out that a fiery monster was pounding down the river towards them. Then the 'monster' appeared, as suddenly as an apparition . . . the *Anson Northup*, shrouded by swirling steam and woodsmoke, rounded the final bend and bore down on the Red River Settlement. The Red River was in its annual flood, but even the tumult of the rushing water was drowned by the violent thrashing of the *Northup*'s stern paddlewheel. The Hudson's Bay Company colours rose above the fort walls to greet the Stars and Stripes flying from the prow of the ungainly vessel. . . . Horses with buckskin riders, oxdrawn two-wheeled carts from the fields, and cautious Indians clad in feathers, leggings, and moccasins streamed to the fort landing. Children thronged at the riverside to see 'an enormous barge, with a watermill on its stern' emerging from the wilderness like a demon churning up water and spitting sparks."

The HBC's response to this daring incursion threatening its transportation system was once more in character: the Company bought out the *Anson Northup* to assert its monopoly over the water route, then raised the freight rates to prohibitive levels on any goods carried for its competitors. But there was a hurdle: American law at that time did not allow foreigners to own U.S.-based properties. No problem. Simpson recruited the best man to head the secret partnership that controlled the small but vital one-boat line: Kittson, the displaced free trader from Pembina, who was now mayor of St Paul. To sweeten the deal, Simpson promoted Kittson to "Commodore"—a rare rank in those parts.

The most important piece of cargo ever carried by the little sternwheeler was a printing-press that would give the community its first newspaper, the *Nor'Wester*. Edited by two young Englishmen, William

Coldwell and William Buckingham, who had been reporters for Toronto newspapers, the weekly took up the cause of Red River's annexation by Canada. It was becoming increasingly clear that either the Canadian or the British government would soon have to take decisive action against the HBC's charter. Red River historian Alexander Ross must have sensed the impending power-shift when he astutely remarked that instead of fighting to preserve Red River, the Hudson's Bay Company was treating its once-treasured colony with "the cool and languid care of a stepmother."

Sir George Simpson in his later years

CHAPTER 14

DEATH OF A TITAN

Like a latter-day King Lear raging against his own
mortality, Simpson was now dragging himself painfully
across the land he had once ruled.

BY THE 1850s, SIR GEORGE SIMPSON must have been aware, however reluctant he may have been to admit it, that his brand of absolute power could no longer hold men or causes. Now that he was in his mid-sixties, the coils of wrath having retreated deep inside him, he assumed the mantle of the fur trade's elder statesman and turned his attention to profitable investments on his own account.

With free trade a reality not only at Red River but spreading like a flash fire through the Company's once insulated territories, the HBC's days of dominance were clearly numbered. Yet its daily operations ticked on as methodically as before.

As in the past, the Company treated a shift in its commercial environment as a circumstance to be carefully co-opted, not as a reason for any sudden switch in strategies.

The Hudson's Bay Company's 152 posts, manned by 45 Chief Factors and Traders, 5 surgeons, 154 clerks and postmasters, and 1,200 servants, plus the crews of the inland canoes, York boats and seagoing supply ships, were conducting business as usual. Dividends of the British shareholders (in 1850 only 4 of the 232 proprietors had Canadian addresses) were still rolling in at such a profitable rate that the stock was listed in London at premiums of 220 to 240 percent. When Sir John Pelly, who had been the Company's British Governor for thirty years, died in 1852,* he was replaced by Andrew Colvile, which reduced Simpson's influence not one whit.

The overseas Governor's burden had been reduced somewhat by the appointment in January 1849 of Andrew's son Eden Colvile as Associate Governor of Rupert's Land, to be resident at Red River. Although the younger Colvile's remuneration (£1,000 annually) was deducted from Simpson's salary, his presence at least relieved the senior Governor of having to handle the daily goings-on at the settlement that had always worn his patience to a nub. Only eight years out of Eton and Cambridge, the young Colvile proved equal to his assignment and became such an enthusiastic Bay man that he was later appointed to the Company's London Committee, and from 1872 to 1889 was its Deputy Governor and then its Governor. (The Colviles, father and son, spent no fewer than seventy-nine years directing the HBC's affairs.)

Simpson still sallied forth on his annual inspection tours, but they had evolved into royal processions, staged more for show than specific purpose. His declining energies were concentrated on building up his private portfolio in Montreal's expanding banks, railway companies, canal construction firms, shipping lines and other enterprises. A shrewd assessor of each business proposition's risk-reward ratio, Simpson purchased (from the estate of Sir Alexander Mackenzie) some of the most desirable land in the centre of Montreal (between what are now Dorchester and Sherbrooke streets) and subdivided it into small building lots; he was first a director of the Bank of British North America and was later associated with the Bank of Montreal. He became part of the syndicate that built the original Beauharnois Canal, invested heavily in the commercial boat operations that dominated the Ottawa River, was one of the founders of the Montreal Mining Company set up to explore Lake Superior's north shore, and was a co-sponsor of the railway line between Montreal and Lachine that was expanded to the U.S. border and eventually bought out by the Grand Trunk. He also purchased a

---

* Pelly had been so influential that Company wags suggested the HBC's Latin motto, PRO PELLE CUTEM (roughly translated as "A skin for a skin"), should really have been changed to PRO PELLY CUTEM. Certainly, no other HBC Governor is so amply commemorated on the Canadian landscape. Wherever northern explorers went they affixed his name to the geography as a mark of gratitude for the Company's co-operation: the Pelly River in the Yukon; Pelly Bay on the Arctic Coast in the Keewatin District; Pelly Island on the Arctic Coast in the Mackenzie District; Pelly Lake on the Back River in Keewatin; Pelly Mountain on Victoria Island in the Franklin District; and Pelly Point on Victoria Island, to mark the farthest point reached by HBC explorer Dr John Rae in his search for traces of Sir John Franklin's lost expedition.

The Simpson home at Lachine, near Montreal

partnership in the enterprises of Hugh Allan, the shipping magnate who was Montreal's wealthiest businessman at the time. When the Allan Line bid against the Canadian Steam Navigation Company for a valuable mail contract, Simpson was assigned the task of lobbying the two Canadian politicians responsible for awarding the tender: Premier Francis Hincks and John Ross, Solicitor-General for Canada West. As in most of his political pressure plays, Simpson used the services of his trusted go-between, Stewart Derbishire, then the provincial government's Queen's Printer. Simpson loved handing out buffalo tongues to his favourite legislators, and when one politician jokingly complained that acceptance of such wilderness delicacies might undermine his credibility, Derbishire assured him, with a twinkle in his eye, that "Sir George . . . pleaded his cause with many tongues." Simpson gave away birchbark canoes, boxes of cheroots, Indian tents and, more than once, large sums of money. Hincks and Ross collected "10,000 golden reasons" between them when Simpson was trying to get a tugboat contract for the Allan Line, a bribe that helped make Ross a staunch supporter of the HBC and all its works.

Although Simpson's name appeared on the prospectus of nearly every important new Montreal business venture, his major concern remained conduct of the HBC's overseas operations. That no longer meant dashing from one wilderness outpost to the next trying to catch some hapless Chief Trader with an incomplete inventory tally. Instead, it required intense lobbying in both London and Montreal to keep the politicians on both sides of the Atlantic aware of why the Company and its royal charter still ought to be accorded such extraordinary privileges.

One of his problems was that the fur trade itself, at least in beaver hats, had declined precipitately almost from the instant Prince Albert, Queen Victoria's consort, had appeared at a public function in 1854 wearing a topper not of beaver felt but of silk. A trend towards the much less expensive substitute swept European society, forcing the HBC to trade for secondary animals such as marten, lynx, fox, wolf, otter and even swans for what were called "fancy" furs.

That switch was disruptive enough, but what was really at stake was the continued existence of the Hudson's Bay Company as a continent-spanning monopoly. As usual, the most intense campaign against the Company originated at Red River. The local activist Donald Gunn officially complained to Philip Vankoughnet, president of Canada West's Executive Council, that the HBC was charging up to 400 percent mark-up on goods sold in its stores. The Red River colonists also sent petitions to Westminster claiming that "Hudson's Bay Company's clerks, with an armed police, have entered into settlers' houses in quest of furs, and confiscated all they found. One poor settler, after having his goods seized, had his house burnt to the ground, and afterwards was conveyed prisoner to York Factory. . . . On our annual commercial journeys into Minnesota we have been pursued like felons by armed constables, who searched our property, even by breaking open our trunks; all furs found were confiscated."

This was followed up with a formal request that Red River be either incorporated into Canada or allowed to establish its own independent government. Even George Moffatt, who had been one of the useful intermediaries in the 1821 amalgamation negotiations, quietly informed Simpson that he intended to move a motion in the Canadian Legislative Council calling for abolition of the HBC's monopoly. A British Army major named Robert Carmichael-Smyth, who visited the Prairies, came back with the recommendation that a railway ought to be built across the empty territory as the "great link required to unite in one powerful chain the whole English race." He added that all this could be achieved with the utmost economy by using convict labour. Just such a scheme (minus the convicts) was proposed by a Toronto group of promoters led by Allan Macdonell, who had pioneered mining developments north of Lake Superior. He based his approach on the advantages of building "a highway across the Continent, westward, thereby establishing a short route to the possessions in India, as well as other Asiatic Marts." Macdonell's idea was to purchase from the HBC (at a quantity discount, of course) a sixty-mile-wide strip of land across its territory to build the railway and grow food for its construction crews. He was denied his wish because the government of the day judged his scheme to be visionary but premature; in the longer run, its effect was to draw attention to the potential uses of the vacant hinterland.

The main problem Canada's politicians had in dealing with the HBC was that they were not daring enough to confiscate its land and did not have the necessary funds to buy it. Their solution was to fight the Company on the legally slippery ground that its charter was no longer valid and that as heirs of the French who had originally claimed most of its real estate, they had full rights to all the territory west of Lake of the Woods. George Brown, editor of the reformist Toronto *Globe*, was still championing his version of manifest destiny, which meant acquiring Rupert's Land from the HBC. Brown was now able to rally not only his own Clear Grit supporters but some of the most articulate Quebec politicians in his crusade. Simpson's spy Derbishire reported that he had overheard the *Globe* editor complaining to a Toronto bookstore proprietor that the HBC had debauched the Indians by importing, in one year alone, a million hogsheads of liquor into the fur trade. That kind of propaganda was reinforced by the continuing agitation at Red River and formal resolutions of the Canada West Executive Council calling ever more urgently for the country to reach out to the Pacific.

Free traders had meanwhile infiltrated all the Company's territories except two of its northernmost districts, and nearly as many goods were flowing in and out of Red River through St Paul as via York Factory. In October 1846, Chief Factor John Swanton, then in charge of Fort Garry, informed Simpson that Lieutenant Colonel C.F. Smith, commanding officer of an American cavalry unit stationed in the Dakota plains, had notified him that the Métis would no longer be allowed to run buffalo south of the border and that he intended to build a military post in the Red River Valley. These belligerent gestures were enough for Simpson and his London principals to persuade the Colonial Secretary to dispatch a detachment of 120 officers and men of the Royal Canadian Rifles to defend the Company's interests. The presence of the troops strengthened the Company's hand, though they actually did nothing except escort a band of twenty visiting Sioux away from the settlement in case of attack by local Métis. This irrelevant show of force

George Brown, founding editor of the Toronto Globe

only angered the settlers, who set up the Assiniboia Committee to monitor the Company's actions and safeguard their own interests.

It was not a powerful or even representative group, but the Committee organized the settlers' anti-HBC campaign, which was rapidly accelerating where it really mattered—in London, among the British politicians and bureaucrats who would soon be responsible for dealing with the Company's request that its licence be renewed before it expired, in May 1859. Late in the summer of 1856, Simpson had warned the London Committee that the Company was "... in a very critical position, the authorities being overawed by the numerical strength of the Halfbreed race; so that, at any moment an unpopular measure or accidental collision might lead to a general rising against the Company and the destruction of their establishments. In the meantime, by tact and forebearance, we contrive to maintain the peace and are making large returns—a state of things which may continue one, two or more years, although at all times liable to be interrupted suddenly."

But the London Committee could be of only limited assistance in helping to avert this portent. British public opinion was swinging against the Company, not so much for any specific Canadian reasons but because it had so clearly become an anachronism. The East India Company was in the process of being wound up, the Royal African

Company was long gone, and the originating justification for these and other royally chartered enterprises—to encourage exploration of unknown continents by rewarding groups of investors in such ventures with trading monopolies—had become irrelevant. The HBC was under attack in the British House of Commons by the influential social reformer (and future prime minister) William Ewart Gladstone, who despised monopolies in any form. "In England," wrote Jan Morris in her monumental history of the period, "the trend of empire was against the Company. The radical imperialists wanted all of Canada open to settlement. The evangelists wanted every valley exalted, the financial community resented the tight-lipped and privileged manner of the Company. . . . Even Lord Palmerston thought commerce was not enough in itself as justification of empire."

THE ISSUE CAME TO A HEAD when Henry Labouchere (afterwards Lord Taunton), Secretary of State for the Colonies in Lord Palmerston's first administration, called for a Select Committee of the House of Commons to investigate the case for renewing the HBC's trading monopoly—and appointed himself its chairman. Among that august body's nineteen members were some of the great notables of British politics at the time: Sir John Pakington, a former Secretary of State for War and for the Colonies; Lord John Russell, the great Whig leader who had been prime minister from 1846 to 1852; Lord Stanley, later the Earl of Derby; Gladstone, who had already been Colonial Secretary under Peel; Robert Lowe, later Viscount Sherbrooke, one of the leading classicists of his time and subsequently Chancellor of the Exchequer; John Arthur Roebuck, the radical free trader and disciple of John Stuart Mill; and Edward Ellice, son of the veteran parliamentarian and former Nor'Wester who had become one of the HBC's staunchest advocates. It was the senior Ellice who would act throughout the hearings as the Company's counsel for the defence.

And so the Hudson's Bay Company and its charter were put on trial at last. The committee sat eighteen times and cross-examined twenty-five witnesses, asking 6,098 questions. The transcript of its hearings covered 450 pages. First to be heard was John Ross, the former Solicitor-General for Canada West, who had already been bribed at least once by Simpson and was president of the Grand Trunk Railway. His testimony was so favourable that the Governor later congratulated him on his "able handling" of the parliamentarians' questions. Even though he wanted the Grand Trunk to cross the West, Ross was quite definite in advocating that the HBC remain the continent's landlord. "I think it would be a very great calamity if their control and power in that part of America were entirely to cease," he told the committee. "My reason for forming that opinion is this: during all the time that I have been able to observe their proceedings there, there has been peace within the whole territory. The operations of the Company seem to have been carried on, at all events, in such a way as to prevent the Indian tribes within their borders from molesting the Canadian frontier; while, on the other hand, those who have turned their attention to that quarter of the world must have seen that, from Oregon to Florida, for these last thirty years or more, there has been a constant Indian war going on between the natives of the American territory, on the one side, and the Indian tribes on the other. Now, I fear very much that if the occupation of the Hudson's Bay Company, in what is called the Hudson's Bay territory, were to cease, our fate in Canada might be just as it is with Americans in the border settlements of their territory."

Next on the witness stand was William Henry Draper, later Chief Justice of Ontario, representing the Macdonald-Cartier government's claims to the great lone land. Associated with the Family Compact so influential in governing the colony, Draper was also a friend of Simpson's; in fact, the Governor had just recently arranged a job for his son. After lauding the HBC, Draper went on to advocate a tougher line on colonization: "I do not think that the interests of a trading company can ever be considered as compatible with the settlement of the province ... I hope you will not laugh at me as very visionary, but I hope to see the time, or my children may live to see the time, when there is a railway going all across that country and ending at the Pacific."

There followed bishops, explorers, army officers, admirals and retired employees, all testifying to the essential decency of the Company's stewardship, emphasizing how HBC Factors had often saved Indian bands from starvation, and repeatedly stressing the differences between the relatively benign occupation of the Canadian Prairie and the savage Indian wars of the American West. But two bits of evidence damaging to the HBC did emerge from the preliminary testimony. Dr John Rae, the Orkney surgeon who had spent most of his life in the Company's service as a doctor, trader and explorer,* testified that its servants were forced to pay a 50-percent mark-up for goods they bought on their own accounts, while Indians were charged the equivalent of 300 percent over British costs. Other testimony confirmed that the HBC was still using large quantities of rum in its Indian trade. Ellice admitted that liquor was employed, but blamed its necessity on American competition.

---

*For a description of Rae's incredible career, see *Company of Adventurers*, Chapter 15.

One of the most telling attacks was the brief from the Aborigines' Protection Society, which claimed that the HBC charter had "given unlimited scope to the cupidity of a Company of traders, placing no stint upon their profits, or limits to their power . . . [with the result that] the unhappy race we have consigned to their keeping, and from whose toil their profits are wrung, are perishing miserably by famine, while not a vestige of an attempt has been made on the part of their rulers to imbue them with the commonest arts of civilized life, or to induce them to change the precarious livelihood obtained by the chase for a certain subsistence derived from cultivation of the soil."

Several hostile witnesses, including A.K. Isbister, the chief British advocate for the people of Red River, and Richard Blanshard, the first governor of Vancouver Island, condemned the Company as a barrier to enlightenment and civilization, stressing its obnoxious monopoly and tyrannical ways. Unlike the previous witnesses who had praised the HBC as a universally benevolent force, these critics were specific, show-ing with actual examples why the lack of competition meant the loss of freedom for the 158,000 inhabitants (11,000 of them whites and Mixed Bloods) of the HBC's licensed territories.

The main issue before the Parliamentary Committee was not so much the Company's past reputation as its future credibility, especially in terms of its own insistence that there could never be any economically viable settlements in its territories beyond its trading posts and the already established enclaves at Red River, Fort Langley and Victoria.

On February 26 and again on March 2, 1857, the politicians appeared in full regalia, puffed up with self-importance as they welcomed to the stand the witness whose testimony they believed would decisively sway their verdict. As he stepped tentatively into that Westminster committee room, Sir George Simpson looked all of his biblical span of threescore and ten years. He felt uncomfortable in his surroundings. His rectitude had always been taken for granted, but here were these politicians in their dandy vestments, none of whom would last an hour hiking up a stiff portage, asking *him* to account for his actions—to justify what he considered to be the Company's natural position. He had never felt himself accountable to anyone except the HBC's proprietors, and he was not about to indulge these popinjays with his confidence. Yet there was nothing for it but to keep his temper as he resigned himself to answering what he expected would be silly little questions.

As it turned out, the questions were chillingly sensible, and, for the first time, Simpson must have felt publicly humiliated by his performance.

When Labouchere, the committee chairman, asked the Governor to describe how suitable the Company's territories might be for cultivation and colonization, Simpson replied: "I do not think that any part of the Hudson's Bay territories is well adapted for settlement; the crops are very uncertain."

"Would you apply that observation to the district of Red River?"

"Yes."

"Why so?"

"On account of the poverty of the soil, except on the banks of the river. The banks of the river are alluvial, and produce very fair crops of wheat; but these crops are frequently destroyed by early frosts; there is no certainty of the crops. We have been under the necessity of importing grain within these last 10 years from the United States and from Canada, for the support of the establishment."

A little later, when asked whether he was familiar with the characteristics of the Pacific Coast, Simpson answered confidently: "Yes. I have gone along the coast from Puget's Sound to the Russian principal establishment at Sitka."

"Do you believe that coast to be altogether unfit for colonization?"

"I believe it to be quite unfit for colonization."

This was a careless assertion for Simpson to make since previous testimony had already confirmed that the HBC's Fort Langley, near the mouth of the Fraser—which Simpson had just described as worthless— was enjoying great success as a Company farm. More damaging still to his credibility had been his cursory dismissal of the agricultural future of Red River and his later direct reference to the uselessness of the land around Fort Frances.

"If I understand you rightly," interjected one of the committee members, reaching into his briefcase for a book, "you think that no portion of Rupert's Land is favourable for settlement, but that some portions might be settled?"

"Yes."

"In your very interesting work of a *Journey Round the World*, I find at page 45 of the first volume this description of the country between the Lake of the Woods and the Rainy Lake: 'From Fort Frances downwards, a stretch of nearly 100 miles, it is not interrupted by a single impediment, while yet the current is not strong enough materially to retard an ascending traveller. Nor are the banks less favourable to agriculture than the waters themselves to navigation, resembling, in some measure, those of the Thames near Richmond. From the very brink of the river there rises a gentle slope of green-sward, crowned in many places with a plentiful growth of birch, poplar, beech, elm, and oak. Is it too much for the eye of philanthropy to discern through the vista of futurity this noble stream, connecting, as it does, the fertile shores of two spacious lakes, with crowded steamboats on its bosom and populous towns on its borders?' I suppose you consider that district favourable for population?"

"The right bank of the river is favourable, with good cultivation; that is to say, the soil is favourable; the climate is not; the back country is a deep morass, and never can be drained, in my opinion."

"Do you see any reason to alter the opinion which you have there expressed?"

"I do see that I have overrated the importance of the country as a country for settlement."

"It is too glowing a description, you think?"

"Exactly so; it is exceedingly beautiful; the bank is beautifully wooded, and the stream is very beautiful. . . ."

"Will you allow me to remind you of one other sentence in your interesting work. It is at page 55 of volume 1: 'The soil of Red River Settlement is a black mould of considerable depth, which, when first tilled, produced extraordinary crops . . . even after 20 successive years of cultivation, without the relief of manure or of fallow, or of green crop it still yields from 15 to 25 bushels an acre! The wheat produced is plump and heavy; there are also large quantities of grain of all kinds, besides beef, mutton, pork, butter, cheese, and wool in abundance.' "

Not an exchange to make the earth move, but enough to plant a seed of doubt in the minds of the parliamentarians about Simpson's—and the Hudson's Bay Company's—believability. Gladstone later noted in his autobiography that the HBC Governor "in answering our questions had to call in the aid of incessant coughing."

In other testimony the hearings revealed that the Company's shareholders had been enriched by dividends totalling £20 million. Even though the HBC had been praised for many of its practices, the most generous-minded among its proponents based their defence mainly on the notion that whatever its corporate sins, the Company had at least prevented the slaughter typical of the American frontier. This was a valid if slightly simplistic point of view, but hardly a rallying cry stirring enough to justify prolonging the HBC's despotic powers over such a large and potentially lucrative chunk of geography. "The disclosures laid bare by this accumulation of testimony, letters, petitions, memorials and other evidence produced before the Parliamentary Select Committee, made the deepest kind of a public sensation," wrote Gustavus Myers in his *History of Canadian Wealth*. "For nearly two centuries the Hudson's Bay Company had represented itself in England as the grand evangel of religion, colonization, and civilization among the Indians; for nearly two centuries it had assiduously spread abroad its pretended reputation; and by insisting long enough upon its assumed virtues had been credited with them by the large mass of the unknowing. Now the truth was revealed, and bad as it was, yet it was regarded as undoubtedly only part of the whole. Imminently threatened, as the Hudson's Bay Company now was, with judicial and legislative extinction, it had to adopt some hurried expedient to save itself."

That expedient proved to be the production of one last witness before the committee adjourned to write its report. He was Edward ("Bear") Ellice, now in his mid-seventies, still respected by the parliamentarians and very much a force within the HBC's governing councils. He had been associated with the Canadian fur trade for half a century and, after a rambling lecture on its historical importance, electrified the committee with his reply to the chairman's question: Would it be difficult to make an arrangement between the Canadian Government and the Company for the extension of settlement into Hudson's Bay territory?

"Not only would there be no difficulty in it," replied the Bear, as if on cue, "but the Hudson's Bay Company would be [only] too glad to make a cession of any part of that territory for the purposes of settlement, upon one condition, that Canada shall be at the expense of governing it and maintaining a good police and preventing the introduction, so far as they can, of competition within the fur trade."

"You think it would be advantageous to the Company to withdraw, as it were, to the more Northern part of their territory, and leave for gradual settlement the Southern portion of their country?"

"I am of [the] opinion that the existence and maintenance of the Hudson's Bay Company for the purpose of temporarily governing this country, until you can form settlements in it, is much more essential to Canada and to England than it is to the Company of Adventurers trading into Hudson's Bay."

After that exchange, the committee's report was a foregone conclusion. As if by magic, the future of the Canadian West had suddenly become negotiable. The committee's majority recommendations, though mildly phrased, were hard-boiled in their intent: the Company must surrender its claims to Vancouver Island immediately and to the adjacent mainland (where a colony was to be created) soon afterwards; the Red River and Saskatchewan districts were to be annexed eventually to Canada; only those portions of the Indian territory considered unsuitable for settlement were to remain under the HBC's monopoly control for another twenty-one years. The Company of Adventurers could no longer claim, as it had in the original charter, to be "true and absolute Lords and proprietors" of the land beyond the westering sea. In the hush of that wood-panelled committee room, it seemed as if the epitaph of the sprawling enterprise had been written.

Edward ("Bear") Ellice, still a force within the HBC in his mid-seventies

But such a pessimistic interpretation was based on an underestimation of the HBC's boundless pragmatism. If the impatient realm of Canada had transcontinental pretensions, that was fine: the Company would sell its land at the highest bid. No corporate officer adopted this unexpected detour with greater enthusiasm than Simpson himself, calculating that the Company's assets should fetch about £1 million cash, including £408,000 for its posts. His prescription for survival was simplicity itself: the HBC would pocket the money and continue to maintain its trading dominance within its territories, but as a private enterprise rather than an odious and "privileged" monopoly. The only problem was that this happy formula required a purchaser with ready funds—and there was none available. While the Macdonald-Cartier government was issuing brave declarations on the issue (mainly to disarm George Brown's more militant supporters), its treasury was bare, and London was not about to make the purchase of HBC lands a burden on the British taxpayer.

That, roughly, was the situation in 1859, when the Company's position was renewed on sufferance. Since neither Canada nor Britain would vote the funds required to govern the Indian territory, the Hudson's Bay Company continued to operate much as before. Its ever-staunch defence of the status quo had triumphed, one more time.

SIR GEORGE SIMPSON RECOVERED QUICKLY from his parliamentary ordeal, but the illnesses that had periodically plagued him now came on more frequently and with debilitating consequences. Waves of fatigue left him so weak he could hardly dress without help. Doctors kept leeching him, but his pulse remained abnormally slow. He was liable to bouts of fainting and occasional seizures. He had suffered two mild apoplectic strokes in 1851 and two years later was devastated by the terminal illness of his beloved Frances; her delicate health had broken after the birth of their second son in 1850.

The Governor could still work up the energy for his annual visits inland, but as one of his former comrades-in-arms, Edward Ermatinger, remarked: "Our old Chief, Sir George, . . . tottering under the infirmities of age, has seen his best days. His light canoe, with choice of men, and of women too! can no longer administer to his gratification."

In the early summer of 1858, feeling a bit more chipper, Simpson travelled west for the first time by train, from New York through Chicago and Milwaukee to St Paul. His companion was none other than the Bear, come from England to spend time with his favourite compatriot. A few years Simpson's senior, Ellice had heard about the wonders of the American railroads, and the two old men sat nodding at one another, assuring themselves that they had come by rail to investigate the possibility of using this southern supply route as a replacement for York Factory on Hudson Bay. Simpson did briefly visit the Council meeting at Norway House and, after some ill-tempered remarks, retreated the way he had come.

Before the following season's inland journey, he penned a confidential letter to the London Committee. Suffering from periods of near-total blindness, he had somehow shrunk into himself, and his clothes hung loosely on his once-imposing frame. "In February next, I shall have completed forty years Service with the Hudson's Bay Company," he wrote. "During that very long period I have never been off duty for a week at a time, nor have I ever allowed Family ties and personal convenience to come in competition with the claims I considered the Company to have on me. . . . It is high time, however, I rested from incessant labour. Moreover, I am unwilling to hold an appointment, when I cannot discharge its duties to my own satisfaction. I shall therefore make way for some younger man, who I trust may serve the Compy. as zealously and conscientiously as I have done." Before receiving a reply he set off westward on his annual inspection tour, but when he reached St Paul he was too ill and too exhausted to continue. After a few days' rest he returned to Lachine.

NOT FAR FROM LACHINE on August 1 of that summer, two other old men met for their final reunion. Eighty-three-year-old Simon Fraser, who had explored the restless river named after him, visited the house of his old friend John McDonald of Garth, who had fought every battle in the Northwest worth fighting. There the two Nor'Westers composed a memorandum. "We are the last of the North West partners," it began, "we have known one another for many years—which of the two survives the other we know not—we are both aged—we have lived in mutual esteem and fellowship—we have done our duty in the stations allotted to us without fear, or reproach—we have survived many dangers—we have run many risks—we can not accuse one another of anything mean or dirty through life—nor done any disgraceful actions—nor wrong to others—we have been feared, loved and respected by natives—we have kept our men under subordination—we have thus lived long lives— and as this is probably the last time we meet on earth—we part as we have lived in sincere friendship and mutual good will."

McDonald of Garth lived another seven years; Fraser died destitute three years later. The most worthy of the Nor'Westers, David Thompson, had passed away two years earlier. After completing his service in the Fur Country and for another decade mapping the Canadian-American border, he had spent most of thirty years trying to eke out a living as a freelance surveyor.* He mapped the Eastern Townships for the British American Land Company and most of the Muskoka Lakes country and, as he became poorer, various street and lot locations in Montreal for anyone who would pay him enough for a meal.

Carrying his surveying tripod on his back, trying to find sustenance for himself and his thirteen children, Thompson eventually had to sell his precious instruments and even pawned his winter coat. "Offered Lake Superior chart to a friend for five dollars," he scribbled in one of the final pages of his journal. "He would not take the chart but gave me the five dollars. A good relief, for I have been a week without a penny."

Despite his failing eyesight, Thompson started to edit his journals for publication and devised an elaborate scheme for financing his writings. He decided to try recruiting a group of patrons who would pay him a dollar a day for the maintenance of his family during his literary endeavours—in return for half the profits from the book. There were no takers. So at seventy-four, half blind and without sponsors, he started to write the memoir of his adventurous life.

Before the work was completed Thompson died on February 16, 1857, in privation at Longueuil, Quebec. The thirty-nine parts of his personal journals were not published until 1916 and then only because of the inspired sponsorship of Dr Joseph Burr Tyrrell, the Canadian mining engineer and explorer who had retraced Thompson's journeys and found his astronomical observations faultless.

WALKING IN THE SIBILANT RAIN falling hard on the granite blocks of the Lachine Canal, Sir George Simpson was most likely unaware of these and many similarly plaintive episodes. Reflecting on how alone he really was, he realized that Frances, John George McTavish, McLoughlin, Ogden, Rowand, Pelly and many others who had shared his life were dead. Ellice would live another four years, but the two men would never meet again. Somehow it didn't seem fair that they had all abandoned him. Like a latter-day King Lear, raging against his own mortality, Simpson was now dragging himself painfully across the land he had once ruled.

---

*During the War of 1812 Thompson became an ensign in the Sedentary Militia but stayed at home when his unit was called into service, limiting his defence contributions to the invention of a sled-mounted gun that was never used.

Rather than at Lachine, he spent much of his time on nearby Dorval Island, where he had purchased a large summer home four years earlier. One of his few remaining pleasures was to attend Sunday services at St Stephen's Anglican Church, so that he could stamp out as noisily as possible whenever he disagreed with the sermon.

At this point, his ordered life was enlivened by a distinguished visitor. The Prince of Wales, the future Edward VII but then an awkward eighteen-year-old, was on his way to be the officiating dignitary at the opening of the Victoria Bridge spanning the St Lawrence. Simpson decided to give him a treat and called out his Iroquois paddlers from Caughnawaga one last time. Having put in a lifetime's apprenticeship at playing the *grand seigneur*, Simpson scurried around for weeks beforehand, making certain that details of the magnificent tableau he intended for the travelling prince would be exactly right.

On August 29, 1860, His Royal Highness inspected a military parade on the Champ de Mars in a thunderstorm, then at noon was driven to Hudson's Bay House at Lachine and welcomed under eight triumphal arches made of pine boughs. As the sun burst from behind the clouds, the royal entourage left their carriages and set out in two barges belonging to the frigate HMS *Valorous* (anchored downstream from the rapids in Montreal Harbour) towards the wharf at Dorval Island, a quarter of a mile away. Near the foot of the island Simpson had assembled a flotilla of ten birchbark voyageur canoes, their HBC flags flapping in the summer wind. Each was manned by twelve Iroquois in full regalia of red flannel shirts, blue trousers and round caps decorated with dyed feathers pretending to be ostrich plumes.

As soon as the Prince's barge pushed off, the canoes darted out to meet him. Chanting voyageur songs, the paddlers allowed the royal party to pass among them. Then, suddenly wheeling around in perfect formation, the colourful convoy escorted the Prince to his landing place, where Sir George was waiting.

Simpson's island home had been temporarily rented out to Lieutenant-General Sir Fenwick Williams, commander-in-chief of the British forces in Canada, and it was he who acted as host for the ensuing luncheon. Simpson had devised a guest list of forty, inviting only those he considered socially worthy of meeting His Royal Highness. That meant mostly visiting celebrities, such as the Colonial Secretary, the Duke of Newcastle; the British Minister to Washington, Lord Lyons; the Marquess of Chandos; the Earl of Mulgrave, Lieutenant-Governor of Nova Scotia; Admiral Sir Alexander Milne, Commander-in-Chief of the North American and West Indies station; Lord Hinchingbrooke, heir to the Earl of Sandwich; Major-General Robert Bruce of the

The grand canoe reception on the St Lawrence given by Simpson for the Prince of Wales

Prince's staff; and only three women—his niece, his private secretary's wife (the artist Frances Ann Hopkins) and her sister, one of the four other daughters of the Arctic explorer F.W. Beechey.

At four-thirty, the party embarked in the Indians' canoes, the Prince in one and Newcastle and Simpson in another. They wheeled about perfectly in line and crossed to Caughnawaga, where the Iroquois paddlers showed off their passengers to the people of the village, more than two thousand of them watching along the St Lawrence shore. With twilight painting the scene a golden amber, Simpson and his Prince were paddled back to Lachine, where they parted.

That day in the sun with the future king had been Sir George Simpson's formal farewell. Only two days later, still flushed with the exhilaration of the royal occasion, the Governor was stricken with apoplexy. On the morning of September 6, his attending physician, Dr William Sutherland from Montreal, came into his sick room to hear Simpson say: "Well, doctor, this is the last scene of all . . ."

"Yes, Sir George. Where would you wish to be buried?"

"In the Montreal Cemetery, of course."

"Would you wish to have a monument erected over your grave?"

"There is a monument there already."

"Would you wish any particular inscription to be put on it?"

"That," said the dying Sir George, in his last words and final show of temper, "is the business of my executor, not yours . . ."

By morning he was dead.*

The Caughnawaga canoemen, chanting a wild but doleful dirge, crossed the river to escort the cortège from his house to the landing, where a special train was waiting, and Simpson's body was borne by railway car to Montreal. He was buried beside Frances under a simple headstone. The surest sign of his greatness was that those who felt most diminished by his passing were his enemies.

---

*The official cause of Simpson's death was stated to have been "haemorrhagic apoplexy, attended with epileptiform convulsions" but historian Frits Pannekoek maintains he died from tertiary syphilis. Simpson's estate was worth more than £100,000; his residence was sold to the Sisters of St Ann, who demolished it in 1888 to make room for a convent. It was at what is now 1300 St Joseph Boulevard in Lachine, where the only reminder of the fur trade is a small warehouse on the other side of the canal, now a lively fur-trade museum run by Parks Canada. Simpson's summer house on Dorval Island stood for another eighty years. When it was finally torn down in 1939 as a safety hazard, its rubble was carted away in thirty-one scow loads, at two dollars each.

The Hudson's Bay Company's centuries-old monopoly was threatened by the arrival of settlers in the west.

CHAPTER 15

Surrender

" What? Sequester our very tap-root? Take away the fertile lands
where our buffaloes feed? Let in all kinds of people to squat and
settle and frighten away the fur-bearing animals they don't kill
and hunt? Impossible!"

—HBC Governor H.H. Berens to the Colonial Secretary, 1863

THE LITTLE EMPEROR was dead, but his Company still ruled the West. Although the HBC's monopoly was not renewed in 1859, its charter remained the object of universal envy and its commerce continued much as before.

Sir George Simpson's successor as Governor of Rupert's Land was Alexander Grant Dallas, a capable if colourless businessman who had started his career in China with the powerful trading house Jardine, Matheson & Company. He had spent most of the five years before his appointment as the Company's main representative on Vancouver Island as President of the Council. During James Douglas's term as Governor of British Columbia, the two men quarrelled but made up long enough for Dallas to marry Douglas's second daughter, Jane.

Dallas moved the centre of operations to Red River from Lachine, sensing that the influx of land-hungry migrants into the once-isolated Selkirk Settlement would become the HBC's most sensitive dilemma. "As the country comes to be occupied without our leave," he grouched, "they will bye and bye not even give us thanks."

For the moment, fur sales continued to bring in 10- and 15-percent annual dividends, despite the best efforts of the free traders who had invaded the Company's territory. But the Bay men themselves, deprived of Simpson's disciplinarian leadership, had gone soft. Many of them insisted that salutes be fired whenever they left or arrived at a fort and that Company servants doff their caps to them. Some dined on white linen, wielded monogrammed silverware, sent their sons to English or

Alexander Grant Dallas

Scottish schools and their daughters to Toronto or Montreal to be tutored in singing and the piano.

The HBC's Governors realized only too well that they could not maintain their feudal proprietorship much longer. No private corporation could hope to possess the moral authority or spend the funds necessary to govern a region the size of Rupert's Land, once it had been settled. As they scrutinized their long-term prospects, the London-based Committeemen were not at all dismayed. The change in circumstances would gain them a potentially hefty profit on their land—an asset they had not previously considered valuable except as free range for fur-bearing animals. The trick was to win the highest price possible, even though the new Canadian nation lacked the necessary money and the mother country didn't want to spend it. The negotiations that ensued were long and convoluted because the Canadians thought that Rupert's Land should be surrendered without payment, and yet there was really no faction prepared to tackle the Company head on.

The issue tightened into a more serious matter than satisfying the already well-heeled HBC shareholders with the emergence of not very subtle aspirations by American annexationists to grab the virgin territory—that, and the increasingly loud urgings of ambitious railway promoters to use a Canadian land route to connect Europe with the Orient. The mainland of British Columbia had achieved colonial status in 1858, and that provided an incentive for the provinces favourably disposed towards Confederation to pump for the inclusion of the vast empty lands between Canada West and the Pacific Coast. "There can be no question," thundered George Brown's *Globe*, "that the injurious and demoralizing sway of that Company over a region of four millions of square miles, will, ere long, be brought to an end, and that the destinies of this immense country will be united with our own. It is unpardonable that civilization should be excluded from half a continent, on at best but a doubtful right of ownership, for the benefit of two hundred and thirty-two shareholders."

Until the 1864 meetings at Charlottetown and Quebec City's St Louis Hotel, Canadian politics was deadlocked between Brown's Clear Grits and John A. Macdonald's oddly named Liberal-Conservatives, because the two leaders had almost nothing in common except their mutual dislike. The largely agricultural and French-Catholic Canada East and the commercially enterprising Protestant Canada West shared equal representation in the Legislative Assembly. Decisions required a double majority (of the two provincial caucuses) as well as overall approval, and that system stifled new initiatives. British free-trade policies had ended the preferential treatment of Canada's exports. Then on March 17, 1866, Washington permitted the lapse of the Reciprocity Treaty of 1854 (which had allowed free U.S.–Canada trade in most commodities), causing the Canadian economy to suffer a severe recession.

The American Civil War had just ended, and the U.S. government was intent on using British North America as the "Achilles heel of the Empire" to exert pressure on London. The Irish vote was too essential to American politicians for them to prevent the unruly Fenians from carrying out raids across the Canadian borders. These forays were based on the Fenians' erroneous conviction that harassing Canadians would prompt the English to "free" Ireland.* While most Americans

---

*The Fenians did make half a dozen forays into Canada, but none lasted longer than forty-eight hours. For years their followers would gather at border taverns to sing the rowdy anthem:

We are a Fenian brotherhood,
skilled in the arts of war,
And we're going to fight for Ireland,
the land that we adore.

Many battles have we won
along with the boys in blue,
And we'll go and capture Canada,
for we've nothing else to do.

viewed Canada "with an indifference at times amounting to bene-volence," many U.S. politicians genuinely believed that citizens of the nascent Canadian state required help to escape the yoke of British imperialism—and recognized no contradiction in the fact that they were attempting to substitute their own. Washington had even dispatched agents northward to measure the strength of the annexation mood. Israel Andrews, who had been sent to Montreal, enigmatically reported that "if people had more brains and officials weren't corrupt, the future would be clearer."

Others had no such doubts. The *New York Herald* was calling for annexation, "peaceably if possible, forcibly if necessary." Most Ameri-cans saw the largely unoccupied plains of the Canadian Midwest as a happy hunting ground for their frontier desperadoes, who could shoot buffalo, Indians and each other just as well north as south of the 49th parallel. Because no one else was actively claiming the land and the Hudson's Bay Company just hunkered there assiduously gathering furs, "the British prairies had now become part of the American horizon." During his 1865 tour, a Boston journalist named Charles Carleton Coffin extolled the region's fertile belt as "boundless savannas fragrant with flowers in spring time, and warming with verdure in summer"— with no visible limit to its agricultural and mineral potential.

One of the main agitators for the American takeover of the HBC's real estate was James Wickes Taylor. A special agent of the U.S. Treasury Department, Taylor was stationed in the Midwest for most of the 1860s, part of the time at Red River (where he was later accredited as U.S. Consul between 1870 and 1893), with orders to promote the progress of American interests. His annexationist views never wavered as he reported that here "was an area large enough to make five states equal in every way to Minnesota." When Taylor was asked by the House of Representatives to analyse commercial relations between the two countries, he overstepped his mandate and drafted an act for the admission to the Union of Nova Scotia, New Brunswick, Canada East, Canada West and "the territories of Selkirk, Saskatchewan and Columbia," proposing to pay the HBC $10 million for the surrender of its claims. The measure was formally introduced in Congress by Nathaniel Prentiss Banks of Massachusetts in July 1866, given two readings, then relegated to the Committee on Foreign Affairs for what turned out to be permanent study. Two years later, the U.S. Senate passed a resolution offering $6 million for the HBC's territorial rights, but it too was shelved.

At Red River itself, which by the late 1860s had a population of more than ten thousand (only sixteen hundred of them whites), the

The HBC's prairie lands became a prime target of American annexationists.

mood was more difficult to read. Because absorption by either the U.S. or Canada was bound to inundate the settlement with newcomers who would eventually outnumber the Mixed Bloods and relegate them to a minority position, annexation by any outside agency had limited appeal. The Canadian lobby was led by a blond giant named Dr (later Sir) John Christian Schultz, who had arrived at Red River in 1861, bought into the weekly *Nor'Wester* and founded the small but noisy Canadian Party. An acquaintance once remarked that in Schultz, "fate had manufactured a scoundrel out of material meant by nature for a gentleman," but he was an effective propagandist, uniting the pan-Canadian sentiments of Toronto Orangemen with local anti-HBC agitation, portraying the Company as a relic of empire obstructing Canada's inland aspirations.

It was less as a response to such trouble-making than as a defensive measure against the threat of American manifest destiny veering northward that John A. Macdonald finally acted. "I would be quite willing, personally," he wrote as late as March 1865, "to leave that whole [HBC] country a wilderness for the next half century, but I fear if Englishmen do not go there, Yankees will." He accused the Hudson's Bay Company of "spoliation and outrage" but was well aware, as his biographer Donald Creighton has pointed out, "that the only way in which British North America could ensure its survival as a separate autonomous power in North America was through the union of all its territories in a single transcontinental state."

Any proposed step by the Canadian government to absorb Rupert's

Land was, at least initially, regarded by most Montreal politicians as part of a plot by Brown and his followers to disrupt the delicate political balance between Canada East and Canada West. After the Charlottetown and Quebec conferences of 1864 had dispelled much of this suspicion, and as the act of Confederation moved closer, French Canada's politicians, particularly George-Etienne Cartier, came around to accepting the notion that compensation would have to be paid to the HBC for its unexpired rights. "Canada," wrote an eloquent Macdonald in an official note to the British government, "looks forward with interest to the day when the valley of the Saskatchewan will become the back country of Canada, the land of hope for the hardy youth of the provinces when they seek new homes in the forest . . . when Canada will become the highway of immigration from Europe to those fertile valleys."

The British North America Act, the statute enacted by Westminster on March 29, 1867, providing for Canadian independence, contained a clause to allow Rupert's Land into the forthcoming Confederation. Later that year, during the first sitting of the country's new parliament, Public Works Minister William McDougall, who had been an active Clear Grit under Brown and had changed party affiliations so often he was nicknamed "Wandering Willie," moved a seven-part resolution calling for action on the Rupert's Land issue. British Columbia made building a railway the condition of entering Confederation, and international financiers were pressuring Ottawa to push the rails westward. The time had come to settle the issue of the Hudson's Bay Company's lands once and for all.

SUCCESSIVE BRITISH COLONIAL SECRETARIES, governed by their own pressing priorities, had spent inordinate time and energy on the issue of nationalizing the HBC, but the burdensome corporate dinosaur never seemed long off their agendas. Immediately after the 1857 parliamentary hearings, the British government decided to dispatch an independent expert to Rupert's Land to help sort out some of the contradictory testimony by investigating at first hand what was really there. Chosen for the assignment (co-sponsored by the Royal Geographical Society) was Captain John Palliser of the Waterford Militia, who had written a book on a similar mission to the western plains of the United States, where he had wrestled a bear, shot a prize panther and been tossed on the horns of an enraged bull buffalo. Accompanied by a botanist, a doctor, an astronomer and an artillery officer turned naturalist, the Palliser expedition surveyed the land-mass between Lake Superior and the Pacific, reporting back on the location of fertile valleys, coal deposits, valuable forests and a possible railway route.*

At the end of his three-year study, Palliser drew up a comprehensive plan for a new Crown colony bounded by the 49th and 54th parallels, strongly recommending that it be created promptly to prevent its loss as a British possession. When the government of the day approached the HBC with the Palliser plan, the Company's response was handled by Edward ("Bear") Ellice, who replied matter-of-factly: "The Hudson's Bay Company are quite willing to dispose of their territory and their establishments. It is a question of a million of money. If either this Government or the Government of Canada wish to take the affair into their own hands I can tell them the cost of the undertaking. But in my mind, as far as the maintenance of order and peace throughout that vast territory is concerned, that is the smallest part of the question." The "million of money" quoted by the Bear was precisely that: £1,000,000 cash.

The Colonial Secretary who first tested the HBC's mettle by issuing an ultimatum to its governor was Sir Edward George Earle Lytton Bulwer-Lytton, who came into office with the Derby-Disraeli government of 1858. A popular novelist (now mainly remembered as author of *The Last Days of Pompeii*), he was nearly stone deaf and suffered from a severe speech defect—political handicaps he overcame by minutely rehearsing every speech and lip-reading his opponents' replies. Determined to create the colony sketched out by Palliser, he threatened to remove the HBC's trading rights unless the Company agreed to test the validity of its charter before the Privy Council, hinting that the verdict was almost certain to be negative. That danger was removed when Lord Palmerston returned to power, and the Duke of Newcastle moved into the Colonial Office.

Unlike his predecessors, Newcastle had at least been to Canada, as one of Sir George Simpson's guests during the Prince of Wales's Montreal visit in 1860. He was an informed and intelligent advocate of

---

*One memorable entry in Palliser's diary concerns his meeting with an Indian chief at Fort Frances on Rainy Lake. As translated by a local free trader, the chief's message was sadly prescient: "I know that you have come straight from the Great Country, and we know that no men from that country ever came to us and lied. I want you to declare to us truthfully what the Great Queen of your country intends to do to us when she will take the country from the Fur Company's people. All around me I see the smoke of the white men to rise. The Long Knives [the Americans] are trading with our neighbours for their lands and they are cheating them and deceiving them. Now, we will not sell nor part with our lands."

colonizing Rupert's Land. Realizing that neither Canada nor England would invest the required capital, he turned to the private sector, particularly to the British financiers anxious to build a railway and telegraph system across the upper part of North America.

Enter Edward Watkin. A former manager of the Manchester, Sheffield, and Lincolnshire Railway, Watkin had been hired by two of London's most reputable merchant bankers, Glyn, Mills & Company* and Baring Brothers, to help resolve the problems of Canada's troubled Grand Trunk Railway, which they had financed. He studied the situation and quickly decided that the best prescription for the Grand Trunk's salvation was to build a railway from the Atlantic to the Pacific. As a first step, he organized the Atlantic and Pacific Postal and Telegraph Company, requesting a ten-mile-wide right-of-way across Rupert's Land for telegraph poles and a wagon road, presumably a precursor of the railway line. On November 17, 1862, the Duke of Newcastle, who heartily endorsed the idea, visited Henry Hulse Berens, then Governor of the HBC, to sound him out on the Watkin proposal.

The twentieth man to hold the office since Prince Rupert of the Rhine, Berens, who was also a director of the Bank of England, had spent thirty years gracing the HBC Committee, upholding a staunch family tradition. His great-grandfather Herman Berens had been a member of the Committee from 1765 to 1794; his grandfather Joseph Berens, Sr., from 1776 to 1795; and his father, Joseph Berens, Jr., from 1801 to 1822. The Colonial Secretary approached the touchy issue at hand as moderately and gently as he could. He presented the promoter's idea of slashing a strip across the heart of the HBC territory as a patriotic gesture to tie the Empire together. Berens's reply was as indignant as it was emotional. "What?" he blustered. "Sequester our very tap-root? Take away the fertile lands where our buffaloes feed? Let in all kinds of people to squat and settle and frighten away the fur-bearing animals they don't kill and hunt? Impossible! Destruction—extinction—of our time-honoured industry. . . ."

That emphatic defence of his turf having been delivered, the Governor reverted to type and, shrewdly squinting at the Duke, queried: "If these gentlemen are so patriotic, why don't they buy us out?"

"What is your price?" calmly inquired the Colonial Secretary.

"Well, about a million and a half."

The price had gone up because Berens could sense that Newcastle's determination to tame Canada's West would attract the necessary

---

*Glyn, Mills, which originally opened its doors on January 5, 1754, had been the Hudson's Bay Company's bankers since 1777.

funds. He was right. Less than a month later, Watkin and his banking principals appeared in Berens's office (which the promoter derisively described as being dingy, the old wooden chairs black with age and the table covered with a faded green cloth), and the deal was cut. The purchasers set only one, highly reasonable, condition: before spending £1,500,000, they wished to examine the Company's books.

In response, Berens produced an eighty-five-year-old accountant named Mr Roberts, who insisted that the ledgers not be removed from Hudson's Bay House. One item Watkin gleaned from his brief inspection of the balance sheets was that the Company had disposed of one thousand acres of prime land in the heart of San Francisco just before the 1849 gold rush for only £1,000, because two Factors had quarrelled over its disposition.

The sales agreement was concluded on June 15, 1863. To raise the large amount of cash demanded by the Governor required greater assets and more risk than were represented by the two bankers backing Watkin. The financial conglomerate that came up with the £1,500,000 called itself the International Financial Society. Incorporated only a month earlier by a consortium of City bankers, the IFS would eventually float debentures that financed a land company in Mauritius and the building of railways in Eastern Europe, but its HBC investment was handled as a share flip. The IFS paid the purring HBC proprietors £300 for each share of £100 par value, up to the £1.5 million total. The Company was then immediately recapitalized (an elegant term for having its stock watered) at £2 million, and the shares were sold to the public in £20 units. Thus the HBC's stock, which had been purchased for three times its nominal value, had quadrupled in price with no real change in revenue prospects having taken place. The transactions left the International Financial Society's owners with a net gain of £300,000; then, having disposed of its shares, the IFS faded from the scene. For the first time since the Company's founding in 1670, HBC stock was now widely distributed among seventeen hundred shareholders, each one of whom expected a hefty return. The *Times* of July 3, 1863, called the plan "one of the most important proposals, both in a financial and national sense, ever introduced on the London money market."

Perhaps the only man in London who despaired of the Company's sale to a group of promoters was Edward Ellice. When one of the IFS negotiators met the Bear, then bent with age and only months away from death, in a London arcade, he reported that the old man had confronted him for some moments without speaking, in a state of confused abstraction. "Then he passed on, like a man endeavouring to recollect a long history of difficulty, and to realize how strangely it had all ended."

Sir Edmund Walker Head

The prospectus that had attracted so many eager shareholders listed the Company's assets at £370,000 in cash; £1,023,500 in physical plant such as trading posts, ships and offices; and 1.4 million square miles, or 896 million acres of land. "The Southern District will be opened to European Colonization under a liberal and systematic scheme of land settlement," spouted the offering circular. "The Company can, without creating any new and costly establishments, inaugurate a new policy of colonization and at the same time dispose of mining grants."

That pledge meant very little, but shareholders were reassured by the quality of the new Committeemen who took over the Company's direction. (The only important holdover from the former board was Eden Colvile, whose lengthy tenure and experience at Red River provided essential continuity.) In addition to three of the City's best-known merchant bankers—James Hodgson, John Henry Schröder and Daniel Meinertzhagen—the Company's new Deputy Chairman, Curtis Miranda Lampson, a former American fur trader who had moved to London in 1830, was one of the City's most able financiers. On the Duke of Newcastle's suggestion, Sir Edmund Walker Head was installed as Governor of the reconstituted HBC. He had served as Lieutenant-Governor of New Brunswick and later as Governor-in-Chief of British North America (1854–61). An Oxford honours graduate in classics, an author, poet and philologist, Head was a thoughtful statesman, genuinely concerned with developing Rupert's Land in an orderly fashion. But he soon found himself overwhelmed by Edward Watkin's impatience. The promoter had hurried to Canada as an agent of the new Company and on his own authority had dispatched surveyors into the field, ordered two hundred tons of copper wire and let a contract (with Hugh Allan's Montreal Telegraph Company) for construction of the line from Fort Garry to Jasper House.

Head could not condone such outrageous flouting of his authority, particularly since Watkin's own reports made it clear that the Canadian government had expressed no intention of helping finance construction of the telegraph line. The Company did send Dr John Rae, the retired HBC Chief Factor and Arctic explorer, to survey the route, but absence of government support had already killed the project. What the minor crisis did accomplish was to reactivate Canada's official pressure on the British Colonial Office to resolve the Hudson's Bay territorial dispute. "What a glorious program it would be," Macdonald later wrote to Charles Tupper, his chief Nova Scotia lieutenant, "to go down to Parliament next session with Nova Scotia pacified, Newfoundland voluntarily joining and the acquisition of Hudson's Bay."

A powerful Canadian delegation, headed by Cartier and McDougall, arrived at London's Westminster Palace Hotel during October 1868 in a mood for serious bargaining about expropriating the new HBC. Earl Granville, the Colonial Secretary in the Gladstone government, had thoroughly absorbed the department's files on the issue and had decided to act much more quickly and decisively than any of his predecessors. Correctly estimating that the Company and the Canadian delegates would reach their usual impasse, he presented both parties with a twelve-paragraph ultimatum on March 9, 1869, noting with a touch of deliberate sarcasm that his conditions would no doubt be found unacceptable to both sides, but that on further consideration they might realize that breaking the deadlock would benefit each of their joint and separate interests. The Canadians were the first to capitulate, and after that the Company had no choice; Granville had made it crystal clear that no other alternative was or would be available. Despite loud protests from HBC shareholders, who regarded the Colonial Secretary's terms as a betrayal of their trust, the deal was approved. On November 19, 1869, the Hudson's Bay Company signed the Deed of Surrender (which became valid on July 15, 1870) that extinguished its much-coveted monopoly rights.

While there was no direct charge to the Treasury of the United Kingdom, it did agree to guarantee a loan to the Canadian government of £300,000 (then the equivalent of $1,460,000) that was to be the HBC's cash compensation. Among the other conditions of the transfer (apart from such trivialities as paying for the aging telegraph wire stored at York Factory) the HBC was allowed to retain:

1. A grant of more than forty-five thousand acres around its 120 existing trading posts. Only four of these forts were in what was then considered to be the fertile belt, but the acreage around Fort Garry alone had immediate cash value.
2. A right to claim, during the ensuing fifty years, blocks of land set out for settlement within its former territory, not to exceed one-twentieth of the fertile area. (This was defined as the region bounded on the south by the American border, on the west by the Rocky Mountains, on the north by the North Saskatchewan River, and on the east by Lake Winnipeg, Lake of the Woods and the waters connecting them.) This grant amounted to seven million acres of some of the best agricultural land in Western Canada.
3. A guarantee of the continuance of its trade without hindrance and with no special taxes or tariffs.

Enemies of the Company interpreted the surrender as the HBC's death blow. "The old lion has been shorn of its mane," one of them gloated, "his roar is no longer heard in the great North-West." The Company's original charter may have been reduced to a decorative parchment, but the HBC was still the largest private landholder in Western Canada—and had been handed a rich ransom for relinquishing holdings that, from the Canadian point of view, it ought never to have been allowed to possess. Most significantly, the Company had been relieved of the responsibility of administering those lands just when settlement was promising to make that function dangerous and expensive.

The terms of sale were routinely ratified by Canada's Parliament, and the physical takeover was slated for December 1, 1869, with William McDougall being named Lieutenant-Governor of Rupert's Land. When he arrived at the frontier village of Pembina, instead of being greeted by a delegation of delighted former colonials, he was handed a proclamation signed by Louis Riel forbidding him to enter Red River. The brief and bitter rebellion that followed has been thoroughly documented and is well beyond the scope of this volume, but the uprising was a perfectly appropriate response to the Company's treatment of what should have been its most valued constituency—the field hands holding down the ground its London proprietors had sold to satisfy their shareholders.

In 1863, when the International Financial Society purchased the HBC, the Company's servants in North America were notified so tardily they felt, as one of them remarked, as if they had been "sold like dumb driven cattle." It was only when they threatened to resign in a body that their plight finally caught London's attention. The Committeemen realized how effectively their own fur traders could compete if they should choose to organize themselves as independents. Governor Head intended to discontinue the winterers' 1821 Deed Poll (which guaranteed them 40 percent of profits), placing all employees on straight salaries. But faced with mounting opposition from across the Atlantic, he agreed to pay a lump-sum settlement of £157,055 to terminate the practice of shared ownership—and specifically excluded the Canadian-based personnel from future land sale profits.

Six years later, when the Company gave up its territory to Canada, neither the citizens of Red River nor the HBC traders scattered across Rupert's Land were officially notified of the proceedings leading to the sale. William Mactavish, the last Governor of Rupert's Land, complained to a Métis acquaintance during the final phase of the negotiations: "I can guarantee nothing. Times are changing. I myself know nothing. Am I still the governor? It seems that everything gets settled in London, but they don't tell me anything."

Least consulted and most directly affected of all were the Indian peoples. As land sales rather than fur barters became the HBC's prime concern, their traditional way of life lost its *raison d'être*, and hunger was the result. Indians begging for food at white settlements became a common sight, as did the sad spectacle of natives having to subsist on a meagre diet of gophers caught by pouring water down their holes and snaring the tough little animals as they emerged. On April 13, 1871, Chief Sweet Grass and a delegation of Plains Cree from the Edmonton and Carlton House districts came in stately procession to address W.J. Christie, the Chief Factor at Edmonton, asking him to transcribe and submit a petition to the Governor at Fort Garry. "We heard our lands were sold and we did not like it," went the proclamation. "We do not want to sell our lands; it is our property, and no one has a right to sell them. Our country is getting ruined of fur bearing animals, hitherto our sole support, and now we are poor and want help—we want you to pity us. We want cattle, tools, agricultural implements, and assistance in everything when we come to settle—our country is no longer able to support us."

Indian claims to the grasslands were gradually muffled, and the interracial fur-trade partnership that had shaped day-to-day contact over most of a continent for much of two centuries was irrevocably severed. A native heritage was regarded as a liability, not an asset, as tent towns grew into villages and villages expanded into towns and cities. The buffalo herds were gone, their mournful bellowing replaced by the echoing hoots first of steamboats and then of locomotives. York boats rotted on the riverbanks, and Sir John A. Macdonald boasted to his friend Sir Hastings Doyle, Lieutenant-Governor of Nova Scotia: "We have quietly and almost without observation annexed all the country between here and the Rocky Mountains."

The last meeting of the Northern Department of Rupert's Land was held at Norway House in July 1870. Only seventeen years later, no further commissioned officers were appointed by the HBC and, four years after that, all of the time-honoured titles of the fur trade were withdrawn. But for this one final occasion, the Chief Factors and Chief Traders sat around the great oak table where Sir George Simpson had once ruled, and where generations of their predecessors had traded quips and empires.

They must have felt as if they were living out the final act in some much-told tale, these ordinary men caught in extraordinary circumstances. Later in life, nodding by a fireside back in the Highlands, England or Montreal, they must have had trouble remembering the details of all those glory days and earthy nights. Like some greybeard who runs his forefinger along his duelling scar as he recalls the bravado of his youth, each of them must have given thanks to his deity for having survived—and yet not on any account would he have forgone the experience.

Descending the Fraser River

Shoppers at Fort Edmonton, 1866

EPILOGUE

BY THE EARLY 1870s, the Company of Adventurers could look back on the century of its greatest glory and its deepest humiliation. The Hudson's Bay Company had come perilously close to being wiped out by the Nor'Westers but had broken through to exploit a continent.

The final blow to its monopoly had come, not from competing fur traders, as its successive Governors had always expected, but from settlers determined to farm the best of its lands. Writing privately to Sir George Simpson, then still at the height of his authority, Peter Skene Ogden, the most daring of his Chief Factors, put the case bluntly: "You are I presume fully aware that the Fur trade and Civilization can never be blended together and experience teaches us that the former invariably gives way to the latter."

The HBC's grand design was thus shattered by an orderly evolution towards colonization and nationhood, with Louis Riel rushing the process in Manitoba and the wild gold stampedes of the Fraser and Cariboo regions escalating displacement of the old order in British Columbia. The other element in the Company's retreat was the dramatic downturn in the fur trade itself. The public's growing boredom with the fashion of beaver hats had become epidemic, and although there was an enduring demand for specialty pelts, even this commerce was threatened by the rapid growth in popularity of nutria—the fur of the coypu rats harvested in the fresh waters of South America, particularly in Brazil and Argentina. Towards the end of the nineteenth century, trappers had marketed three million nutria pelts in direct competition with the HBC. At the same time, fur farming was becoming a popular industry in Eastern Canada and Western Europe.

Faced with these and other discontinuities in its traditional trading patterns, the Company's operating philosophy—not for the first or last time—was turned on its head. The final fur brigade passed down to York Factory in 1871, and although some pelts continued to be exported through Hudson Bay for another four years, by 1875 Upper Fort Garry had become headquarters for the Northern Department and the once-great tidewater depot at York Factory languished as a minor trading post.

Except for local trapping, the HBC switched into selling off its huge tracts of real estate—to the very settlers who had broken its monopoly. Until the railways came, the Company operated a transportation system over the prairie river networks, then turned to retailing and merchandising, feeding and supplying the farmers who had purchased its land. Within a decade of the HBC's unfrocking in 1869, its shareholders were raking in more dividends than ever, while many a Prairie settler wanting to cut winter firewood still had to ask permission from the HBC to do so—and pay for the privilege.

At the close of this second of three volumes of the HBC's history, the Company had surrendered its vaunted monopoly only to emerge as Western Canada's largest private landlord. This bit of fiscal acrobatics serves as a perfect example of the Hudson's Bay Company's remarkable ability to meet each new crisis by transforming itself into a very different kind of corporate beast. That Darwinian instinct for survival was never more evident than in the HBC's dramatic jettisoning, during late 1986 and early 1987, of its fur-auction houses and Northern Stores Division, spinning off its very soul to evolve in new directions. With all its current problems and despite a grievous debt load, the HBC remains Canada's ninth-largest company, employing 41,000 people and enjoying annual revenues of nearly $6 billion.

THE FUR TRADE, which was finished as a major industry by 1870, had been North America's first transcontinental enterprise. It provided the momentum for exploration of the once-mysterious hinterland and set in place a transportation matrix that shaped the new Canadian nationality. Even if the motivation for this march westward by the fur companies was mainly an attempt to crush potential and existing rivals, occupation of the empty territory kept the Yanks out just long enough for Canada to claim its own interior destiny.

Although it was the movement of settlers from or through what is now Ontario and Quebec that turned the fur preserve into a farm belt, the West never was a child of the East. Because of their founding connection with the Hudson's Bay Company, what have become Canada's four western provinces are quite distinct in origin from Quebec or Ontario. As Professor Leslie H. Neatby has pointed out, the Prairie provinces are the children of the Bay as surely as Central Canada is the

The first HBC retail store, which opened in Vancouver in 1887

offspring of the St Lawrence. This fact—and, more significantly, the ignorance and insensitivity of Eastern Canadians in treating most Westerners with condescension as country cousins—has been and remains a severely divisive influence within Canada's Confederation.

The Hudson's Bay Company's trading methods left Canada's Indians in a position of dependence from which they have yet to emerge. But if the native peoples found themselves internal exiles in their own land, at least the HBC's greed for ever more furs, which required constant harnessing of the Indian labour force, prevented the kind of indiscriminate slaughter of the native peoples that fouled the American frontier.

Yet that verdict of virtue by inadvertence or by comparison with some other, much worse fate, seems unfair. The HBC's traders were no saints, but neither were they sinners. Only rare individuals possess the inner balance to wield great power without becoming personally distorted or slightly unhinged in the process. It is not the existence of authority but its use and abuse that disrupt the common patterns of behaviour and test the tensile strength of character. Considering that for most of two centuries the HBC reigned over its huge empire with virtually no public accountability, its Governors, officers and servants cannot be charged with any great burden of shame. It was a proudly feudal institution operating at a time of burgeoning populism, and it survived by adjusting to shifting circumstances at the last possible moment.

How the Company spawned its own dynasty of merchant princes who turned a marginal remnant of burned-out fur traders into the country's largest department store organization, transplanted its monopoly from the West into Canada's North, and how that third HBC empire barely managed to revive itself—these are some of the tales that remain to be told in my third volume.

The Hudson's Bay Company, as portrayed in this book, represents the ultimate Canadian case history. Fur was an extractive industry, carried on by an overseas-based monopoly strictly for the gain of its private shareholders. That condition—a multinational corporation grabbing Canada's most profitable natural resources for the one-way benefit of its owners—has characterized Canadian commerce ever since. No nation that has moved past colonial status owns a smaller proportion of its profitable assets.

At the same time, the Indians who surrendered their freedom for the sake of possessions that promised to improve their living standards also foreshadowed the dominant ethic that would shape Canadian society. That rush to sacrifice economic and cultural independence on the altar of potential material gain was never more evident than during the free-trade negotiations between Canada and the United States during the late 1980s.

Because the fur trade set the pattern for Canada's initial economic evolution, the fate of the Indians who became its willing victims runs with us all.

APPENDICES

Chronology

1670
The Hudson's Bay Company is founded
May 2 as the "Company of Adventurers of England Tradeing into Hudsons Bay."

1746
At Culloden, 1,200 Scotsmen die, and the British begin to dismantle the clan system. Many Scots emigrate.

1750
Sir Atwell Lake, eldest son of Sir Bibye Lake (Governor, 1712–1743), is appointed Governor; is succeeded in 1760 by Sir William Baker.

1754
Anthony Henday is the HBC's first white employee to see the Rockies, but the Company makes no move to consolidate his findings for half a century.

1768
Huge decline in HBC trade due to the competitiveness of the Montreal-based "pedlars."

1770
Bibye Lake, another son of Sir Bibye Lake, is appointed HBC Governor.

1774
HBC builds first inland trading post, Cumberland House, on the Saskatchewan River.

1775
War breaks out in the Thirteen Colonies. Americans invade Canada, lay siege to Quebec and temporarily capture Montreal. Simon McTavish moves from Albany to Montreal.

1776
The "pedlars" regroup in Montreal, sometimes using the name North West Company; they establish their main supply base at Grand Portage at the western end of Lake Superior.

1778
Peter Pond, exploring the Athabasca Delta, taps a rich new source of furs and establishes a post. Capt. James Cook lands at Nootka Sound, Vancouver Island, and gets sea otter pelts from inhabitants. William Tomison is appointed Inland Master of the HBC. John Paul Jones tries to kidnap the 4th Earl of Selkirk.

1779
The "pedlars" in Montreal form a sixteen-share partnership of merchants, but the North West Company is restructured three times before emerging in 1783 as a permanent entity.

1780s–1790s
The HBC and NWC establish inland posts, in fierce competition. Peter Fidler and Philip Turnor map the interior of the continent.

1781–1782
Smallpox kills many Plains Indians.

1782
Samuel Wegg is appointed Governor of the HBC.

1785
In February, the NWC's Beaver Club is established in Montreal; it is disbanded on March 5, 1827.

1786
HBC appoints William Tomison chief at York Factory, with responsibility for inland posts. "Most likely date" for George Simpson's birth.

1788
British independent trader John Meares builds first trading post at Nootka Sound on land purchased from Chief Maquinna.

1789
Alexander Mackenzie sets off from Fort Chipewyan on June 3 to explore "the Grand River" (later the Mackenzie) and on July 14 reaches the Arctic Ocean.

1790
McTavish, Frobisher & Co. dominates the newly formed North West partnership, with Simon McTavish holding controlling interest. Philip Turnor, HBC surveyor, arrives ill-equipped in Athabasca and hears Indians' complaints re NWC traders.

1792–1794
Capt. George Vancouver surveys the Pacific Coast for the Royal Navy, from April 1792 until late in 1794

1793
Alexander Mackenzie, NWC partner, sets out from the Peace River on May 9 to find a river route to the Pacific; he reaches the ocean July 21 at Dean Channel. The Nor'Westers now control 78 percent of Canadian fur sales.

1794
Intense feuding surfaces between Alexander Mackenzie and Simon McTavish; Mackenzie wants merger of NWC with the HBC. Fort Edmonton is established by William Tomison, Inland Chief of the HBC near the older NWC Fort Augustus.

1797
David Thompson defects from the HBC to the NWC. Russian-American Company is formed to trade in furs from Alaska.

1798
Breakaway Montreal traders coalesce as the New North West Company, dubbed the XY Company.

1799
Sir James Winter Lake, son of Sir Atwell Lake, is appointed Governor; despite rapid expansion, the HBC has only 498 men posted in North America. The Nor'Westers build a wooden canal to bypass the portage at Sault Ste Marie. Mackenzie and McTavish square off in a power play at the NWC annual conclave; Mackenzie loses. Upon his father's death, Thomas Douglas becomes the 5th Earl of Selkirk.

1800
John Jacob Astor dispatches his first chartered vessel to trade in China. Alexander Mackenzie joins the XY Company, which becomes popularly known as "Alexander Mackenzie & Co."

1801
NWC resolution makes Simon Fraser a full partner, to take effect in 1802.

1802
Alexander Mackenzie is knighted by George III and very nearly gains control of the HBC. HBC's Peter Fidler, assigned to establish Nottingham House post near Fort Chipewyan, is harassed by Nor'Westers Archibald Norman McLeod and Samuel Black.

1803
NWC headquarters is moved from Grand Portage, which has become U.S. territory, to Fort William. British Parliament on Aug. 11 passes the Canada Jurisdiction Act aimed at regulating lawless conflict between HBC and NWC. NWC's McTavish establishes four outlaw posts on Hudson Bay; they last three years. In the Louisiana Purchase, the U.S. buys from France a huge tract west of the Mississippi.

1804
U.S. President Thomas Jefferson dispatches Lewis and Clark expedition to the Pacific Coast. Lord Selkirk visits Montreal. Simon McTavish of the NWC, foe of the XY Company's Alexander Mackenzie, dies on July 6; NWC and XY Company agree to merge, Nov 5.

1804–1821
The NWC consistently ships more furs than the HBC, yet both sides suffer losses and low profits due to increased costs, overtrapping and fierce competition.

1805
Meriwether Lewis and William Clark reach the Pacific Ocean, overland, on Nov. 14. Mackenzie, who had reached the Pacific in July 1793, leaves Montreal to live in Britain.

1806
At the annual Fort William conclave, a new resolution is adopted prohibiting Nor'Westers from taking Indian wives. HBC servants have by now opened sixty inland stations.

1807
William Mainwaring is appointed Governor of the HBC. David Thompson, his wife and family cross the Rockies on mapmaking journey. Selkirk marries Jean Wedderburn.

1808
May-June-July: Simon Fraser makes his 850-mile journey to the Pacific down the river now named for him.

1809
Andrew Wedderburn (later known as Colvile) reorganizes the financially sluggish HBC to combat the NWC competition, as proposed by Colin Robertson, and institutes "the Retrenching System." Masters of the HBC posts are given increased flexibility and power in trade, and a share in profits. NWC builds Fort Gibraltar on the future site of Winnipeg. Between 1809 and 1815, the HBC pays no dividends.

1811
Lord Selkirk, major HBC stockholder, on March 6 reaches agreement to buy more than 74 million acres, or 116,000 square miles, for 10 shillings to establish a settlement at Red River. On July 26, the first shipload of settlers is under way. Great flood of the Red River. John Jacob Astor's men establish Astoria at the mouth of the Columbia River in March; the NWC's David Thompson arrives there in mid-July. HBC profits are £57,860, compared with a loss of £19,000 in 1809.

1812
U.S. declares war on Britain and closes border. Joseph Berens, Jr., is appointed HBC Governor. On July 17, the British seize Michilimackinac from the Americans with the help of NWC voyageurs. On Aug. 30, Miles Macdonell and first settlers reach Red River. On Oct. 1, the Corps of Canadian Voyageurs is formed; is disbanded March 14, 1813. Cuthbert Grant, at nineteen, is sent out to the Qu'Appelle River as an NWC clerk.

1813
NWC lays siege to, then buys, Astoria. It is then officially proclaimed British by Capt. Black of HMS *Racoon*. Americans capture and burn York (Toronto). HBC surveyor Peter Fidler lays out Red River lots in narrow strips in the Lower Canadian way, upsetting Métis.

1814
Demand for fur revives on London markets. The Treaty of Ghent defines the boundary between Canada and the United States. John McLoughlin, physician at Fort William, is named an NWC partner.

1815
Red River Governor Miles Macdonell surrenders himself to the NWC at Fort Gibraltar; most settlers abandon Red River after houses are burned, but return to their farms after meeting HBC Chief Factor Colin Robertson en route to Athabasca. Robert Semple is appointed new Governor of Red River. Selkirk receives initial proposal from William McGillivray re HBC-NWC amalgamation.

1816
Former Nor'Wester John Clarke leads HBC brigade into Athabasca. Ill-equipped and faced with NWC hostility, sixteen men starve. The first permanent HBC post of the Athabasca Country, Fort Wedderburn, opens. On June 19, Semple and twenty others are shot and their bodies mutilated at Seven Oaks by a troop of NWC adherents led by Cuthbert Grant. Settlers flee. Selkirk and his mercenaries seize Fort William on August 12 and arrest several NWC partners for their complicity in the massacre. Severe cold spells mark this a "year without a summer."

1817
Lord Selkirk stays thirteen summer

weeks at the Red River Colony. Royal proclamation is made on May 1 against "open warfare in the Indian territories."

1818
On October 11 in the Athabasca Country, the HBC's Colin Robertson is kidnapped by Nor'Wester Samuel Black. Selkirk is embroiled in court challenges to his Red River aspirations.

1819
Post-war depression hits British North America and the U.S. Selkirk leaves England in September for Pau, France.

1820
Lord Selkirk and Alexander Mackenzie die within twenty-seven days of each other. Colvile dispatches George Simpson to Rupert's Land; Simpson sets out overseas to Montreal, Fort William and Athabasca. John McLoughlin and Angus Bethune head via Montreal to London to negotiate on behalf of the NWC's unhappy wintering partners.

1821
On March 26, the amalgamation agreement between the HBC and NWC is signed. The British Parliament on July 2 grants the combined companies under the HBC name a twenty-one-year monopoly of the fur trade in British North America west of Upper Canada. HBC now controls more than 3 million square miles of land. Amalgamation of the two companies' 173 posts begins. The NWC wintering partners converge on Fort William by July 10 to learn of the changes. The HBC men converge on Norway House, and HBC Committeeman Nicholas Garry presents the new arrangements. George Simpson becomes Governor of the new Northern Department. Traders of both companies later meet at York Factory. Swiss settlers arrive at the Selkirk Settlement, but most soon leave for the U.S. Alexander I of Russia issues an imperial edict restricting shipping and fur trading on the northwest coast of North America.

1822
John Henry Pelly is appointed Governor of the HBC. Simpson embarks on snowshoe trek across the Athabasca, Slave and Peace regions. HBC forms the Buffalo Wool Co., which fails, as do the later tallow export and sheep wool companies.

1823
John Rowand establishes HBC's Northwest headquarters at Fort Edmonton, near the present Alberta Legislature.

1824
Simpson appoints John McLoughlin Chief Factor of the Columbia Department, and visits Astoria. Headquarters is moved from Astoria to Fort Vancouver, a hundred miles up the Columbia River. A chain of posts is eventually established from the Columbia north to Alaska, and the shoreline is patrolled by Company vessels. Anglo-Russian Treaty fixes boundary of Alaska at 54°40'. James Douglas marries Amelia Connolly. The original profit-sharing agreement of the 1821 amalgamation agreement falls apart; former NWC agents lose their votes and influence in HBC affairs, and must post bond to cover legal expenses. In the 1824 reorganization, former Nor'West agent Edward Ellice joins the HBC's Committee and continues to prosper, unlike his former NWC colleagues.

1825
William McGillivray dies, leaving his brother Simon with onerous debts. Simpson pioneers the Carlton Trail.

1826
George Simpson is officially named Governor of both the Northern and Southern departments. Severe flood at Red River.

1828
HBC dividends reach 20 percent, up from 4 percent in 1824. Simpson again ventures to the Pacific. Cuthbert Grant is named Warden of the Plains by Simpson.

1830
Simpson marries his cousin Frances and honeymoons in a canoe.

1831
Construction begins on Lower Fort Garry.

1832
The Simpsons move into Lower Fort Garry ("the Stone Fort").

1833
Simpson transfers management operations to Lachine; Frances returns to England, until 1845.

1835–1837
Upper Fort Garry is started in 1835 to replace an older fort damaged in 1826 flooding. Smallpox on the Plains; by 1837 an estimated three-quarters of the Plains Indians die.

1836
HBC steamer *Beaver* goes into service on Pacific Coast. Selkirk family on May 4 trades its lands for £84,000 worth of HBC stock. Upper Fort Garry becomes the administrative centre of Assiniboia.

1837
Economic depression hits low point.

1838
HBC licensed monopoly is renewed for another twenty-one years by the British government. Simpson travels to St Petersburg. Samuel Black, former tormentor of HBC men, is named one of the Company's Chief Factors.

1839
Andrew Colvile becomes HBC Deputy Governor. Simpson is appointed Governor-in-Chief of Rupert's Land. James Douglas is appointed Chief Factor of the Columbia Department.

1840
Red River's population has increased to 4,369 from less than 300 in 1818. John Henry Pelly is created a baronet.

1841–1842
Simpson is knighted; he circles the world, from London, via Halifax, Boston, Montreal, Fort Vancouver,

California, Hawaii, Alaska, Siberia and Europe; nineteen months, nineteen days later, he is back in London. Upper Canada is renamed Canada West; Lower Canada becomes Canada East. Limits are imposed on the beaver catch in the interests of conservation.

1843
Fort Victoria is established by James Douglas at the southern tip of Vancouver Island. Final HBC anti-liquor regulation is approved by Council at Red River on June 17. Norman Kittson attempts to lure fur trade from Fort Garry to his U.S. post at Pembina.

1846
Oregon Treaty establishes the 49th parallel as the boundary between American and British territory west of the Rockies, with Vancouver Island to be British.

1849
Sayer Trial at Red River opens the market for free traders in fur. Gold fever hits California. Cuthbert Grant is fired by Simpson. Andrew Colvile's son Eden is named Associate Governor of Rupert's Land. Richard Blanshard is appointed Governor of the Colony of Vancouver Island, granted to the HBC by the British government.

1850
Foss-Pelly scandal and trial at Red River.

1851
James Douglas is appointed Governor of Vancouver Island, following Richard Blanshard's resignation.

1852
Sir John Pelly dies, and Andrew Colvile, HBC Deputy Governor since 1839, is appointed Governor.

1853
Frances Simpson dies.

1856
John Shepherd is appointed Governor of the HBC.

1857
HBC licence comes due for renewal.

Parliamentary hearings inquire into the HBC's position and practices. David Thompson dies impoverished in Longueuil. John Palliser begins a major study of lands between Lake Superior and the Pacific.

1858
Colony of British Columbia is created. Discovery of gold on the Fraser River attracts a rush of Americans into British territory. Henry Hulse Berens is appointed Governor of the HBC.

1859
HBC has retained its territorial rights but has lost its licence to exclusive trade. The *Anson Northup* reaches Fort Garry from Minnesota on June 10. First major Canadian rail project, the Grand Trunk, is completed between Lévis, opposite Quebec City, and Sarnia.

1860
Simpson entertains the Prince of Wales in Lachine on Aug. 29, dies on Sept. 7. Alexander Grant Dallas succeeds him and moves headquarters from Lachine to Red River. United States has 30,000 route-miles of rail track. Gold fever pulls miners to the Cariboo Country.

1862
Simon Fraser dies destitute. British Crown takes back from the HBC all rights over Vancouver Island.

1863
Edward Watkin, supported by the International Financial Society of London, buys out all HBC stock on June 15. The London Committee is reorganized; Sir Edmund Walker Head is appointed HBC Governor. James Douglas is knighted by Queen Victoria.

1864
Negotiations towards Confederation take place in Quebec City and Charlottetown.

1866
U.S. allows 1854 Reciprocity Treaty to lapse; Canadian economy suffers severe recession. Fenians raid northward across the Canada-U.S. border.

1867
BNA Act is enacted at Westminster on March 29; Clause 146 makes provision for the admission of Rupert's Land and Northwest Territories into the new Confederation.

1868
The Earl of Kimberley is appointed Governor of the HBC. Canadian delegation arrives in London to begin negotiations for HBC lands.

1869
HBC signs Deed of Surrender on April 9, agreeing to surrender Rupert's Land to the Crown. HBC gains cash settlement, and keeps its 120 posts and land concessions. William McDougall, appointed Lieutenant-Governor of Rupert's Land and the Northwest Territories, sets out for Red River; is turned back at Pembina by armed Métis.

1870
Sir Stafford Northcote, later Earl of Iddesleigh, is appointed Governor of the HBC. Northern Department of Rupert's Land holds its final meeting at Norway House. Rebellion at Red River under Louis Riel.

1874
Final York boat brigade arrives at York Factory.

1875
Upper Fort Garry becomes the head-quarters of the Northern Department.

1885
Louis Riel hanged at Regina for high treason after Northwest Rebellion of that year.

1886–1887
During the winter, tribes starve in the Northwest "owing to the destruction of game."

1887
No further commissioned officers are appointed by the HBC.

Resource People

The more than two hundred men and women kind enough to have helped distil and synthesize the early history of the Hudson's Bay Company were listed in Appendix Seven of *Company of Adventurers*. They, together with the people listed below, have contributed energy and information to the books. Most of the descriptions or titles given in the listings apply to the individuals at the time of their interviews, as do their places of residence. Most have been interviewed either by Camilla Newman or by me, and transcripts of these conversations have been donated to the Hudson's Bay Company Archives in Winnipeg. We wish to express our gratitude for the time, concern and perceptions shared with us, and look forward to continuing the interviews for the third volume in this trilogy. The hope common to all those involved in the preparation of the series is that these first-hand insights will help make the chronicles of the HBC true to life.

Del Anaquod
Former president, Federation of
Saskatchewan Indians
Regina

Boris Atamanenko
Director, Peace River Centennial
Museum
Peace River, Alta.

Timothy Ball
Department of Geography
University of Winnipeg
Winnipeg

Graeme A. Beare
Nepean, Ont.

Mark Blumes
CEO, Mark's Work Wearhouse
Calgary

Malvina Bolus
Editor, *The Beaver*, 1958–1972
Victoria

R.H. (Bob) Cheshire
Former manager, HBC
Northern Stores division
Former general manager, HBC Fur
Trade Department
Victoria

F. G. Cooch
International Scientific Affairs
Management of Wildlife Sciences
Conservation and Preservation
Government of Canada
Hull, Que.

Alan Cooke
Director, Hochelaga Research Institute
Montreal

Shirley Dawe
Former vice-president, HBC
Toronto

Timothy Dubé
Archivist, British Archives
Manuscript Division
Public Archives Canada
Ottawa

Tristan Easton
Senior clerk to Chief Justice
Allan McEachern
Supreme Court of British Columbia
Vancouver

Robin A. Fisher
Department of History
Simon Fraser University
Burnaby, B.C.

Russell W. Fridley
Director, Minnesota Historical Society
St Paul, Minn.

John S. Galbraith
Former professor, British Empire
history,
University of California at
Los Angeles
San Diego, Calif.

E.J. (Scotty) Gall
Head of HBC transport,
Western Arctic, 1923–1966
Victoria

Betty Gibb
and Interlibrary Loan staff
McPherson Library
University of Victoria
Victoria

Kathleen Gillespie
Archivist, Lord Selkirk
Association of Rupert's Land
Winnipeg

Hon. Elijah Harper
Minister of Northern and Native
Affairs, Manitoba
Winnipeg

Patricia Harpole
Chief librarian, Minnesota Historical
Society
St Paul, Minn.

Richard Harrington
Wilderness photographer
Toronto

Robert W. Herber
Former HBC executive
Former president, Holt Renfrew
Toronto

H. Albert Hochbaum
Artist and naturalist
Delta, Man.

A. Rolph Huband
Vice-president and secretary, HBC
Toronto

Dorothy Jorre de St. Jorre
Spent girlhood at York Factory
Victoria

David Kilgour
MP, Edmonton Strathcona
Ottawa

George Kosich
President, HBC
Toronto

Walter O. Kupsch
Geologist
Saskatoon

W. Kaye Lamb
Dominion Archivist, retired
Vancouver

Sandra Leland
Tape transcription typist
Genie Computing
Victoria

Allan G. Levine
Historian
Winnipeg

John Levy
Former president, Zeller's
Vancouver

Charles B. Loewen
President
Loewen, Ondaatje, McCutcheon
Son-in-law of former HBC
managing director Philip A. Chester
Toronto

Michael Lubbock
Former HBC employee
Ottawa

Charles A. Macdonell
Macdonell, McNaught, Sutcliffe &
Hougestol
Grande Prairie, Alta.

Hon. Allan McEachern
Chief Justice, Supreme Court of
British Columbia
Vancouver

W.D.C. (Don) Mackenzie
W.D.C. Mackenzie Consultants
Former HBC director
Calgary

Don McLean
Gabriel Dumont Institute of Native
Studies and Applied Research
Regina

Hugh MacMillan
Archives Liaison Officer
Archives of Ontario
Toronto

C.A.M. MacRae
Simpson's executive, retired
Scarborough, Ont.

Duncan MacRae
Executive officer, HMCS *Malahat*
Esquimalt, B.C.

D.W. Mahaffy
Senior vice-president
Finance and Administration, HBC
Toronto

H.H.G. (Herbert) Moody
Builder of HBC downtown stores
Victoria

Jean Morrison
Supervisor, Library & Research
Services
Old Fort William
Thunder Bay

James Richard (Dick) Murray
Managing director, HBC, retired
Victoria

Tom Naylor
Department of Economics
McGill University
Montreal

Peter F.S. Nobbs
Vice-president, Corporate Finance
Midland Bank Canada
Former HBC treasurer
Toronto

Ruth Oakes
Wife of former HBC employee
Harry Oakes
Victoria

Yukie Orenstein
Researcher
Don Mills, Ont.

Muriel Oslie
Peace River, Alta.

William Palk
Former managing director
Eaton's Winnipeg store
Toronto

John de B. Payne
Former director
Public Relations, HBC
Montreal

C.F. (Frank) Platt
Former HBC employee
S.S. *Mackenzie River*
Victoria

Carol Preston
Managing Editor
The Beaver
Winnipeg

Arthur J. Ray
Department of History
University of British Columbia
Vancouver

Gail Revesz
Victoria Microfilm
Victoria

Robin Roberts
Tape transcription typist
Victoria

Iain Ronald
Former executive vice-president, HBC
Toronto

Alex Ross
Head, 20th Century Records
HBC Archives
Winnipeg

Abraham Rotstein
Dept. of Political Economy
University of Toronto
Toronto

Reginald Roy
Department of History
University of Victoria
Victoria

Chesley Russell
Former HBC employee
Sidney, B.C.

Anne Schaan
Tape transcription typist
Victoria

Sidney S. Schipper
Director
Management Internship Division
Canadian Council for Native Business
Toronto

Joe Segal
President
Kingswood Capital Corp.
Former chairman, Zeller's
Vancouver

Derrick Sewell
Department of Geography
University of Victoria
Victoria

C. Richard Sharpe
Chairman & CEO
Sears Canada
Toronto

Ron Sheen
Former HBC executive
Victoria

George Yale Simpson
Great-great-grandson of
Sir George Simpson
Victoria

Hal C. Sisson
Lawyer
Peace River, Alta.

Shirlee Anne Smith
Keeper, HBC Archives
Winnipeg

Allen Sprecht
Archivist
Sound and Moving Images Division
Provincial Archives of British Columbia
Victoria

Mary Louise V. Stathers
Genealogist, fur-trade families
Great-great-granddaughter of
Sir George Simpson
Vancouver and Squamish, B.C.

Donald M. Stewart
Collector of coins, fur-trade tokens,
medals, paper money
Victoria

Victoria M. Stewart
Lake St Louis Historical Society and
Macdonald Stewart Foundation
Montreal

Blair Stonechild
Head, Dept. of Indian Studies
Saskatchewan Indian
Federated College
Regina

Maurice F. Strong
Former HBC clerk
Crestone, Colorado

Kenneth R. Thomson
Thomson Newspapers Ltd.
Proprietor, 76 percent, HBC
Toronto

J. Donald Tigert
Director, Burns Fry Ltd.
Toronto

John A. Tory
President, Thomson Corp.
Toronto

Murray Turner
Former promotion manager
HBC, Winnipeg
Toronto

Glenn and Trish Warner
Bathurst Inlet Lodge
Bathurst Inlet, N.W.T.

George A. Whitman
Former director of External Relations
HBC, Winnipeg
Vice-president
North West Company Inc.
Victoria

Donald O. Wood
Former HBC executive
Winnipeg and Toronto
President
Crowntek Communications Inc.
Markham, Ont.

Peter Wood
Former executive vice-president, HBC
Toronto

J.J. (Woody) and Kay Wood
Former HBC factor and his wife
Victoria

Jordan Zinovich
Fur-trade historian
New York

Chapter Notes

ACKNOWLEDGEMENTS

P. xii. "At the heart of good history. . .":
Stephen Schiff, *The New York Times
Book Review*, 4 May 1986, p. 19.

PROLOGUE

P. xvi. "HE WAS EVERY MAN'S
FRIEND. . .": Tombstone inscription
on the grave of Henry Fuller (Twelve-
Foot) Davis, in Grant MacEwan, *Fifty
Mighty Men*, p. 170.

P. xvi. "Bury me with my feet pointing
downhill. . .": Henry Fuller (Twelve-
Foot) Davis to Colonel Jim Cornwall,
related by High Prairie, Alta., bailiff
Sam Harris to Hal Sisson of Peace
River, written out by Hal Sisson 12
Sept. 1957, and forwarded to author
for use in this volume.

P. xvi. "the management of their
affairs. . .": Andrew Freeport, to Lord
Palmerston, in Douglas MacKay, *The
Honourable Company*, p. 259.

P. xvii. "at the edge of a frozen sea":
Joseph Robson in Peter C. Newman,
Company of Adventurers, p. 145.

P. xix. "cloak to protect the trade. . .":
Anon. [NWC Montreal partner], in
Daniel Francis, *Battle for the West*,
p. 113.

P. xx. "It was a bitter war. . .": from
Frederick Merk, ed., *Fur Trade and
Empire*, p. x.

P. xx. Re arms inventory of Columbia
Department: list reproduced in Donald
H. Clark, "Iron Interpreters," *The
Beaver*, September 1954, p. 51.

P. xxi. "Between 1821 and 1869, it
was the skill. . .": W. Kaye Lamb, in
Malvina Bolus, ed., *People and Pelts*,
pp. v-vi.

P. xxi. "sniping redskins. . .": in
F.G. Roe, "The Hudson's Bay Com-
pany and the Indians," *The Beaver*,
September 1936, p. 11.

P. xxii. "striking contrast between
British and American Indian rela-
tions. . .": Frederick Merk, ed., *Fur
Trade and Empire*, p. xxxiv.

P. xxii. "the parenting effect of
water. . .": Clark Blaise, quoted in
Peter C. Newman, "The Unknown
Element," *Saturday Night*, 100th Anniversary Issue/January 1987, p. 176.

P. xxiii. "Water is very special to
Canadians. . .": Derrick Sewell, quoted
in Peter C. Newman, "The Unknown
Element," *Saturday Night*, 100th Anniversary Issue/January 1987, p. 176.

P. xxiii. "The waterways were almost
miraculous. . .": Chester Martin, in
his Introduction to George Simpson,
Journal of Occurrences. . ., p. xviii.

P. xxiv. "I hate the sight of these
forts. . .": Frederick Ulric Graham,
while travelling with Simpson, in K.C.
Tessendorf," George Simpson, Canoe
Executive," *The Beaver*, Summer 1970,
p. 40.

CHAPTER 1
THE NOR'WESTERS

P. 4. "toward making Yonge Street a
better road": Marjorie Wilkins
Campbell, *The North West Company*,
p. 114.

P. 5. "the North West Company was
the forerunner. . .": Harold A. Innis,
The Fur Trade in Canada, p. 262.

P. 6. "The rivalry was not between two
commercial enterprises. . .": Daniel
Francis, *Battle for the West*, p. 49.

P. 7. "as if it were drawn by a dead horse.": ibid., p. 67.

P. 7. "Sometimes one or two partners. . .": Washington Irving, *Astoria*, p. 9.

P. 8. "the swelling and braggart style": ibid., p. 17.

P. 8. "hyperborean nabobs": ibid., p. 9.

P. 10. "McTavish is entirely unequalled. . .": Patrick C.T. White, ed., *Lord Selkirk's Diary 1803-1804*, p. 204.

P. 10. McTavish loved "good wine, good oysters. . .": David MacMillan, "'The Marquis' — King of the fur trade," *Canadian Banker*, July/August 1978, p. 29.

P. 14. "In those days we dined. . .": George T. Landmann, from *Adventures and Recollections*, in Clifford P. Wilson, "The Beaver Club," *The Beaver*, March 1936, p. 20.

P. 17. "They ascended the rivers in great state. . .": Washington Irving, *Astoria*, p. 10; also quoted in *Canadian Geographical Journal*, January 1948, p. 14.

P. 19. "At night *bourgeois* and clerks danced. . .": Marjorie Wilkins Campbell, in Leslie F. Hannon, *Forts of Canada*, [Ch. 16, opening page; unpaginated].

P. 20. "What did the Indian women get in return. . .": Margaret Atwood, *Days of the Rebels 1815/1840*, pp. 50-51.

P. 21. "I gave the Chef de Canard's widow. . .": Archibald McLeod, diary entry, in Walter O'Meara, *The Savage Country*, p. 131.

P. 21. "This Indian brought his daughter. . .": James McKenzie, journal entry 9 April 1800, in Jennifer S.H. Brown, *Strangers in Blood*, pp. 84-85.

P. 21. "[The Gros Ventres] appear to be destitute. . .": Alexander Henry the Younger, journal entry 1811, in

Walter O'Meara, *The Savage Country*, p. 165.

P. 22. "Liard's daughter took possession of my room. . .": Alexander Henry the Younger, journal entry 1 January 1801, in Ogden Tanner, *The Canadians*, p. 42.

P. 22. "I gathered up the remaining bones. . .": Alexander Henry the Younger, journal entry, in Frank Rasky, *The Taming of the Canadian West*, p. 90.

P. 22. "The union which has been formed between us. . .": Daniel Williams Harmon, journal entry, in W. Kaye Lamb, ed., *Sixteen Years in the Indian Country*, pp. 194-95.

P. 23. Harmon was not the only Nor'Wester. . .: Sylvia Van Kirk, letter to the author, 8 June 1987.

CHAPTER 2
THE MAGNIFICENT RIVER RATS

P. 25. "not only hanging on by their hands and feet but by their 'eyebrows'": H.M.S. Cotter, "The Birch Bark Canoe," *The Beaver*, July 1922, p. 10.

P. 26n. the work "may be unfavourably compared with. . .": Alan Cooke, "The Ungava Venture of the Hudson's Bay Company, 1830-1843," Ph.D. dissertation, p. 57.

P. 26. "They had the pride of champions. . .": Hugh MacLennan, *The Rivers of Canada*, p. 31.

P. 26. "They sprang from European peasants. . .": ibid., p. 183.

P. 26. "those natural water Dogs": Anon. [Company servant], in Glyndwr Williams, "Cumberland House: The Move Inland," *The Beaver*, Commemorative Issue, p. 31.

P. 26. "It will still be good policy. . .": Ramsay Crooks to John Jacob Astor, about April 1817 [first portion of letter is missing], in a letterbook of the American Fur Company, p. 12; in David Lavender, *The Fist in the Wilderness*, p. 257.

P. 27. "They are not brave; but when they apprehend a little danger. . .": Daniel Williams Harmon, "A Journal of Voyages and Travels in the Interior of North America," in W. Kaye Lamb, ed., *Sixteen Years in the Indian Country*, pp. 197–98.

P. 30. "to serve, obey, and faithfully carry out. . .": in "Contract between Joseph Charron, called Cabanna, of the parish of Verchère at Tetreau [Montreal] and Messrs Alexr. MacKenzie and Company, before the Notary of the Province of Lower Canada. . .Drawn and passed in Montreal in the office of the undersigned notary in the year one thousand eight hundred and two, the fifth of April in the morning. . ." Original in the collection of Donald M. Stewart, Victoria, B.C.

P. 30. "Their minds were agitated with these scruples. . .": Duncan McGillivray, journal entry, in Grace Lee Nute, *The Voyageur*, p. 50.

P. 32. "One man's face. . .": John J. Bigsby, *The Shoe and Canoe*, Vol. 1, pp. 132–33.

P. 33. "You really had to keep your tongue. . .": Hugh Mackay Ross, *The Apprentice's Tale*, p. 123.

P. 34. "No camel train across Asia Minor. . .": Leslie F. Hannon, *Redcoats and Loyalists*, p. 81.

P. 38. Re Chief Solomon Voyageur's portage feat: Nanuwan of Chiboogama, "Solomon Voyageur," p. 162.

P. 38. "Their song is like the murmur of the river. . .": J.G. Kohl, in Marius Barbeau, "Voyageur Songs," p. 15.

P. 41. "It was a small square building. . .": Deposition of Alexander Fraser, in [John Halkett], *Statement respecting the Earl of Selkirk's Settlement upon the Red River. . .*[London, 1817], pp. xcv-xcvii.

P. 41. "They have a softness and delicacy. . .": Walter O'Meara, *The Savage Country*, p. 26.

P. 42. "It is questionable whether [Napoleon] Bonaparte. . .": Thomas L. McKenney, in Donna Brinkworth, "Voyageur Life Review," p. 18.

P. 43. "On the second night of the contest. . .": Duncan McGillivray, journal entry, in Grace Lee Nute, *The Voyageur*, p. 66.

P. 44. "Take the scrapings from the driest outside corner. . .": H.M. Robinson, *The Great Fur Land*, in Douglas MacKay, ed., "The HBC Packet," *The Beaver*, September 1934, p. 8.

P. 44. "It tasted like meat. . .": William Campbell, in the *Winnipeg Free Press*, 10 August 1934, ibid.

P. 45. "one ought to have his Blood composed of Brandy,. . .": Ogden Tanner, *The Canadians*, p. 31.

P. 45. "Their arrival at Lachine. . .": W. George Beers, in Edgar Andrew Collard, *Montreal: The Days That Are No More,* p. 181.

P. 47. "They talked incessantly. . .": Joseph McGillivray, journal entry, in Grace Lee Nute, *The Voyageur*, p. 164.

P. 48. "I have now been forty-two years in this country.": Anon., by Alexander Ross, journal entry, ibid., pp. 207-8.

CHAPTER 3
BIG MACK

P. 52. "Beaing then sixteen years of age. . .": Peter Pond, journal entry, in Hugh MacLennan, *The Rivers of Canada*, p. 184.

P. 52. "We met the next morning eairley. . .": Peter Pond, journal entry, in Ogden Tanner, *The Canadians*, p. 23.

P. 53. "It is celebrated for the view. . .": Lt. John Henry Lefroy, in George F.G. Stanley, ed., *John Henry Lefroy: In Search of the Magnetic North*, pp. 64-65.

P. 56. "At one moment Mackenzie is hard put. . .": W. Kaye Lamb, ed., *The Journals and Letters of Sir Alexander Mackenzie,* p. 499.

P. 57. "The English Chief was very much displeased. . .": Alexander Mackenzie, journal entry, in Maurice Hodgson, "The Exploration Journal as Literature," *The Beaver,* Winter 1967, p. 8.

P. 57. "We sat down and without loss of time. . .": George T. Landmann, journal entry, in Clifford P. Wilson, "The Beaver Club," *The Beaver,* March 1936, p. 21.

P. 61. "It was evident that these waters emptied themselves. . .": Alexander Mackenzie, journal entry, in Hugh MacLennan, *The Rivers of Canada,* p. 199.

P. 61. "I also urged the honour of conquering disasters. . .": Alexander Mackenzie, journal entry, in Donna Brinkworth, "Voyageur Life Review, Old Fort William staff report, 6 Feb, 1982."

P. 63. "This magnificent theatre of nature. . .": Alexander Mackenzie, journal entry, in Ogden Tanner, *The Canadians,* p. 58.

P. 64. Ships "as big as islands": Alexander Mackenzie, journal entry, ibid., p. 59.

P. 65. Putting "a period to all my anxiety. . .": Alexander Mackenzie, journal entry, ibid., p. 61.

P. 66. "I determined to proceed. . .": Alexander Mackenzie, journal entry, in Walter Sheppe, *First Man West,* p. 164.

P. 66. "My companion's hair being greased. . .": Alexander Mackenzie, journal entry, in Ogden Tanner, *The Canadians,* p. 62.

P. 66. "In the house there were several chests. . .": Alexander Mackenzie, *Voyages from Montreal. . .,* pp. 298-99.

P. 67. "Here my voyages of discovery. . .": Alexander Mackenzie, journal entry, in Walter Sheppe, *First Man West,* pp. 276-77.

P. 67n. "The object of this last. . .": sign posted by Meriwether Lewis, 23 March 1806.

P. 67n. "Mr. M'Kenzie with a party. . .": David McKeeham to Meriwether Lewis, 7 April 1807, in Donald Dean Jackson, ed., *Letters of the Lewis and Clark Expedition,* 1st ed. Urbana, Ill.: University of Illinois Press, 1962, pp. 401-2.

P. 68. "Mackenzie introduced a new reality. . .": Hugh MacLennan, *The Rivers of Canada,* p. 35.

P. 69. "Last fall I was to begin copying. . .": Alexander Mackenzie, letter to Roderick McKenzie, in Roy Daniells, *Alexander Mackenzie and the North West,* p. 161.

P. 69. "I am fully bent. . .": Alexander Mackenzie, letter to Roderick McKenzie, ibid., p. 162.

P. 71. Forget "that which we seldom lose sight of": Alexander Mackenzie, journal entry, in W. Stanford Reid, *The Scottish Tradition in Canada,* p. 37.

P. 71. "The old North West Company. . .": Alexander Henry the Elder, journal entry, in Roy Daniells, *Alexander Mackenzie and the North West,* p. 169.

P. 72. "These voyages will not, I fear. . . .": Alexander Mackenzie, journal entry, ibid., pp. 170-71.

P. 73. "You know him to be vindictive. . .": John Fraser, letter to Simon McTavish, in Daniel Francis, *Battle for the West,* p. 76.

P. 74. Exchange between Joseph Maurice Lamothe and James King: in Arthur S. Morton, *A History of the Canadian West to 1870-71,* p. 513.

P. 75. "In a vault beneath this church. . .": tablet at Chiswick parish church in London, England.

P. 76. "I have at last been over-taken. . .": Alexander Mackenzie, letter to Roderick McKenzie, in Roy Daniells, *Alexander Mackenzie and the North West,* p.185.

P. 76. "Most of the prominent events. . .": Alexander Mackenzie, letter to Roderick McKenzie, ibid., p. 184.

P. 76. "Lady Mackenzie is sitting by me. . .": Alexander Mackenzie, letter to Roderick McKenzie, ibid., p. 186.

P. 76. "In a longer vista of time. . .": Alexander Mackenzie, journal entry, ibid., p. 198.

CHAPTER 4
STORMING OF THE WEST

P. 79. "We had to pass where no human being. . .": Simon Fraser, journal entry, in Margaret A. Ormsby, *British Columbia: A History,* p. 37.

P. 81. Fraser's River "is one of the basic political and economic facts. . .": Bruce Hutchison, *The Fraser,* pp. 6–7.

P. 82. "These Indians had heard of fire arms. . .": Simon Fraser, journal entry, ibid., pp. 40–41.

P. 82. "their singing makes a terrible racket. . .": Simon Fraser, journal entry, in Frank Rasky, *The Taming of the Canadian West,* p. 57.

P. 82. "however kind the savage may appear. . .": Simon Fraser, journal entry, ibid.

P. 83. "In a sense the Fraser does not flow at all. . .": Hugh MacLennan, *The Rivers of Canada,* p. 249.

P. 83. "a desperate undertaking!": Simon Fraser, journal entry, in Bruce Hutchison, *The Fraser,* p. 44.

P. 83. "even for one person side-ways. . .": Simon Fraser, journal entry, in Frank Rasky, *The Taming of the Canadian West,* p. 67.

P. 83. "We cut steps. . .": Simon Fraser, journal entry, ibid.

P. 83. "Here the channel contracts. . .": Simon Fraser, journal entry, in Corday MacKay, "With Fraser to the Sea," p. 6.

P. 84. "I have been for a long period. . .": Simon Fraser, journal entry, in Margaret A. Ormsby, *British Columbia: A History,* p. 37.

P. 84. "steps. . .formed like a ladder. . .": Simon Fraser, journal entry, ibid.

P. 84. "singing a war song, beating time. . .": Simon Fraser, journal entry, in W. Kaye Lamb, ed., *The Letters and Journals of Simon Fraser 1806–1808,* pp. 105 and 108.

P. 85. "Elliott Coues's description of Thompson. . .": Richard Glover, ed., introduction to *David Thompson's Narrative 1784–1812,* p. xiii.

P. 85. "the white flower of a blameless life": Richard Glover, ibid., p. xii.

P. 87. Thompson could "create a wilderness and people it. . .": John J. Bigsby, *The Shoe and Canoe* , Vol. I, pp. 113–14.

P. 87. "Writers on the Indians always compare them. . .": David Thompson, journal entry, in Frank Rasky, *The Taming of the Canadian West,* p. 80.

P. 87. "Once after a weary day's march. . .": David Thompson, journal entry, ibid.

P. 88. "No dove is more meek. . .": David Thompson, journal entry, ibid., p. 79.

P. 88. "may perhaps be correctly diagnosed. . .": Richard Glover, ed., introduction to *David Thompson's Narrative 1784–1812,* p. xii.

P. 89. "for all I had seen in their service. . .": David Thompson, journal entry, in E.E. Rich, *Hudson's Bay Company, 1670–1870,* Vol. 2, p. 147.

P. 94. "Thus I have fully completed the survey. . .": David Thompson, in J.B. Tyrrell, "David Thompson: Explorer," *Maclean's*, 21, no. 5 (March 1911), p. 75.

P. 95. "He dined here last night . . .": James Gallatin, in Lucy Kaveler, *The Astors*, p. 1.

P. 99. "Oregon was the specific prize. . .": Kenneth A. Spaulding, ed., *The Fur Hunters of the Far West*, p. xx.

P. 99. "They fitted up a large but light bark canoe. . .": Washington Irving, in Edgar Andrew Collard, *Montreal: The Days That Are No More*, pp. 180–81.

P. 100. "I fear we are in the hands of a lunatic!": Alexander MacKay, in Lucy Kavaler, *The Astors*, p. 18.

P. 100. "On perceiving him, the captain ordered. . .": Gabriel Franchère, journal entry, in Gordon Speck, *Northwest Explorations*, p. 281.

P. 103. "Mr. Pillet fought a duel with Mr. Montour. . .":in Marjorie Wilkins Campbell, *The North West Company*, p.191.

P. 104. "While I breathe. . .": John Jacob Astor, in Lucy Kavaler, *The Astors*, p. 20.

P. 104. "There, I told you she would pay it,. . .": John Jacob Astor, ibid., p. 21.

P. 105. "It might have been better if she had had only six guns. . .": John McDonald of Garth, in Barry Gough, "The 1813 Expedition to Astoria," *The Beaver*, Autumn 1973, p. 46.

P. 105n. "coarse" "illiterate": Sylvia Van Kirk, *"Many Tender Ties,"* p. 202.

P. 105n. "I should offend your modesty. . .": Alexander McKenzie [sic], HBCA, F.3/2, fo. 194, ibid., p. 280.

P. 106. "The expense attending the sending of our own vessels. . .": William McGillivray, in Hilary Russell, "The Chinese Voyages of Angus Bethune," *The Beaver*, Spring 1977, p. 31.

P. 106n. On "all foreign vessels trad-

ing in China. . .": Hilary Russell, ibid.

CHAPTER 5
HOWLING WITH THE WOLVES

P. 109. "When you are among wolves, howl.": Colin Robertson, his motto, in Frank Rasky, *The Taming of the Canadian West*, p. 141.

P. 109. " 'The Honourable Company'. . . opposed the liquor trade. . .": Robert MacDonald, *The Owners of Eden*, p. 5.

P. 110. "That applied particularly to the liquor trade. . .": Frank B. Walker, address to the Atikokan Kiwanis Club, 1 May 1951, and in interview with the author.

P. 112. "Good Sir, it grieves us to see. . .": William Tomison's petition, in E.E. Rich, *Hudson's Bay Company, 1670–1870*, Vol. 2, p. 227.

P. 112. Complaint that "the Canadians is [sic] going through the Barren Ground. . .": William Tomison to the London Committee, in Daniel Francis, *Battle for the West*, p. 79.

P. 112. "The Company's function should be to strip. . .": British Prime Minister Lord Palmerston, in James Morris, *Heaven's Command*, p. 216.

P. 113. "Drunken Indians were among the casual inconveniences. . .": Douglas MacKay, *The Honourable Company*, p. 222.

P. 113. "The love of Rum. . .": Duncan McGillivray, journal entry, in Arthur S. Morton, ed., *The Journal of Duncan M'Gillivray*, p. 47.

P. 113. "Men, women, and children promiscuously mingle. . .": Duncan McGillivray, journal entry, in Marjorie Wilkins Campbell, *The North West Company*, p. 102.

P. 114. "To see a house full of drunken Indians. . .": Daniel Williams Harmon, journal entry, in Craig MacAndrew and Robert B. Edgerton, *Drunken Comportment: A Social Explanation*, p. 104.

P. 114. "Every one knows the passion. . .": Daniel Williams Harmon, journal entry, ibid., p. 102.

P. 114. "Whisky and brandy destroyed the self-respect. . .": Diamond Jenness, *The Indians of Canada*, p. 254.

P. 115. "We may truly say that liquor. . .": Alexander Henry the Younger, journal entry, in Walter O'Meara, *The Last Portage*, p. 135.

P. 115. "The Indians continued drinking. . .": Alexander Henry the Younger, journal entry, ibid., p. 136.

P. 115. She "applied a fire brand . . .": Alexander Henry the Younger, journal entry, in Craig MacAndrew and Robert B. Edgerton, *Drunken Comportment: A Social Explanation*, p. 158.

P. 115. "Little Shell almost beat. . .": Alexander Henry the Younger, journal entry, in Frank Rasky, *The Taming of the Canadian West*, p. 105.

P. 115. Stereotype as "abject supplicant. . .": Robert Hood, journal entry, in C. Stuart Houston, ed., *To the Arctic by Canoe, 1819–1821*, p. 86.

P. 115. "On the subject of alcohol abuse. . .": A. Blair Stonechild, Head, Department of Indian Studies, Saskatchewan Indian Federated College; memorandum to the author, 5 February 1987.

P. 116. "The Indian had never before tasted. . .": Robert MacDonald, *The Owners of Eden*, p. 77.

P. 116. "It is commonly understood that liquor. . .": Robert E. Pinkerton, *The Gentlemen Adventurers*, p. 226.

P. 116. "Indians develop alcoholism at about the same rate as the rest of us. . .": Bruce Cox, letter to the author, 10 September 1986.

P. 116. "Across a continent, the Indian observed. . .": Craig MacAndrew and Robert B. Edgerton, *Drunken Comportment: A Social Explanation*, p. 163.

P. 117. "If it does turn out that. . .": Lillian E. Dyck, "Are North American Indians Biochemically More Susceptible to the Effects of Alcohol?", *Native Studies Review*, 2, no. 2 (1986), pp. 85 and 92.

P. 117. "Some of the principal Indians. . .": Daniel Williams Harmon, journal entry on New Year's Day in New Caledonia, in newsletter, Old Fort William, 19 December 1983, p. 2.

P. 118. "To see drunkenness and debauchery. . .": Alexander Ross, journal entry, in Craig MacAndrew and Robert B. Edgerton, *Drunken Comportment: A Social Explanation*, p. 145.

P. 118. "I'll fix up 'coffin varnish' so strong. . .": Johnny Healy, in Frank Rasky, *The Taming of the Canadian West*, p. 178.

P. 122n. "Colen was right, but for the wrong reasons. . .": Tim Ball, Department of Geography, University of Winnipeg; letter to the author, 16 December 1986.

P. 123. "the most miserable hovel. . .": William Auld, in Daniel Francis, *Battle for the West*, p. 105.

P. 123. "When three-fourths of the people had drunk. . .": Daniel Williams Harmon, in Douglas MacKay, *The Honourable Company*, p. 132.

P. 123. London Committee's instructions "to avoid any discussion. . ." and to "maintain the utmost peace. . .": *London Correspondence Outward—Official*, Public Archives of Canada (PAC), HBC MG20 A6. Albany Factory, 1803.

P. 123. "The great and first objective. . .": HBC London Committee, in E.E. Rich, *Hudson's Bay Company, 1670–1870*, Vol. 2, p. 257.

P. 124. "Then all our people came into the house. . .": James Tate, in Glyndwr Williams, ed., *Hudson's Bay Miscellany 1670–1870*, p. 110.

P. 125. "She was riding her horse. . .": Sylvia Van Kirk, *"Many Tender Ties,"* p. 178.

P. 126. Howse had "explored a Country European feet. . .": William Hemmings Cook, journal entry, in W. Christoph Wolfart, "Joseph Howse," *Dictionary of Canadian Biography*, Vol. VIII, p. 413.

P. 126. Indians felt "a settled dislike for the Canadians. . .": Philip Turnor, in J.B. Tyrrell, ed., *Journals of Samuel Hearne and Philip Turnor,* p. 453.

P. 128. McLeod warned Fidler that. . . "the proprietors of the NWC. . .": Archibald Norman McLeod, in Arthur S. Morton, *A History of the Canadian West*, p. 519.

P. 128. Samuel Black "the strangest man I ever knew. . .": Sir George Simpson in his Character Book, in Glyndwr Williams, ed., *Hudson's Bay Miscellany 1670–1870*, pp. 192–93.

P. 129. "We are so very few — they so numerous!": Peter Fidler, journal entry, in James G. MacGregor, *Peter Fidler,* p. 194.

P. 129. "I told them both to return. . .": Peter Fidler, journal entry, ibid., p. 176.

P. 130. "Some people in reading this Journal. . .": Peter Fidler, journal entry, 21 January 1816, in Samuel Black, *A Journal of a Voyage from Rocky Mountain Portage,* p. xxxii.

P. 130. Black told Fidler that "if he offered to go to us. . .": Peter Fidler, journal entry, in J.G. MacGregor, *Peter Fidler,* p. 178.

P. 130. "They have now given her to a Canadian . . .": Peter Fidler, journal entry, ibid., p. 178.

P. 130. William Auld criticizes "mean and spaniel-like behaviour": ibid., p. 181.

P. 131. Fidler described as "a faithful and interested old servant. . .": HBC note, ibid., p. 255.

P. 131n. "All my money in the funds. . .": Peter Fidler's will, in John Robert Colombo, ed., *Colombo's Canadian Quotations*, p. 192.

P. 131n. "I wouldn't be a darn bit surprised": Marian Wiggins, interview with the author, 18 March 1987, Kinistino, Sask.

P. 134. "Good God! See the Canadians. . .": Colin Robertson, in E.E. Rich, *Hudson's Bay Company, 1670–1870*, Vol. 2, p. 286.

P. 134. HBC's incumbents as "drones and drivellers. . .": Colin Robertson, journal entry, in Frank Rasky, *The Taming of the Canadian West*, p. 141.

P. 134. "When you are among wolves, howl.": Colin Robertson, his motto, ibid.

CHAPTER 6
A FEARFUL INNOCENCE

P. 141. "Madam: It cannot be too much lamented. . .": John Paul Jones, letter to Lady Selkirk, in Mary H.T. Alexander, "Paul Jones and Lord Selkirk," *The Beaver*, June 1943, p. 7.

P. 142. "I frankly acknowledge. . .": Lady Selkirk, in John Morgan Gray, *Lord Selkirk of Red River*, p. 5.

P. 142. "This was a momentous event. . .": Lord Selkirk, letter to John Halkett, 21 June 1813; in Mary H.T. Alexander, "Paul Jones and Lord Selkirk," *The Beaver*, June 1943, p. 7.

P. 142. "Perhaps this may help to explain. . .": John Perry Pritchett, *The Red River Valley*, ibid.

P. 142. Insisting that "only a man whose ruling. . .": [Dugald Stewart], *Outlines of Moral Philosophy, For the Use of Students at the University of Edinburgh* (Edinburgh, 1793), p. 288.

P. 143. "Pass first in fight. . .": Sir James (The Black Douglas), in John Morgan Gray, *Lord Selkirk of Red River*, p. 6.

P. 144. "The destruction was begun in the west. . .": John Prebble, *The Highland Clearances*, p. 78.

P. 145. "but also to the British Empire. . .": Public Archives of Canada, Selkirk Papers, p. 13231, in John Perry Pritchett, *The Red River Valley,* p. 21.

P. 146. "many of the shares were being held in chancery. . .": K.G. Davies, in Dale L. Morgan et al., *Aspects of the Fur Trade,* p. 176.

P. 149. "By God, Sir, if you are bent on doing. . .": Anon., addressing Lord Selkirk, in Beckles Willson, *The Great Company,* p. 143.

P. 149. "The Committee of the Hudson's Bay Company. . .": Simon McGillivray letter, in Arthur S. Morton, *A History of the Canadian West,* pp. 541–42.

P. 149. "governed by the moon" and "a cloak thrown over [his] avaricious designs. . .": in Introduction to George Simpson, *Journal of Occurrences,* p. xx.

P. 150. "I really don't believe Selkirk realized. . .": W. Kaye Lamb, interview with the author, 27 November 1985, Vancouver.

P. 150. "It is a business which I hate. . .": Lord Selkirk, letter to Lady Selkirk, in Selkirk Papers, National Heritage Collection, Public Archives of Canada; and in *Correspondence at St. Mary's Isle,* Vol. 3, p. 405.

P. 152. "Even if the emigrants. . .": "The Highlander" [Simon McGillivray], in Gerald Friesen, *The Canadian Prairies: A History,* p. 73.

P. 152. "The Highlanders were like children. . .": John Prebble, *The Highland Clearances,* pp. 192–93.

P. 155. "victims sacrificed to the sinister views . . .": Willard Wentzel, in L.F.R. Masson, *Les Bourgeois de la Compagnie du Nord-Ouest,* p. 130.

P. 157. "It is, quite simply, the French expression. . .": Don McLean, Gabriel Dumont Institute of Native Studies and Applied Research, Regina, letter to the author, 24 October 1986.

P. 157n. "polyglot jabber": in Rhoda R. Gilman et al., *The Red River Trails,* p. 12.

P. 158. "Lord Selkirk, philanthropist and humanitarian. . .": Don McLean, *A Research Resource Book of Native History,* p. 112.

P. 158n. "When I first went to Moose. . .": J.J. (Woody) Wood, interview with Camilla Newman, 14 October 1986, Victoria.

P. 161. "1. No buffalo to be run. . .": List of regulations, in Ogden Tanner, *The Canadians,* p. 136.

P. 162. "During the whole of the three days. . .": Paul Kane, in J.G. MacGregor, "The Return of the Buffalo: Canada's Purchase of the Pablo Herd," *Alberta Historical Review,* July 1954, p. 4.

P. 163. "Owing to the destruction of game. . .": William T. Hornaday, *The Extermination of the American Bison* (Washington: Government Printing Office, 1889), pp. 526–27.

P. 163. "From the first time they came to scratch. . .": D.A. Dary, *The Buffalo Book,* p. 16.

CHAPTER 7
SHOWDOWN

P. 167. "If we are to be poor . . .": Lady Selkirk letter to Lord Selkirk, in Introduction to George Simpson, *Journal of Occurrences,* p. xxix.

P. 169. "He was able to identify himself. . .": Margaret Arnett MacLeod and W.L. Morton, *Cuthbert Grant of Grantown,* p. 24.

P. 169. Force enough "to crush all the Nor'Westers. . .":Miles Macdonell, in Marjorie Wilkins Campbell, *The North West Company,* p. 210.

P. 171. "Oh for the love of beaver!": Colin Robertson, in Frank Rasky, *The Taming of the Canadian West,* p. 141.

P. 172. Drop their "slow, jog-trot manner" and adopt ". . .the glittering pomposity": in Glyndwr Williams, "The Red River Affair," *The Beaver*, Autumn 1970, p. 42.

P. 172. "The sight of the great fort. . .": Marjorie Wilkins Campbell, *The North West Company*, p. 215.

P. 173. "I will be in my proper glory. . .": Lieutenant Ener Holte, PAC, North West Papers, Holte to Pritchard, 14 April 1816; in George C. McMillan, "The Struggle of the Fur Companies in the Red River Region 1811–1821," p. 99.

P. 174. Exchange between François Firmin Boucher and Governor Robert Semple: Margaret Arnett MacLeod and W.L. Morton, *Cuthbert Grant of Grantown*, p. 48.

P. 175. "The nameless, faceless directors. . .": Don McLean, *A Research Resource Book of Native History*, p. 121.

P. 176. Against "open warfare. . .": Proclamation dated 1 May 1817, issued by the Governor-in-Chief of Canada in the name of the Prince Regent, in Arthur S. Morton, *A History of the Canadian West*, p. 595.

P. 176. Weather data for summer of 1816: Tim Ball, "Selected Periods of Severe Weather and Their Impact on the Operations of the Hudson's Bay Company," unpublished paper delivered at the Fifth Annual Fur Trade Conference, Montreal, May 1985.

P. 178. This "piddling lord":William McGillivray's comment re Lord Selkirk, in Marjorie Wilkins Campbell, *The North West Company*, p. 227.

P. 178. "We landed, and proceeded to the gate. . .": John McNab, in *Statement Respecting the Earl of Selkirk's Settlement*, p. xciii; in Arthur Black, *Old Fort William*, pamphlet prepared by the staff of Old Fort William, Thunder Bay, Ont., p. 38.

P. 178. Determined to "cut up by the roots. . .": Lord Selkirk, in Marjorie Wilkins Campbell, *The North West Company*, p. 228.

P. 179. "The news of Seven Oaks. . .": John Morgan Gray, *Lord Selkirk of Red River*, p. 158.

P. 179. "If ever I am acquitted. . .": Kenneth MacKenzie to Daniel McKenzie, in Jean Morrison, ed., "Famous Personalities of the North West Company," p. 5.

P. 179. "Everything in your expedition. . .": Lady Selkirk, in John Morgan Gray, *Lord Selkirk of Red River*, p. 193.

P. 182. Three were ". . .fatally pricked. . .": in Frank Rasky, *The Taming of the Canadian West*, p. 139.

P. 183. "The lady with the ring in her nose. . .": Colin Robertson, journal entry, ibid., p. 142.

P. 183. "Black the Nor'Wester is now in his glory. . .": Colin Robertson, journal entry, in Agnes C. Laut, *The Conquest of the Great Northwest*, p. 211.

P. 183. "Landing, I dashed. . .": Colin Robertson, journal entry, ibid., p. 213.

P. 184. "I began to arrange all our Posts. . .": Colin Robertson, journal entry, in E.E. Rich, ed., *Colin Robertson's Correspondence Book. . .*, pp. 78–79.

P. 186. "Our opponents have lowered their tone. . .": Colin Robertson, letter to Governor William Williams, in Marjorie Wilkins Campbell, *The Saskatchewan*, p. 144.

P. 187. "Come, [Abbé], put down your name. . .": Colin Robertson exchange with Dr John McLoughlin and Angus Bethune, journal entry, in E.E. Rich, ed., *Colin Robertson's Correspondence Book. . .*, p. 139.

P. 187. "If we are to be poor. . .": Lady Selkirk, letter to Lord Selkirk, in Introduction to George Simpson, *Journal of Occurrences*, p. xxix.

P. 188. A "polar region where even the minimal agriculture. . . ," "a residence for uncivilized man" and "was so completely isolated. . .": John

Strachan, in F.L. Barron, "Victimizing His Lordship: Lord Selkirk and the Upper Canadian Courts," *Manitoba History*, July 1984, p. 21.

P. 188. "For pity's sake, make up your mind. . .": Lady Selkirk, letter to Lord Selkirk, in John Morgan Gray, *Lord Selkirk of Red River*, p. 304.

P. 188. "my honour is at stake. . .": Lord Selkirk, letter to Andrew Colvile, ibid., p. 323.

CHAPTER 8
A MARRIAGE OF
GREAT CONVENIENCE

P. 193. Colony "had been in the Red Sea. . .": Andrew Colvile, in Introduction to George Simpson, *Journal of Occurrences*, p. xx.

P. 194. "To you, I feel that I am solely indebted. . .": Simpson to Andrew Colvile, letter from York Factory, 8 September 1821, in Selkirk Papers, 7374, ibid., p. xli.

P. 194. Opinion that "an enlightened Indian. . .": Simpson to Andrew Colvile, ibid.

P. 195. Passengers were "precious nymphs. . . .": Simpson, in John S. Galbraith, *The Little Emperor*, p. 30.

P. 195. "John Bull merely wanted the opportunity. . .": Simpson, ibid., p. 27.

P. 196. Determined to "show my Governors that I am not wanting. . .": Simpson, to a Mr. Pooler, in K.G. Davies, ed., *Northern Quebec and Labrador Journals and Correspondence, 1819–35*, p. 367n.; MG 19 A-26, Archives of British Columbia, Victoria, B.C.

P. 197. Pledging to "maintain the rights and interests. . .": Simpson, in E.E. Rich, *Hudson's Bay Company, 1670–1870*, Vol. 2, p. 377.

P. 197. "Mr Simpson, a gentleman from England. . .": Willard Wentzel, in Introduction to George Simpson, *Journal of Occurrences*, p. xxxviii.

P. 197. "It has been hinted that you are rather addicted. . .": Simpson, letter to Joseph Greill at Berens House, in Arthur S. Morton, *Sir George Simpson*, p. 45.

P. 199. "they look upon me. . ." and "a little rum operates like a charm. . .": Simpson, in Frank Rasky, *The Taming of the Canadian West*, pp. 147–48.

P. 199. "Black could at first scarcely look me in the face. . .": Simpson, in Frederick Merk, ed., *Fur Trade and Empire*, p. 203.

P. 199. "Come here, Boxer. . .": exchange between Simpson and Simon McGillivray, Jr., in John W. Chalmers, *Fur Trade Governor,* p. 10.

P. 200. "Mr. McGillivray, I should be glad . . .": Simpson to Simon McGillivray, Jr., in Marjorie Wilkins Campbell, *The North West Company*, p. 261.

P. 200. "I arrest you. . :": Amable Grignon to Simon McGillivray, Jr., ibid.

P. 200. Having "got to the blind side. . .": Simpson, in Frank Rasky, *The Taming of the Canadian West*, p. 151.

P. 200. "The English are up. . .": Joseph Bouché, in George Simpson, *Journal of Occurrences,* p. 180.

P. 201. "On one side were the North Westers, the Cavaliers. . .": K.G. Davies, "From Competition to Union," *Minnesota History*, 40, no. 4 (Winter 1966), p. 166.

P. 202. "By 1821, the Hudson's Bay Company had become. . .": ibid.

P. 204. "a very serviceable man. . .": Charles Greville's description of Edward Ellice, in Dorothy E.T. Long, "The Elusive Mr. Ellice," *Canadian Historical Review*, Vol. 23 (1942), p. 48.

P. 204. "I never could see why the Bear. . .": Emily Eden, in Sir Herbert Maxwell, *Life and Letters of George William Frederick, 4th Earl of Clarendon* (2 vols., London, 1913), Vol. 2, p. 232.

P. 205. "all bunkum. . .": Selkirk, in John Morgan Gray, *Lord Selkirk of Red River*, pp. 329–30.

P. 205. "A very poor creature, vain. . .": Simpson, about Angus Bethune, in Glyndwr Williams, ed., *Hudson's Bay Miscellany, 1670–1870*, p. 178.

P. 207. "Simon Pure and I settled it. . .": Andrew Colvile, in *Correspondence at St. Mary's Isle.*

P. 207. "Amalgamation? This isn't amalgamation. . .": Anon. [NWC winterer], in Beckles Willson, *The Great Company*, p. 433.

P. 208. "The union of the North West and Hudson's Bay companies. . .": John S. Galbraith, *The Hudson's Bay Company as an Imperial Factor*, p. 14.

P. 209. "At the [foot] of this magnificent fall. . .": Nicholas Garry, journal entry, in "From the Diary of Nicholas Garry," *The Beaver*, March 1931, p. 168.

P. 210. "To the most worthy. . .": inscription on Samuel Black's ring, in Marjorie Wilkins Campbell, *The North West Company*, p. 273.

PP. 210–11. "I avail myself of the opportunity. . . .": William McGillivray, letter to John Strachan 26 July 1821, in Strachan Papers, Archives of Ontario, Toronto.

P. 211. "Our dinner table was a hard rock. . .": Nicholas Garry, journal entry, in "From the Diary of Nicholas Garry," *The Beaver*, March 1931, p. 168.

P. 212. "I was not insensible. . .": Nicholas Garry, in Leslie F. Hannon, *Redcoats and Loyalists, 1760/1815*, unpaginated.

P. 213n. "Heaven is as near England. . .": Rev. James Evans, in W.B. Ready, "Norway House," *The Beaver*, March 1949, p. 34.

P. 214. "For another quarter of a century. . .": Chester Martin, Introduction to George Simpson, *Journal of Occurrences*, p. iv.

P. 214. Lamented that "the fur trade is forever lost. . .": William McGillivray, letter to John Strachan, 26 July 1821, in Strachan Papers, Archives of Ontario, Toronto.

P. 214. "The feudal state of Fort William. . .": Washington Irving, *Astoria*, p. 11.

CHAPTER 9
THE BIRCHBARK NAPOLEON

P. 218. "Evidently uncertain. . .": John Tod, "Reminiscences of 1821," [Amalgamation dinner at York Factory], microfiche in British Columbia Provincial Archives, Victoria, B.C., A/8/30/T56, from original in Bancroft Library, University of California at Berkeley.

P. 218. Simpson "all bows and smiles": John Tod, "Reminiscences of 1821," microfiche in British Columbia Provincial Archives, Victoria. A/8/30/T56, from original in Bancroft Library.

P. 219. "One of them still bore. . .": John Tod, "Reminiscences of 1821," microfiche in British Columbia Provincial Archives, Victoria. A/8/30/T56, from original in Bancroft Library.

P. 220. Simpson "built upon the Egyptian model. . .": John Henry Lefroy, in George F.G. Stanley, ed., *John Henry Lefroy: In Search of the Magnetic North*, p. 6.

P. 221. "Simpson represented in purest distillation. . .": John S. Galbraith, "The Little Emperor," *The Beaver*, Winter 1960, p. 22.

P. 222. "It had occurred to me that philanthropy. . .": Simpson, in Frank Rasky, "The counting-house clerk who tamed the fur pirates," *Liberty* (Montreal), June 1962, p. 54.

P. 222. "nine out of ten men are captivated. . .": Simpson, ibid., p. 54.

P. 223. "His Excellency miscalculates. . .": Thomas Simpson, in J.W. Chalmers, "A Family Affair," *Alberta Historical Review*, Spring 1960, pp. 2–3.

P. 223. "In no colony. . .": John McLean, *John McLean's Notes of a Twenty-Five Years' Service in the Hudson's Bay Territory* (London: Richard Bentley, 1849), Vol. 2, p. 235.

P. 223. "Clothed with a power so unlimited. . . .": John McLean, in E.E. Rich, *Hudson's Bay Company, 1670–1870*, Vol. 3, p. 467.

P. 223. "They may learn that from the moment. . .": John McLean, in Charles Bert Reed, *Masters of the Wilderness*, p. xxv.

P. 224. "Simpson must have been one of the best-hated. . .": Alan Cooke, review of John S. Galbraith's *The Little Emperor: Governor Simpson of the Hudson's Bay Company*, in *Archivaria*, 30, no. 2 (June 1977), pp. 124–25.

P. 225. "That all Chief Factors. . .": Item 139, "Minutes of a Council held at York Factory Northern Department of Ruperts Land, 5 July 1823," in R. Harvey Fleming, ed., *Minutes of Council*, p. 57.

P. 225. "The Northwest is beginning. . .": NWC clerk Willard Wentzel, journal entry, 30 July 1820, in George Simpson, *Journal of Occurrences*, p. 2.

P. 226. "The Table Appointments throughout. . .": Simpson, in John A. Hussey, "'Unpretending' but not 'Indecent': Living Quarters at Mid-19th Century HBC Posts," *The Beaver*, Spring 1975, p. 12.

P. 226. "The late arrangements. . .": Simpson, 1822 letter to London, in Introduction to George Simpson, *Journal of Occurrences*, p. lvi.

P. 226. "Two Nez Percés Chiefs arrived. . .": Simpson, journal entry, 9 April 1825, in Frederick Merk, ed., *Fur Trade and Empire*, p. 136.

P. 227. "an Indian brought me a Beaver skin. . .": George Gladman, letter to Simpson, in Arthur J. Ray, "Some conservation schemes of the Hudson's Bay Company, 1821–50: An examination of the problems of resource management in the fur trade," *Journal of Historical Geography*, 1:1 (January 1975), p. 55.

P. 227. "[If] it be found that gentlemen disregard. . .": Simpson, ibid., p. 57.

P. 227n. "RESOLVED that the Indians be treated with kindness. . .": Resolution No. 40, "Rules and Regulations Drawn Up at the Council Meeting of Red River 17th June, 1843, signed by George Simpson, Governor," Hudson's Bay House Library, File: Liquor.

P. 230. "It is strange that all my ailments. . .": Simpson, letter to John George McTavish, in John S. Galbraith, "The Little Emperor," *The Beaver*, Winter 1960, p. 25.

PP. 230–31. "While at Sitka, I took a bath. . .": Simpson, in K.C. Tessendorf, "George Simpson, Canoe Executive," *The Beaver*, Summer 1970, p. 40.

P. 231. "As we wafted along. . .": Chief Trader Archibald McDonald, in K.C. Tessendorf, "George Simpson, Canoe Executive," *The Beaver*, Summer 1970, p. 40.

P. 232. "through the noonday stillness. . .": G.M. Trevelyan, in Barbara Tuchman, *Practicing History*, p. 61.

P. 233. "I believe there is nothing known. . .": Simpson, arriving at Split Lake, letter to McTavish, 20 August 1824, B 239 c, HBA.

P. 233. "He was such a figure. . .": Simpson, of John McLoughlin, in Frederick Merk, ed., *Fur Trade and Empire*, p. 23.

P. 233. "to give the Dr. an opportunity. . .": Simpson, ibid.

P. 234. "Some of the people were so numbed. . .": Simpson, in Grace Lee

Nute, "Jehu of the Waterways," *The Beaver*, Summer 1960, p. 16.

P. 234. "The water was too wide. . .": Simpson, ibid.

P. 234. "they will lose their scalps. . .": Simpson, in J.F. Klaus, "Early Trails to Carlton House," *The Beaver*, October 1985, p. 33.

P. 234. "I got on my old charger 'Jonathan,'. . .": Simpson, journal entry, in Grace Lee Nute, "Jehu of the Waterways," *The Beaver*, Summer 1960, p. 16.

P. 235. "unremitting exertion. . ." and "masterly arrangements and decisive measures. . .": Council to Simpson, 9 July 1825, in R. Harvey Fleming, ed., *Minutes of Council*, pp. 136–38.

P. 235. "The commodity has been a great consolation. . .": Simpson, 9 April 1825, in Frederick Merk, ed., *Fur Trade and Empire*, p. 136.

P. 235. "made whitened countenances. . .": Simpson, in Willard E. Ireland, "Simpson's 1828 Journey: A review of the tenth volume of the Hudson's Bay Record Society," *The Beaver*, September 1948, p. 43.

P. 236. "nearly amphibious. . .": Simpson, in E.E. Rich, ed., *Part of Dispatch from George Simpson Esq., Governor of Ruperts Land*, p. 34.

P. 236. "Many of our principal Clerks. . .": Simpson, letter to Andrew Colvile, 1826, HBCA.

P. 237. "From what I have seen of you. . .": Simpson to Chief Factor Angus Cameron, in Malvina Bolus, ed., *People and Pelts,* p. 87.

P. 238. "The walls and ceiling. . .": Paul Kane, in Douglas MacKay, *The Honourable Company*, p. 250.

P. 238. "Jigs, reels, and quadrilles. . .": *Harper's Magazine*, October 1860.

P. 240. "any man who is not dead. . .": John Rowand, in Marjorie Wilkins Campbell, *The Saskatchewan*, p. 166.

P. 240. "We know only two powers. . .": John Rowand, ibid., p. 167.

P. 240. "actually cried. . .": Colin Fraser, in Douglas MacKay, *The Honourable Company*, p. 250.

CHAPTER 10
THE VICEROY

P. 243. "No man is more appreciative. . .": Chief Factor John Stuart to Donald Smith, in John S. Galbraith, "The Little Emperor," *The Beaver*, Winter 1960, p. 22.

P. 244. "lords of the lakes and forests. . .": often cited, as in John S. Galbraith, *The Little Emperor*, p. 18.

P. 244. "They could outvote me. . .": Simpson, in Douglas MacKay, *The Honourable Company*, p. 283.

P. 244. "The few individuals who compose it. . .": Simpson, in John McLean, *John McLean's Notes of a Twenty-Five Years' Service in the Hudson's Bay Territory*, pp. 333–34.

P. 244. "Keep your temper. . .": Simpson to McTavish, in E.E. Rich, ed., *Part of Dispatch from George Simpson, Esq.*, introduction by W. Stewart Wallace, p. xiv.

P. 245. "as a feat of memory. . .": Glyndwr Williams, ed., *Hudson's Bay Miscellany, 1670–1870*, p. 166.

P. 245. "generous to extravagance. . .": Simpson, entry in his Character Book re John George McTavish, in Glyndwr Williams, ed., *Hudson's Bay Miscellany, 1670–1870*, p. 171.

P. 245. "will not tell a lie. . .": Simpson, entry in his Character Book re John Rowand, ibid., p. 182.

P. 245. Antoine Hamel: "A stout strong illiterate common kind of fellow. . .": Simpson, No. 42 in his Character Book, ibid., p. 215.

P. 245. Charles Ross: "A good classical scholar. . .": Simpson, No. 71 in his Character Book, ibid., p. 225.

P. 245. Thomas Dears: "A flippant, superficial, trifling creature. . .": Simpson, No. 18 in his Character Book, ibid., p. 205.

p. 246. Leslie Bryson: "An Irishman. . .": Simpson, No. 11 in his Character Book, ibid., pp. 202–3.

P. 246. Francis Ermatinger: "A stout active boisterous fellow. . .": Simpson, No. 22 in his Character Book, ibid., pp. 206–7.

P. 246. John Clarke: "A boasting, ignorant low fellow. . .": Simpson, No. 4 in his Character Book, ibid., pp. 171–72.

P. 246. Colin Robertson: "A frothy trifling conceited man. . .": Simpson, No. 1 in his Character Book, ibid., pp.169–70.

P. 250. "The reason for this situation. . .": David McNab, "The Colonial Office and the Prairies in the Mid-Nineteenth Century," *Prairie Forum*, 3:1 (1978), p. 22–23.

P. 251. "When we assert. . .": Alexander Kennedy Isbister et al., *A Few Words on the Hudson's Bay Company. . .*, London, [n.d.], pp. 1–2.

P. 251. "Not a sound can be heard. . .": Anon., in Daniel Francis, *Battle for the West*, p. 161.

P. 254. "Few can overmatch me. . .": Simpson, in Alice M. Johnson, "Simpson in Russia," *The Beaver*, Autumn 1960, p. 4.

P. 254. "head of the most extended Dominions. . .": Simpson, ibid.

P.254. "retired at 11.": Simpson, ibid.

P. 255. "Indeed, I have not observed. . .": Simpson, ibid.

P. 255. "An extraordinary-looking, ferret-eyed. . .": Simpson, of Baron Ferdinand Petrovich von Wrangell, ibid., p. 11.

P. 255. "Wrangell and I are very thick. . .": Simpson, ibid.

P.255. "While we defiled through the gates. . .": Simpson, in Douglas MacKay, *The Honourable Company*, p. 214.

P. 259. Simpson as "father of the fur trade" and "fathered seventy sons between the Red River and the Rocky Mountains. . .": Grant MacEwan, *Fifty Mighty Men*, p. 53.

P. 260. "the White Fish diet of the district. . .": Simpson, to John George McTavish, 12 November 1822, B239, HBA.

P. 260. "private or separate entrance to my apartments. . .": Simpson, letter to John George McTavish, 12 Nov. 1822, in R. Harvey Fleming, ed., *Minutes of Council,* p. 424.

P. 260. "Simpson continually violated. . .": Sylvia Van Kirk, letter to the author, 8 June 1987, p. 5.

P. 260. "My family concerns I leave entirely. . .": Simpson, letter to John George McTavish, 12 Nov. 1822, in R. Harvey Fleming, ed., *Minutes of Council,* p. 424.

P. 261. "Pray keep an eye on the commodity. . .": Simpson, in Sylvia Van Kirk, "Women and the Fur Trade," *The Beaver*, Winter 1972, p. 13.

P. 261 "He was utterly ruthless. . .": Irene Spry, interview with the author, Ottawa, 1984.

P. 261. "I have not got over. . .": Chief Factor Nicol Finlayson, in Frank Rasky, *The Taming of the Canadian West*, p. 115.

P. 262. "Connubial alliances are the best security. . .": Simpson, 18 May 1821, in Marjorie Wilkins Campbell, *The North West Company*, p. 262.

P. 262. "all officers or servants. . .": *Minutes of Council for 1821,* Resolution No. 75, PAC, HBCA (microfilm), MG20, B 135 K 1.

P. 262. "petty coat politicians. . .", "a stout good looking Dame" and "persuasion and cunning": Simpson, in Sylvia Van Kirk, "Women and the Fur Trade," *The Beaver*, Winter 1972, p. 10.

P. 262. He "led the stampede. . .": John E. Foster, "The Indian-Trader in the Hudson Bay Fur Trade Tradition," in Jim Freedman and Jerome Barkow, eds., *Proceedings of the Second Congress, Canadian Ethnology Society*. Ottawa: National Museums of Canada, 1975, p. 581.

P. 263. "The coming of white women. . .": Sylvia Van Kirk, "Women and the Fur Trade," *The Beaver*, Winter 1972, p. 21.

P. 264. "Let me know if you have any fair cousin. . .": Simpson to McTavish, 5 December 1829, B 135 C/2, HBA, in Sylvia Van Kirk, "Women and the Fur Trade," *The Beaver*, Winter 1972, p. 14.

P. 264. "I see you are something like myself, shy. . .": Simpson, ibid.

P. 265. "I owe it all to Geordy": John George McTavish, to Donald McKenzie, in Margaret Arnett MacLeod, "The Riddle of the Paintings," *The Beaver*, December 1948, p. 10.

P. 265. Frances Simpson "was always terrified to look. . .": Frances Simpson, in Sylvia Van Kirk, "Women and the Fur Trade," *The Beaver*, Winter 1972, p. 16.

P. 265. "What could be your aim. . .": John Stuart to Simpson, HBCA, E.24/4, fo. 12, in Sylvia Van Kirk, *"Many Tender Ties,"* p. 188.

P. 265. "who got stupid, but shook hands. . .": letter from R. Clouston to D. Ross, 20 Nov. 1847, PABC, D. Ross Correspondence.

P. 266. "On either side are stupendous rocks. . .": Frances Simpson, in John W. Chalmers, *Fur Trade Governor: George Simpson, 1820–1860*, p. 118.

P. 266. "To cross this baffled the skill. . .": Frances Simpson, in Grace Lee Nute, ed., Introduction to "Journey for Frances," *The Beaver*, December 1953, p. 54.

P. 267. "old and weather beaten. . .": Frances Simpson of Chief Trader Thomas McMurray, in Sylvia Van Kirk, "Women and the Fur Trade," *The Beaver*, Winter 1972, p. 17.

P. 267. "The reception I here met with. . .": Frances Simpson, in Grace Lee Nute, ed., "Journey for Frances," Part 3, *The Beaver*, June 1954, p. 14.

P. 268. "Robertson brought his bit of Brown. . .": Simpson, in E.E. Rich, ed., *Colin Robertson's Correspondence Book*, p. cxxiii.

P. 269. "I am most heartily tired of Red River. . .": Simpson, to John George McTavish, in Sylvia Van Kirk, "Women and the Fur Trade," *The Beaver*, Winter 1972, p. 19.

P. 270. "Lord have mercy. . .": Simpson, in John W. Chalmers, *Fur Trade Governor: George Simpson 1820–1860*, p. 125.

CHAPTER 11
GALAHADS OF THE PACIFIC

P. 273 "Necessity has no laws": Peter Skene Ogden in Simpson, Character Book, in Peter Skene Ogden, *Peter Skene Ogden's Snake Country Journals*, Vol. 1 (1824-25 and 1825-26), Introduction by Burt Brown Barker, p. xix.

P. 273. "An imperial tide lapped the shores. . .": Barry M. Gough, "The Character of the British Columbia Frontier," *B.C. Studies*, 32 (Winter 1976-77), p. 29.

P. 274. "you could walk across on their backs. . .": Anon. Early explorer, in Peter Farb, *Man's Rise to Civilization*, p. 126.

P. 275. "the very scum of the country. . .": Simpson, in John McLoughlin, *The Letters of John McLoughlin*, First Series, introduction by W. Kaye Lamb, pp. lx-lxi.

P. 278. "everything appears to me on the Columbia. . .": Simpson, ibid., p. xxv.

P. 278. "In behalf of the Honourable. . .": Simpson, in Frederick Merk, ed., *Fur Trade and Empire*, p. 124.

P. 278. "to identify our claim to the soil. . .": Simpson, journal entry, ibid.

P. 278. "I got home safe. . .": Finan McDonald, in Peter Skene Ogden, *Peter Skene Ogden's Snake Country Journals*, Vol. 1 (1824-25 and 1825-26), Introduction by Burt Brown Barker, p. xxxvii.

P. 279. "A keen, sharp, off hand fellow. . .": Simpson, Character Book, ibid., p. xix.

P. 279. "Necessity has no laws": Peter Skene Ogden, ibid., p. xix.

P. 279n. "It is scarcely credible. . .": Peter Skene Ogden, journal entry, 29 April 1829, ibid., p. xv.

P. 281. "I would most willingly sacrifice. . .": Peter Skene Ogden, journal entry, *Peter Skene Ogden's Snake Country Journals*, Vol 3. (1827-28 and 1828-29), introduction by David E. Miller and David H. Miller, p. xxxii.

P. 283. "This life makes a young man sixty. . .": Peter Skene Ogden, journal entry, in Anon., "Ogden's Journals," *Oregon Historical Quarterly*, 11, pp. 216-17.

P. 283. "There remains now only one man living. . .": Peter Skene Ogden, journal entry, ibid., p. 390.

P. 283. "This is certainly a most horrid life . . .": Peter Skene Ogden, in Glyndwr Williams, "Peter Skene Odgen," *Dictionary of Canadian Biography*, Vol. 8, p. 661.

P. 287. The White-Headed Eagle: often cited, as in Dorothy Nafus Morrison, *The Eagle & The Fort*, p. 162.

P. 287. "a bump of curiosity. . .": Jedediah Smith, in Richard Dillon, *Siskiyou Trail*, p. 83.

P. 288. "rather *outré*, even for Vancouver": John McLoughlin, journal entry, in Bruce Hutchison, "When a Canadian Ruled Oregon," *Maclean's*, 30 April 1955, p. 58.

P. 288. "an unscrupulous hireling. . .": Hall Jackson Kelley, in Richard Dillon, *Siskiyou Trail*, p. 144.

P. 288. She "probably felt sad. . .": Hall Jackson Kelley, ibid.

P. 290. "eatables and drinkables. . .": Simpson, in John McLoughlin, *The Letters of John McLoughlin*, First Series, introduction by W. Kaye Lamb, p. lxxv.

P. 290. "never did a change of system": Simpson, ibid.

P. 291. "Captain Davidson's talent. . .": Simpson, ibid., p. lxxxvi.

P. 292. "overawing the natives": Simpson, ibid., p. xix.

P. 293. "I am not aware. . .": McLoughlin to Simpson, 7 March 1842, HBCA, B.223/b/29, fo. 73.

P. 294. "justifiable homicide": Simpson, in Dorothy Nafus Morrison, *The Eagle & The Fort*, p. 115.

P. 294 "Instead of conducting the examination. . .": McLoughlin to Simpson, ibid., p. 117.

P. 296. "Gentlemen, I will serve you no longer": McLoughlin, in Daniel Francis, *Battle for the West*, p. 154.

P. 296. "By British demagogues, I have been represented. . .": McLoughlin, in Bruce Hutchison, "When a Canadian Ruled Oregon," *Maclean's*, 30 April 1955, p. 58.

P. 296. "I might better have been shot. . .": McLoughlin, in John McLoughlin, *The Letters of John McLoughlin*, First Series, introduction by W. Kaye Lamb, p. lxii.

P. 297. "The Hudson's Bay Company has been with you. . .": Peter Skene Ogden to Tiloukaikt, in Herbert Dunk,

"The Spirit of the Fur Trader As Exemplified by Peter Skene Ogden," *The Beaver*, June 1930, p. 19.

P. 298. "Your words are weighty. . .": Tiloukaikt to Peter Skene Ogden, ibid.

CHAPTER 12
BRITISH COLUMBIA'S
MULATTO KING

P. 301. Douglas "a cold brave man. . .": John Sebastian Helmcken, "Reminiscences," Vol. 3, p. 63, in Barry M. Gough, "Sir James Douglas As Seen by His Contemporaries: A Preliminary List," *B.C. Studies*, 44 (Winter 1979-80), p. 47.

P. 302. "Old Square-Toes": Anon. Civil servant, in Barry M. Gough, ibid., p. 48.

P. 302. Shilling to "spend as he liked": in Mary Elizabeth Colman, "The Mulatto King of B.C.," *Maclean's*, 15 April 1952, p. 17.

P. 302. "Douglas . . . would step around . . .": Joseph Watt, in "General Joel Palmer's Narratives," ms., 1878, p. 14; PA 58, H.H. Bancroft Library, University of California, Berkeley.

P. 302. "His Excellency, James Douglas. . .": in J.S. Galbraith, "Bulwer-Lytton's Ultimatum," *The Beaver*, Spring 1958, p. 20.

P. 302. "the peculiar advantage of being. . .remote. . .": in Mary Elizabeth Colman, "The Mulatto King of B.C.," *Maclean's*, 15 April 1952, p. 46.

PP. 302-3. "A day highly suggestive of the past. . .": James Douglas, memorandum, 19 March 1869; Public Archives of British Columbia, Governor Douglas, Correspondence Outward, Miscellaneous Letters November 30, 1859, to December 8, 1863, pp. 130-31; in Margaret A. Ormsby, *British Columbia: A History*, pp. 82-83.

P. 305. "Though the Governor is a wonderfully clever man. . .": Lieutenant Charles William Wilson, in Barry M. Gough, "Sir James Douglas As Seen by His Contemporaries: A Preliminary List," *B.C. Studies*, 44 (Winter 1979-80), p. 49.

P. 305. "The place itself appears to be a perfect 'Eden'. . .": James Douglas, letter to James Hargrave, 5 February 1843, *The Hargrave Correspondence*, p. 420, in Margaret A. Ormsby, *British Columbia: A History*, p. 80.

P. 305. would "not give one of the bleakest knolls. . .": Hon. John Gordon, in Walter N. Sage, *Sir James Douglas and British Columbia*, p. 18.

P. 306. "settlements of resident colonists. . .": ibid., p. 143.

P. 306. "the land there as may be necessary. . .": ibid.

P. 309. "They arrived in large numbers. . .": Chief Trader W.H. McNeill, in T.A. Rickard, "The Discovery of Gold in B.C.," *The Beaver*, March 1942, p. 47.

PP. 309-10. "The entire population of San Francisco. . .": H.B. Hobson, in Walter N. Sage, *Sir James Douglas and British Columbia*, p. 207.

P. 312. "I trust and think he is. . .": Herman Merivale to Sir Edward Bulwer Lytton, 7 Aug.1858, Bulwer Lytton Papers, D/EK101, Hertfordshire Record Office, Hertford.

P. 312n. "If the name of New Caledonia. . .": Queen Victoria to British Colonial Secretary, in A.C. Benson and Viscount Esher, eds., *The Letters of Queen Victoria* (London, 1908), Vol. 3, p. 296.

P. 314. "He wanted to serve his country. . .": Amor de Cosmos, editorial, 11 December 1858, *British Colonist*, Victoria.

P. 315. Allowed to "look on":
New Westminster, B.C., *British Columbian*, 12 March 1864.

P. 315. "You probably think me unjustly severe. . .": John Tod, to Edward Ermatinger, 22 March 1870; Ermatinger Papers, Public Archives of British Columbia, in Barry M. Gough, "Sir James Douglas As Seen by His Contemporaries: A Preliminary List," *B.C. Studies*, 44 (Winter 1979-80), p. 50.

CHAPTER 13
UNRAVELLING THE FUR MONOPOLY

P. 320. "assumed the power to enact tariffs. . .": Toronto Board of Trade petition, in Beckles Willson, *The Great Company*, p. 471.

P. 321. "There is a strange revolution. . .": James Douglas, PAC, Hargrave Papers, 26 February 1840.

P. 321. "A good wife must be clean and industrious. . .": Sylvia Van Kirk, *"Many Tender Ties,"* p. 147.

P. 323. "They struggled to recreate the English rural parish. . .": Frits Pannekoek, "The Anglican Church and the Disintegration of Red River Society, 1818-1870," in Carl Berger and Ramsay Cook, eds., *The West and the Nation: Essays in Honour of W.L. Morton*, p. 75.

P. 324. "our excellent Liturgy. . ." and "heathens. . .": Rev. David Jones, in Sylvia Van Kirk, *"Many Tender Ties,"* p. 154.

P. 324. Little good other "than filling the pockets and bellies. . .": Simpson, letter to London Committee, in Frederick Merk, ed., *Fur Trade and Empire*, p. 181.

P. 324n. "What was most remarkable. . .": Frits Pannekoek, in *The West and the Nation: Essays in Honour of W.L. Morton*, p. 74.

P. 325. "a female of notoriously loose character. . ." and ". . . kept Mistress of the highest personage at this station. . .": Herbert Beaver, report to HBC London Committee, in Sylvia Van Kirk, *"Many Tender Ties,"* p. 155.

P. 325. "Sire, if you wish to know. . .": Exchange between Herbert Beaver and John McLoughlin, in Dorothy Nafus Morrison, *The Eagle & the Fort*, pp. 88-89.

P. 326. Type who "must always have a sweetheart. . .": Mrs Robert Logan re Sarah Ballenden, PAM, Records of the General Quarterly Court of Assiniboia, "Foss vs. Pelly, 16-18 July 1850," pp. 185-86, 203.

P. 327. "Writs were carried. . .": Alexander Ross, quoted by Frits Pannekoek, in *The West and the Nation: Essays in Honour of W.L. Morton*, p. 79.

P. 327. "All the inhabitants thought it proper. . .": Simpson to J. Black, 18 December 1850, HBCA, D. 4/71, fos. 265-66d.

P. 327. "Today the Bishop and his sister. . .": Eden Colvile, letter to Simpson re visit from Rt. Rev. David Anderson, in Sylvia Van Kirk, *"Many Tender Ties,"* p. 227.

P. 328. "I entreat you, for my sake. . .": John Ballenden, letter to Simpson, 5 December 1851, HBCA, D.5/32,f. 323.

P. 328. "if there is such a thing as dying of a broken heart. . .": Alexander Ross, letter to Simpson, 1 August 1851, HBCA, D.5/31, f. 206.

P. 329. "neither the Ishmaelite wildness. . .": W.L. Morton, *Manitoba: A History*, p. 67.

P. 330. Turned the ship "out of the bed of the river. . .": from report in the *Manitoban*, in Theodore Barris, *Fire Canoe: Prairie Steamboat Days Revisited*, p. 30.

P. 331. "are a distinct sort of beings. . .": Simpson, in Frederick Merk, ed., *Fur Trade and Empire*, p. 198.

P. 331. "A halfbreed whose name must long recall to mind. . .": Simpson, in his Character Book, in Glyndwr Williams, ed., *Hudson's Bay Miscellany, 1670–1870*, pp. 209–11.

P. 332. "You are the great soldier and leader. . .": James Dickson to Cuthbert Grant, in Margaret Arnett MacLeod, "Dickson the Liberator," *The Beaver*, Summer 1956, p. 6.

P. 333. "They are not too fond of the country. . .": Wemyss Simpson, re the 6th Regiment of Foot (the Royal Warwickshires), in W.E. Ingersoll, "Redcoats at Fort Garry," *The Beaver*, December 1945, p. 16.

P. 336. Jurors recommended mercy "as it appeared that he thought he had a right. . .": Jury foreman Donald Gunn, PABC, Ross Papers, Report of A. Ross, in W.S. Wallace, *Dictionary of Canadian Biography*, Vol. 1, p. 251.

P. 338. "a lumbering old pine-basket. . .": Capt C.P.V. Lull, re the *Anson Northup,* in Molly McFadden, "Steamboats on the Red," *The Beaver*, June 1950, p. 31.

P. 338. "Within moments there was pandemonium. . .": Theodore Barris, *Fire Canoe: Prairie Steamboat Days Revisited*, p. 19.

P. 339. "the cool and languid care. . .": Alexander Ross, in Ogden Tanner, *The Canadians*, p. 138.

CHAPTER 14
DEATH OF A TITAN

P. 343. "Sir George. . .pleaded his cause. . .": Stewart Derbishire, in John S. Galbraith, *The Little Emperor*, p. 175.

P. 343. "10,000 golden reasons. . .": Simpson to Derbishire, 7 March 1854, D-4/82, HBA.

P. 344. "Hudson's Bay Company's clerks. . .": *Report of the Select Committee of the House of Commons on the Hudson's Bay Company*, British Parliament, 1857, , pp. 34ff.

P. 344. "great link required to unite. . .": Major Robert Carmichael-Smyth, *A Letter from Major Robert Carmichael-Smyth to his friend the Author of "The Clockmaker" containing thoughts on the subject of a British Colonial Railway Communication between the Atlantic and the Pacixc*, London, 1849, p. 6.

P. 345. "a highway across the Continent. . .": Text of proposition by Allan Macdonell and others, Province of Canada, *Journals of Legislative Assembly*, 2 June 1851.

P. 346. Company "in a very critical position. . .": Simpson to Sir John Shepherd, 2 August 1856, HBC. Series A.12/8.

P. 347. "In England, the trend of empire. . .": James (Jan) Morris, *Heaven's Command*, p. 127.

P. 347. Congratulated on "able handling. . .": Simpson to John Ross, in John S. Galbraith, *The Little Emperor*, p. 198.

P. 348. "I think it would be a very great calamity. . .": John Ross, in Sir Edward Watkin, *Canada and the States* (London, 1887), pp. 140–41.

P. 348. "I do not think that the interests. . .": William Henry Draper, in Douglas MacKay, *The Honourable Company*, p. 269.

P. 349. Charter had "given unlimited scope to the cupidity. . .": Brief from the Aborigines' Protection Society, in Gustavus Myers, *A History of Canadian Wealth*, p. 135.

PP. 350–51. Sequence beginning, "I do not think that any part of the Hudson's Bay territories. . .": interchange between Parliamentary Committee Chairman Henry Labouchere and Simpson, in Douglas MacKay, *The Honourable Company*, pp. 264ff.

P. 351. Governor "in answering our questions. . .": William Ewart Gladstone, in James (Jan) Morris, *Heaven's Command*, p. 128.

P. 351. "The disclosures laid bare. . .":
Gustavus Myers, *A History of Canadian
Wealth*, p. 142.

P. 352. "Not only would there be no
difficulty. . .": Edward ("Bear") Ellis,
in Douglas MacKay, *The Honourable
Company*, p. 272.

P. 354. "Our old Chief, Sir George. . .":
Ermatinger to James Hargrave,
8 November 1853, in John S. Galbraith,
The Little Emperor, p. 189.

P. 355. "In February next, I shall
have completed forty years. . .":
Simpson, ibid., p. 203.

P. 355. "We are the last of the North
West partners. . .": Simon Fraser and
John McDonald of Garth, joint memo-
randum, reprinted in the *Montreal Daily
Star*, 9 November 1935.

P. 356. "Offered Lake Superior
chart. . .": David Thompson, journal
entry, in Frank Croft, "David Thompson's Lonely Crusade to Open the
West," *Maclean's*, 9 November 1957,
p. 43.

P. 356. Re Thompson's death: David
Thompson was buried in the Landell
family plot, his son-in-law being a
Landell, in the oldest section of Mount
Royal cemetery in Montreal.

P. 358. "Well, doctor, this is the last
scene. . .": Exchange between Simpson and his physician Dr William
Sutherland, in "Sir George Simpson's
Case," *American Journal of Insanity*, 19,
no. 3, January 1863, p. 261.

CHAPTER 15
SURRENDER

P. 361. "What? Sequester our very
tap root? . . .": HBC Governor Henry
Hulse Berens, in Beckles Willson, *The
Great Company*, p. 474.

P. 361. "As the country comes to be
occupied. . .": Alexander Grant Dallas,
in Daniel Francis, *Battle for the West*,
p. 173.

P. 363. "There can be no question. . .":
Globe editor George Brown, in Robert
M. Hamilton and Dorothy Shields,
eds., *The Dictionary of Canadian Quotations
and Phrases* (Toronto: McClelland and
Stewart, 1979), p. 442.

P. 363n. *"We are a Fenian brother-
hood. . ."*: in D.J. Goodspeed, "The
Day Canada Became a Nation,"
Maclean's, 1 December 1962, p. 69.

P. 364. Viewed Canada "with an
indifference. . .": Edgar W. McInnis,
The Unguarded Frontier (New York:
Doubleday Doran & Co., 1942), p. 5.

P. 364. Reported that "if people had
more brains. . .": Israel Andrews, in
William R. Manning, *Diplomatic Cor-
respondence of United States, Canada
Relations, 1784–1860*, Vol. 4, 1849–1860
(Washington, 1945), No. 2087, p. 311.

P. 364. Annexation "peaceably if possible. . .": *New York Herald* item, in
D.J. Goodspeed, "The Day Canada
Became a Nation," *Maclean's*,
1 December 1962, p. 69.

P. 364. "the British prairies had now
become. . .": James G. Snell, "The
Frontier Sweeps Northwest," p. 398.

P. 364. "boundless savannas. . .":
C.C. Coffin, 1865, quoted, ibid.,
p. 382.

P. 364. Here "was an area large
enough. . .": James Wickes Taylor,
J.W. Taylor letters, 25 November 1868,
4th (unnumbered) page, in Lois M.
Burgess, "Influences Affecting the
Transfer of Rupert's Land," p. 124.

P. 365. "fate had manufactured a
scoundrel. . .": Anon., re John Christian Schultz, in W.L. Morton, *Manitoba: A History*, p. 110.

P. 365. "I would be quite willing. . .":
John A. Macdonald, March 1865, in
Donald Creighton, "Old Tomorrow,"
The Beaver, Winter 1956, p. 10.

P. 365. "spoliation and outrage": John
A. Macdonald, in Beckles Willson,
The Great Company, p. 415.

P. 365. "that the only way in which British North America. . .": Donald Creighton, "Old Tomorrow," *The Beaver*, Winter 1956, p. 8.

P. 366. "Canada looks forward with interest. . .": John A. Macdonald, in Douglas MacKay, *The Honourable Company*, p. 280.

P. 367. "The Hudson's Bay Company are quite willing to dispose. . .": Edward ("Bear") Ellice, letter to Labouchere, 30 September 1856, HBA, A-7/2, in John S. Galbraith, *The Hudson's Bay Company as an Imperial Factor*, p. 340.

P. 367n. "I know that you have come. . .": Indian chief at Fort Frances, in George Bryce, *The Remarkable History of the Hudson's Bay Company*, p. 338.

P. 368. "What? Sequester our very tap-root?. . .": HBC Governor Henry Hulse Berens, in Beckles Willson, *The Great Company*, p. 474.

P. 368. "If these gentlemen are so patriotic. . .": HBC Governor Henry Hulse Berens to the Duke of Newcastle, British Colonial Secretary, quoted, ibid., p. 474.

P. 369. "Then he passed on. . .": IFS negotiator regarding Edward ("Bear") Ellice, quoted, ibid., pp. 479–80.

P. 371. "The Southern District will be opened. . .": 1863 Prospectus, in James Dodds, *The Hudson's Bay Company, Its Position and Prospects*, p. 76.

P. 371. "What a glorious program it would be. . .": John A. Macdonald,

2 January 1869, letter to Charles Tupper, PAC, Macdonald Papers, Letter Book No. 12, 13 October 1868 - 17 July 1869, p. 353.

P. 372. "The old lion has been shorn. . .": Anon., in Seymour Freedgood, "Hudson's Bay: Return to Greatness," *Fortune*, August 1958, p. 75.

P. 373. "sold like dumb driven cattle. . .": Anon., in Daniel Francis, *Battle for the West*, p. 176.

P. 373. "I can guarantee nothing. . . .": Governor William Mactavish, in Ogden Tanner, *The Canadians*, p. 140.

P. 374. "We heard our lands were sold. . .": Proclamation of Chief Sweet Grass and Plains Cree to Chief Factor W.J. Christie, 13 April 1871, in "Extract of a Despatch - W.J. Christie, Esq., Chief Factor to Lieut. Gov. Archibald, bearing date, Edmonton House, 13th April 1871," in Report of Indian Branch, *Sessional Papers*, 7, no. 22 (1872), pp. 33–34.

P. 374. "We have quietly and almost without observation. . .": John A. Macdonald to Sir Hastings Doyle, PAC, John A. Macdonald Papers, Vol. 515, 16 June 1869.

EPILOGUE

P. 377. "You are I presume fully aware. . .": Peter Skene Ogden to Simpson, 10 March 1849, in HBCA, D-5/24.

Bibliography

This listing is a selection from the books and articles consulted during the writing of this volume. Several sources listed in *Company of Adventurers*, the first volume of this three-book series, were again pertinent and are therefore included here for ready reference by the reader. The Chapter Notes, in a separate appendix, provide specific information on the author's sources of individual quotations throughout the text.

Adams, Gary. "Art and Archeology at York Factory." *The Beaver*, Summer 1982: 38–42.

Akrigg, G.P.V. and Helen B. Akrigg. *British Columbia Place Names*, Victoria: Sono Nis Press, 1986.

Alexander, Mary H.T. "Paul Jones and Lord Selkirk." *The Beaver*, June 1943: 4–7.

Allen, Robert S. *Peter Fidler and Nottingham House, Lake Athabasca, 1802–1806*. History and Archeology series, no. 69. Ottawa: National Historic Parks and Sites Branch, Parks Canada, 1983.

Alwin, John A. "Colony and Company Sharing the York Mainline." *The Beaver*, Summer 1979: 4ff.

Arrowsmith, William A. "Northern Saskatchewan and the Fur Trade." Master's thesis, University of Saskatchewan, 1964.

Atwood, Mae. *In Rupert's Land: Memoirs of Walter Traill*. Toronto: McClelland and Stewart, 1970.

Atwood, Margaret. *Days of the Rebels, 1815/1840*. Canada's Illustrated Heritage. Toronto: Natural Science of Canada, 1977.

Baergen, William Peter. "The Fur Trade at Lesser Slave Lake, 1815–1831." Master's thesis, University of Alberta, 1967.

Barbeau, Marius. "Voyageur Songs." *The Beaver*, June 1942: 15–19.

Barker, Burt Brown, ed. "McLoughlin Proprietary Account with Hudson's Bay Company." *Oregon Historical Quarterly*, 45, no. 1 (March 1944): 1–7.

Barr, William. "On to the Bay." *The Beaver*, Autumn 1985: 43–53.

Barris, Theodore. *Fire Canoe: Prairie Steamboat Days Revisited*. Toronto: McClelland and Stewart, 1977.

Barron, F. Laurie, and James B. Waldram, eds. *1885 and After: Native Society in Transition*. Proceedings of a conference, University of Saskatchewan, Saskatoon, May 1985. Regina: Canadian Plains Research Centre, University of Regina, 1986.

Begg, Alexander. *Alexander Begg's Red River Journal and Other Papers Relative to the Red River Resistance of 1869–1870*. Edited, with introduction, by W.L. Morton. The Champlain Society, Vol. 34. Toronto: The Champlain Society, 1956.

Berger, Carl, and Ramsay Cook, eds. *The West and the Nation: Essays in Honour of W.L. Morton*. Toronto: McClelland and Stewart, 1976.

Bigsby, John Jeremiah. *The Shoe and Canoe, or Pictures of Travel in the Canadas*. 2 vols. London: Chapman & Hall, 1850; New York: Paladin Press, 1850.

Birk, Douglas A. "John Sayer and the Fond du Lac Trade: The North West Company in Minnesota and Wisconsin." In Thomas C. Buckley, ed., *Rendezvous: Selected Papers of the Fourth North American Fur Trade Conference, 1981:* 51–61.

Bishop, C.A. *The Northern Ojibway and the Fur Trade: An Historical and Ecological Study.* New York: Holt, Rinehart & Winston, 1974.

Black, Samuel. *A Journal of a Voyage from Rocky Mountain Portage in Peace River to the Sources of Finlays Branch and North West Ward in Summer 1824.* Edited by E.E. Rich; assisted by A.M. Johnson; introduction by R.M. Patterson. HBRS, Vol. 28. London: Hudson's Bay Record Society, 1955.

Black-Rogers, Mary. "'Starving' and Survival in the Subarctic Fur Trade: A Case for Contextual Semantics." Paper delivered at the Fifth North American Fur Trade Conference, Montreal, 1985.

Blake, Anson S. "The Hudson's Bay Company in San Francisco." *California Historical Society Quarterly,* Part 1: 28, no. 2: 97–112; Part 2: 28, no. 3: 243–58.

Blegen, Theodore C. *The Voyageurs and Their Songs.* St. Paul, Minn.: Minnesota Historical Society, 1966.

Bolus, Malvina, ed. *People and Pelts: Selected Papers of the Second North American Fur Trade Conference, 1970.* Winnipeg: Peguis Publishers, 1972.

Boon, Thomas C.B. "The Archdeacon and the Governor." *The Beaver,* Spring 1968: 41–49.

Bowes, Gordon E., ed. *Peace River Chronicles.* Vancouver: Prescott Publishing, 1963.

Bowsfield, Hartwell. *Louis Riel: The Rebel and the Hero.* Toronto: Oxford University Press, 1971.

——— , ed. *Fort Victoria Letters, 1846–1851.* Introduction by Margaret A. Ormsby. HBRS, Vol. 32. Winnipeg: Hudson's Bay Record Society, 1979.

Boyce, Gerald E. "Canadian Interest in the Northwest, 1856–1860." Master's thesis, University of Manitoba, 1961.

Brinkworth, Donna. "Voyageur Life Review." Old Fort William staff report, 6 February 1982: 18.

Brown, Jennifer S.H. *Strangers in Blood: Fur Trade Company Families in Indian Country.* Vancouver: University of British Columbia Press, 1980.

——— . "Linguistic Solitudes and Changing Social Categories." In Judd, Carol M., and A.J. Ray, eds., *Old Trails and New Directions: Papers of the Third North American Fur Trade Conference.* Toronto: University of Toronto Press, 1980.

Bryce, George. *Mackenzie, Selkirk, Simpson.* Toronto: Morang & Co., 1911.

——— . *The Old Settlers of Red River.* Manitoba Historical and Scientific Society, Transaction no. 19, Season 1885–86. Winnipeg: Manitoba Daily Free Press, 1885.

——— . *The Remarkable History of the Hudson's Bay Company.* London: Sampson, Low, Marston, 1910.

Bryce, Mrs. George. *Early Red River Culture.* Historical and Scientific Society of Manitoba, Transaction no. 57, Feb. 1901. Winnipeg: Manitoba Free Press, 1901.

Buckley, Thomas C., ed. *Rendezvous: Selected Papers of the Fourth North American Fur Trade Conference, 1981.* St Paul, Minn.: North American Fur Trade Conference, 1984.

Bumsted, J.M. *The People's Clearance: Highland Emigration to British North America, 1770–1815.* Edinburgh: Edinburgh University Press; Winnipeg: University of Manitoba Press, 1982.

——— , ed. *The Collected Writings of Lord Selkirk*: see entry under Douglas, Thomas.

——— . "The Affair at Stornoway, 1811." *The Beaver*, Spring 1982: 52–58.

——— . "Lord Selkirk's Highland Regiment and the Kildonan Settlers." *The Beaver*, Autumn 1978: 16ff.

——— . "The Quest for a Usable Founder: Lord Selkirk and Manitoba Historians, 1856–1923." *Manitoba History*, 1981, no. 2: 2ff.

——— . "Settlement by Chance: Lord Selkirk and Prince Edward Island." *Canadian Historical Review*, 59, no. 2 (June 1978).

Burgess, Lois M. "Influences Affecting the Transfer of Rupert's Land: Some Aspects of the Attitudes of Five Governments and Peoples to the Transfer of Rupert's Land from the Hudson's Bay Company to Canada, July 15th, 1870." Master's thesis, University of Ottawa, 1963.

Burns, Flora Hamilton. "Holiday 1856 in Honolulu." *The Beaver*, Autumn 1965: 4–11.

Calloway, Colin G. "Foundations of Sand: The Fur Trade and British-Indian Relations, 1783–1815." Paper delivered at the Fifth North American Fur Trade Conference, Montreal, 1985.

Cameron, Alan. "Ships of Three Centuries." *The Beaver*, Summer 1970: 4–21.

Campbell, Marjorie Wilkins. *McGillivray: Lord of the Northwest.* Toronto: Clarke, Irwin, 1962.

——— . *The North West Company.* Toronto: Macmillan of Canada, 1957.

——— . *The Nor'Westers: The Fight for the Fur Trade.* Toronto: Macmillan of Canada, 1974.

——— . *Push to the Pacific.* Toronto: Canadian Jackdaw, 1968.

——— . *The Saskatchewan.* Rivers of America series, Hervey Allen and Carl Carmer, eds. Toronto: Rinehart & Co., 1950.

Catchpole, A.J.W. "Evidence from Hudson Bay Region of Severe Cold in the Summer of 1816." In Harington, C.R., ed. *Syllogeus 55: Climatic Change in Canada 5— Critical Periods in the Quaternary Climatic History of Northern North America.* National Museum of Natural Sciences, National Museums of Canada. Ottawa: Queen's Printer, 1985.

Chalmers, John W. *Fur Trade Governor: George Simpson, 1820–1860.* Edmonton: Institute of Applied Art, 1960.

——— , ed. *The Land of Peter Pond.* Boreal Institute for Northern Studies, occ. publ. no. 12. Edmonton: University of Alberta, 1974.

——— . "They Travelled with the Governor." *Montana*, Spring 1960: 11–21.

Cline, Gloria Griffen. *Peter Skene Ogden and the Hudson's Bay Company.* Norman, Okla.: University of Oklahoma Press, 1974.

Coates, K.S., and W.R. Morrison. "Northern Visions: Recent Writing in Northern Canadian History." *Manitoba History*, 10 (Autumn 1985): 2–9.

Coats, R.H., and R.E. Gosnell. *Sir James Douglas.* The Makers of Canada, Vol. 20. Toronto: Morang & Co., 1908.

Cole, Jean Murray. *Exile in the Wilderness: The Biography of Chief Factor Archibald McDonald, 1790–1853.* Don Mills, Ont.: Burns & MacEachern, 1979.

Collard, Edgar Andrew. *Montreal: The Days That Are No More.* Toronto: Doubleday Canada Ltd., 1976.

Colombo, John Robert, ed. *Colombo's Canadian Quotations*. Edmonton: Hurtig Publishers, 1974.

Cooke, Alan. "The Ungava Venture of the Hudson's Bay Company, 1830–1843." Ph.D. dissertation, Cambridge, 1969.

Copland, A. Dudley. *Coplalook: Chief Trader, Hudson's Bay Company, 1923–1939*. Winnipeg: Watson & Dwyer Publishing, 1985.

Coues, Elliott, ed. *New Light on the Early History of the Greater Northwest: The Manuscript Journals of Alexander Henry, Fur Trader of the Northwest Company, and of David Thompson, Official Geographer and Explorer of the Same Company, 1799–1814*. 3 vols. New York: Francis P. Harper, 1897. Facsimile reprint. 2 vols. Minneapolis: Ross & Haines, 1965.

Coutts, Robert. "York Factory: Three Hundred Years of History on the Shore of Hudson Bay." *Newest Review*, 9, no. 9 (May 1984): 9–12.

Cowles, Virginia. *The Astors*. New York: Alfred A. Knopf; Toronto: Random House of Canada, 1979.

Cree, Muriel R. "For Crown and Fur Trade." *The Beaver*, September 1934: 46–49.

Creighton, Donald. *The Passionate Observer: Selected Writings*. Edited by Ramsay Derry. Toronto: McClelland and Stewart, 1980.

Croft, Frank. "David Thompson's Lonely Crusade to Open the West." *Maclean's*, 9 November 1957: 20ff.

Crowe, Keith J. *A History of the Original Peoples of Northern Canada*. Arctic Institute of North America. Kingston and Montreal: McGill–Queen's University Press, 1974.

Cumming, Carman. "The Plot to Buy the Canadian Northwest." *The Beaver*, Autumn 1984: 4–9.

Daniells, Roy. *Alexander Mackenzie and the North West*. London: Faber and Faber, 1969.

Dan Sha [newspaper published monthly by Ye Sa To Communications Society], Whitehorse, Yukon Territory.

Dary, D.A. *The Buffalo Book*. Chicago: Swallow Press, 1974.

Davidson, Donald C. "Relations of the Hudson's Bay Company with Russian American Company in the North West Coast 1829–67." *British Columbia Historical Quarterly*, 5, no. 1 (January 1941): 33–38.

Davidson, Gordon Charles. *The North West Company*. University of California Publications in History, Vol. 7. Berkeley: University of California Press, 1918. Reprint. New York: Russell & Russell, 1967.

Davies, K.G., ed. *Northern Quebec and Labrador Journals and Correspondence, 1819–35*. Introduction by Glyndwr Williams. HBRS, Vol. 24. London: Hudson's Bay Record Society, 1963.

——— , ed. *Peter Skene Ogden's Snake Country Journals*, Vol. 2: see entry under Ogden, Peter Skene.

Dawson, Will. *The War That Was Never Fought*. Princeton: Auerbach Publishers, 1971.

Dempsey, Hugh A., ed. "David Thompson on the Peace River." *Alberta Historical Review*, Winter 1965: 1–10; Spring 1966:14–21; Autumn 1966:14–19.

Denison, Merrill. *Canada's First Bank: A History of the Bank of Montreal*. 2 vols. Toronto: McClelland and Stewart, 1966, 1967.

Den Otter, A.A. "Transportation and Transformation: The Hudson's Bay Company, 1857–1885." *Great Plains Quarterly*, 3, no. 3 (Summer 1983): 171–85.

Dickenson, John A. "Old Routes and New Wares: The Advent of European Goods in the St. Lawrence Valley." Paper delivered at the Fifth North American Fur Trade Conference, Montreal, 1985.

Dictionary of Canadian Biography. Toronto: University of Toronto Press, (Vol. 1) 1966; (Vol. 2) 1969; (Vol. 3) 1974; (Vol. 4) 1979; (Vol. 6) 1983; (Vol. 8) 1985; (Vol. 9) 1976; (Vol. 10) 1972; (Vol. 11) 1982.

Dillon, Richard. *Siskiyou Trail: The Hudson's Bay Company Route to California*. New York: McGraw-Hill, 1975.

Dobbin, Murray. *The One-And-A-Half Men: The Story of Jim Brady and Malcolm Norris, Métis Patriots of the Twentieth Century*. Vancouver: New Star Books, 1981.

Dodds, James. *The Hudson's Bay Company, Its Position and Prospects*. London: Edward Stanford, 1866.

Douglas, Thomas (5th Earl of Selkirk). *The Collected Writings of Lord Selkirk, 1799–1809*. Writings and Papers of Thomas Douglas, Fifth Earl of Selkirk, Vol. 1, edited by J.M. Bumstead. Manitoba Record Society Publications, Vol. 7. Winnipeg: Manitoba Record Society, 1984.

——— . *Lord Selkirk's Diary 1803–04*. Edited by Patrick C.T. White. Champlain Society, Vol. 35. Toronto: The Champlain Society, 1958.

Duckworth, Harry W. "The Last Coureurs de Bois." *The Beaver*, Spring 1984: 4–12.

Duff, Wilson. *The Indian History of British Columbia, Volume 1: The Impact of the White Man*. Ministry of Provincial Secretary and Government Services, British Columbia Provincial Museum, Anthropology in British Columbia Memoir no. 5, 1964. Reprint, 1980. Victoria, B.C.: Queen's Printer, 1980.

Dunae, Patrick A. *Gentlemen Emigrants: From the British Public Schools to the Canadian Frontier*. Vancouver: Douglas & McIntyre, 1981.

Duncan, Janice K. *Minority without a Champion: Kanakas on the Pacific Coast,*

1788–1850. Portland, Ore.: Oregon Historical Society, 1972.

Dunk, Herbert. "The Spirit of the Fur Trader As Exemplified by Peter Skene Ogden." *The Beaver*, June 1930: 18–19.

Durnford, Hugh, ed. *Heritage of Canada*. Montreal: Reader's Digest Association (Canada) with the Canadian Automobile Association, 1978.

Dye, Eva Emery. "A Hero of Old Astoria." *Oregon Historical Quarterly*, 12 (1911): 220–23.

Eckert, Allan W. *Gateway to Empire*. Toronto: Little, Brown & Co. (Canada), 1983.

Eliot, T.C. "The Surrender at Fort Astoria in 1818." *Oregon Historical Quarterly*, 14, no. 4 (December 1918): 272–82.

Evans, Elwood. *The Re-Annexation of British Columbia to the United States: Right, Proper and Desirable*. Address delivered by the Hon. Elwood Evans before the Tacoma Library Association, Olympia, W.T., Jan. 18, 1870. Reprint. Victoria, B.C.: Morriss Printing Co., 1965.

Farb, Peter. *Man's Rise to Civilization: The Cultural Ascent of the Indians of North America*. 2nd rev. ed. New York: E.P. Dutton, 1968.

Fidler, Peter. *Notebook, 1794–1813*. Photostat copy of manuscript from the British Museum, London, [n.d.]. From the papers of J.B. Tyrrell at Robarts Library, Toronto.

Finnie, Richard. "Trading into the North-west Passage." [Re Scotty Gall's west-to-east transit of North West Passage.] *The Beaver*, December 1937: 46–53.

Fisher, Robin A. "Arms and Men on the Northwest Coast." *B.C. Studies*, 29 (Spring 1976): 29ff.

Fitzharris, Tim. *The Island: A Natural History of Vancouver Island*. Toronto: Oxford University Press, 1983.

Flanagan, Thomas. *Riel and the Rebellion: 1885 Reconsidered*. Saskatoon: Western Producer Prairie Books, 1983.

——— , ed. *The Diaries of Louis Riel*. Edmonton: Hurtig Publishers, 1976.

Fleming, R. Harvey, ed. *Minutes of Council, Northern Department of Rupert Land, 1821-31*. General editor, E.E. Rich. Introduction by H.A. Innis. HBRS, Vol. 3. Toronto: Champlain Society for the Hudson's Bay Record Society, 1940.

Foster, J.E. "The Métis: The People and the Term." *Prairie Forum*, 3, no.1 (Spring 1978): 79-90.

Fountain, Paul. *The Great North-West and the Great Lake Region of North America*. London: Longmans, Green, and Co., 1904.

Francis, Daniel. *Battle for the West: Fur Traders and the Birth of Western Canada*. Edmonton: Hurtig Publishers, 1982.

——— . *Discovery of the North: The Exploration of Canada's Arctic*. Edmonton: Hurtig Publishers, 1986.

Francis, Daniel, and Toby Mortantz. *Partners in Furs: A History of the Fur Trade in Eastern James Bay, 1600-1870*. Kingston and Montreal: McGill-Queen's University Press, 1983.

Francis, R. Douglas, and Howard Palmer, eds. *The Prairie West: Historical Readings*. Edmonton: University of Alberta Press, Pica Pica Press, 1985.

Fraser, Simon. *The Letters and Journals of Simon Fraser*: see entry under Lamb, W. Kaye.

French, C.H. "'Uplands,' the Ancient H.B.C. Farm on Vancouver Island." *The Beaver*, January 1921: 5.

Freuchen, Peter. *It's All Adventure*. Garden City, N.Y.: Halcyon House, 1941.

Fridley, Russell, ed. *Aspects of the Fur Trade: Selected Papers of the 1965 North American Fur Trade Conference*. St Paul, Minn.: Minnesota Historical Society, 1967.

Friesen, Gerald. *The Canadian Prairies: A History*. Toronto: University of Toronto Press, 1984.

Friesen, J., and H.K. Ralston, eds. *Historical Essays on British Columbia*. Institute of Canadian Studies, Carleton University, Ottawa. Carleton Library No. 96. Toronto: McClelland and Stewart, 1976.

Fulford, Roger. *Glyn's, 1753-1953*. London: Macmillan & Co., 1953.

Galbraith, John S. *The Hudson's Bay Company as an Imperial Factor 1821-69*. Berkeley and Los Angeles: University of California Press, 1957.

——— . *The Little Emperor: Governor Simpson of the Hudson's Bay Company*. Toronto: Macmillan of Canada, 1976.

——— . "Conflict on Puget Sound." *The Beaver*, March 1951: 18-22.

——— . "The Enigma of Sir George Simpson." *The Beaver*, Spring 1976: 4-9.

——— . "George N. Sanders, 'Influence Man' for the Hudson's Bay Company." *Oregon Historical Quarterly*, 53, no. 3 (Sept. 1952): 159-76.

——— . "The Hudson's Bay Company under Fire, 1847-1862." *Canadian Historical Review*, 30, no. 4 (December 1949): 322-35.

——— . "The Hudson's Bay Land Controversy, 1863-1869." *Mississippi Valley Historical Review*, 36, no.3 (Dec.1949): 457-78.

——— . "John Edward Fitzgerald versus the Hudson's Bay

Company: The Founding of Vancouver Island." *British Columbia Historical Quarterly*, 16, no. 3–4 (Sept., Oct. 1952): 191–207.

——— . "Land Policies of the Hudson's Bay Company, 1870–1913." *Canadian Historical Review*, 32, no.1 (March 1951): 1–21.

——— . "The Little Emperor." *The Beaver*, Winter 1960: 22–28.

Gall, E.J.(Scotty). "Travelling in the Old Days." *Moccasin Telegraph*, Commemorative Issue, 30, no. 1 (Winter 1970): 40–41.

——— , as related to A. Dudley Copland. "Wreck of the 'Emma Jane.' " *The Beaver*, Summer 1970: 52–55.

Garry, Nicholas. *The Diary of Nicholas Garry, Deputy-Governor of the Hudson's Bay Company: a detailed narrative of his travels in the Northwest Territories of British North America in 1821.* Originally composed, edited and annotated from his grandfather's original manuscript by Francis N.A. Garry,1900. Edited for this edition with added material by W.J. Noxon. Toronto: Canadiana House, 1973.

Gates, Charles M., ed. *Five Fur Traders of the Northwest.* Introduction by Grace Lee Nute. Foreword by Theodore C. Blegen. St Paul, Minn.: Minnesota Historical Society, 1965.

Giffen, Naomi Musmaker. *The Roles of Men and Women in Eskimo Culture.* Chicago: University of Chicago Press, 1930.

Gilman, Rhoda R., Carolyn Gilman and Deborah M. Stultz. *The Red River Trails: Oxcart Routes between St Paul and the Selkirk Settlement, 1820–1870.* St Paul, Minn.: Minnesota Historical Society, 1979.

Gingras, Larry. *Medals, Tokens and Paper Money of the Hudson's Bay Company.* [n.p.]: Canadian Numismatic Research Society, 1975.

Glazebrook, G. de T. "A document concerning the union of the Hudson's Bay Company and the North West Company." *Canadian Historical Review*, 14 (1933): 183–88.

Glover, Richard, ed. *David Thompson's Narrative 1784–1812:* see entry under Thompson, David.

——— . "The difficulties of the Hudson's Bay Company's penetration of the west." *Canadian Historical Review*, 29 (1948): 240–54.

Gluek, Alvin C. *Minnesota and the Manifest Destiny of the Canadian Northwest: A Study in Canadian-American Relations.* Toronto: University of Toronto Press, 1965.

——— . "Imperial Protection for the Trading Interests of the Hudson's Bay Company." *Canadian Historical Review*, 37 (1956): 119–40.

Godsell, Philip H. *Arctic Trader: The Account of Twenty Years with the Hudson's Bay Company.* New York: G.P. Putnam's Sons, 1932.

Goldring, Philip. "Governor Simpson's Officers: Elite Recruitment in a British Overseas Enterprise, 1834–1870." *Prairie Forum*, reprinted from *Journal of the Canadian Plains Research Center*, 10, no. 2 (Fall 1985).

——— . "Labour Records of the Hudson's Bay Company, 1821–1870." *Archivaria*, 11 (Winter 1980–81): 53–86.

Goossen, N. Jaye. "The Relationship of the Church Missionary Society and the Hudson's Bay Company in Rupert's Land, 1821 to 1860, with a case study of Stanley Mission under the direction of the Rev. Robert Hunt." Master's thesis, University of Manitoba, 1974.

Gough, Barry M. *Gunboat Frontier: British Maritime Authority and Northwest Coast Indians, 1846–90*. Vancouver: University of British Columbia Press, 1984.

——— . "British Policy in the San Juan Boundary Dispute, 1854–72." *Pacific Northwest Quarterly*, April 1971: 59–68.

——— . "Canada's 'Adventure to China,' 1784–1821." *Canadian Geographical Journal*, Dec. 1976/Jan. 1977: 28.

——— . "Sir James Douglas As Seen by His Contemporaries: A Preliminary List." *B.C. Studies*, 44 (Winter 1979–80): 32–50.

——— . " 'Turbulent Frontiers' and British Expansion: Governor James Douglas, the Royal Navy, and the British Columbia Gold Rushes." *Pacific Historical Review*, 41, no. 1 (February 1972): 15–32.

Gray, John Morgan. *Lord Selkirk of Red River*. Toronto: Macmillan of Canada, 1963.

Great Plains Research Consultants. *Fort St. James: Costuming and Animation*. Parks Canada, Microfiche Report Series 85, 1983.

Guemple, Lee. *Alliance in Eskimo Society*. Proceedings of the American Ethnological Society, 1971, Supplement. Seattle: University of Washington Press, 1972.

Hannon, Leslie F. *Redcoats and Loyalists, 1760/1815*. Canada's Illustrated Heritage. Toronto: McClelland and Stewart, 1978.

Harding, Chris. "Bucking the Ice-Floes in Late Summer Trip from York to Severn." *The Beaver*, October 1920:16–17.

——— . "The Monetary System of the Far Fur Country." *The Beaver*, June 1921: 2–4.

Harmon, Daniel Williams. *A Journal of Voyages and Travels in the Interior of North America, between the 47th and 58th Degree of North Latitude. . .* Edited by Daniel Haskel. Andover, Vt., 1820. Reprint. American Explorers Series. New York: Allerton Book Co., 1922.

——— . *Sixteen Years in the Indian Country: The Journal of Daniel Williams Harmon*. W. Kaye Lamb, ed. Toronto: Macmillan of Canada, 1957.

Harper-Fender, Ann. "A Transaction-Cost Analysis of the Hudson's Bay Company." Paper delivered at the Fifth North American Fur Trade Conference, Montreal, 1985.

Harvey, Sanford Stephen. "The Part Played by the Hudson's Bay Company in Western Canadian Education, 1821–1869." Master's thesis, University of Manitoba, 1955.

Henderson, Anne Matheson. *Kildonan on the Red*. Winnipeg: Lord Selkirk Association of Rupert's Land, [n.d.].

Henry, Alexander [the Elder]. *Travels and Adventures in Canada and the Indian Territories between the Years 1760 and 1776*. New York. 1809. Ann Arbor, Mich.: University Microfilms, Inc., 1966. Reprint. Edmonton: Hurtig Publishers, 1969.

Henry, Alexander [the Younger]. *Journals*: see entry under Coues, Elliott, ed., *New Light on the Early History of the Greater Northwest. . .*

Hildebrandt, Walter. *The Battle of Batoche: British Small Warfare and the Entrenched Métis*. Studies in Archeology, Architecture and History, National Historic Parks and Sites Branch, Parks Canada. Ottawa: Environment Canada, 1985.

Hind, Henry Youle. *Narrative of the Canadian Red River Exploring Expedi-*

tion of 1857 and of the Assiniboine and Saskatchewan Exploring Expedition of 1858. London,1860, 2 vols. Reprint. Edmonton: M.G. Hurtig Ltd., 1971.

——— ."Red River Settlement and the Half-Breed Buffalo Hunters." Canadian Merchants Magazine and Commercial Review, 3 (1858): 9–17.

Holbrook, Stewart H. The Columbia. Rivers of America series, Carl Carmer, ed. New York: Rinehart and Co., 1956.

Holman, Frederick V. "Some Important Results from the Expeditions of John Jacob Astor to, and from, the Oregon Country." Oregon Historical Quarterly, 12 (1911): 206–19.

Holmgren, Eric J. "Fort Dunvegan and the Fur Trade on the Upper Peace River." In Thomas C. Buckley, ed., Rendezvous: Selected Papers of the Fourth North American Fur Trade Conference, 1981. St Paul, Minn.: North American Fur Trade Conference, 1984.

Homick, Teresa M. A Social History of Fort St. James, 1896. Parks Canada, Microfiche Report Series 144, 1984.

Honigmann, John J. Ethnography and Acculturation of the Fort Nelson Slave. Yale University Publications in Anthropology, no. 33. New Haven: Yale University Press, 1946.

Hornaday, William T. The Extermination of the American Bison. Smithsonian Institution, Report of the National Museum, 1886–87, pp. 369–548. Washington: Government Printing Office, 1889.

Houston, C. Stuart, ed. To the Arctic by Canoe, 1819–1821: The Journals and Paintings of Robert Hood, Midshipman with Franklin. Arctic Institute of North America. Montreal: McGill–Queen's University Press, 1974.

Howard, Joseph. Strange Empire: Louis Riel and the Métis People. Introduction by Martin Robin. Orig. publ. New York: William Morrow & Co., 1952, as Strange Empire; A Narrative of the Northwest. Reprint. Toronto: James Lewis and Samuel, 1974.

Hudson's Bay Company. "Sir George Simpson Centennial Celebration, Fort St. James, 17th September, 1928; Unveiling of Tablet, Simpson Pass on the High Road from Banff to Windermere, B.C., 20th September, 1929." Pamphlet.

——— . "Souvenir of the 250th Anniversary Dinner to the London Staff, Prince's Hotel, St. James's, 3 May 1920." Pamphlet, [n.p., n.d.].

Hughes, Ken. "Boundless Horizon: Line or Curve." Newest Review, 9, no. 5 (January 1984): 3–6.

Hunter, Archie. Northern Traders: Caribou Hair in the Stew. Victoria, B.C.: Sono Nis Press, 1983.

Hutchison, Bruce. The Fraser. Rivers of America series. Toronto: Clarke, Irwin, 1950.

——— . "When a Canadian Ruled Oregon." Struggle for the Border, Part 5. Maclean's, 30 April 1955: 24, 52–58.

Ignatieff, Nicholas. "The Influence of the Fur Trade of the Pacific North West on Anglo-Russian Negotiations Proceeding from the Ukase of 1821 to the Treaty of 1825." Master's thesis, University of Manitoba, 1963.

Illerbrun, W.J. "A Selective Survey of Canadian-Hawaiian Relations." Pacific Northwest Quarterly, 63, no. 3 (July 1972).

Inglis, Richard I., and James C. Haggarty. "Cook to Jewitt: Three Decades of Change in Nootka Sound." Paper delivered at the Fifth North American Fur Trade Conference, Montreal, 1985.

Innis, Harold A. The Fur Trade in Canada: An Introduction to Canadian Economic History. New Haven: Yale University Press, 1930.

——— . *Peter Pond, Fur Trader and Adventurer*. Toronto: Irwin & Gordon Ltd., 1930.

Irving, Washington. *Astoria*. Philadelphia,1836. Reprint. Portland, Ore.: Binfords & Mort, 1967.

Jardine, Matheson. *Jardine, Matheson & Company: An Historical Sketch*. Privately published. Hong Kong: Jardine, Matheson & Co. Ltd., [n.d.].

Jenness, Diamond. *The Indians of Canada*. 7th ed. Toronto: University of Toronto Press, 1977.

Jessett, Thomas E., ed. *Reports and Letters of Herbert Beaver, 1836-1838: Chaplain to the Hudson's Bay Company and Missionary to the Indians at Fort Vancouver*. Portland, Ore.: Champoeg Press, 1959.

Johansen, Dorothy O. "Ogden's Snake Country Journals." *The Beaver*, September 1951: 46-47.

Johnson, Alice M., ed. *Saskatchewan Journals and Correspondence: Edmonton House, 1795-1800; Chesterfield House, 1800-1802*.HBRS, Vol. 26. London: Hudson's Bay Record Society, 1967.

——— . "Simpson in Russia." *The Beaver*, Autumn 1960: 4-12.

——— . "System and Regularity." *The Beaver*, Summer 1960: 36-39.

Judd, Carol M., and Arthur J. Ray, eds. *Old Trails and New Directions: Papers of the Third North American Fur Trade Conference, 1978*. Toronto: University of Toronto Press, 1980.

Judson, Katherine B. "The British Side of the Restoration of Fort Astoria." *Oregon Historical Quarterly*, 20 (1919): 243-60, 305-30.

Kane, Paul. *Wanderings of an Artist among the Indians of North America from Canada to Vancouver's Island and Oregon through the Hudson's Bay Company's Territory and Back Again*.

Orig. publ. 1859. Reprint. Edmonton: M.G. Hurtig Ltd., 1968.

Kavaler, Lucy. *The Astors: A Family Chronicle of Pomp and Power*. New York: Dodd, Mead & Co., 1966.

Karamanski, Theodore J. *Fur Trade and Exploration: Opening the Far Northwest, 1821-1852*. Vancouver: University of British Columbia Press, 1983.

Karklins, Karlis. *Nottingham House: The Hudson's Bay Company in Athabasca, 1802-1806*. History and Archeology series, no. 69. Ottawa: National Historic Parks and Sites Branch, Parks Canada, 1983.

Kaye, Barry. "Some Aspects of the Historical Geography of the Red River Settlement from 1812 to 1870." Master's thesis, University of Manitoba, 1967.

——— . "Origins of Wheeled Transport in Western Canada." *Great Plains Quarterly*, 4, no. 2 (Spring 1984): 121-34.

Kennedy, John. "The Squire Takes a Musk-Ox." *The Beaver*, Summer 1985: 20-29.

Kerr, D.G.G. *Sir Edmund Head: A Scholarly Governor*. Toronto: University of Toronto Press, 1954.

Keswick, Maggie. *The Thistle and the Jade: A Celebration of 150 Years of Jardine, Matheson & Co*. London: Octopus Books, 1982.

Kilbourn, William. *The Making of the Nation: A Century of Challenge*. Illustrated Canadian Library. First ed., Canadian Centennial Publishing Co. Ltd., 1965. Rev. ed. Toronto: McClelland and Stewart, 1973.

Klaus, J.F. "Early Trails to Carlton House." *The Beaver*, October 1985: 32-38.

Klimko, Olga. *Pastlog No. 5: The Archeology and History of Fort Pelly 1, 1824-1856*. Regina: Saskatchewan Culture and Recreation, 1983.

Krech, Shepard, III, ed. *The Subarctic Fur Trade: Native Social and Economic Adaptations*. Vancouver: University of British Columbia Press, 1984.

——— . "The Early Fur Trade in the Northwestern Subarctic: The Kutchin and the Trade in Beads." Paper delivered at the Fifth North American Fur Trade Conference, Montreal, 1985.

Lamb, W. Kaye, ed. *The Journals and Letters of Sir Alexander Mackenzie*: see entry under Mackenzie, Alexander.

——— , ed. *The Letters and Journals of Simon Fraser 1806–1808*. Toronto: Macmillan of Canada, 1960.

——— , ed. *Sixteen years. . . .*: see entry under Harmon, Daniel Williams.

——— . "S.S. *Beaver*: Vice-regal Yacht of 1858." *The Beaver*, Winter 1958: 10–17.

Laut, Agnes C. *The Conquest of the Great Northwest*. New York: George H. Doran, 1918.

Lavender, David. *The Fist in the Wilderness*. Garden City, N.Y.: Doubleday & Co., 1964.

——— . *Land of Giants: The Drive to the Pacific Northwest 1750–1950*. Reprint. Lincoln, Neb. University of Nebraska Press, Bison Books, 1979.

Lefroy, John Henry. *Letters:* see entry under Stanley, George F.G., ed., *John Henry Lefroy: In Search of the Magnetic North. . .*

Libby, David, and William Schneider. "Fur Trapping on Alaska's North Slope." Paper delivered at the Fifth North American Fur Trade Conference, Montreal, 1985.

Lillard, Charles. *Seven Shillings a Year: The History of Vancouver Island*. Ganges, B.C.: Horsdal & Schubart, 1986.

Lindsay, Debra. "The Hudson's Bay Company-Smithsonian Connection and Fur Trade Intellectual Life: Bernard Rogan Ross, a Case Study." Paper delivered at the Fifth North American Fur Trade Conference, Montreal, 1985.

Links, J.G. *The Book of Fur*. [n.p.]: James Barrie, 1956.

Lockyer, H.T. "The Rise of H.B.C. Vancouver Retail Establishment." *The Beaver*, December 1920: 20–22.

Longley, R.S. "Cartier and McDougall, Canadian Emissaries to London, 1868–9." *Canadian Historical Review*, 26, no. 1 (March 1945): 25–41.

Lower, J. Arthur. *Canada on the Pacific Rim*. Toronto: McGraw-Hill Ryerson, 1975.

MacAndrew, Craig, and Robert B. Edgerton. *Drunken Comportment: A Social Explanation*. Chicago: Aldine Press, 1969.

McCarty, Richard Frances. "Fort Assiniboine, Alberta, 1823–1914: Fur Trade Post to Settled District." Master's thesis, University of Alberta, 1976.

McCloy, T.R. "Fur-trade Biographies." *British Columbia Historical Quarterly*, July-October 1951: 203–12.

McDonald, Archibald. *Peace River: A Canoe Voyage from Hudson's Bay to Pacific, by Sir George Simpson; in 1828. (Journal of the late Chief Factor, Archibald McDonald, . . . who accompanied him.)* Orig. ed., Ottawa: J. Durie & Son, 1872. Edited and with notes by Malcolm McLeod. Reprint. Edmonton: M.G. Hurtig, 1971.

MacDonald, Janice E. *The Northwest Fort: Fort Edmonton*. Edmonton: Lone Pine Publishing, 1983.

MacDonald, Robert. *The Owners of Eden*. Calgary: Ballantrae Foundation, 1974.

MacEwan, Grant. *Fifty Mighty Men.* Saskatoon: Western Producer Prairie Books, 1975.

——— . *Marie Anne: The Frontier Adventures of Marie Anne Lagimodière.* Saskatoon: Western Producer Prairie Books, 1984.

MacGhee, Robert. "In the Land of the Plank Houses." *Canadian Heritage,* May-June 1984: 13–17.

McGillivray, Duncan. *The Journal of Duncan McGillivray of the North West Company at Fort George on the Saskatchewan, 1794–5.* Edited by A.S. Morton. Toronto: University of Toronto Press, 1929.

MacGregor, James G. *John Rowand: Czar of the Prairies.* Saskatoon: Western Producer Prairie Books, 1978.

——— . *The Land of Twelve-Foot Davis.* Edmonton: Institute of Applied Arts, 1952.

——— . *Peter Fidler: Canada's Forgotten Surveyor 1769–1822.* Toronto: McClelland and Stewart, 1966.

McHugh, Tom. *The Time of the Buffalo.* New York: Alfred A. Knopf, 1972.

MacKay, Corday. "Pacific Coast Fur Trade." *The Beaver,* Summer 1955: 38–42.

——— . "With Fraser to the Sea." *The Beaver,* December 1944: 3–7.

MacKay, Douglas. *The Honourable Company: A History of the Hudson's Bay Company.* 1936. Indianapolis and New York: Bobbs-Merrill, 1936. 2nd ed., revised to 1949 by Alice MacKay. Toronto: McClelland and Stewart, 1949.

——— . "The HBC Packet." *The Beaver,* September 1934: 8.

——— . "Men of the Old Fur Trade." *The Beaver,* June 1937: 7–9.

McKelvie, B.A. "Coal for the Warship." *The Beaver,* June 1951: 8–11.

——— . "Successor to Simpson." *The Beaver,* Sept. 1951: 41–45.

MacKenzie, A.E.D. "Baldoon." *The Beaver,* Autumn 1972: 48–51.

Mackenzie, Alexander. *The Journals and Letters of Sir Alexander Mackenzie.* W. Kaye Lamb, ed. Hakluyt Society, Extra Series No. 41. Cambridge: Cambridge University Press, 1970.

——— . *Voyages from Montreal, on the River St. Laurence, through the Continent of North America, to the Frozen and Pacific Oceans; in the Years, 1789 and 1793. With a Preliminary Account of the Rise, Progress, and Present State of the Fur Trade of That Country.* London, 1801. Reprint. Edmonton: M.G. Hurtig, 1971.

Mackie, J.D. *A History of Scotland.* Revised ed. by Bruce Lenman and Geoffrey Parker. London: Allen Lane, Penguin Books Ltd., 1978.

Mackinnon, C.S. "Some Logistics of Portage La Loche (Methy)." *Prairie Forum,* 5, no. 1 (1980): 51–65.

MacLaren, Roy. *Canadians on the Nile, 1882–1898: Being the Adventures of the Voyageurs on the Khartoum Relief Expedition and Other Exploits.* Vancouver: University of British Columbia Press, 1978.

McLaughlin, Merlyn. "Imperial Aspects of the North West Company in Western Canada to 1870." Ph.D. dissertation, University of Colorado, 1951.

McLean, Don. *1885: Métis Rebellion or Government Conspiracy?* Gabriel Dumont Institute of Native Studies and Applied Research. Winnipeg: Pemmican Publications, 1985.

——— . *A Research Resource Book of Native History.* Regina: Gabriel Dumont Institute of Native Studies and Applied Research, 1981.

McLean, John. *John McLean's Notes of a Twenty-Five Years' Service in the*

Hudson's Bay Territory. W. Stewart Wallace, ed. Champlain Society, Vol. 19. Toronto: The Champlain Society, 1932.

MacLennan, Hugh. *The Rivers of Canada.* Toronto: Macmillan of Canada, 1974.

MacLeod, Margaret Arnett. "The Riddle of the Paintings." *The Beaver,* December 1948: 7–11.

MacLeod, Margaret Arnett, and W.L. Morton. *Cuthbert Grant of Grantown: Warden of the Plains of Red River.* New introduction by W.L. Morton. Carleton Library No. 71. Toronto: McClelland and Stewart, 1974.

McLoughlin, John. *The Letters of John McLoughlin from Fort Vancouver to the Governor and Committee.* First Series, 1825–38 (HBRS, Vol. 5). Second Series, 1839–44 (HBRS, Vol. 6). Third Series, 1844–46 (HBRS, Vol. 7). Edited by E.E. Rich, with introductions by W. Kaye Lamb. London: The Champlain Society for the Hudson's Bay Record Society, 1941, 1943 and 1944.

McMillan, George Cameron. "The Struggle of the Fur Companies in the Red River Region, 1811–1821." Master's thesis, University of Manitoba, 1955.

Macnaughton, John. *Lord Strathcona.* Makers of Canada Series. London: Oxford University Press, 1926.

McNeil, Kent. *Native Rights and the Boundaries of Rupert's Land and the North-Western Territory.* Studies in Aboriginal Rights No. 4. Saskatoon: University of Saskatchewan, 1982.

Maloney, Alice Bay. "California Rendezvous." *The Beaver,* December 1944: 32–37.

Martig, Ralph Richard. "The Hudson's Bay Company Claims 1846–1869." Ph.D. thesis, University of Illinois, 1934.

Masson, L.F.R. *Les Bourgeois de la Compagnie du Nord-Ouest, Récits de voyages, lettres et rapports inédits relatifs au Nord-Ouest canadien.* 2 vols. Quebec, 1889, 1890.

Mazour, A.G. "The Russian American and Anglo-Russian Conventions 1824–25: An Interpretation." *Pacific Historical Review,* 14 (1945): 303ff.

Meilleur, Helen. *A Pour of Rain: Stories from a West Coast Fort.* Victoria, B.C.: Sono Nis Press, 1980.

Merk, Frederick, ed. *Fur Trade and Empire: George Simpson's Journal Entitled Remarks Connected with the Fur Trade in the Course of a Voyage from York Factory to Fort George and Back to York Factory 1824/25.* Introduction by Frederick Merk. Orig. ed., Cambridge, Mass.: Harvard Historical Studies, 1931. Revised ed. Cambridge, Mass.: Harvard University Press, Belknap Press, 1968.

Millard, Peggy. "Company Wife." *The Beaver,* Spring 1985: 30–39.

Miquelon, Dale. "A Brief History of Lower Fort Garry." *In Canadian Historic Sites: Occasional Papers in Archeology and History, No. 4:* 1–41. National Historic Sites Service, National and Historic Parks Branch, Department of Indian Affairs and Northern Development. Ottawa: Queen's Printer, 1970.

Mitchell, Elaine Allen. "Edward Watkin and the Buying-Out of the Hudson's Bay Company." *Canadian Historical Review,* 34, no. 3 (September 1953): 219–44.

——— . "A Red River Gossip." *The Beaver,* Spring 1961: 4–11.

——— . "Sir George Simpson: 'The Man of Feeling.' " In Malvina Bolus, ed., *People and Pelts: Papers of the Second North American Fur Trade Conference, Winnipeg, 1970:* 98–99.

Winnipeg: North American Fur Trade Conference, 1972.

Moccasin Telegraph, 30, no. 1 (Winter 1970). Commemorative issue, HBC 300th Anniversary.

Montgomery, Franz. "Notes and Documents: Alexander Mackenzie's Literary Assistant." *Canadian Historical Review*, 18 (September 1937): 301-3.

Morgan, Dale L.,et al. *Aspects of the Fur Trade: Selected Papers of the [First] North American Fur Trade Conference, St. Paul, Minn., 1965*. St Paul, Minn.: Minnesota Historical Society, 1967.

Morgan, Lewis Henry. *The Indian Journals, 1859-62*. Edited with an introduction by Leslie A. White. Ann Arbor: University of Michigan Press, 1959.

Morice, Adrien Gabriel. *History of the Northern Interior of British Columbia, formerly New Caledonia (1660-1880)*. Toronto: William Briggs, 1904.

Morris, James (Jan). *Heaven's Command: An Imperial Progress*. London: Faber and Faber, 1973.

——— .*Farewell the Trumpets: An Imperial Retreat*. London: Penguin Books, 1978.

Morrison, Dorothy Nafus. *The Eagle & The Fort: The Story of John McLoughlin*. New York, 1979. 2nd ed. Portland, Ore.: The Press of the Oregon Historical Society, Western Imprints, 1984.

Morrison, Jean, ed. "Famous Personalities of the North West Company." Educational Resource Kits compilation. Thunder Bay, Ont.: Old Fort William, 1981.

Morse, Eric W. *Fur Trade Canoe Routes of Canada/Then and Now*. Department of Indian Affairs and Northern Development, National and Historic Parks Branch. Ottawa: Queen's Printer, 1969.

Morton, Anne. "Charles Elton and the Hudson's Bay Company." *The Beaver*, Spring 1985: 22-29.

Morton, Arthur S. *A History of the Canadian West to 1870-71*. London, 1939. 2nd ed. Edited by Lewis G. Thomas. Toronto: University of Toronto Press, 1973.

——— . *Sir George Simpson: Overseas Governor of the Hudson's Bay Company*. Toronto: J.M. Dent & Sons (Canada), 1944.

——— , ed. *The Journal of Duncan M'Gillivray. . .*: see entry under McGillivray, Duncan.

——— . "Did Duncan McGillivray and David Thompson Cross the Rockies in 1801?" *Canadian Historical Review*, 18 (March 1937): 12-27.

——— . "The Place of the Red River Settlement in the Plans of the Hudson's Bay Co., 1812-1825." Canadian Historical Association, *Annual Report*, 1929: 103-9.

Morton, W.L. *Manitoba: A History*. 2nd ed. Toronto: University of Toronto Press, 1967.

——— , ed. *Alexander Begg's Red River Journal. . .*: see entry under Begg, Alexander.

——— . "The Canadian Métis." *The Beaver*, September 1950: 3-7.

Myers, Gustavus. *A History of Canadian Wealth*. Vol. 1. Orig. publ. 1914. Reprint. Introduction by Stanley Ryerson. Toronto: James Lewis & Samuel, 1972.

Nanuwan of Chiboogama. "Solomon Voyageur." *The Beaver*, March 1929: 162.

Newcombe, C.F. *The First Circumnavigation of Vancouver Island*. Archives of British Columbia, Memoir No. 1. Victoria, B.C.: King's Printer, 1914.

Newman, Peter C. *Company of Adventurers*. Toronto: Viking, 1985.

Nicks, Trudy. "Native Responses to the Early Fur Trade at Lesser Slave Lake." Paper delivered at the Fifth North American Fur Trade Conference, Montreal, 1985.

Norcross, E. Blanche. *The Company on the Coast*. Nanaimo, B.C.: Nanaimo Historical Society, 1983.

North, Robert Carver. *Bob North*. New York: G.P. Putnam's Sons, 1929.

Nute, Grace Lee. *The Voyageur*. Orig. ed., 1931. Reprint. St Paul, Minn.: Minnesota Historical Society, 1955.

——— . *The Voyageur's Highway: Minnesota's Border Lake Land*. St Paul, Minn.: Minnesota Historical Society, 1951.

——— , ed. *Documents Relating to Northwest Missions, 1815–1827*. St Paul, Minn.: Minnesota Historical Society, 1942.

——— . "Jehu of the Waterways." *The Beaver*, Summer 1960: 15–19.

——— . "Simpson as Banker." *The Beaver*, Spring 1956: 51–52.

——— , ed. "Journey for Frances." *The Beaver*, December 1953: 51–54; March 1954: 12–17; June 1954: 12–18.

Ogden, Peter Skene. *Peter Skene Ogden's Snake Country Journals*. Vol. 1, 1824–25 and 1825–26, edited by E.E. Rich (HBRS, Vol. 13). Vol. 2, 1826–27, edited by K.G. Davies (HBRS, Vol. 23). Vol. 3, 1827–28 and 1828–29, edited by Glyndwr Williams (HBRS, Vol. 28). London: Hudson's Bay Record Society, 1950, 1961 and 1971.

Oleson, Robert Valdimar. "The Commissioned Officers of the Hudson's Bay Company and the Deed Poll in the 1870s, with particular emphasis on the Fur Trade Party, 1878–1879." Master's thesis, University of Manitoba, 1977.

Oleson, Sigurd F. *Reflections from the North Country*. New York: Alfred A. Knopf, 1976.

O'Meara, Walter. *The Last Portage*. Boston: Houghton Mifflin Co., 1962.

——— . *The Savage Country*. Boston: Houghton Mifflin Co., 1960.

Ormsby, Margaret A. *British Columbia: A History*. Toronto: Macmillan of Canada, 1958.

Ostenstad, W.L. "A Lucrative Contract: The HBC and the Pacific Ice Trade." *The Beaver*, Winter 1977: 36–40.

Pannekoek, Frits. "The Historiography of the Red River Settlement 1830–1868." *Prairie Forum*, 6, no.1 (1981): 75.

Parks Canada. *Wild Rivers: Saskatchewan*. Parks Canada, Department of Indian and Northern Affairs. Ottawa: Queen's Printer, [n.d.].

Parnell, C. "Ballantyne the Brave." *The Beaver*, December 1941: 4–6.

Patterson, R.M. *The Dangerous River*. Sidney, B.C.: Gray's Publishing Ltd., 1966.

Paul, E.K. "H.B.C. and Vancouver Island." *The Beaver*, September 1923: 441–45.

Pedley, Rev. J.W. *Biography of Lord Strathcona and Mount Royal*. Toronto: J.L. Nichols, 1915.

Pendergast, Russell Anthony. "The XY Company 1798 to 1804." Ph.D. dissertation, University of Ottawa, 1957.

Peterson, Jacqueline, with John Anfinson. "The Indian and the Fur Trade: A Review of Recent Literature." *Manitoba History*, 10 (Autumn 1985): 10–18.

Peterson, Jacqueline, and Jennifer S.H. Brown. *The New Peoples: Being and Becoming Métis in North America*. Manitoba Studies in Native

History, no.1. Winnipeg: University of Manitoba Press, 1985.

Pethick, Derek. *James Douglas: Servant of Two Empires*. Vancouver: Mitchell Press, 1969.

Phillips, Basil Harry. "Lord Selkirk, Colonizer-Idealizer." Master's thesis, Acadia University, 1962.

Phillips, Paul Chrisler. *The Fur Trade*. Vol. 2. Norman, Okla.: University of Oklahoma Press, 1961.

Phillips, R.A.J. *Canada's North*. Toronto: Macmillan of Canada, 1967.

Pinkerton, Robert E. *The Gentlemen Adventurers*. Toronto: McClelland and Stewart, 1931.

Pitseolak, Peter, and Dorothy Eber. *People from Our Side*. Edmonton: Hurtig Publishers, 1975.

Prebble, John. *The Highland Clearances*. New York: Penguin Books, 1967.

Pritchett, John Perry. *The Red River Valley 1811–1949, A Regional Study*. New Haven: Yale University Press, 1942.

Rasky, Frank. *The Taming of the Canadian West*. Toronto: McClelland and Stewart, 1967.

Rawlinson, H.E. "The Portrait of Chief Factor John Rowand." *The Beaver*, Summer 1962: 36ff.

Ray, Arthur J. *Indians in the Fur Trade: Their Role as Trappers, Hunters, and Middlemen in the Lands Southwest of Hudson Bay, 1660–1870*. Toronto: University of Toronto Press, 1974.

——— . "The Northern Great Plains: Pantry of the Northwestern Fur Trade, 1774–1885." *Prairie Forum*, 9, no. 2 (1984): 263–80.

Redekop, Linda, and Wilfred Gilchrist. *Strathcona County: A Brief History*. [Edmonton]: W. Gilchrist, 1981.

Reed, Charles Bert. *Masters of the Wilderness*. Fort Dearborn Series, Chicago Historical Society.

Chicago: University of Chicago Press, 1914.

Reid, W. Stanford. *The Scottish Tradition in Canada*. Toronto: McClelland and Stewart, 1976.

Reksten, Terry. *"More English Than the English": A Very Social History of Victoria*. Victoria, B.C.: Orca Book Publishers, 1986.

Rich, E.E. *The Fur Trade and the Northwest to 1857*. The Canadian Centenary Series. Toronto: McClelland and Stewart, 1967.

——— . *History of the Hudson's Bay Company, 1670–1870*. Vol. 1, 1670–1763 (HBRS, Vol. 21); Vol. 2, 1763–1870 (HBRS, Vol. 22). London: Hudson's Bay Record Society, 1958, 1959.

——— . *Hudson's Bay Company, 1670–1870*. Vol. 1: 1670–1763; Vol. 2: 1763–1820; Vol. 3: 1821–1870. Toronto: McClelland and Stewart, 1960.

——— , ed. *Colin Robertson's Correspondence Book, September 1817 to September 1822*. HBRS, Vol. 2. London: Champlain Society for the Hudson's Bay Record Society, 1939.

——— , ed. *Journal of Occurrences in the Athabasca Department. . .*: see entry under Simpson, George.

——— , ed. *A Journal of a Voyage from Rocky Mountain Portage. . .*: see entry under Black, Samuel.

——— , ed. *The Letters of John McLoughlin*: see entry under McLoughlin, John.

——— , ed. *London Correspondence Inward from Eden Colvile, 1849–1852*. Introduction by W.L. Morton. HBRS, Vol. 19. London: Hudson's Bay Record Society, 1956.

——— , ed. *Part of Dispatch from George Simpson, Esq., Governor of Ruperts Land . . .*: see entry under Simpson, George.

—— , ed. *Snake Country Journals. . .*: see entry under Ogden, Peter Skene.

Roberts, Leslie. *The Mackenzie*. Rivers of America Series. Toronto: Rinehart & Co., 1949.

Robertson, Arthur. "Journey to the Far North, Summer 1887." Part 1: *The Beaver*, Spring 1985: 10-21. Part 2: *The Beaver*, Summer 1985: 45-55. Part 3: *The Beaver*, Autumn 1985: 34-42.

Robertson, Colin. *Letters 1817-22*: see entry under Rich, E.E., ed., *Colin Robertson's Correspondence Book. . .*

Robin, Martin. *The Rush for Spoils: The Company Province, 1871-1933*. Toronto: McClelland and Stewart, 1972.

Roe, Frank Gilbert. *The Indian and the Horse*. Norman, Okla.: University of Oklahoma Press, 1955.

—— . *The North American Buffalo: A Critical Study of the Species in its Wild State*. Toronto: University of Toronto Press, 1951.

Rohner, R.P., and E.C. Rohner. *The Kwakiutl Indians of British Columbia*. New York: Holt, Rinehart and Winston, 1970.

Ross, Alexander. *The Fur Hunters of the Far West*. London, 1855. New ed. Edited by Kenneth A. Spaulding. Norman, Okla.: University of Oklahoma Press, 1956.

—— . *The Red River Settlement, its Rise, Progress and Present State, with Some Account of the Native Races and its General History to the Present Day*. London, 1856. Reprint. Edmonton: Hurtig Publishers, 1972.

Ross, Eric. *Beyond the River and the Bay: Some Observations on the State of the Canadian Northwest in 1811 with a View to Providing the Intending Settler with an Intimate Knowledge of That Country*. Toronto: University of Toronto Press, 1970.

Ross, Frank E. "The Retreat of the Hudson's Bay Company in the Pacific Northwest." *Canadian Historical Review*, 18 (September 1937): 262-80.

Ross, Hugh Mackay. *The Apprentice's Tale*. Winnipeg: Watson & Dwyer Publishing, 1986.

Rostecki, Randy R. "Winnipeg Land Politics in the 1870s." *The Beaver*, Spring 1985: 42-48.

Ruggles, Richard I. "Mapping the Interior Plains of Rupert's Land by the Hudson's Bay Company to 1870." *Great Plains Quarterly*, 4, no. 3 (Summer 1984): 152-65.

Russell, R.C. *The Carlton Trail*. Saskatoon: Modern Press, 1955.

Sage, Walter N. *Sir James Douglas and British Columbia*. Univ. of Toronto Studies, History and Economics, 6, no. 1. Toronto: University of Toronto Press, 1930.

—— . "Sir James Douglas, K.C.B.: The Father of British Columbia." *British Columbia Historical Quarterly*, July 1947: 211-27.

Saskatchewan Department of Culture and Youth. *Fort Carlton Historic Park*. Historic Booklet No. 1. 2nd ed. Edited by Brenda J. Stead. Museums Branch, Museum of Natural History, Wascana Park, Regina, 1976.

Schilz, Thomas F. "Brandy and Beaver Pelts: Assiniboine-European Trading Patterns, 1695-1805." *Saskatchewan History*, 37, no.3 (Autumn 1984): 95-102.

Sealey, D. Bruce. *Cuthbert Grant and the Métis*. Agincourt, Ont.: Book Society of Canada, 1976.

Selkirk, 5th Earl of. *Lord Selkirk's Diary 1803-04*: see entry under Douglas, Thomas.

Selwood, H. John. "Mr. Brydges' Bridges." *The Beaver*, Summer 1981: 14-21.

——— . "Urban Development and the Hudson's Bay Company, 1870–1918." Paper delivered at the annual meeting of the Learned Societies, Winnipeg, 1986.

Selwood, H. John, and Evelyn Baril. "Land Policies of the Hudson's Bay Company at Upper Fort Garry: 1869–1879." *Prairie Forum*, 2, no. 2 (November 1977).

Seton, Ernest Thompson. *The Arctic Prairies*. New York: Charles Scribner's Sons, 1911.

Sheppe, Walter, ed. *First Man West: Alexander Mackenzie's Journal of His Voyage to the Pacific Coast of Canada in 1793*. Montreal: McGill University Press, 1962.

Simpson, George. *Journal. . . 1824/25.*: see entry under Merk, Frederick, ed., *Fur Trade and Empire. . .*

——— . *Journal of Occurrences in the Athabasca Department by George Simpson, 1820 and 1821, and Report.* Edited by E.E. Rich, with introduction by Chester Martin. The Champlain Society, Vol. 1. London: The Champlain Society for the Hudson's Bay Record Society, 1938.

——— . *London Correspondence Inward from Sir George Simpson, 1841–42.* Edited by Glyndwr Williams, with introduction by John S. Galbraith. HBRS, Vol. 29. London: Hudson's Bay Record Society, 1973.

——— . *Narrative of a Journey Around the World. . . 1841 and 1842.* 2 vols. London, 1847. Republished as *An overland journey round the world, during the years 1841 and 1842*, edited by Adam Thom and Archibald Barclay. Philadelphia, 1847.

——— . *Part of Dispatch from George Simpson, Esq., Governor of Ruperts Land, to the Governor & Committee of the Hudson's Bay Company, London, March 1, 1829. Continued and completed March 24 and June 5, 1829.*

[Also referred to as *Simpson's 1828 Journey to the Columbia.*] Edited by E.E. Rich, with introduction by W. Stewart Wallace. HBRS, Vol. 10. London: The Champlain Society for the Hudson's Bay Record Society, 1947.

——— . Re centennial celebration: see entry under Hudson's Bay Company.

——— . Re court case on sanity at deathbed: see entry under Superior Court, Montreal.

Sloan, W.A. "The Native Response to the Extension of the European Traders into the Athabasca and Mackenzie Basin, 1770–1814." *Canadian Historical Review*, 60 (1979): 281–99.

Smith, Arthur D. Howden. *John Jacob Astor: Landlord of New York*. New York: Blue Ribbon Books, 1929.

Smith, Dorothy Blakey. *James Douglas: Father of British Columbia*. Toronto: Oxford University Press, 1971.

Smith, James K. *Wilderness of Fortune*. Vancouver: Douglas & McIntyre, 1983.

Smith, Mary Larratt. *Prologue to Norman: The Canadian Bethunes*. Oakville, Ottawa: Valley Editions, Mosaic Press, 1976.

Snell, James G. "The Frontier Sweeps Northwest: American Perceptions of the British American Prairie West at the Point of Canadian Expansion (circa 1870)." *Western Historical Quarterly*, 11, no. 4 (October 1980): 381–416.

Somerset, H. Somers. *The Land of the Muskeg*. London: William Heinemann, 1895.

Spaulding, Kenneth A., ed. *The Fur Hunters of the Far West:* see entry under Ross, Alexander.

Speck, Gordon. *Northwest Explorations*. Edited by L.K. Phillips. Portland, Ore.: Binfords & Mort, 1954.

Sprenger, George Herman. "Coping with Competition: The Reorganization of the Hudson's Bay Company after the Monopoly." In *Proceedings of the Second Congress, Canadian Ethnology Society*. Jim Freedman and Jerome H. Barkow, eds. National Museum of Man Mercury Series, Canadian Ethnology Service, Paper no. 29, 1975.

——— . "The Métis Nation: Buffalo Hunting vs. Agriculture in the Red River Settlement (circa 1810–1870)." *Western Canadian Journal of Anthropology*, Special Issue: The Fur Trade in Canada, 2, no. 1 (1972): 158–78.

Stacey, C.P. "The Hudson's Bay Company and Anglo-American Military Rivalries during the Oregon Dispute." *Canadian Historical Review,* 18 (September 1937): 281–300.

Stanley, George F.G. *The Birth of Western Canada: A History of the Riel Rebellions.* Toronto: University of Toronto Press, 1961.

——— , ed. *John Henry Lefroy: In Search of the Magnetic North—A Soldier-Surveyor's Letters from the North-West, 1843–1844.* Toronto: Macmillan of Canada, 1955.

——— . "The Fur Trade Party." Part 1, "Storm Warnings," *The Beaver,* September 1953: 35–39. Part 2, "United We Stand. . .", *The Beaver,* December 1953: 21–25.

Stefansson, Vilhjalmur. *My Life with the Eskimo.* New York: Macmillan Co., 1913.

Stevenson, Alex. "The Beaver at Waikiki: The Hudson's Bay Company Operations in Hawaii." *North,* 25, no. 6 (November-December 1978): 48–51.

Stewart, Susan. "Sir George Simpson: Collector." *The Beaver,* Summer 1982: 4–9.

Stobie, Margaret R. "Backgrounds of the Dialect Called Bungi." *Historical & Scientific Society of Manitoba Transactions*, Series 3, no. 24 (1967–8): 65–77.

——— . "The Bremner Furs." *The Beaver,* Summer 1985: 36–44.

Superior Court, Montreal: Sir George Simpson's Case. The Rev. John Flanagan, Plaintiff, vs. Duncan Finlayson et al., Defendants. Mss. Case. Testimony reprinted in *American Journal of Insanity*, 19, no. 3, Utica, Vt., January 1863: 249–321.

Syms, E. Leigh, and Pamela Smith. "Unbuttoning the History of Fort Rivière Tremblante." *The Beaver,* Spring 1984: 26–30.

Tanner, Ogden. *The Canadians.* Old West series. Alexandria, Va.: Time-Life Books, 1977.

Tate, Merze. "Great Britain and the Sovereign of Hawaii." *British Columbia Historical Quarterly,* 31 (1962): 327–48.

Tessendorf, K.C. "George Simpson, Canoe Executive." *The Beaver,* Summer 1970: 39–41.

Thomas, Greg. "Dramatic Interpretation: 'The Foss-Pelly Scandal' at Lower Fort Garry." *Dawson and Hind Quarterly*, 11, no. 3 (Fall 1983): 26–33.

Thomas, Greg, and Ian Clarke. "The Garrison Mentality and the Canadian West—The British-Canadian Response to Two Landscapes: The Fur Trade Post and The Ontarian Prairie Homestead." *Prairie Forum*, 4, no. 1 (1979): 83ff.

Thomas, Lewis G. *The Prairie West to 1905: A Canadian Sourcebook.* Toronto: Oxford University Press, 1975.

Thompson, David. *David Thompson's Narrative, 1784–1812.* Edited by J.B. Tyrrell. Toronto, 1916. Edited and with introduction and notes by Richard Glover. Champlain Society, Vol. 40. Toronto: The Champlain Society, 1962.

——— . *New Light on the Early History. . .*: see entry under Coues, Elliott, ed.

Thrum, Thomas G. "History of the Hudson's Bay Company's Agency in Hawaii." *18th Annual Report* , Hawaii Historical Society,1910; read at the Spring Meeting, 25 May 1911. Honolulu, 1911.

Traver, Lillie A. "Early Negotiations for the Acquisition of the Hudson's Bay Territory by the Union Government of Canada." Master's thesis, McGill University, 1928.

Tuchman, Barbara W. *Practicing History: Selected Essays*. New York: Alfred A. Knopf, 1981.

Tulchinsky, Gerald J.J. *The River Barons: Montreal Businessmen and the Growth of Industry and Transportation, 1837–53*. Toronto: University of Toronto Press, 1977.

Turnor, Philip: see entry under Tyrrell, J.B., ed. *Journals of Samuel Hearne and Philip Turnor. . . .*

Tway, Duane C. "The Influence of the Hudson's Bay Company upon Canada, 1870–1889." Ph.D. dissertation, University of California at Los Angeles, 1963.

——— . "The Wintering Partners and the Hudson's Bay Company, 1863 to 1871." *Canadian Historical Review*, 33, no. 1 (March 1952): 50–63.

——— . "The Wintering Partners and the Hudson's Bay Company, 1867–1879." *Canadian Historical Review*, 41, no. 3 (September 1960): 215–23.

Tyrrell, J.B., ed. *Journals of Samuel Hearne and Philip Turnor between the Years 1774 and 1792*. Champlain Society, Vol. 21. Toronto: The Champlain Society, 1934.

——— . "David Thompson and the Columbia River." *Canadian Historical Review*, 18 (March 1937): 12–27.

——— . "David Thompson: Explorer." *Maclean's*, 21, no. 5 (March 1911): 64–75.

Usher, Peter J. *Fur Trade Posts of the Northwest Territories, 1870–1970*. Northern Science Research Group, Department of Indian Affairs and Northern Development. Ottawa: Queen's Printer, 1971.

Van Kirk, Sylvia. *"Many Tender Ties": Women in Fur-Trade Society in Western Canada, 1670–1870*. Winnipeg: Watson & Dwyer Publishing, 1981.

——— . "'The Reputation of a Lady': Sarah Ballenden and the Foss-Pelly Scandal." *Manitoba History*, no. 11 (Spring 1986): 4–11.

——— . "Women and the Fur Trade." *The Beaver*, Winter 1972: 4–21.

Van Stone, James W. *Athapaskan Adaptations: Hunters and Fishermen of the Subarctic Forests*. Chicago: Aldine Press, 1974.

Walbran, Capt. John T. *British Columbia Coast Names, 1592–1906*. Ottawa, 1909. 2nd reprint. Introduction by G.P.V. Akrigg. Vancouver: J.J. Douglas, 1971.

Waldo, Fullerton. *Down the Mackenzie through the Great Lone Land*. New York: Macmillan Co., 1923.

Wallace, W. Stewart. *The Pedlars from Quebec*. Toronto: Ryerson Press, 1954.

——— , ed. *Documents Relating to the North-West Company*. Champlain Society, Vol. 22. Toronto: The Champlain Society, 1934.

——— , ed. *John McLean's Notes of a Twenty-Five Years' Service in the Hudson's Bay Territory:* see entry under McLean, John.

Watson, Robert. "James Douglas and Fort Victoria." *The Beaver*, September 1931: 271–75.

West, John. *The Substance of a Journal during a Residence at the Red River Colony*. London, 1824. New York: Johnson Reprint, 1966.

Wheeler, Robert C. *A Toast to the Fur Trade: A Picture Essay on Its Material Culture*. Edited by Ardis Hillman Wheeler. St Paul, Minn.: Wheeler Productions, 1985.

White, Bruce M. "Montreal Canoes and their Cargoes." Paper delivered at the Fifth North American Fur Trade Conference, Montreal, 1985.

White, Patrick C.T., ed. *Lord Selkirk's Diary 1803–1804*: see entry under Douglas, Thomas, *Lord Selkirk's Diary*. . . .

Whymper, Frederick. *The Heroes of the Arctic*. London: Society for Promoting Christian Knowledge, 1875.

Williams, David R. *". . . The Man for a New Country": Sir Matthew Baillie Begbie*. Sidney, B.C.: Gray's Publishing, 1977.

Williams, Glyndwr, ed. *Hudson's Bay Miscellany, 1670–1870*. HBRS, Vol. 30. Winnipeg: Hudson's Bay Record Society, 1975.

——— , ed. *London Correspondence Inward from Sir George Simpson, 1841–42:* see entry under Simpson, Sir George.

——— , ed. *Peter Skene Ogden's Snake Country Journals,* Vol. 3: see entry under Ogden, Peter Skene.

——— . Articles in *The Beaver*, Commemorative Issue 1670–1970, publ. 1970.

——— . "Governor George Simpson's Character Book." *The Beaver*, Summer 1975: 4–18.

Willson, Beckles. *The Great Company, Being a History of the Honourable Company of Merchants-Adventurers Trading into Hudson's Bay*. Toronto: Copp, Clark Co., 1899.

Wilson, Clifford P. *Northern Treasury: Selections from The Beaver*. Toronto: Thomas Nelson & Sons, [n.d.].

——— . "The Beaver Club." *The Beaver*, March 1936: 19–24.

——— ."The Emperor at Lachine." *The Beaver*, September 1934: 18–22.

——— . "The Emperor's Last Days." *The Beaver*, December 1934: 49–51.

——— . "Sir George Simpson at Lachine." *The Beaver*, June 1934: 36–39.

Wolk, Jack. "The North West Company and the Hudson's Bay Company Forts: 1810 to 1830." *Manitoba Archeological Quarterly* , 6, no. 3 (July 1982): 26–45.

Wonders, William C., ed. *Canada's Changing North*. Carleton Library No. 55. Toronto: McClelland and Stewart, 1971.

Wood, Kerry. *The Map-Maker: The Story of David Thompson*. Toronto: Macmillan of Canada, 1955.

Woodcock, George. *Gabriel Dumont: The Métis Chief and His Lost World*. Edmonton: Hurtig Publishers, 1975.

——— . *The Hudson's Bay Company*. Toronto: Collier-Macmillan Canada Ltd., 1970.

Yerby, J.C. *The Subarctic Indians and the Fur Trade, 1680–1860*. Vancouver: University of British Columbia Press, 1986.

Young, Gregg A. "The Organization of the Transfer of Furs at Fort William: A Study in Historical Geography." Photocopy. Thunder Bay Historical Museum Society Papers and Records, 1974: 29.

Illustration Credits

Cover
Governor George Simpson and Chief Trader Archibald McDonald descending the Fraser in 1828
Painted by A. Sherriff Scott
Hudson's Bay Company

Frontispiece (PP. viii–ix)
Canoe Manned by Voyageurs
Oil painting by Frances Ann Hopkins
National Archives of Canada C-2771

P. xviii
At the Portage
National Archives of Canada C-82974

P. xxii
Buckboard, Macleod
Watercolour, pen and ink by William Armstrong
Courtesy of the Royal Ontario Museum, Toronto, Canada

P. xxv
Moose Factory, Hudson's Bay
Coloured engraving
Courtesy of the Royal Ontario Museum, Toronto, Canada

P. 2
Watercolour
National Archives of Canada C-8711

P. 4
Shooting the Rapids, ca. 1879.
Oil painting by Frances Ann Hopkins, wife of the Secretary to HBC Governor George Simpson
National Archives of Canada C-2774

P. 11
Oil painting
National Archives of Canada C-164

P. 14
McCord Museum of Canadian History, McGill University, Montreal

P. 15
Oil painting, 1806, by William Berczy
McCord Museum of Canadian History, McGill University, Montreal

PP. 18–19
Old Fort William, Thunder Bay, Ontario

P. 20
A Christmas Ball in Bachelor's Hall, York Factory, 1843
Hudson's Bay Company

P. 24
Canoes in a Fog, Lake Superior, 1869.
Oil painting by Frances Ann Hopkins
Collection of Glenbow Museum, Calgary, Alberta

P. 29
Running a Rapid on the Mattawa River
Engraved by C. Butterworth Sc. (after Mrs. F.A. Hopkins)
National Archives of Canada C-13585

P. 31
Old Fort William, Thunder Bay, Ontario

P. 34
The Spring Brigade Leaves Montreal for the West
By Franklin Arbuckle, R.C.A. This illustration shows the departure of a canoe brigade in the early 1820s, after the North West Company had been absorbed by the Hudson's Bay Company
Hudson's Bay Company

P. 36
Adapted from map showing route of voyageurs, *Horizon Canada* magazine, vol. 2, no. 23, p. 539.

P. 39
Voyageurs at Dawn, 1871
Oil painting by Frances Ann Hopkins
National Archives of Canada C-2773

P. 46
Winter Travelling in Dog Sleds
Oil painting, ca. 1850, by Paul Kane
Courtesy of the Royal Ontario Museum, Toronto, Canada

P. 50
Oil on canvas by Sir Thomas
Lawrence
The National Gallery of Canada,
Ottawa

P. 53
Watercolour, 1825, by Captain George
Back
National Archives of Canada C-2477

P. 55
Public Record Office, Kew,
Richmond, Surrey, England; Reference
CO 700 America North and South 49;
Crown copyright

P. 68
Provincial Archives of British
Columbia, cat. no. HP6460

P. 77
George Hunter/Miller Services Limited

P. 78
Painting by John Innes
Native Sons of British Columbia, Post
#2

P. 80
Provincial Archives of British
Columbia cat. no. pdp 2258

P. 94
Pen and ink drawing by C.W. Jefferys
National Archives of Canada C-70258

P. 95
Provincial Archives of British
Columbia, cat. no. HP44971

P. 97
A View of New York Taken from Veahawk
Coloured aquatint
Courtesy of the Royal Ontario
Museum, Toronto, Canada

P. 101
The Oregon Historical Society, neg.
no. ORHI21682 and ORHI60033

P. 108
Courtesy of The New-York Historical
Society, New York City

P. 111
*Blackfoot Indian Encampment, Foothills of
the Rocky Mountains*
Watercolour by William Armstrong

Courtesy of the Royal Ontario
Museum, Toronto, Canada

P. 113
Courtesy of The New-York Historical
Society, New York City

P. 132
Oil painting, ca. 1821, attributed to
G.S. Newton
National Archives of Canada C-8984

P. 135
*Cold Night Camp on the Inhospitable Shores
of Lake Winipesi in Oct. 1821*
Watercolour on pencil with pen and
ink outline, by Peter Rindisbacher
National Archives of Canada C-1925.

P. 136
From a painting ascribed to Raeburn
National Archives of Canada C-1346

P. 139
Independence National Historical
Park Collection, Philadelphia

P. 151
Office of the Sheriff of the Judicial
District of York, Toronto, Ontario;
print provided by Metropolitan
Toronto Library

P. 154
List of Men belonging to the Red
River Settlement arriving in Hudson's
Bay in 1811 and Brought from York
Factory, July 1812
National Archives of Canada, Miles
Macdonell, MG 19, E4, Vol. I,
File 2, p. 151.

P. 156
Watercolour/mixed media, ca. 1822,
by Peter Rindisbacher
Hudson's Bay Company Collection,
Environment Canada Parks, Lower
Fort Garry National Park

P. 157
Lithograph in colour
Print provided by Metropolitan
Toronto Library: T 15959

P. 160
Half Breeds Running Buffalo
Oil painting, ca. 1850, by Paul Kane
Courtesy of the Royal Ontario
Museum, Toronto, Canada

P. 162
Data provided by Hudson's Bay
Company Library

PP. 164–65
*Birch Bark Canoe Being Carried on a Red
River Cart*, 1847
Pen and ink drawing by George E.
Finlay; Collection of Glenbow
Museum, Calgary, Alberta

P. 166
Pen and ink drawing by C.W. Jefferys
National Archives of Canada C-73663

P. 168
Hudson's Bay Company Archives,
Provincial Archives of Manitoba
(upper)
Presbyterian Church in Canada
Archives (lower)

P. 170
Watercolour thought to be by Lord
Selkirk, copied by A.R. Winning
National Archives of Canada C-8714

P. 171
National Archives of Canada C-624

P. 177
From Bryce, *Life of Lord Selkirk*,
Musson Book Co.

P. 180
Archives of Ontario (upper and lower)

P. 185
Engraving
National Archives of Canada C-19202

P. 192
French River Rapids
Oil painting, ca. 1850, by Paul Kane
Courtesy of the Royal Ontario
Museum, Toronto, Canada

P. 195
Miniature courtesy of Mrs. M.
Porritt, Halfway House, South Africa

P. 198
Watercolour, ca. 1832, by Captain
George Back
National Archives of Canada C-15251

PP. 206-7
Edward Ellice (left): National Archives
of Canada C-2835.
William McGillivray (middle): Oil

painting, 1820, attributed to Sir
Martin Shee; National Archives of
Canada C-167. Simon McGillivray
(right): Oil painting attributed to R.R.
Reinagle; National Archives of
Canada C-176

P. 215
*The Barracks and Entrance to
Penetanguishene Harbour from Matchedash
Bay*
Watercolour by George Russell
Dartnell
Courtesy of the Royal Ontario
Museum, Toronto, Canada

P. 216
*Governor of Rupert's Land, George
Simpson, on a tour of inspection*
HBC's 1926 calendar painting by L.L.
Fitzgerald.
Hudson's Bay Company Archives,
Provincial Archives of Manitoba

P. 225
Cumberland House
From a sketch taken by the Henry
Youle Hind expedition of 1858;
Hudson's Bay Company Archives,
Provincial Archives of Manitoba

P. 228
Manitoubah Sailing on River, 1863
Oil painting by W.G.R. Hind;
National Archives of Canada C-13976

P. 237
Provincial Archives of British
Columbia, cat. no. HP42416

P. 239
Fort Edmonton
Oil painting, ca. 1850, by Paul Kane
Courtesy of the Royal Ontario
Museum, Toronto, Canada

P. 242
From a painting by Stephen Pearce for
the Hudson's Bay Company
Hudson's Bay Company

P. 249
Oil painting by Henry Perronet
Briggs, R.A.
Hudson's Bay Company Archives,
Provincial Archives of Manitoba

P. 250
Hudson's Bay Company

P. 253
Provincial Archives of British
Columbia, cat. no. HP75480

P. 258
Lithograph, ca. 1857, by G.H.
Burgess
Bishop Museum, Honolulu, Hawaii

P. 263
Indian Women in Tent
By P. Rindisbacher
West Point Museum Collections,
United States Military Academy

P. 264
Courtesy of Mrs M. Porritt, Halfway
House, South Africa

P. 269
Hudson's Bay Company

P. 272
Return of a War Party
Oil painting, ca. 1850, by Paul Kane
Courtesy of the Royal Ontario
Museum, Toronto, Canada

P. 280
Provincial Archives of British
Columbia, cat. no. HP4274

P. 282
Nezperee Indian (Paul Kane's
designation)
Oil painting, ca. 1850, by Paul Kane
Courtesy of the Royal Ontario
Museum, Toronto, Canada

P. 283
The Oregon Historical Society, neg.
no. ORHI 10126 #735

P. 284
The Oregon Historical Society, neg.
no. ORHI 248

P. 286
From *Maclean's*, 30 April 1955, p. 25.
Reprinted with permission—The
Toronto Star Syndicate

P. 288
The Denver Public Library, Western
History Department

P. 292
Vancouver City Archives

P. 299
Collection of Glenbow Museum,
Calgary, Alberta

P. 300
Provincial Archives of British
Columbia, cat. no. HP 2656

P. 304
Provincial Archives of British
Columbia, cat. no. HP 2659

P. 310
Provincial Archives of British
Columbia, cat. no. HP51782

P. 311
Provincial Archives of British
Columbia, cat. no. HP10110

P. 313
Provincial Archives of British
Columbia, cat. no. HP759

P. 318
The Dakota Boat
Oil on canvas (87.0 × 112.6 cm) by
W. Frank Lynn (1835–1906);
Collection of The Winnipeg Art
Gallery; Donated by Mr & Mrs Sam
Cohen G-71-94; Photograph courtesy
The Winnipeg Art Gallery, Ernest P.
Mayer

P. 322
Hudson's Bay Company

P. 334
Provincial Archives of British
Columbia, cat. no. HP4107

P. 335
Provincial Archives of Manitoba

P. 337
Engraving, 1859, by A. Rochester
Fellow;
Provincial Archives of Manitoba

P. 340
Copy of a daguerrotype by Notman;
Notman Photographic Archives

P. 343
Hudson's Bay Company

P. 346
Engraving
National Archives of Canada C-11333

P. 353
Engraving, 1878
Hudson's Bay Company Archives,
Provincial Archives of Manitoba

P. 358
Illustrated London News, 13 October
1860
Print provided by Metropolitan
Toronto Library

P. 360
Identified on painting as ''Fort Garry,
Winnipeg'' (location not verified), oil
painting by W. Frank Lynn;
Hudson's Bay Company

P. 362
Provincial Archives of British
Columbia, cat. no. HP57906

P. 365
Indian Camp—Sunset
Oil on canvas (51.6 × 92.0) by
Frederick Arthur Verner (1836–1928);
Photograph courtesy The Winnipeg

Art Gallery, Ernest P. Mayer; Private
Collection, Winnipeg

P. 370
After the painting by George
Richmond, R.A.
Hudson's Bay Company

P. 375
*Governor George Simpson and Chief Trader
Archibald McDonald descending the Fraser
in 1828*
Painted by A. Sherriff Scott
Hudson's Bay Company

P. 376
Photo courtesy Frederic Remington
Art Museum, Ogdensburg, N.Y.

P. 379
Hudson's Bay Company

P. 380
Buffalo Skull
Sketch, ca. 1850, by Paul Kane
Courtesy of the Royal Ontario
Museum, Toronto, Canada

Index